CREAM OF THE CROP

Other Books by the Authors

Herant Katchadourian

Fundamentals of Human Sexuality, 5th ed.
(translated into French, Spanish, Portuguese, and Chinese)

Human Sexuality—Sense and Nonsense

Biology of Adolescence

Human Sexuality: A Comparative and Developmental Perspective
(editor) (translated into Spanish)

Fifty: Midlife in Perspective (translated into Greek)

Careerism and Intellectualism Among College Students
(with John Boli)

John Boli

New Citizens for a New Society:
The Institutional Origins of Mass Schooling in Sweden

Institutional Structure: Constituting State, Society, and the Individual
(with George M. Thomas, John W. Meyer, and Francisco O. Ramirez)

Careerism and Intellectualism Among College Students
(with Herant Katchadourian)

Cream of the Crop

The Impact of Elite Education
in the Decade After College

HERANT KATCHADOURIAN
AND
JOHN BOLI

BasicBooks
A Division of HarperCollins*Publishers*

Figure 4.2 from *An M.B.A.'s Guide to Self-Assessment and Career Development* by James G. Clawson and David D. Ward. Copyright © 1985 by Prentice-Hall, Inc. Reprinted by permission.

Designed by Ellen Levine

Library of Congress Cataloging-in-Publication Data
Katchadourian, Herant A.
    Cream of the crop : the impact of elite education in the decade after college / Herant Katchadourian and John Boli.
    p. cm.
    Includes bibliographical references and index.
    ISBN 0–465–04343–7
    1. College graduates—United States—Attitudes—Longitudinal studies. 2. College graduates—Employment—United States—Longitudinal studies. 3. Universities and colleges—United States—Admission. 4. Minority college graduates—United States—Longitudinal studies. I. Boli, John, 1948– . II. Title.
LB2424.K38 1994
378'.01'0973—dc20   94–12174
                                                                    CIP

94 95 96 97 ❖/RRD 9 8 7 6 5 4 3 2 1

To the participants of the cohort follow-up study—be they Careerists, Intellectuals, Strivers, or Unconnected—this book is gratefully and affectionately dedicated.

Contents

List of Figures and Tables

FIGURES

TABLES, Appendix A

Preface

What does it take to "make it" today in the most affluent country in the world? What constitutes success in the career and personal lives of professional men and women as they come of age in contemporary American society? How do they reconcile the competing demands of career and family? Do these demands allow any time and energy for cultivating the life of the mind, social concerns, and other pursuits beyond the self?

Every spring, some 100,000 eagerly expectant high school seniors receive acceptance letters from the most highly selective fifty or so private and public colleges and universities in the country, fulfilling a dream for which they have worked diligently since they were children and bringing joy and relief to their families. But for all concerned, the event also marks the need for new commitments, which they willingly undertake with the hope that joining the "educational elite" will not only broaden their minds but also lead to fulfilling careers, financial security, and higher social status, even enhance their chances of finding desirable mates.

How realistic are these hopes and expectations?

We address this question based on an in-depth study of a representative sample of men and women in one preeminently elite institution—Stanford University. We begin with the experiences of these women and men while they were in college and follow the trajectory of their lives during the decade following graduation.

Three major issues constitute the central focus of this book. The first addresses general questions: What does education in elite institutions mean for the lives of their graduates? Does it guarantee occupational and financial success, as is commonly supposed? Does it produce "the leaders of tomorrow"? Does it produce truly educated people who bring breadth and depth to their working and private lives?

Our second issue is determining the primary beneficiaries of this educational process. Is this path open to all who are academically qualified or only to a select few? How inclusive are these institutions as they seek out the "best and the brightest" among the nation's youth? We are specially concerned with three groups that have been, until recently, largely excluded from membership in the educational elite: women, disadvantaged ethnic minorities, and members of lower socioeconomic groups. Taking gender as an example, is elite education as gender-neutral as the prevailing ideology in these institutions claims? How different are men and women after college in their advanced education, occupational choices, professional accomplishments, and personal lives? Where do we find genuine equality, and where does gender still make a difference? If gender equality is to be found anywhere, it should be within elite educational institutions because the young people they educate have successfully passed through many selective filters and are all highly competent, motivated, and capable. Similar assumptions would apply to ethnicity and social class.

Elite education thus represents a best-case scenario for the working out of meritocratic principles by providing the optimal conditions for equality to be realized. It holds the promise for women as well as for men, for members of ethnic minorities as well as for the white majority, for the children of the poor as well as the rich, that anyone with the ability and willingness to work hard can not only get on board but travel first-class. To what extent is this prospect a tangible reality?

Finally, we turn to the more specific differences between individuals that go beyond gender, ethnicity, and socioeconomic class. While ultimately each person is unique, we have looked for their discernible and meaningful common features. These features allow us to describe distinctive patterns by which women and men make career and personal choices and consolidate them into stable life patterns. To these issues we address a third set of questions: How does variation in young people's orientations to conventional career success and the love of learning for its own sake affect their early adult lives? Is the intellectualism that elite institutions are supposed to foster mere gloss, or do we find that those who deeply absorb this approach to life look different from those who do not? Does the single-minded pursuit of professional advancement and financial gain in fact lead to greater success in conventional terms? What are the costs and benefits of these different orientations? What price does careerism exact in young adult life? Do the intellectually oriented suffer in their careers? Is it possible to "have it all," that is, to put great effort into developing a career while also making the life of the mind a central concern?

Some may wonder why we have chosen to focus on the educational elite. After all, this group represents but a fraction of the entire age cohort of a given generation. Why dwell on them? Is this book yet another excursion into the "lives of the rich and famous," or those destined to join their ranks? Is it an exercise in social voyeurism, or a paean to those who climb to the top of the heap? Some people may be offended by the mere reference to, let alone our seeming acceptance of, an educational elite. Would it not be better, they may argue, to focus instead on the enormous social disparities that divide our nation, and on the lives of those who suffer because of it?

The educational elite is obviously a very small segment of the population, but the influence and potential social impact of its members go far beyond their numbers. The professional and managerial elites which they join occupy the upper reaches of private and public power structures. So it is important to know what they are like, whatever one may think or feel about them. Hence, this book examines who these men and women are and how they got to where they are.

That we call them the "cream of the crop" (somewhat tongue-in-cheek) and dwell at length on their achievements (as well as their failures) is not meant to glorify their accomplishments at the expense of those who pursue other paths either by going to nonelite institutions or forgoing college altogether (whether by choice or, more often, lack of choice). There are, indeed, many honorable and socially useful ways of living and working. It is not for us to say which ways are "better."

If we focus on the realities of our world—the way things are rather than the way we might like them to be—we come to understand the processes whereby members of the educational elite move into the upper reaches of American society. The consequences of such membership are enormous. Historically, elite educational institutions have largely catered to the children of the social elite. They still do, but that is no longer their only focus. They are an effective vehicle for upward social mobility for more of their students than ever before. Hence, we look at the elite educational process not only as it maintains the status quo but also as it brings about social change. We hope this book will speak to everyone who has a stake in the coming of age of the nation's youth.

Acknowledgments

We have incurred many debts in connection with this work. The largest is to the participants in the cohort study who took part in the follow-up investigation ten years later. Donald Kennedy, president emeritus of Stanford University, has been a steadfast supporter of this project in both its phases. We have also received generous support from the provosts James Rosse and Gerald Lieberman, who provided release time to the senior author and institutional support for the conduct of the study. Additional funding was provided by the Carnegie Corporation. We are particularly grateful to its president, David Hamburg, and vice president Barbara D. Finberg for their encouragement. John Boli would also like to thank QNAB, Inc., of Helsingborg, Sweden, for computer resources.

Several members of the original interview team conducted some of the follow-up interviews; we acknowledge their contributions in our chapter notes. A group of readers read the entire manuscript, and others parts of it. We are grateful for their insightful comments and criticisms. Among them are several members of the interview team and a number of the study participants. They are, in alphabetical order, Raymond Bacchetti, Anne Coxon, Jean Fetter, Elizabeth Hirschhorn, Jeff Kirkpatrick, Sally Mahoney, Victor Menon, James Montoya, Stephen Peeps, and Jean Joyce Williams. We would like to thank Ruth Schneider and the members of her staff at the Career Planning and Placement Center at Stanford University: Kathy Campbell, Lance Choy, Laura Dominguez, Lynne Dotson, Anne Greenblatt, Al Levin, and Marlene Scherer-Stern. We are especially grateful for the expert advice we received from John Krumboltz, Albert Hastorf, and George Vaillant. President Gerhard Casper, former presidents Richard W. Lyman and Donald Kennedy of Stanford, David P. Gardner, former president of the University of California, and Roger C. Heyns, former chancellor of the University of California at Berkeley, provided insightful comments on chapter 10.

A great deal of effort went into the preparation of the manuscript, for which we would like to thank Laurie Burmeister, Stacey Campbell, and Ben Wang. Our editor at Basic Books, Jo Ann Miller, helped and guided us through the whole process.

Finally, our wives, Stina and Lisbeth, sustained us from the gestation to the birth of this book. Through countless discussions about its sundry aspects, their thoughts and words have become freely intermingled with our own.

CREAM OF THE CROP

CHAPTER 1

Crossing the Twenties

"Mr. Genochio is on the phone to Japan," says the executive secretary in a hushed voice. "He will be with you in a few minutes." True enough, Mr. Genochio emerges soon from his office, walking with the deliberate steps of a man confidently on his way to the top. Dressed in a dark suit and bold striped blue shirt, he is the quintessence of the successful young business executive.

Ten years ago, Mr. Philip Genochio was plain Phil, a Stanford University senior about to graduate with a bachelor's degree in economics.[1] He was almost a stranger to money then, having worked his way through college in three years to save the expense of a fourth and still ending up $10,000 in debt. Phil's father was a salesman for a small construction company, his mother a housewife. Neither of them had gone to college: But since the eighth grade, Phil knew what he wanted and how to get it. After Stanford, he went to Yale Law School and worked as a corporate attorney for three years. Then he went to Harvard for an M.B.A. and became an investment banker in New York. At the age of thirty-one, he now makes well over $250,000 a year.[2]

Poised and enormously self-confident, Philip Genochio is pleased and at ease with his career success, "being on the leading edge, setting the pace." He has worked hard to get where he is and still puts in eighty-hour weeks. In addition to the financial rewards, he enjoys "the challenge and the collegial atmosphere of working with senior executives."

Looking out the window of his forty-fifth-floor office with a commanding view of the New York skyline, Philip Genochio reflects on his education and career. He has always set his sights very high. As a freshman, he thought he might become a senator or a member of the cabinet. In his senior year, he contemplated being on the U.S. Supreme Court.

Phil was pleased to get into Stanford, though he was not satisfied with everything there. The math courses were "depressing." Most of the courses in economics, his major, were "useless and poorly taught." Were he to do it again, he would try to "obtain specific skills useful in the marketplace." Nonetheless, he picked his courses with care, evaluating them by several criteria: their contribution to his long-range plans, the requirements they fulfilled, and his interest in their subject matter. Eventually, Stanford did serve its function of moving him on to the next step of his career trajectory. As he puts it, "College is one important step out of ten that I have taken, of twenty that I hope to take before I die." His future is wide open. "I'm still not sure what my career is," he muses, reflecting on the boundless opportunities he sees ahead. "I can now tackle just about any job that comes my way." There is no trace of self-consciousness in his voice. He is almost amused at how far he has come already.

During his climb up the career ladder, Phil relied on not just a single mentor but "a council of elders who have been superimportant." Most of all, he relied on himself. "I have fully committed myself to every task that I have undertaken. And I have taken advantage of every opportunity that has come my way," he sums up. "I am an opportunist," is how he had characterized himself back in college.

There are strong moral reservations, and an altruistic streak, beneath Philip Genochio's careerist armor. It bothers him that his "ethical standards have degraded over time." "Living up to my ethical expectations was tough enough as a lawyer," he complains. "In the business world, it's far worse." As an example of the ethical dilemmas he faces, Philip explained that his current boss is under fire and possibly on his way out. So, on the one hand, he must remain loyal to the man, but on the other, he must avoid getting damaged himself by the association.

Philip's vision of the future combines a pair of objectives. At the peak of his career, in a decade or so, he hopes to be a CEO or managing partner making "one million dollars plus a year." After he has secured his future financially, he would like to "spearhead an organization to solve social or environmental problems. Maybe help Third World countries with their economic problems. Maybe work for the government."

Philip Genochio has managed his personal life with as much forethought and determination as his career. He dated his future wife for five years and got married when he was thirty because he wanted to get his career on track first. As with his career, he knew exactly what he wanted.

He says:

> There are two kinds of women. There are women who are similar to
> me. They are hard-driving, career-type people for whom careers are
> superimportant. I find these women very stimulating to have around,
> but not the kind of person I would want to marry. I want to have a
> family, I want my children to spend time with their parents. I want
> someone for whom the concept of family is more important than
> their career. That's the profile of my wife. I am very content with
> that. I am the exception these days with respect to that. I look at
> some of my friends and the strain on them, having a kid, both trying
> to crank in the world, leaving no time for each other. It is very diffi-
> cult. For us, so far, it has been very easy, as our understanding for the
> future is very consistent.

Philip found in Claire what he was looking for. She is an attractive, vivacious, intelligent woman who works for a bank, where she makes $50,000.
She is in charge of running the household while he helps with various
chores. They are very happy together and fully committed to each other.
"This is it," he says confidently. Although Claire will take primary responsibility for the care of their children, Philip does not want to be an absen-
tee father. He has seen too many executives drive themselves relentlessly
and wreck their family lives, ending up as "losers." And if there is one
thing Philip Genochio does not want, it is to be a loser.

Outside of his work and marriage, Philip has little time for much else.
"I have not read a book for a long time," he says unapologetically. He certainly appreciates the life of the mind—"It is great to know Socrates," he
concedes—yet he feels little urgency at the moment to pursue it. He faults
in part his undergraduate education ("Stanford didn't prepare me for such
pursuits"), while admitting that back in college he saw humanists as
"losers." His musical tastes run to rock. His wife has gotten him interested
in art, and he has tried his hand at painting.

Philip Genochio is fascinated by social and political issues but, unless
they relate to his business, only at a rather abstract level. He has no time
now to be personally involved but expects to be more fully engaged with
social issues in the future. As a Catholic, he attends church occasionally
and tries to uphold the ethical values inculcated in him by his family,
though the demands of the marketplace make this difficult. Whatever time
the Genochios can spare in their busy lives they like to spend outdoors; fly
fishing and bird hunting are his favorite activities.

Alicia Turner, the subject of our next profile, is a very different sort of person. She came to her interview in a flowery dress complemented by large earrings of miniature fruit. Alicia teaches elementary school students with learning disabilities in one of the most disadvantaged communities in Atlanta. She is a black woman who earns about one-tenth of what Philip Genochio makes, but in her work she is as accomplished and successful as he is in his. Alicia Turner's example is an alternative success story, marked by dedication to public service. We do not present her as representative of women, blacks, schoolteachers, or any other group. She represents no one but herself.[3]

Alicia grew up in a lower-middle-class family in Alabama. Her father has a small furniture refinishing business, and her mother is a schoolteacher. She did well at a private girls' school, leading to her acceptance at Stanford. Although her academic goals were rather vague, her career goals were highly ambitious: "to make the most money, to get the best job, to be the most successful person." Engineering was to be the means to these ends, but Alicia never made it through the freshman math sequence. Her first year ended on a mixed note of disillusionment and self-consolation: "I was searching for external happiness, since I felt so alienated and alone. Nonetheless, I did have fun!"

Just before returning for her sophomore year, Alicia was involved in a serious car accident. She escaped unscathed, but the experience left her with "a sense that my life had a definite purpose, even if I did not know it." "My priorities changed," recalls Alicia. "Making money didn't appeal to me anymore."

There was little guidance from her parents, who said only, "We just want you to be happy." It was just as well. "Had my parents tried to push me, I would have rebelled," says Alicia. Yet "lack of parental involvement" in her education was one of the problems she faced in college, along with "lack of motivation." The motivational turnaround occurred in a conference with her anthropology teacher. "He gave me the first words of encouragement I had received since high school. The next quarter, I applied myself for the first time at Stanford. I got an A in a class and decided on a major!" She chose communications.

Despite Alicia's resolve to do better, her extensive commitments to many social organizations—for instance, up to twenty hours a week with the gospel choir, tutoring disadvantaged children on Saturdays—left her little time to study. "These experiences were crucial to the process of rebuilding my self-esteem, which had been shattered by less than satisfactory academic performance," she explains. These involvements moved Alicia from "observer" to "participant" in college life, but they took their toll. Her optimistic and cheerful exterior masked dissatisfaction with her academic performance and disillusionment with Stanford for making her feel like a "second-class citizen."

Alicia finally admitted to herself, "If I am going to graduate, I have to get on the stick and stay there." She was helped by the unstinting love of her family, especially her mother. A number of others, mostly black faculty and staff members, stood by her. But most important was the sustenance she received from her faith. Her senior year, she said, was just "me, the Lord, the books, and a few close friends. I didn't have time for much else. But study I did."

Yet, at graduation, Alicia still felt at a loss:

> I didn't know what to do when I came, and I didn't know what to do when I left. So for five years after graduation I worked at small jobs, mainly as an office temporary. It was a time for me to have fun. But I wanted to settle down. I wanted to know what I wanted to do; it was just a process of finding out what it was. I don't consider that a waste of time. With the temporary service, I worked at retail, at a bank, in marketing, in customer service, and my final job at an insurance company. It was a good experience.

Nevertheless, Alicia was clearly not satisfied. "I went to college for four years, I went to college prep school before then. What was all that for?" The only workplace in which she felt at ease was the insurance company, where she met Ruby, a black woman who was vice president of the company. "One day she took me aside," says Alicia, "and said to me, 'You have a degree from Stanford? What are you doing here?' I really respected her for what she had achieved in her work and personal life. So when she said, 'Look, you really have to figure out what you want to do with your life,' it meant a lot to me."

Alicia felt inspired but was still unclear about what to do. She finally found direction from her involvement in Sunday school at church. After discovering that she enjoyed teaching and was good at it, she took a shortcut past regular teacher training by entering a federally funded training course for special reading programs. The course led to a teaching position that turned out to be a perfect match for her. She had found her calling. "The first day I went to teach my class," recalls Alicia, "I was so happy, I was jumping with joy."

Alicia developed into a superb teacher, not only effective in the classroom but involved in the personal lives of her students. "I make home visits," says Alicia. "I present workshops for parents. I am trying to bridge the gap between home and school in a variety of ways."

Two women supervisors took over as Alicia's mentors. "They trained me. They constantly supported me, constantly encouraged me. They have written letters of recommendation for me. And right now what they are saying is, 'Why haven't you done graduate work? You really need to go back to school, not just stay at the level where you are.' " Alicia has begun studying part-time for a master's degree in educational administration and plans to seek a doctorate in early childhood education. In ten years, she hopes to be the director of a "Head Start–type program for preschoolers." But she would also be perfectly content just to teach for the rest of her life.

Alicia now earns $26,000 a year. She says, "It's adequate. That's all I can say about it. I can eat. I have a place where I can live, and I have clothes to wear. I can barely make ends meet, and I don't live extravagantly. But I am self-sufficient." Though she would welcome a little more money, she loves what she is doing. "I feel appreciated," she says, "and someone has to be there for the children." Inspired by her vision of Christian service, she uses her experience at Stanford to help those less fortunate. "I am able to introduce my children to the world because I was exposed to it at Stanford. I encourage my students to dream big dreams. I share a global perspective with them. I discourage them from setting limits for themselves. I try to help them develop a desire for learning about the people and the world around them."

Alicia is not yet married but has a special friendship with Michael, a physicist. They have the same ethnic background and have known each other since she was in college and he was a graduate student. During the last year or so they have gotten closer. He has just moved to New York, and she is considering doing the same. Perhaps, together in New York, they would have "a more, you know, serious relationship."

Alicia is "ready to do the family thing," and Michael may be the man. "He is head and shoulders above anyone else I have known," she says. Though she has dated a few other people, only once before did she feel as close to someone. But when that person went back to his old girlfriend, Alicia felt "kind of burned." For the next five years she dated no one. It got lonely. "I have been faithful to you, Lord," she used to pray. "Where is he?"

The relationship with Michael has had its ups and downs. "There was a point when I was interested and he wasn't; there was a point when he was interested and I wasn't." Now they are more in step. "We complement each other," says Alicia. "He is a Christian. I am a Christian. We share the same moral values. He is such a gem." On the other hand, "I am not sure I want to direct this relationship, to take the bull by the horns. What would it be like to live with him? Is he willing to settle down? I am in a real quandary."

Alicia's intellectual and social concerns are centered in her church. She reads books by pastors and Christian psychologists, "to help me become the kind of person that God wants me to be." She "flips through" *Newsweek.* Thinking back to her college days, Alicia misses "the intellectual exchange" and keeps in touch with her college friends, her link to the wider world.

Philip Genochio and Alicia Turner have distinctive life histories, but they are also good examples of an important segment of the generation of young people who came of age in the 1980s. They are 2 out of a group of 320 students in the Stanford class of 1981—one-fifth of the total—who were chosen at random to participate in a longitudinal study. But Alicia and Philip are part of a much larger group of young adults as well: the several hundred thousand men and women who studied in some fifty select institutions like Stanford in the 1970s and 1980s. It is these institutions that produce the educational elite of the United States, the wide range of young professionals whose prestigious degrees and driving ambition rapidly propel them up the career ladder to positions of leadership.

There are over twelve million students enrolled in some form of postsecondary education in the United States, and well over forty million young adults who came of age in the same decade as Alicia and Philip.[4] It is mainly the members of the educational elite, however, who will occupy the top professional positions in business, law, medicine, academics, science, politics, and other such arenas.[5] There are, of course, some others outside of the educational elite who also attain prominence in these fields but the likelihood of their doing so is much lower.

PURPOSE OF THE BOOK

Our purpose is to describe the life trajectories of the educational elite as exemplified by the Stanford class of 1981, during the ten years following graduation. We presented our findings about this group during their college years (the "cohort study") in an earlier book, *Careerism and Intellectualism among College Students* (1985). Here we discuss the results of our second study of this remarkable group (the "follow-up study"), using information gathered in 1990 and 1991 in an extensive questionnaire survey of 70 percent of the original cohort study sample of 320 students and intensive interviews with one hundred members of that sample.

However diverse have been the career choices of the men and women we discuss here, most of them are now rising members of this country's professional elite. Their lives raise a number of important questions for all members of their generation. What is their conception of success? What makes them successful? Can success be measured? Is it only a matter of objective attainments like money and position? Is it a function of career accomplishment as judged by deals closed, patients cured, cases won, books written, paintings exhibited? Or does it lie in the more subjective sense of satisfaction derived from work performed conscientiously and well? Is it personal gain or social utility? What really counts, the impact of what you do, or the motivation for doing it?

The personal lives of the educational elite raise important questions as well. How and when have these young men and women formed intimate relationships? Do career considerations so dominate their lives that marriage is only one of many goals? How does having children fit into their lives, and what are their attitudes toward child rearing? How satisfied are they with their personal lives? How do they juggle the demands of family life and career? What sort of relationships do they have with their parents? What do they do for fun? Can they have fun, given their family and career demands? And what about the life of the mind for these highly educated professionals? What are their intellectual interests, social concerns, and religious and philosophical beliefs? Is there still room for maintaining the ideals of a university education ten years after graduation?

A preview of our findings yields the following conclusions. The educational elite moves into the ranks of the occupational elite during the decade after graduation from college. The great majority accomplish this following graduate study in a professional school, typically in law, business, medicine, or engineering, and enter prestigious and lucrative positions in these fields. Though not yet at the peak of their careers, their annual income is well over three times the national average for all adults, and one-third higher than for other college graduates. Nonetheless, a substantial minority of one in four does not pursue further study after college and goes into other occupations, including teaching and full-time child rearing.

Two-thirds of the members of the educational elite come from upper-middle-class families. By age thirty most have established themselves at the same socioeconomic level as their parents. For others, joining the educational elite represents upward social mobility. Half of those from middle-class families, and all of those from lower socioeconomic backgrounds, have already risen above the levels of their families of origin by the end of the decade after college.

The educational elite are concerned with more than making a good living. Most receive nonmonetary rewards from their work and would still work even if they did not need the money. Generally, they feel highly content, committed, and competent in their careers.

Gender equality is central to the career ideology and practice of the educational elite. Although some gender differences persist in career choice and level of satisfaction, the traditional divisions between women and men have largely disappeared. Professional women generally share the same very high career aspirations and expectations as men. Some areas, however, such as teaching and full-time child rearing, continue to be primarily the domain of women.

Two-thirds of the educational elite marry by the end of the decade after college. Most of those who are single expect to marry or live with someone. Close to one in ten of their marriages has ended in divorce after ten years. Most marriages aspire to be egalitarian partnerships, with shared responsibilities for housework, although women still tend to carry more than their share of the burden. A smaller group of women have primary charge of the household; a few men in the study have taken on that role.

About a third of the couples have one or more children. The arrival of children has a compelling impact on their lives: parenthood represents the single most important challenge in meshing career and family life, especially for women. A substantial number avoid the issue by choosing either career or motherhood. The majority manage both through accommodation and compromise, along with considerable conflict.

The demands of career and family life leave little time for much else. Intellectual interests are generally set aside, at least for the time being. Social involvements usually involve sports, travel, and hobbies. Political engagement tends to be minimal. The majority are not actively involved with religious institutions, although some become involved upon the arrival of children.

The majority continue to express high levels of satisfaction with their college experience a decade after graduation. Over nine in ten would attend Stanford again and most say it was well worth the money. Virtually all attest to the tremendous impact of their undergraduate experience on their lives and point to its continuing influence in opening doors and enhancing their careers and social standing. There are some, nonetheless, who remember their college experience less positively and are highly critical of its institutional values. Many more show considerable discrepancy between the values they profess and their behavior.

The life patterns of the educational elite during the decade after college show remarkable consistency but not uniformity. Although some of the diversity in all the facets of their lives reflects the effects of gender and ethnicity, more often it reflects their varied orientations to the academic and career dimensions of college life.

THE COHORT STUDY

The central purpose of our earlier cohort study was to learn how under-graduates make academic and career choices. Why do they choose the courses they take, the majors they enter, the careers they decide to pursue? What role do parents, professors, the job market, life goals, and other factors play in their academic and career decisions? Which college experiences do they find meaningful, and which are seen as better off forgotten? How do these experiences orient them to the lives they intend to build?

To answer these questions, a set of studies was initiated by Herant Katchadourian when he was vice provost and dean of undergraduate studies at Stanford University; John Boli joined him as director of research. The most ambitious of our projects was a longitudinal study of a randomly chosen cohort of freshmen constituting 20 percent of the class of 1981. These 320 students exactly matched the entire class in gender composition (56 percent men; 44 percent women) and ethnic distribution (22 percent minorities).[6] They were studied during each of their four undergraduate years through questionnaires and interviews in the spring of each academic year.[7]

Strong concerns had emerged in the late 1970s that college students were excessively career-oriented. Educators feared that the American vision of a liberal education—the pursuit of knowledge for its own sake—and the full development of the individual not only occupationally but also psychologically and socially were not being achieved. As we stated at the time:

> Who would have thought that over a mere decade or so careerism would replace radicalism as the central concern of educators? The dominant image of the 1960s college student was a disheveled, surly, and alienated youth tearing away at the fabric of higher education. The 1980s image is a tidy, cheerful, and self-centered student milking higher education for all it's worth to get ahead in the world. Such stereotypes are misleading if generalized, but they are not meaningless if they capture the spirit of the times. The villain in this unfolding drama is "careerism," its victim "intellectualism."[8]

To explore these issues, we developed a typology based on two scales measuring student careerism and intellectualism. The scales were built from a variety of questionnaire items dealing with such topics as reasons for attending college, characteristics desired in a major, and characteristics desired in a career. For example, items that indicated intellectualism included attending college to learn to think critically, gain exposure to different viewpoints, and obtain a general liberal education. Attending college to obtain specialized preparation for a career, acquire marketable skills, or prepare for professional school reflected careerism. If students indicated that they chose their majors on the basis of the intellectual challenge or intrinsic interest of the subject matter, they received higher scores on the intellectualism scale. If they chose majors for more instrumental purposes, as a way to get into a prestigious graduate program or to enter a lucrative profession, they got higher careerism scores. Similarly, choosing a career because it required creativity and originality, or was intellectually challenging and provided an opportunity to be of service to others, raised their intellectualism scores, whereas career aspirations motivated by job security, social status and prestige, or high income raised their careerism scores.

We expected careerism and intellectualism to be negatively correlated, so that students high on the careerism scale would be low on the intellectualism scale, and vice versa. That turned out not to be the case. In fact, there was no relationship between the two. Students high in careerism were as likely to be high as to be low in intellectualism.

Since the two scales are entirely independent of each other, we were able to create a typology by simply cross-tabulating them. Those with high intellectualism scores and low careerism scores we designated Intellectuals. Their opposite numbers, with low intellectualism scores and high careerism scores, we named Careerists. Those who scored high on both measures— students devoted to pursuing both intellectual and career interests—were labeled Strivers, and their opposites who scored low on both measures were called the Unconnected (figure 1.1).

FIGURE 1.1
Schematic Representation of the Typology (*four cells*)

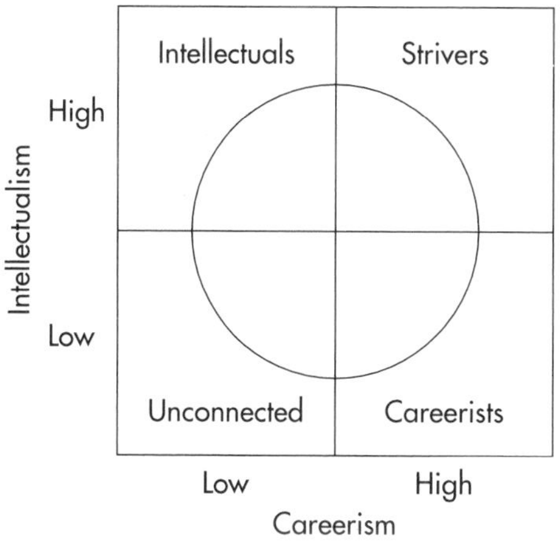

These labels, like all other labels that purport to describe human behaviors, fail to do full justice to the people they represent. Each label is likely to have connotations beyond its intended meaning. Moreover, how well the labels fit the students varies. About two-thirds of the students clearly fit one of the four types, and our interview reports generally confirmed their placement according to the quantitative scales. But a substantial number, perhaps as many as one-third, belong to a more amorphous group (encompassed by the circle in figure 1.1) among whom the distinctions are much less striking than among the "core" groups of Careerists, Intellectuals, Strivers, and the Unconnected.[9]

THE FOLLOW-UP STUDY

The follow-up study largely replicated the methodology of the cohort study to produce information consistent with what had been gathered earlier. Inevitably, the two studies differ in some aspects. In the follow-up study, we were no longer dealing with undergraduates making academic and career decisions but with young men and women fairly well established in their careers and personal lives. Our subjects were no longer students in the same college milieu but adults scattered all over the country. Instead of meeting them year after year over a four-year period, we now had only one chance to study them.

Although the follow-up sample is only 70 percent of the original group, it remains highly representative of the class of 1981. The follow-up respondents match the original class exactly in terms of sex, and very closely in terms of parental social class. The follow-up group is slightly lower in ethnic minorities. Asian-Americans, African-Americans, and Hispanics each represented 6 percent of the entering class of 1981. The proportion of Asian-Americans remains about the same in the follow-up, but we have only 4 percent African-Americans and just under 4 percent Hispanics now.

Follow-up questionnaires were mailed to the study participants in the spring of 1990.[10] Interviews were conducted mainly during the first six months of 1991. The cohort study participants had been interviewed by a team of Stanford administrators; some were members of the faculty and others had regular contact with undergraduates as part of their duties. This team could not be called upon for the follow-up study. Some interviewers were no longer at Stanford, and most of the rest could not take the time to go off-campus to conduct interviews. We were able to engage five members of the earlier cohort study team to conduct interviews with some fifteen participants who had been their subjects earlier.[11] The remaining eighty-five interviews were conducted by the senior author, including the participants he had interviewed during their undergraduate years. What may have been lost in terms of continuity between the two sets of interviewers was compensated for by the greater consistency that resulted from having the same person interview most of the subjects.

As in our previous book, we make extensive use of interview materials in this volume. The biographical vignettes and profiles are intended to provide a human texture to the disembodied quantitative responses, helping us to probe more deeply into the outlook and attitudes of the complex and vital men and women who represent the American educational elite.

THE EDUCATIONAL ELITE

The United States has the largest and most diverse system of higher education in the world. Of its 3,000 institutions of postsecondary education, about 2,100 are baccalaureate-granting universities and colleges. The rest are two-year community colleges and comparable facilities.[12] The United States leads the world in the ratio of its population that goes to college, with 5,225 enrollments per 100,000 a year. (Canada is next with 3,539 enrollments per 100,000.)[13] "We have created the world's first system of universal access to higher education," says a leading educator, Ernest Boyer. "It provides entrance somewhere to virtually all who wish to enroll and offers an almost unlimited choice of subjects to be studied." [14]

Universal access to this system does not mean freedom of access to all parts of it. This is a matter of great importance because of the enormous disparity in quality—real as well as perceived—among these institutions.[15] In conveying students to their educational and career stations, these vehicles of learning are as different at their extremes as a horse-drawn carriage from an automobile.

In principle, the best institutions would be those that have the best faculties, the best staff, the best facilities, the best programs, and the best students. Unfortunately, as in other social arenas, the criteria for assessing educational quality are far from clear, and some commonly used criteria have little to do with the quality of education as such. The quality of academic programs varies considerably not only between schools of comparable quality but even within a given university. Similarly, there is no common yardstick for identifying the "best" students. Admissions officers rely heavily on grade point averages and standardized test scores, but whether such "objective" criteria are the best measures of student quality is a matter of ongoing debate.

Despite such uncertainties, there is a fair consensus about which institutions constitute the upper crust of the American educational system. The term normally used to describe them is not "elite" but "highly selective," or "select." A select institution can pick and choose among its applicants since its applicant pool is two to ten times greater than the number of freshmen it admits each year. Conversely, these are the institutions most avidly selected by hopeful high school seniors.

The word *elite* is derived from the verb "to choose"; hence, it means "choice," or "select." Because of its association with political and social class hierarchies, *elitism* may have pejorative connotations. Yet, when unencumbered with such associations, the term describes the virtually universal phenomenon of some members of a social group separating themselves out for special recognition. In practice, what makes elitism "good" or "bad" is the basis on which such selectivity is exercised. In a meritocratic society, special skills or personal accomplishments (rather than considerations like family origin) constitute the basis of membership in an elite group. It is in that sense that we use the term here.

As in any free-market economy, what is most sought after in education is given the highest value, and vice versa. Being highly selective thus becomes synonymous with being the best. We do not mean to imply that quality is simply a function of popularity. But it is fair to assume that if high-achieving students work hard to get into a particular college, and their parents are willing to spend large sums of money to make their attendance possible, there must be a good reason for these commitments. The questions then become: What are the expected benefits that justify such heavy investment? To what extent are these expectations fulfilled?

The cohort and follow-up studies provide ample material with which to address these questions. Stanford University meets the most stringent criteria of selectivity.[16] It is widely regarded as one of the outstanding universities in the country.[17] Moreover, Stanford students constitute a typical segment of the educational elite. For example, in a survey of 3,600 Stanford and Harvard alumni conducted in 1986 by Yankelovich, Skelly, and White, graduates of these two schools turn out to be remarkably similar in personal characteristics and in their opinions on a wide range of social issues.[18]

WHO EDUCATES THE EDUCATIONAL ELITE?

What schools produce this educational elite? Is it indeed meaningful to claim that an educational elite exists at all? Though Americans may find the idea of a social elite incompatible with the ideals of a democratic society, stratification is obviously central to the social fabric of American society, as of most others. The places where people live, the restaurants where they eat, the sections of the airplane they occupy, all include areas that are considered "choice." Just so, a small number of colleges and universities comprise the institutions of "choice" in the American educational system. Whether they in fact provide the best education available, or the best graduates, is hardly the issue. The fact remains that they are seen as the elite institutions and their graduates are treated differently from those of the huge number of nonelite schools.

Ernest Boyer informs us that "there are probably fewer than 50 colleges and universities in the United States today that can be considered highly selective, admitting less than half the students that apply."[19] Many of these schools are well known, but some are not. Historically, the Ivy League has set the standard of academic excellence. Its eight institutions (Brown, Columbia, Cornell, Dartmouth, Harvard, Pennsylvania, Princeton, and Yale) include some of the oldest and most distinguished universities in America. They share a number of distinctive features, including highly selective admissions, an undergraduate emphasis on liberal arts, large financial endowments, high tuition, and high prestige.[20] There is, of course, no formal evaluation system that definitively identifies the elite institutions, but these characteristics place the Ivy League schools, other private institutions like Stanford, and a few public universities such as the University of California at Berkeley, on the list of the best in virtually every college guide.[21] And the lists in the college guides are in fact fairly reliable sources for identifying the elite schools—for it is primarily informal social perceptions that account for the classification of institutions.

In most social arenas, the elite upper crust (whether it be individuals, families, or organizations) has exclusive associations, "clubs," whose members carefully regulate membership to exclude unworthy aspirants. The elite educational institutions also have something of a club in the little-known body called the Consortium on Financing in Higher Education (COFHE). Based in Cambridge, Massachusetts, it collects and provides information to its member institutions and provides a forum for discussion of common problems and interests. Its thirty-two members represent the most select private institutions of higher learning in the country. Eighteen of them are universities, including the Ivy League schools and private institutions like Stanford, MIT, Cal Tech, Duke, and the University of Chicago. The other fourteen are liberal arts colleges, including six of the Seven Sisters of the Northeast (the historically all-female counterparts of the Ivy League: Barnard, Bryn Mawr, Mount Holyoke, Radcliffe, Smith, and Wellesley; the seventh, Vassar, has declined membership), plus first-rate colleges like Amherst, Williams, Swarthmore, and Pomona.[22] Though non-COFHE private institutions may offer as good an education for less money, they are generally not as highly regarded, in part because of the company they do not keep.

There are also select institutions in the public sector. For example, the faculty of UC Berkeley ranks with the very best by any academic measure. Although private schools constitute the majority of select institutions, select public schools account for the majority of enrollments because of their size. Thus, the total undergraduate student body of the COFHE members comes to about 100,000, while the undergraduate population at UC Berkeley alone is about 22,000. The public sector, after all, educates over 80 percent of all college students.

The select public institutions do not have a formal organization like COFHE, but there is informal agreement as to which of them are of higher standing. Richard Moll has called ten of these schools "the public Ivys," and he designates another nine as "the best of the rest."[23] Adding these nineteen institutions from the public sector to the thirty-two COFHE members yields fifty-one select institutions of higher learning. Their total enrollment of about 410,000 students produces 87,000 graduates a year, constituting 7 percent of those graduating from college in a given year and amounting to less than 3 percent of young adults in the same age groups.[24]

HOW DO YOU JOIN THE EDUCATIONAL ELITE?

If the very idea of an educational elite annoys some people, the process of joining it mystifies many more. Perhaps the most common perception is that the educational elite are the children of the rich who are admitted to rich schools and then go on to get the best jobs to stay rich. There is a lot of truth to this perception, but it takes more than affluence to join the educational elite. Increasing numbers of men and women have been joining it who do not come from affluent families but do have the requisite abilities and credentials.

Hence, the educational elite simultaneously serves to help the affluent to maintain their position and allows others to use it as a meritocratic vehicle for upward social mobility (see chapter 5). Since the race to join the educational elite is open (at least more open than it used to be), the burning question that animates prospective applicants is "How do I get in?"

Unfortunately, there is no simple answer, and there are many wrong answers commonly bandied about. What select institutions are looking for in their applicants is a combination of shared characteristics (such as good grades and test scores) and more individual attributes and accomplishments. Some colleges could otherwise fill their classes with students who received nothing but "A"s in high school.

By the same token, these select institutions are not only choosing their applicants but they are also being chosen by them. Most everyone applies to more than one school, and many are accepted by more than one. In making their choices, applicants rely on a variety of considerations ranging from academic reputation to the quality of the social life, the cost, and the location, including the weather.

Though no one who does not meet a set of basic requirements gets admitted to these institutions, there are a great many who meet the requirements but do not get in, either because they did not apply or they applied and were rejected. The failure to apply is often due to misconceptions. For example, many parents do not realize that selective colleges practice "need-blind" admissions, whereby applicants are chosen irrespective of ability to pay; the institution offers a financial aid package that includes loans, grants, and student employment. (About 40 percent of Stanford students availed themselves of such aid at the time of the cohort study, and the proportion has grown higher since.) Nevertheless, the cost of elite higher education still constitutes a major burden that falls most heavily on families who are too well off to qualify for aid but not affluent enough to forgo it. Applicants are also discouraged by myths about "quotas," "connections," and so on. Among those who are admitted, there are considerable differences in aptitudes and accomplishments, even within one institution. No wonder there is so much mystification and gnashing of teeth when rejection letters are mailed out each spring.

Admissions officers make choices according to guidelines set by faculty committees, administration policies, and their own judgments. Because those who cut the timber do not build the houses, there is often some tension over the discrepancies between the admissions office's choices and the type of student the faculty wants. Institutions of higher learning are also sensitive to the sentiments of alumni, donors (if private), and state legislatures (if public), as well as larger social forces (demographics, public opinion) in setting their admissions objectives. The dramatic increase in the proportion of ethnic minorities (mainly Asian-Americans) at Stanford between the time of the cohort study and the follow-up reflects the interplay of these influences.

How does an institution like Stanford choose its entering class?[25] The primary criterion for admission to Stanford is academic excellence, and the single most important credential is the transcript of coursework, which shows where the student studied, what courses he or she took, and what grades were received. Performance in core academic courses (English, science, foreign language, history) obviously counts more than the grade for driver education. Strong performances in accelerated honors and advanced placement courses are especially noteworthy. High test scores are important but do not guarantee admission. There are no minimum requirements for grade point averages, test scores, or class rank in high school, but the majority of those admitted have done very well on all counts (see page 350, note 16). These objective measures are supplemented by more subjective assessment through letters of recommendation from counselors, teachers, and principals; these letters reveal, among other things, how well applicants have used the resources within their particular schools and communities.

Next to academic excellence, applicants are assessed for evidence of sustained commitment and leadership, as well as for special talents. Hence, contributions and accomplishments in areas such as public service, student government, journalism, debate, athletics, and the arts are taken into consideration. Exceptional achievements in any one area may be very important but will not ensure admission.

Applicants' essays are scrutinized for writing skills as well as for reflections of personal qualities. (Stanford does not conduct personal interviews.) Finally, some special consideration may be given to the qualified children of alumni and faculty, as well as other applicants, to help obtain a geographically and ethnically diverse student body. Such consideration exerts only a minor influence; yet it may make the difference, all else being equal, in the admission of one applicant over another. Ultimately, it is the judgment of admission officers, based on all these factors, that carries the day. There is no formula, and their judgments are certainly fallible.

One last condition for joining the educational elite is rarely mentioned or explicitly required: mental health. The period of late adolescence is often a time of considerable psychological turmoil. Normally, this turmoil constitutes no more than the growing pains of becoming adult, but sometimes serious mental illness is evident. The requirements for joining the educational elite are so demanding that it is highly unlikely that a seriously disturbed young adult could make it. One does encounter an occasional psychotic break (or suicide) in these select student populations, but it is relatively rare; the seriously disturbed usually do not even get far enough to apply to these institutions. Admissions officers do not directly assess the psychological health of applicants, but their assessments of academic and social measures very much reflect the level of the person's psychological strength and weakness. Nonetheless, the educational elite is not immune to serious mental problems and some get admitted despite them (see chapter 8).

Just as Stanford students, their distinctive characteristics notwithstanding, are part of the larger educational elite, the elite is also very much part of a still larger cohort of individuals of similar age. Hence, they are subject to the same social trends, political issues, cultural developments, and economic swings that affect the corresponding segment of the national population. Therefore, we need to look at the cultural context in which our study participants came of age.

THE BOOMERS' TAIL

In the 1980 census of the U.S. population, our participants were in the twenty- to twenty-four-year-old group; in 1990 they were in the thirty- to thirty-four-year-old age bracket. This segment of the American population is exactly half male, half female. It is 77 percent white, 11 percent black, 9 percent Hispanic, and 3 percent Asian-American. About 40 percent never went to college; the rest did, but only 23 percent graduated, and only 5 percent obtained advanced degrees. Some 67 percent are married and 9 percent divorced, leaving 24 percent who have never married; most of those married have children, so about half are parents. The members of the educational elite are clearly quite different from their same age cohorts on most counts.

As important as demographics are historical events and cultural trends. Since the turn of the century, journalists and social commentators have labeled successive generations with catchy monikers intended to capture the flavor of the era. The first of these was the GI Generation, born between 1901 and 1924. They endured the Depression, fought World War II, and are deemed to have fostered an ethic of hard work and self-denial that as great-grandparents today they still often favor. Their children, born between 1925 and 1942, became the Silent Generation; they came of age during the cold war and settled into careers and child rearing in the placid, prosperous, and materialistic 1950s.

World War II veterans were responsible for the "baby boom" of the postwar period. This fertility bulge added some seventy million children to the U.S. population between 1946 and 1964. In cultural terms, the Baby Boomers more properly encompass those born between 1943 and 1960, accounting for the age group currently in their early thirties to late forties.[26] The participants in our study thus constitute the tail end of the Boomers.

The Baby Boomers have been prominent players in far-reaching cultural movements. The boom's early progenies, including the "victory babies" conceived at the end of the war, are popularly imaged as the "Dr. Spock" generation, reared under child-centered principles and disdained as the most indulged youngsters in history. They went to college in the 1960s, were key players in the so-called sexual revolution, and fueled the fires of the civil rights and antiwar movements.

Though accounting for only a fraction of this generation, the hippies and yippies among them added flamboyant color to the cultural landscape; the Beatles, the Rolling Stones, and Bob Dylan set the tone of their musical legacy. The "generation gap" battle was largely a confrontation between these early Boomers and the GI Generation that was in command, epitomized by presidents Johnson and Nixon. The Silent Generation, parents of the Boomers, were caught in between, spectators but hardly mediators in the culture wars of the time.

The early Boomers included not only Janis Joplin, Angela Davis, and David Harris (the former Stanford student body president who became the most famous draft resister of all), but also Bill Bradley, Rush Limbaugh, and Oliver North. Joining the counterculture and waging struggles for peace and civil rights were the preoccupations of only a portion of the generation.

After the mid-1970s, the Boomers underwent a remarkable transformation. The early Boomers turned inward, searching for the inner peace and harmony that had not been a by-product of their outward efforts. Their radical political ideology and countercultural lifestyle were diluted and transformed; to their bemused horror, they became part of the establishment they once so vigorously decried.

Those in the Boomers' tail, including our participants, were hardly touched by the 1960s cultural revolution. Instead, they redirected the turn inward into an unabashed quest for career success, while a small segment continued the youthful tradition of rebellion as punks, skinheads, and heavy-metal nihilists. Careerism was especially characteristic of the educational elite, for whom spiked hair and nail-studded boots were little more than curiosities they did not understand and certainly did not wish to adopt.

With the expansive, deficit-financed economy of the 1980s and the national obsession with reaffirming the greatness of America and the reality of the American dream, which had been so thoroughly questioned in the 1960s and 1970s, the Boomers' tail thus forsook yippiedom for yuppiedom.[27] Young urban professional—the yuppie image was in fact applicable primarily to the educational elite, though it came to be a symbol for an entire generation. It was not an image they applied to themselves, except in a self-ironic way. Nonetheless, despite being a caricature, the yuppie image of single-minded careerism, conspicuous consumption, and me-first narcissism (as Christopher Lasch anticipated it) captured an important aspect of the decade.[28]

A 1984 *Time* magazine review of *The Yuppie Handbook* by Marissa Piesman and Marilee Hartley (1984) provides a portrait of the yuppie stereotype:

> Who are all these upwardly mobile folk with designer water, running shoes, pickled parquet floors and $450,000 condos in semi-slum buildings? Yuppies, of course . . . upscale young singles and dual career couples gathered in or near big cities. . . . Yuppies are dedicated to the twin goals of making piles of money and achieving perfection through physical

fitness and therapy. The Yuppie wakes to a digital alarm, sets down the dog food for the akita and jogs for the beta-endorphins before putting in a typically grueling day at the office, followed by an hour of therapy and meeting of the condo board. There is no time for sex, so for many Yuppies celibacy is a way of life. Yuppies eat tortellini, tuna sashimi and chef's salad and favor restaurants with ceiling fans and dark green walls. No instant food ever passes Yuppie lips.[29]

The successors to the Boomers are the Baby Busters, born between the mid-1960s and early 1970s and ranging at the time of the follow-up study from older teenagers to those in their late twenties. They were born as the boom went bust—fertility rates dropped rapidly from their historic highs. They are popularly defined by contrast with the Boomers—not by who they are, but by who they are not. Their less sharply defined, nebulous public image is full of contradictions. They have been called angry, optimistic, complacent, sober, frivolous, and idealistic.[30]

Such an amorphous popular image can hardly generate a label that sticks. Sometimes they are called Xers, after the novel by Douglas Coupland, *Generation X* (1991). "Twentysomethings" is a say-nothing imitation of the "thirtysomething" label that had meaning for the Boomers. The term "13ers" is a reference to the number of generations since the time of the founding of the American Republic.[31] Though a more positive image is sometimes proclaimed (the Upbeat Generation), most of the labels are downbeat: they are the slacker, Nowhere, Boomerang, New Lost, or MTV Generation. This is a group with "few heroes, no anthems, no style to call their own."[32]

Generation X's main gripe is said to be directed at the mess left by the Boomers. Racially and ethnically more diverse than previous generations, more often the children of divorced parents, frequently latchkey children in dual-career families reared by television, "they feel paralyzed by the social problems they see as their inheritance: racial strife, homelessness, AIDS, fractured families and federal deficits."[33] Their all-black clothes seem to mourn their forlorn youth. The caps they wear backwards point to an idyllic past that is closed off to them.

These media images are obviously overdrawn, more bleak and far-reaching than is justified. Their very existence is under question. "Disaffected, bored Twentysomethings exist only in the fervid imaginations of a few writers and pop psychologists," charges one commentator.[34] As always, the bulk of the nation's youth at any given time are preoccupied with the daily business of going to school, working, getting settled. They are not hippies, yuppies, or Xers. But the stereotype captures a reality, the tenor of the times. Thus, when one speaks to college students, including those in select institutions, many of the concerns of self-proclaimed Xers are shared by them.

The members of the educational elite we have studied stand at the cusp between the Boomers' tail and Generation X. They were born around 1960, the milestone that marks the shift of these generations. They came of age in the late 1970s and early 1980s as yippiedom was giving way to yuppiedom, as political change was yielding to career success as the primary concern of young people. Very few of them were political or cultural revolutionaries, but some of them seem to have been harbingers of the Xers that followed them. In some respects, the generation of our participants constitutes something of a throwback to the pre-Boomer period of the 1950s, with their conventional career choices, focus on prosperity, and political apathy. They are very different from that generation, however, with respect to their gender roles.

As members of the educational elite, our participants were well positioned to avoid the economic and social problems that have troubled the Xers. Yuppiedom was still within their reach if they chose to pursue it, and no matter what their level of alienation from established structures, they left college with skills and credentials sufficient to open most career doors almost in spite of themselves. Hence, while they were no more immune to the cultural trends of the times than any other segment of their generation, they constitute a privileged class for whom failure—be it occupational, social, or personal—was something they would almost have to have worked at. As we shall see, very few of them did so. Their overall success, as defined in conventional terms, is overwhelming.

So far we have spoken quite generally about our cohort of the educational elite without differentiating between men and women. This is no oversight. Even though some differences persist between these groups, the similarities are by far more dominant. The majority of these women work at demanding careers, and there is a strong ideological commitment in this group to gender equality. One of the most striking social trends of recent decades—the tremendous push for women's equality in all sectors of society—is clearly reflected in the coming of age of our participants. Spawned in the 1960s along with many other civil rights efforts, the modern women's movement has generated sweeping changes in the lives of young adult women. In no segment of the population is this more evident than among the educational elite.

COMING OF AGE

Understanding the cultural and historical context in which our participants reached adulthood is essential but in itself insufficient. No matter which generation we look at, there are developmental patterns through which individuals progress at various paces. The length of time it takes to become an adult can vary greatly. For example, as the professional requirements for advanced formal education have risen, those currently entering high-level professions commonly extend their transition into full adulthood to five or even ten years after graduation from college. But no matter how long the process, some of its basic features remain fairly constant.

Our earlier cohort study focused on academic and career choices, two of the major issues facing youth in college. With the follow-up study, we have moved beyond that framework. Most college-student studies comparable to ours do not have a longitudinal component. Thus, the body of research most relevant to this stage of our work are the life-cycle studies that look at adult development across the life span.

Over two dozen longitudinal studies of human development have been conducted to date in the United States, some starting as far back as the 1920s.[35] Only some of these investigations cover the same age period as that covered in our study, and most of them deal with personality development, which is not the focus of our investigation. Nonetheless, some of the basic issues they deal with concern us as well.

No matter how we look at it, human development shows a fairly orderly, if not always uniform, pattern through the life span. Two basic and seemingly contradictory processes shape these developmental patterns: constancy and change. The men and women in our study who are now in their early thirties are, in some ways, the same individuals from the day of their birth until the day they die. But at the same time, their personal characteristics and the circumstances of their lives are obviously very different from the time of their infancy and will continue to change into their old age.

This combination of constancy and change applies to the three basic dimensions of our lives: the biological, psychological, and social spheres. Biologically, our genetic endowment was set at the time of conception (which determined, among other things, our sex). Yet the processes of growth and aging continue to transform our bodies throughout our lives. At the psychological level, our cognitive abilities, emotional makeup, and personalities were also set to some extent at birth (in part based on our genetic endowment). These aspects of our selves also continually change during our lives (including our gender identity or sense of masculinity and femininity). The question of the relative stability and change of various personality functions is one of the most contested issues in developmental psychology.[36] Third, our social circumstances (such as socioeconomic class or marital status) are likely to persist in some ways while changing in others. Our social roles (including gender roles) shift over time, largely shaping our interactions with others in the workplace and at home.

What complicates matters further—thereby making life more interesting—is that these three major streams do not flow on a parallel course but constantly intermingle, so much so that it becomes impossible to determine their exact contributions to a particular developmental event or even a single act. As we follow the unfolding stories of Philip Genochio, Alicia Turner, and their peers, we must bear in mind that their lives are in a state of constant flux, while some core elements of their identities persist. We also need to remember that our participants are now in their early thirties, that is, at a particular stage in their lives that will inevitably change.

Another puzzle in developmental studies relates to the segmentation of the life span into discrete stages, especially in adulthood. Like a river that flows from its source to its destination, each life is clearly a single and continuous entity. Yet the same river looks very different when it starts as a gentle mountain stream then rushes through rapids, cascades down a precipice, meanders through plains and spreads out in a delta. An individual's life also looks very different during its journey. But beyond such metaphors, can we reliably divide the life span into predictable stages?

The historical roots of this idea go far back. Both Plato and Aristotle conceived of life as divisible into stages. Perhaps the best-known literary reference to life stages is Shakespeare's seven ages of man.[37] While the concept of life stages is ancient, our modern ideas about these stages are relatively new. For instance, we now take it for granted that the human life span is "naturally" divided into childhood, adolescence, adulthood, and old age. But childhood as we understand it only appeared in early modern times, whereas during the late Middle Ages children over the age of six or seven were treated like miniature adults.[38] "Adolescence" is a term coined early in this century.[39] The concept of adulthood as a phase of life (apart from aging) is even more recent and remains the most nebulous, despite the common practice of dividing it into young adulthood, middle age, and late adulthood. In fact, even the onset of adulthood can be delineated only with difficulty, given the variability in the rate of biological maturation and our modern culture's extended period of psychosocial development.[40]

Adulthood is now generally considered to begin as physical maturation is reached and the obligatory phase of schooling is completed around age eighteen. The eligibility to vote further confirms a young person's standing as an adult citizen. Yet many other "adult" behaviors may already be in progress before age eighteen, including driving a car, working for pay, getting married or having children (which one million teenagers do each year). When we consider the process of becoming adult in other historical periods and across different cultures, the differences become bewildering.

Most theorists of adult development currently also conceive of the life cycle as divided into stages. But no two investigators agree on what these stages consist of, their age ranges, or the developmental issues that characterize them. Some investigators even deny the existence of stages in adult development altogether.[41]

Despite these disagreements among researchers, the notion of discrete adult life phases with characteristic concerns continues to appeal to many people, as evidenced by the enormous popularity of Gail Sheehy's *Passages* (1974) some years back. Whether such phases constitute a natural sequence or are simply artifactual constructions we impose on the seamless course of life—to gain a sense of order and control over an inherently disorderly world—may hardly matter to many, yet it remains an issue of scholarly concern.

Our cohort and follow-up studies cover the age period from eighteen to thirty-two. According to the best-known theory of life-cycle development, Erik Erikson's, this period encompasses two discrete stages, which Erikson defines by their respective phase-specific tasks.[42] Though Erikson does not ascribe specific ages to his life stages, the first stage we are concerned with corresponds to what he designates as adolescence, the next to young adulthood.

The phase-specific task of adolescence is the consolidation of the sense of ego identity, which can be simply defined as the answer to the question, "Who am I?" The preliminary steps of this task are dealt with in earlier phases of life, and its residues continue to be dealt with in subsequent phases. Yet the issue of identity comes to a head during adolescence and must be adequately addressed to avoid the problem of "identity confusion," which will otherwise linger on.

Young adulthood is primarily concerned with reconciling the contradictory demands of intimacy and isolation. Developing intimacy involves the establishment of close bonds with others, most often a member of the opposite sex, typically in marriage or some equivalent; isolation is the condition resulting when intimacy is not achieved (often seen as failure) or not desired (when we distance ourselves from those harmful to us).

A theorist who is more specifically concerned with career development in young adulthood is Daniel Levinson.[43] A decided stage theorist, Levinson envisages the life cycle as consisting of periods of rapid change alternating with periods of relative stability. Although he focuses mainly on the midlife transition, he has also studied the decade of the twenties, culminating with the age thirty transition to full adulthood. Some of the issues Levinson discusses are relevant to our study and will be discussed later.

The investigation most similar to ours in terms of its sample is the Grant study, whose subjects consisted of a cohort of Harvard undergraduates who were studied while in college and at intervals for the next thirty-five years. As prime members of the educational elite, they resemble our participants in their career choices and accomplishments. But the Grant subjects were all men who graduated in the early 1940s; the major account of their lives, George Vaillant's *Adaptation to Life,* was published in 1977, when they were in their late fifties.[44] The focus of the Grant study was on how individuals adapt to the challenges and tribulations of life through psychological defense mechanisms, a focus that is only marginally comparable to our own. Our study is virtually unique in its focus on the educational elite, female as well as male, in this postindustrial, postmodern era. Nonetheless, we will have further occasion to refer to these and other studies.

This chapter and the next provide the background of our studies over the past fourteen years and a summary of the findings conveyed in our earlier book. Then we move into two sets of issues that are basic to the lives of young adults: career and family. In chapters 3, 4, and 5, we examine career choice and preparation, patterns of career consolidation, and career success and satisfaction. In chapters 6, 7, and 8, we look at the same sequence on the more personal side: marital choice and its alternatives, patterns of family life and parenthood, marital satisfaction, and the integration of career with family life. In chapter 9, we turn to issues beyond career and family: the life of the mind, social concerns, and the search for meaning through religious or secular avenues. Finally, chapter 10 takes a broad overview of the impact of their Stanford education on the lives of these members of the educational elite in the decade after college and describes how the participants see the future shaping up ahead of them over the next decade.

CHAPTER 2

Four Pathways

For the half of American youth who go to college, the experience occurs during a key developmental period during which they are transformed from late teenagers to young adults. During their undergraduate years, they are expected to make educational and career choices that will shape their adult lives. The many goals of American higher education do not make this an easy matter; the narrow and clear goal of preparing for a career is not easily reconciled with the broad but vaguer goal of becoming an "educated person" through a diverse liberal curriculum. Nonetheless, many students try to reconcile these aims, particularly those in the educational elite, who can usually devote themselves full-time to their studies without the burdensome jobs that other students must take on to support themselves.

For those who enjoy the luxury of full-time college study right after high school, the undergraduate experience has a life cycle of its own. The freshman year is a time of introduction to higher learning. The sophomore year is a period of exploration and definition of academic purpose, normally leading to a decision on an academic major and a narrowing of occupational options. As juniors, students pursue in-depth study and consolidation of knowledge in their chosen fields. Then, as seniors, they aim for closure and integration of their educational experience and make final career decisions that will lead to either work or graduate education.

In crossing this terrain, students leave a bewildering variety of footprints. Even in a highly selective institution like Stanford, students now come from diverse backgrounds. Their academic agendas may be tentative or fully formed. They may stay on course or switch paths. Parents, professors, peers, and prospects in the job market intersect with personal preferences and chance events to shape their decisions. In the meantime, they are becoming adults and learning how to cope with the obligations and demands placed on full members of society.

The typology we developed in the cohort study imposes some order on this variety of patterns by identifying four distinct pathways through the undergraduate experience. Our four types do not constitute, however, distinct student corps marching in lockstep down these four paths. Yet although variety exists within the four types, each has a great influence on the students' academic and career decisions. For instance, some career paths, like teaching, are almost unthinkable to Careerists, but others, like medicine, are highly attractive to them; for Intellectuals, the opposite holds.

In our earlier book, we described in detail the background characteristics, academic and career choices, evaluations of the undergraduate experience, and other characteristics of the four types. Our questionnaires provided the data for our primary analyses, but to obtain a greater understanding, we relied heavily on the interview material. From this material, we profiled a number of individuals for each type. We have taken six of these biographical accounts and added two more to constitute the profile group in this volume. These eight individuals will serve as our primary biographical examples, although we will also hear the voices of numerous other participants.[1]

In this chapter we restrict ourselves to the experiences of the profile group while they were in college. The unfolding stories of their lives will then run as common threads through the rest of the book.

CAREERISTS

Martin MacMillan grew up in a small town in the Midwest.[2] Polite and reserved in manner, he came to college with the clear purpose of becoming a doctor. His father, an uncle, and several cousins are physicians. Dr. Robert MacMillan, Martin's father, is a general practitioner. He has been a role model and the dominant influence in his son's life. When Martin refers to him as "a great guy," admiration and love resonate in his voice. Yet Martin yearned to become a physician not just to imitate his father. He saw medicine as an opportunity to practice an exciting profession and help people.

Early in his freshman year, Martin plunged into the required premedical courses. His objective was clear: get through the courses he needed with the best grades he could get so as to be admitted to the medical school of his choice. He applied himself diligently to his courses, irrespective of his interest in their content. Only rarely did Martin deviate from this strategy, for instance, by taking a course on Shakespeare, which he enjoyed thoroughly.

Martin was socially and politically conservative. He often found himself at odds with the views and behavior of the more liberal students, who set the tone of college life ("screaming protests about everything"). He was distressed by all the drinking that went on because he never touched a drop. His occasional social involvements were mainly with religious groups. ("My Christian faith has helped maintain my sanity.") He was an avid tennis player, but he had little time for it. "Too much damned sunshine," he noted ruefully. "I hate to study when I could play tennis."

After two years of this relentless pace, Martin was fed up. He complained about the competitive premed atmosphere. His classes were a "depersonalized, disjointed mess." The premedical requirements allowed him too little time to take courses of more personal interest. Everything he did was geared toward furthering his chances of getting into medical school.

Some of Martin's fraternity brothers in engineering were as career-oriented as he was. But they were happy studying what they wanted. Martin was not. The tough courses in chemistry and physics, with no apparent connection to medicine, felt like a senseless and brutal obstacle course he had to get through.

Nonetheless, Martin managed to satisfy some of his intellectual interests. His interest in aging was sparked by the declining health and eventual death of his grandmother, whom he loved dearly. By the end of his junior year, he noted, his focus had "shifted a little more toward people-oriented concerns." His senior year brought further relief. Martin became a resident associate in a dorm, "the best experience of my time here." Having to work with other students broadened his social perspective. "It was a lesson in tolerance, an exercise in looking for the good in people, having to be a mandatory friend." He ventured into courses in Chinese culture and drama. He took part in a musical production, his first such experience since coming to college. But these isolated experiences at this late date hardly resulted in a broad and coherent liberal education. His preoccupation with medical school and the uncertainty of getting accepted continued to plague him.

Though Martin ended up feeling quite positive about his college experience ("I feel sadness at the prospect of leaving Stanford"), he was well aware of the narrowness of his education. He said, "If I could do it over, I would first of all get a clear idea of what I wanted out of my education apart from going into medicine, and find somebody to help me." He wished he had not played the game "too safe" and had made bolder choices, such as taking more challenging courses in philosophy and literature rather than being satisfied with introductory-level offerings in psychology and sociology. And he fervently wished that the world of premeds had been different.

Our second profile Careerist, Cynthia Eastwood, was a bright, cheerful, and enthusiastic freshman imbued with boundless energy.[3] She came to college from an affluent community in southern California. Her high school is not known for its academic excellence, and Cynthia had not really expected to get into Stanford. But once in, she loved it ("a very special place").

Like a coiled spring let loose, Cynthia wholeheartedly threw herself into athletics. She was an accomplished tennis player, and she joined the sailing club, the track program, and the rowing crew. She also joined a sorority and plunged herself into its active social life.

Academics took a backseat. As a freshman, Cynthia "felt totally lost academically." She did not study much and got mediocre grades. Science appealed to her, but she was fearful of the fierce competitiveness and competence of her peers. She tried several majors, but none of them really engaged her interest despite her initial enthusiasm for each. Her electives were picked by the "hit-or-miss approach." Yet, Cynthia seemed to know what she ultimately wanted. She proclaimed, "My primary academic interest is literature, but it is business that I plan to pursue."

In the spring of her senior year, while most of her classmates were hustling around desperately to find jobs, Cynthia simply picked up the telephone and called the president of E. F. Hutton in San Francisco. She introduced herself as a Stanford student interested in finance and asked if there was a possibility that she could have a job that offered experience and a little money. She was invited for an interview and hired on the spot.

Although Cynthia did not show the grim vocational determination of more extreme Careerists, she always assumed that her education would lead to exciting career prospects. Her plan was to get a job and a few years later go to business school. Though quite happy at Stanford, she was itching to get going by her senior year. ("I have a mild case of senioritis.")

CHARACTERISTICS OF CAREERISTS

Men are more likely than women to be Careerists; 70 percent of our Careerists are men, as against 55 percent of men in the sample. Careerists typically choose professions, such as business, law, or medicine, that until recently were male bastions. While there had been a marked increase in the proportion of women entering these professions, by the late 1970s women in these fields were still seen as unusual. Hence, despite their lower numbers, what is noteworthy is the fact that women constitute a significant share of Careerists, and many women Careerists are as single-minded in their pursuit of careers as their male counterparts.

There are no general differences among ethnic groups that seem to determine who becomes a Careerist. Yet, ethnicity intersects with gender among Careerists in two ways: minority men are less likely than majority men to be Careerists, while minority women are more likely than majority women to follow this path. As for family background, the fathers of Careerists are most often middle-level businessmen or professionals, usually college-educated but rarely with degrees beyond the master's level. They have worked hard, consider career success very important, and let their children know it. Careerists' mothers tend to reinforce their husbands' expectations, ensuring that parental emphasis on career success is direct and explicit. Students from these families know exactly what is expected of them. For example, Randy was strongly under the influence of his father, who had always "pounded" into him that he should "be the best," that he "should orient his life toward something that makes lots of money, while avoiding the 'fuzzy' studies that are quite useless occupationally."

Fathers of Careerists encourage their daughters to put careers first also, but when daughters emulate their fathers, they have to cross traditional gender barriers. Jenny is the daughter of an engineer who pushed her into the same field. She went along to please her father but felt "out of place" in this traditionally male profession. Her "heart was never in it."

Some mothers provide their daughters with career role models while others expressly point their daughters toward certain career paths to channel their own unfulfilled ambitions. For instance, Gertrude felt pressured by her mother "to succeed in a male-dominated profession." Her mother had been a teacher but was attending law school; she thought Gertrude, too, "should find something challenging" to excel in.

Similarly, Mrs. Brown had raised Jamila while working as a grocery store clerk. As a single mother, she had great ambitions for her daughter and imbued her with the desire to rise above their lower-middle-class origins. When Jamila entered college, it mattered little to her if she became a doctor, lawyer, or businesswoman. Careers were merely vehicles for getting ahead in the world. She would take the shortest career path to the most comfortable life. Jamila's use of her education as a stepping-stone to career success and little else is typical of Careerists. Each step—choosing courses, deciding on a major—is a way of getting to the next career objective. As one of them said, "I selected biology as the best major for a premed even though I hate my biology courses. They have no relevance or value for me. They are only a means to an end." There is, of course, nothing unusual about majoring in biology, and it can be a fine preparation for medical school. But the value of such a choice is compromised when it is essentially instrumental.

Their singularity of purpose endows some Careerists with almost grim determination. Edward came to college with clear and compelling career objectives. He would make the most of his education by making it lead to the sort of job he wanted. Determined to get as much competitive edge out of being at Stanford as he could, he was committed to making every last course and every last experience count directly toward his career goals.

Just as the value of their education lies not in learning for its own sake but in its contribution to their careers, these careers themselves are often seen as vehicles for the acquisition of material rewards rather than for the intrinsic satisfactions of the work. Typically, Careerists want to make money, a lot of it, and as fast as possible. Making money is in turn seen as the means to a life of financial security and leisure. Peter saw money as the means to happiness in the sense that "it will make comfortable the search for love and happiness." He was not too concerned about the specifics of his occupation—it could be anything that made money. He was also very interested in "gaining power" and would do this by making money.

We have chosen here some of the more extreme examples to make a point. Making money is not the only career objective that motivates Careerists. Martin MacMillan expected to derive much personal satisfaction from practicing medicine in addition to having a healthy income. Similarly, Edward, the engineer, had higher aims. Though he bent everything to his career interests, and definitely wanted to make a good living, his career aims were not subservient to making money. Edward was truly dedicated to his vocation, which evolved in the direction of applying basic scientific research to socially useful purposes, such as harnessing solar energy and protecting the environment.

Perhaps more than any other type, the Careerist orientation is largely formed by the time students come to college and is reinforced in college. Though their parents continue to be a major influence in their lives, Careerists do not become as involved with the faculty as other students. They commonly complain that they know too few faculty members to ask for letters of recommendation, but they are less concerned about missing out on personal intellectual interactions with faculty outside the classroom.

Careerists are especially likely to major in economics and biology in order to pursue careers in business, law, and medicine. Engineering also appeals to them because, unlike most majors, it provides them with professional skills and good job prospects right out of college. But Careerists ignore most career options in humanistic professions—public service, teaching, and so on. These fields simply do not offer enough certainty about career and financial success.

Careerists are fixed in their purposes and less likely than other types to change their career plans in college. If they do make a change, it is likely to be from one of the four mainstream professions to another: business, law, medicine, and engineering. Careerism also appeals to those parents who want their sons and daughters to follow a clear and steady path through college toward a safe, respectable, and lucrative career, with virtually guaranteed jobs and financial independence.

The price Careerists pay is the compromising of their chances for getting a broad, liberal education. As one of them said, "Exposure to the humanities is not part of my plan, and I don't want to dawdle in the 'softer' social sciences. I took one anthropology course, and it was utterly trivial and worthless." The attempt to "game" the system to please admissions committees at graduate schools results in haphazard choices of electives. "I have taken courses from about every field—business schools like that," is the way Ken put it.

Some Careerists lose little sleep over what they are missing. "There is no rhyme or reason for my course selection outside of my major," said Teresa with no visible distress. Yet others do have a genuine interest in liberal learning but are prevented from doing so by the constraints of their major. ("Study overseas? How? Not as an engineer.") The few courses Susan took outside of her major proved to be the highlight of her college career. ("They keep me sane.") Anthony complained about the "big tension in purpose" between his desire to explore a broad-based curriculum and the needs of preprofessional training.

When Careerists fail to live up to parental expectations (typically as premeds), their college experience turns disheartening. Scott found it difficult to explain to his parents that he had not been able to do well enough in the premedical curriculum. In high school he had derived great pleasure from his parents' pride in his academic performance. His parents had always told him that if he worked hard, he would achieve whatever he set his mind to. Yet he found that just making the effort was not sufficient. Diane started college as a poised young woman looking like the model gymnast she was. She had done very well in her small-town high school and plunged into her premedical studies, dropping virtually everything else and sacrificing her desire to become liberally educated. She worked hard and did well for a while. But then she began to lose her motivation. By her senior year, she had gained twenty pounds and become increasingly depressed and obsessed about food. "I haven't felt very good about myself for a long time," she complained. "I was trying so hard to please my parents, and I just couldn't do it anymore."

The effects of careerism extend beyond the classroom. Careerists are less likely to engage in cultural or service-oriented extracurricular activities, but they are keen on athletics and fraternities. They tend to be politically conservative without being politically engaged. "Social and political issues have not interested me," said Jimmy. He claimed that many others like him are not involved because they're interested in their careers, the preparation for which is "what we are paying for."

How do Careerists do in college? Their grades are just about average, and they evaluate their own abilities as average as well, feeling somewhat more competent than other students in technical and mathematical areas closely related to their major fields but far less adequate in the humanities. At graduation, they express average satisfaction with the university experience. They are more satisfied than most students with their training for graduate or professional school—the main reason they were in college— but they are less satisfied than most with their liberal education, courses, and faculty involvement.

INTELLECTUALS

Intellectual Kirsten Buchanan, like Careerist Martin MacMillan, comes from a medical family.[4] Her father is a distinguished endocrinologist, her mother is a nurse, a brother is a cardiologist, a sister is a nurse married to a doctor. Unlike Martin, Kirsten came to college to obtain "a good liberal arts education first and foremost," with the possibility of going to medical school. She credits her father for her interest in the liberal arts. Having been educated in a Jesuit school, Dr. Buchanan wanted to pass on to his children the love of learning that had been inculcated in him.

As a freshman, Kirsten had broad interests ("anything from premed to classics"), and she was full of self-confidence. "It's a matter of knowing what I want to do, not what I can do." When asked what she thought "can do" included, her unaffected and honest response was, "Anything." Kirsten took a broad mix of classes, including the premedical chemistry series, but became rapidly disenchanted with the "cut-throat fashion in which premeds are approaching their education." She abandoned the idea of medicine because it seemed too confining. Instead, she chose to double-major in Spanish and international relations to prepare herself for a career in either international business or the Foreign Service.

Kirsten spent a good part of her sophomore year in the overseas program in Spain. Fluent in Spanish, she made excellent use of local acquaintances and friends. She was very involved with the faculty but also spent a good deal of time following up on her own interests—checking out archives, visiting cathedrals, reading voraciously, and expanding her cultural horizons.

To the very end of her undergraduate days, Kirsten pursued her broad intellectual interests. Her one regret was that the requirements of her double major made it difficult for her to incorporate as many of her own choices into her study schedule as she would have liked. In her senior year, she branched out further into economics and accounting and took calculus "just for fun."

Concurrently with her varied and demanding academic life, Kirsten was active in a variety of student organizations and was an accomplished athlete. She held a steady part-time job and put a lot of energy into her friendships. To test her interest in a possible business career, Kirsten worked one summer for an international company in Spain. Based on that experience, she applied, and was admitted, to a prestigious business school. Her senior-year interviewer, impressed by her intelligence, independence, and self-confidence, was moved to ask, "Can an undergraduate be this self-sufficient?"

Christopher Luce, our second profile Intellectual, is the son of an affluent business executive father and homemaker mother.[5] His strong intellectual orientation was clear before he entered college. In response to a survey sent to prospective freshmen about their academic interests, he wrote, "I love to read!" He then listed an impressive array of authors he had already read, adding apologetically, "I am not trying to impress you, but I really want to be a writer, and I feel to be a good one you have to read the best." He also grudgingly considered the prospect of going into law ("if I have to").

Christopher's educational goals were "to learn as much about everything as I can. I want my education to give me greater appreciation and enjoyment of life." His freshman year proved almost overwhelming: "Like somebody opened a door to a whole new world. Stanford has completely disoriented me. Hooray! Marxist theory, Rousseau, Goethe, Shakespeare, Eliot, Milton—I feel like a kid in a candy store!"

This intellectual exuberance led to a slump in his sophomore year. Christopher could no longer see much purpose in what he was doing. He was "very serious, very unclear, and hence very discouraged." Christopher joined a fraternity and coached a boys' soccer team in a neighboring disadvantaged community. He then went to the overseas campus in England and traveled for several months thereafter. He returned back on track and with a broader perspective on the world and a sharper image of where he fit in.

Though he majored in English, Christopher took a wide array of courses, ranging from the biological to the behavioral sciences, as a "broadening complement to literature." Many of his fraternity brothers were engineers and premeds, and he developed an appreciation of their world as well. "I hated practical people when I came in," he admitted, "and it still makes me angry that engineers don't have more background in the humanities, but now I also wonder whether I shouldn't have more background in *their* fields myself."

The breadth of Christopher's intellectual interests was matched by his active social life. Before getting to college, he had worried about how well he would fit in, but in addition to members of his fraternity he befriended students active in the antinuclear movement and other causes. Especially important were Christopher's relationships with several members of the faculty who became mentors and friends. Yet most compelling of all were the authors Christopher came to admire: "Perhaps no single writer has had quite as big an impact on me as William Faulkner. I have ingested his work until I relate to his stories as if I had lived them myself." Christopher wrote his honors thesis on Faulkner, an experience that convinced him that he wanted to become a scholar.

CHARACTERISTICS OF INTELLECTUALS

Women are overrepresented among Intellectuals by two to one—the exact opposite of their numbers among Careerists. Are women more likely to choose this path because of their intellectual interests, or do they hesitate to single-mindedly pursue careers? Generally, intellectualism for women is not a form of career avoidance but a positive choice to have intellectual values rather than career concerns shape one's life.

Disadvantaged ethnic minorities are relatively scarce in this group, particularly among men: all Intellectual men in our sample are white, even though 15 percent of the men in the sample belong to minority groups. This is not to say that students from ethnic minorities have no intellectual interests or do not value liberal education. Many do. Wanting to get ahead in the world, however, they are not likely to see intellectual pursuits as the shortest route to economic success. Hence, they feel they cannot afford to pursue such aims at the expense of their careers. Those with strong intellectual interests try to combine them with career concerns, thus becoming Strivers.

Intellectuals generally come from more affluent backgrounds than other types, but not from the richest families. The main producers of Intellectuals are upper-middle-class families, financially secure but not wealthy.

Moreover, those at the lower end of the economic ladder are not pre-cluded, though they are less likely to be Intellectuals. Families with yearly incomes of less than $50,000 (1978 dollars), or the lower third of our family income scale, produced 12 percent of our Intellectuals.

Particularly significant factors are the occupational and educational levels of the fathers (but not mothers) of Intellectuals. Children of professors (33 percent) are especially likely to be Intellectuals; those of engineers are far less inclined toward intellectualism (8 percent), and blue-collar workers are virtually absent among these parents. Over one-third of the fathers hold doctoral degrees, and only 9 percent of Intellectuals have fathers who are not college graduates. Unlike the direct influence exerted by Careerist parents, however, the influence of the parents of Intellectuals is more subtle. As Kirsten Buchanan put it, "It's the way I was raised."

The academic strengths of Intellectuals show a curious gender split. Using SAT scores as indicators, women with high scores in both math and verbal areas are most likely to be Intellectuals; men with low scores in both areas are most likely to be in the same group. To the extent that SAT scores provide some measure of aptitude (as admissions committees typically assume), the academically "strongest" of the women and "weakest" of the men tend to end up as Intellectuals. Therefore, intellectualism may be a positive choice for the most competent women and more of a choice by default for relatively less competent men. There are, of course, exceptions among both men and women, and all of these students scored well above the national average in both math and verbal areas.

Intellectuals are just as clear about their purposes in coming to college as Careerists, but their aims are quite different. Their primary objective is to pursue their broad intellectual interests and obtain a good liberal education. They want breadth ("I would love to take every introductory class") as well as depth ("I had four years of French in high school; now I want advanced courses so I can read existentialist authors in the original").

Ironically, Intellectuals tend to feel like a beleaguered minority in the middle of one of the great centers of learning in the country, since their peer culture is not particularly receptive to their intellectual aspirations. Kevin came to Stanford expecting to be surrounded by philosophically oriented intellectual repartee. Instead, the first conversations he heard concerned the chances of being admitted to grad school and the starting salaries that lay beyond. He concluded that too many of the students were "success-oriented at the expense of honesty and depth," resulting in "a superficiality, supercoolness, and avoidance of substantial, satisfying common concerns."

The closer intellectual kinship Intellectuals have with their teachers is an important component in shaping their education. When Susan conveyed her wish to be a writer to her literature professor, he told her, "You already are a writer." Their close interaction with faculty provides Intellectuals with a more individualized, less assembly-line education, with greater depth. As one expressed it: "It's like being right at the crest of a wave of discovery where you can begin to frame what are the root questions and you begin to understand what you really might be testing for. It isn't that I understand how to frame those questions, but they let me participate, and every once in a while I could say something helpful, and I learned a tremendous amount. . . . People get excited with me, and they are respectful of the questions I am trying to ask and of the answers and results I am getting."[6]

Although Intellectuals are primarily drawn to the humanities and interdepartmental programs, some are attracted to the sciences. Irrespective of their particular area of interest, their desire for learning the material for the love of it shines through. Harold double-majored in philosophy and chemistry, completing honors programs in each. His interest in chemistry was primarily intellectual: "It's kind of purely metaphysical. I like reading about a theory and working it out in lab, or maybe just working it out with pencil and paper, and when it works, being able to say, 'Hey, that's neat!'" A medieval philosophy course in his freshman year intrigued him because "every night it's a hundred pages of people who are dead, and you can't ask them what they meant, and that was kind of interesting."

It is no wonder that Intellectuals are generally seen by the faculty and staff interviewers in very positive terms.

> Donna is a bright, independent, and genuinely self-confident young woman who is getting exactly the needed experience that she considers her first priority in undergraduate education. She has a sensible, level-headed approach to academic decision-making, a wish for a broad exposure to ideals combined with a reasonably focused program and a high degree of confidence that college is the place where she can realize her goals.[7]

> Steve is one refreshing, independent, bright, and likeable soul. In many ways he very much resembles the ideal everyone has in mind when they talk about getting a liberal arts education without worrying about a job.[8]

Intellectuals were involved in more extracurricular activities in college than any other group. They became more involved in academically oriented projects (like internships) and in music, drama, and dance. They also spent three times as much time as Careerists in voluntary activities. In their social concerns, they tended to be more reformist than radical.

Even in their friendships, Intellectuals showed a certain seriousness of purpose. There was an intensity to their relationships based on shared intellectual interests. Julie described herself as "intense about everything" and very "serious." When she shared a confidence with a friend, she expected something from the friend in return. Reflective almost to a fault, she constantly evaluated herself, her life, her interests, her friendships, and her academic growth. When she got excited about something she had just read or studied, she wanted to rush out and tell everyone else about it.

Despite the fact that students in this group deemphasized the need for career preparation, many had quite good work prospects by graduation and in fact were choosy about the jobs they were willing to take. One woman received four offers from retailing firms and two from insurance companies but turned them all down, saying, "I want to work around educated people." She turned down a job in Indiana because "I don't want to live and die diesel engines."

Intellectuals were also more likely to allow themselves time to grow into their careers and more willing to live with uncertainties. One man knew that he would never have trouble finding employment, so he wanted to be able to concentrate on broader issues and hoped he would not have to settle down for at least ten years.

At the time of graduation, Intellectuals were the mirror image of Careerists. Where Careerists expressed satisfaction with their career preparation but felt deficient in their liberal education, the Intellectuals were happy with their liberal education but expressed only average satisfaction about career preparation. They generally got higher grades and a larger share of honors, such as election to Phi Beta Kappa and graduation with distinction. They rated their abilities high in domains like literature and the arts but lower in math and the natural sciences. They were specially pleased with their faculty interaction but rated their sense of belonging and general level of contentment as only average. Overall, they got what they came for: a strong, diverse education. But they were much less certain than Careerists that they had strong professional prospects after college.

STRIVERS

Striver George Mehta entered college at the age of sixteen with thirty units of advanced placement credit.[9] He had compiled a straight-A record in high school, with a 97 percent average in his grades, and had won a prestigious science award, just as predicted by his sixth-grade teacher. George's special interest was biology, and he had thought of becoming a doctor. He enrolled in the premedical chemistry sequence as a freshman but also sampled a wide range of courses in art, philosophy, international relations, and geology. He preferred focused seminars over large introductory courses. He got straight "A"s ("cruised through classes easily"). Photography and working for the student radio station took up the rest of his time.

George encountered "stagnation" in his sophomore year; he did not feel academically challenged but did feel compelled to fulfill his major requirements. Chemistry lost its appeal; he retained little of the information once the course was over. ("It is like collecting snowflakes.") Philosophy stayed with him longer and was more stimulating, and he especially enjoyed courses in art. He ended up majoring in biology but could easily have double-majored in art history since he ended up fulfilling most of its requirements.

In his junior year, George was able to take more of the courses he enjoyed. He chose them with care, distinguishing between those that were "stepping-stones" and others that were "valid courses" of intrinsic interest. By the middle of his sophomore year, he had achieved junior-year standing. He could have graduated early (a Careerist would have), but instead he broadened his intellectual horizons further; his fascination with visual thinking led him to take courses in mechanical engineering. He spent his summers as a volunteer for the Sierra Club and worked with emotionally disturbed children at a summer camp. He painted and wrote poetry.

By his senior year, George was trying to focus on a career and his long-term future ("thinking very seriously about my life in great detail"). He had long since given up all thought of going into medicine. "Once you are a doctor, there is only one thing you can be." Instead, he decided to go to business school. A surprising choice, perhaps, but George had his own perspective on business, one that went beyond making money. He hoped to use his background in biology to become involved with environmental problems in industry. He was accepted at a first-rate business school on a generous scholarship. His senior interview report pointed out that, in addition to his broad intellectual interests (which would have easily qualified him as an Intellectual), George had strong career ambitions as well. He aimed to become the president of a major corporation.

Articulate, poised, and attractive, Striver Geraldine Jones seemed destined for the stage even as a freshman.[10] Her father was a scientist turned businessman, her mother an actress. Her parents were divorced, and her mother had been remarried, to a physician. Geraldine chose Stanford because she wanted a "superior education," but her academic and career plans were rather vague. The excellent private school she went to had already inculcated in her the importance of a good liberal education, but linking that to a career turned out not to be an easy task for her.

Geraldine began by enrolling in a wide variety of courses, ranging from the natural sciences to the humanities. She liked science and thought of becoming a doctor, but she felt more strongly drawn to the stage, where she had already done some acting and singing. Science, drama, medicine— three career streams from three parental sources—coursed through Geraldine's mind.

Things got even more uncertain in her sophomore year, when she lost some of her academic zeal. ("I have no motivation.") Pulled in different directions by her diverse talents and interests, she meandered on through various courses while much of her time and energies went into singing in musicals, acting, attending concerts, participating in sports, and getting involved with people. The sense of confusion she conveyed held only glimmers of clarity and purpose.

In her junior year, Geraldine began to see more clearly the various career choices facing her. She began to think more carefully about what she wanted to do, apart from parental expectations. She decided on a mind-boggling combination: to major in environmental engineering and then pursue a master's degree in drama.

Following her junior year, Geraldine went to New York to enroll in drama workshops and take acting lessons. She got a job and supported herself. There were "issues to be sorted out" with her father. They had a long and candid discussion. ("We talked for five days straight.") That greatly helped to clear things up. Geraldine summed up the gains she made during the year by saying, "I believe the force that most strongly shaped this academic year was a long-needed (and continuing) process of maturation."

On returning to college as a senior, Geraldine changed her major to drama. Her academic and career aspirations finally seemed to come together. She felt settled and happy with her choice. She had ranged widely over many subjects, some by choice, some through indecision, yet was still aware of a "vast wealth of things here that I have left untapped." Though grateful that she had been allowed the freedom to seek her own way, she complained that "creative people die a slow death in college, in such a homogenized environment."

At graduation, Geraldine had been accepted for advanced theater study at two first-rate programs. She had a standing job offer from a producer in Paris as well as the prospect of working for the Royal Shakespeare Company. In ten years, she expected to be an actress working in the theater or in film. Geraldine's parting comments were, "I'm guided by what makes me happy and doing things that I enjoy. It's important to me not to be locked in. I need to feel I am experiencing my potential. I need to test myself in all different capacities. It's important to keep myself alive and living."

CHARACTERISTICS OF STRIVERS

Strivers are a hybrid group derived from Careerist and Intellectual stock but with their own distinctive features. While Careerists are mostly men and Intellectuals mostly women, the two genders are equally represented among Strivers. Nonetheless, Striver men are more like Careerists with strong intellectual interests, while Striver women are more like Intellectuals with decided career interests. In either case, getting a good education and a good job are their dual objectives.

> I want to get a good general education, but I do not want to graduate without a marketable skill that will allow me to do something interesting and worthwhile while at the same time earning enough money to do the kinds of things I want to do.[11]

> What I want from my undergraduate education is a good background that will be rigorous, that will enable me to be admitted to a good law school, something I have wanted to do since my junior year in high school. I would like to learn to be constructively critical and to be logical and to balance those things out with some general knowledge of science and some appreciation of the arts.[12]

Ethnic minority students are especially likely to be Strivers, with Asian-Americans of both sexes and Hispanic males leading the way. Correspondingly, the socioeconomic background of Strivers, both minority and non-minority, is generally lower than that of Careerists and Intellectuals. Thus, almost half of our Strivers came from families with yearly incomes of less than $20,000, and most of the few children of blue-collar workers in our sample were Strivers. But this is a bimodal group as well: 39 percent of the children of physicians and 29 percent of students from the top income bracket (over $100,000 per year) are also Strivers.

Bill came from the more typical modest background. His father worked fourteen hours a day in a print shop. Neither parent had gone to college. Their social lives were centered on their small evangelical church. Coming from this sheltered background, Bill felt "socially inexperienced." Yet his horizons expanded rapidly. He was determined to get a good liberal education and equally keen about his "ultimate dream of getting into a J.D.-M.B.A. program" to secure his financial future.

By contrast, Joshua's family had extensive financial interests in the entertainment industry. He had attended a select prep school, traveled widely, and was socially sophisticated. He, too, wanted a good liberal education and a successful career. Having already helped manage some of his father's global enterprises during the summers, Joshua had exercised a level of financial responsibility that many of his peers would never attain.

As measured by SAT scores, Strivers have the weakest academic backgrounds of the four types (while still scoring very high by national standards). Paradoxically, then, the academically least strong of the educational elite are most likely to be the ones to go after the best of both worlds. We were struck by the ambitiousness and boundless enthusiasm of students like Jennifer who spoke over and over again of her exhilaration over being at college. She had discovered a freedom to think about new things, and a lot of her classes she took for their intrinsic interest. She loved to discuss ideologies, philosophies, and personal values.

The breadth of interest and energy of some of the Strivers were breathtaking. Kevin, a big grinning farm boy from Oregon, came to Stanford having done everything from manual labor to assembling a computer. His career interests included farming, the Foreign Service, engineering, and veterinary medicine. At first he felt a bit out of place, but his three quarters at the Stanford overseas campus in Vienna and the University of Vienna found him "attending a concert almost every night and going to a dozen Viennese balls." He traveled through Poland, Hungary, and Yugoslavia; on returning to Stanford, he spoke German, French, Russian, and Romanian. The next summer Kevin worked on an eastern Oregon construction site, living alone in a camper. He had no radio, telephone, or television, so he read twenty-three books in several languages and all of Shakespeare's works. He was a perfect example of the early pioneer American—adventurous, ingenious, and self-reliant.

Not every Striver is a Kevin. More often than not, the quest for breadth overwhelms depth when Strivers spread themselves too thin. "My program has been incoherent, especially in my major," said one. "It would have helped me if things had been more structured. I wanted to get something out of classes that would do something for me personally." Melanie's program of study also appeared aimless. She had come to college for a broad general education and wanted to learn a lot about a lot of things. Not surprisingly, she found it hard to choose a major and was extremely frustrated by the process of narrowing down her interests.

Strivers, a gregarious lot, were often the mainstays of student theatrical productions. Tom spent forty hours a week working on a production. He directed the show, wrote the music, conducted the orchestra, and was involved in all other aspects of it. Brenda could move with ease from a vigorous tennis match at 4:00 P.M. to a faculty dorm dinner at 5:30 P.M. and a pretest chemistry study section at 7:00 P.M. She ran two miles each day, swam on warm days, hardly ever missed the flicks, went to lots of speeches to hear "great people that you would otherwise only read about," played tennis, practiced the piano, played the flute in her dorm's musical production—yet she still worried that she might be missing some opportunities.

In steering their way through college, Strivers were responsive to many influences, including (like Careerists) their parents. Sandy's many and varied interests seemed patterned on his father, a translator for an oil company who "speaks fifteen languages and can play the piano with his toes." Like Intellectuals, they sought close relationships with the faculty and complained when they did not find them. Mark regretted that professors did not provide much direction to students and was disappointed that no member of the faculty had taken a real interest in him. He appreciated the university's efforts to promote student-faculty contact but felt that "such interactions can't be forced."

Strivers are also strongly influenced by their peers, their work experience, and their reading of the future job market. Thus, they are the most open of all groups, embracing everything in sight. It is hardly surprising that they make more varied choices about majors and careers than do Careerists and Intellectuals. They tend to go into engineering somewhat more often than others, but otherwise their choices, especially those of women Strivers, cover the whole gamut.

The most distinctive personal characteristic of Strivers is their enthusiastic optimism and positive outlook, sometimes carried to the point of almost Pollyannaish naïveté: "Every class I have taken here has been my best class." . . . "The brilliance of that man is amazing." . . . "I know I'm getting the best." . . . "All superb in their own ways." Their enthusiasm is so infectious that faculty and staff react to them in reciprocal terms. ("An interview with Yvette is a great way to start the day. This bouncy, almost giddy live wire is about as spirited and zestful a Stanford student as I've ever talked to.")

Nonetheless, many Strivers have their limitations. For instance, Nancy was described as "not an intellectual but one respectful of intellect. She will never be a great student, but she has been able with effort to do good work in hard-for-her courses." Similarly, Greg came across as attractive and eager. "He is full of conflicting and confused feelings and beliefs, but he has intelligence and energy and is an activist; he is also introspective when he allows himself the time, so the confusions will probably sort themselves out."

What also comes across clearly is the healthy and happy cast of their personalities. Strivers are typically the most well rounded of students. They may well be psychologically the healthiest. They fit into the college culture like a hand in a glove. For instance, Sarah impressed us as an extraordinarily well-adjusted, healthy, and balanced person. She was bright but did not come across as a heavy intellectual; she had distinct professional ambitions but was not out to conquer the world; she knew what she wanted in a career yet simultaneously had definite aspirations for her personal life. In short, what was impressive about her was not one or another isolated characteristic but the overall balance and harmony of her life.

Strivers turn out to be the academically least successful students (with notable exceptions). They got lower grades than the other types, and few of them made Phi Beta Kappa. Yet their level of satisfaction with their undergraduate experience is highest of all the groups. When asked what they were taking with them from college, one senior summed it up as "everything."

THE UNCONNECTED

Katherine Johnson was enticed to attend Stanford by a financial aid package with a lower loan burden than that offered by Berkeley.[13] She needed all the help she could get; although she was born into a "solid middle-class family," after her parents divorced (when she was twelve) she was raised by her mother under strained financial circumstances. Having accrued thirty units of advanced placement credit, she hoped to graduate in three years while working at a variety of jobs, starting as a hasher. She no longer counted on help from her mother.

Katherine had broad but rather diffuse academic interests. She enjoyed athletics and was strongly committed to social causes, especially regarding South Africa. One of her main disappointments at Stanford was the "lack of awareness and involvement of other students pretty much caught up in their own worlds."

Katherine had thought of law but changed to "doing something interesting, with little concern for money." As she put it, "I have no desire to get rich, and I am not afraid to be poor."

As Katherine progressed through her undergraduate years, her academic aims remained broad and diffuse. As a junior, she still hoped for "exposure to as many possible ways of viewing the modern world as possible." Her career interests had shifted to teaching high school, though law school remained a possibility. A certain sense of alienation from the mainstream and deep concern for others continued to preoccupy Katherine. In

responding to a question about what books had been particularly significant during the year, she referred to Robert Caro's *The Power Broker:
Robert Moses and the Fall of New York* (1974) and went on to say:

> It reminded me, in the midst of the Stanford country club, that there
> is much to be done "outside." I have lost my fourth good friend to
> the malaise known as "stopping out"—the fourth one who said she
> was going crazy here, though only the second to actually get institu-
> tionalized. Does Stanford know about these people? Where they go
> when they "stop out," and why? Four out of perhaps six real friends
> have stopped out in my three years here, and all four have sought
> psychiatric help. I'm not saying this is a function of being a Stanford
> student, as opposed to going to any school, or just plain living in
> these times (Camus calls this an "unsancrosanct age"). But I wonder
> if Stanford, with its various ways of reaching the student personally
> (The Bridge, advisers, these questionnaires) has any idea that so
> many students are succumbing, "dropping like flies," as my room-
> mate put it. I'd be interested to find out, and interested to know
> what, if anything, is done about it. Can anything be done? I don't
> know. It would make quite an interesting survey.

To the end of her senior year, Katherine remained full of contradictions.
She got excellent grades with seemingly little effort, describing Stanford as
"a perpetual vacation." She could have easily been an honors student; yet
the Political Science Department found her proposal for an honors thesis
"too broad," so she dropped it, apparently without regret.

Katherine continued to be disdainful of the careerist mentality of her
peers and dismayed that even her counterculture friends were running
scared and drifting toward business. "Everyone is flocking to law school,"
Katherine noted. "If I can't do something else, I'll go to law school also."
Yet, at the same time, she was rather bitter that Stanford had failed to
equip her for the job market and disillusioned that a liberal arts education
seemed to lead nowhere. She hoped "to write over the next five to ten
years, while doing some stupid job," but she had a "terrible fear of ending
up as a secretary or bank teller."

His long, thick, heavy mane of hair an emblem of his sense of alienation,
Unconnected David Levy had barely begun his freshman year before he
started thinking of transferring to another college.[14] He claimed to be disenchanted with the "liberal education bias that provides no skills" but
simultaneously denounced as "disgusting" the "highly competitive achievement orientation of achievers and succeeders."

David professed some interest in an undergraduate degree in business, though he had known Stanford did not offer such a program before he arrived. In view of his uncertainty, David took a range of courses to learn about various fields. He dropped out for part of his sophomore year to attend his home-state university. The experience prompted him to head right back; things were worse over there. Finally, he declared English as his major but remained vague about his long-range plans and career aspirations.

During his junior year, the pieces of David's life began to fall into place. He found classes he liked and a co-op student house he felt comfortable living in. He liked the people, the autonomy, and the collaborative decision-making process. He also met a woman who became central to his life.

The high point of David's undergraduate experience was the time he spent at the overseas campus in England. He was glad to be out of the country. "I realized that the United States is not the only viable society, let alone the center of the world," he declared on his return. The courses he took there were excellent and closely tied to his major. Yet even about this successful experience David expressed relatively little enthusiasm. He showed no interest in further travel, no burning desire to see the rest of the world; nor did he manifest the typical nostalgic reactions of students just back from their first trip abroad.

David reached his senior year showing not much satisfaction with either his educational experiences or his career prospects. Though he remained reasonably satisfied with his major, he was not involved with the department. His career prospects had become even vaguer. He thought of teaching English in the Peace Corps, a prospect that did not please his career-oriented parents. He was the third son, and with David's two older brothers still uncertain about career direction, his parents were running out of sons to fulfill their ambitions. He considered working on a kibbutz in Israel. Meanwhile, feeling compelled to become independent of his parents, he hoped "to find some way of supporting myself that I can stand." Graduate school remained a long-range possibility. Though a fairly accomplished guitarist and piano player, he could not see himself as a musician like his father. He had long since lost interest in becoming an accountant like his mother.

In his senior year, David expressed regret about having gone to college right after high school. ("I should have waited until I found what was the point of it.") His freshman adviser, later his departmental adviser, had been helpful in sorting out his courses, but "otherwise I did not seek out many faculty. Apart from the classroom, I probably learned more from other students."

David seemed like the type of student who would have passionate political involvements, yet he described himself as "not very active but very aware." His long hair, worn-out clothes, and general style of relating to others made him look like a throwback to the 1960s. Without the social support for that lifestyle, he could only maintain it on his own.

David remained an enigma to the very last. His senior year interview report concluded:

> It's hard to get a sense of how bright or talented he may be because he is extremely low-key, nonassertive, and not at all lively. I also thought that he's fairly thoughtful and concerned about leading a life that he can feel both contributes to the greater good and is intrinsically satisfying, and until he feels certain that he has found a career line to pursue that is his own choice, he won't begin to pursue it. Establishing independence from his parents is a rather important need at this point, and that pressure on him to get into a standard success-oriented career has led him both not to do so and to feel stymied as to what he really wants to accomplish.

In the final assessment of his college experience, David wrote, "I simply would not attend Stanford again if given the chance. Although there's no campus that I would prefer over Stanford, the financial cost was simply too great." He left "with the realization that I was completely lost as far as my career plans go."

CHARACTERISTICS OF THE UNCONNECTED

The first three types discussed in this chapter present fairly consistent and comprehensible patterns. It is, after all, not difficult to understand why someone would want to be a Careerist or an Intellectual, or try to get the best of both worlds by becoming a Striver. But why would anyone go to all the trouble of getting into a select institution like Stanford and then refuse or fail to connect to either of its main objectives?

The question baffled us for a long time. Since in every race there is a loser, we assumed initially that the Unconnected must be the losers. Yet the Unconnected are not losers, either then or now. Our bafflement about the Unconnected began to clear when we recognized that there are many more reasons for being Unconnected than there are for being any of the other three types.

The Unconnected are thus the most diverse and the least homogeneous

of the four types. They can be subdivided into four subgroups characterized by vastly different motivations and psychological dynamics—as well
as outcomes a decade after college.

The first and largest subgroup among the Unconnected consists of
those who are young for their years when they enter college. The second
are distracted from their academic goals for a variety of reasons. The third
subgroup, by contrast, includes individuals who may be mature beyond
their years but who wish to pursue their destinies on their own terms. The
fourth and smallest subgroup are those persons with serious psychological
problems that make it impossible for them to fully engage in the college
experience (discussed in chapter 8).

It is easy to detect seeds of other orientations in the first subgroup;
some are pointing in a Careerist direction, others toward the Intellectual
experience. But like cars with their engines idling but not in gear, they are
not moving in either direction. Their indecision, procrastination, and
unwillingness to make definitive choices may suggest a developmental lag,
but it is no reflection on either their intelligence or competence. At least
some of them have come to college without being ready for it. Some gave
in to parental pressure, and others simply had nothing better to do.

For many of them, being Unconnected is tied up with the struggle of
identity formation. "Who am I?" is a question they cannot answer, and
without knowing who they are, they cannot act. In Eriksonian terms, they
have not yet consolidated their sense of ego identity. This unresolved
search for personal identity often underlies their academic and career confusion. For instance, Michael struck us as an undergraduate who was at
Stanford but not of Stanford. His interviewer noted:

> He's been a sort of academic drifter always out of the mainstream,
> swirling in his own currents, touched from time to time by the
> momentum of the curriculum and spun into an eddy before drifting
> back into his own personal flow. He seems still to be existentially
> afloat. My guess is that his education and the way he pursued it was a
> way for him to sow many seeds in the soil of his life without having to
> confront any fundamental facts about his motivational goals. This
> may have been astute, a way of giving himself more time to grow up,
> to let nature, in a way, take its course according to which of the seeds
> prospered and what sort of a garden grew.

This is the reason this subgroup of the Unconnected may come across
as less psychologically mature, not as well adapted as the Strivers, less
"adult" than the Careerists. Yet, except for the psychologically disturbed

subgroup, they are not conflicted to the point of being unable to focus on their work.

A variety of factors distract the second subgroup and lead to a failure to connect. Some become distracted from educational and career goals by getting overly involved in social and extracurricular interests. They are out to have fun and cultivate friendships. The Unconnected also include more than their share of varsity athletes, who have to put much time and energy into their sports, leaving little time for academics. As one of them put it: "My grades have been terrible . . . my study habits are terrible. I practice three hours a day and I keep saying I am going to do better next quarter but I do too many other things. I don't see the usefulness in studying. I think I can do anything if I apply myself but it gets me down when I do poorly in my classes. I don't want to face the next year. I don't feel I want to be here. I am just sick of it. But I probably will come back because of the team."[15]

Other students fail to connect because of the disparity between their educational and social background and the Stanford culture. One woman said, "I am lost. My high school was so small, and Stanford seems so big. I am really scared here. I don't know what I want to do."

The appearance of disengagement can also be deceptive. Jimmy came from "a sleepy town in a farming community." He looked as distracted as they come. A hopeless procrastinator, he had yet to declare his major and get an adviser late in his junior year. Notably uncommunicative, he bored the interviewer to tears. Yet by the time Jimmy graduated, he had been admitted to five law schools and had managed to get a fine liberal education as well. A Striver could not have done better.

For the third subgroup, the cause of their unconnectedness lies more often in the institution (or their perception of it) than in themselves. Far from being behind in academic development, they are out of step by being ahead. It is the exceptional competence of some students that seems to lead to unconnectedness; college fails to challenge them sufficiently. Alex came from a select prep school where he had done very well. Having already been away from home and studied in a demanding academic setting, college was hardly a novel experience. In his freshman year, he said, "It isn't right if someone can goof around like I have, cram just before final exams, and pass." Yet that is what he did. In his junior year, he continued to be plagued by lack of motivation. He declared a major in English and found it easy to do well. Writing came naturally for him; he could go through the entire reading list for a quarter during the last week before exams and come out with a very respectable grade.

Ronald was brilliant. He came to Stanford with forty units of advanced placement credits, a math SAT score of 800 and a verbal score of 720. He had an intensely intellectual orientation to life but only the vaguest of career interests—the perfect combination for intellectualism. Yet Ronald did not connect to the institution's intellectual lifelines. He majored in physics, earning straight "A"s, but was not interested in the subject; he took a set of demanding courses in the humanities but expressed little enthusiasm for them. Had Stanford treated Ronald more like a graduate student than an undergraduate, he might have connected more easily.

Others in this group showed exceptional maturity and psychological health despite an appearance of indecisiveness. Joel, for example, was an unusually relaxed individual, one who seemed to "have his head together." He was remarkably calm, patient, trusting, straightforward, and self-aware. It is hard to explain why some people's indecisiveness seems dangerously linked to confusion while a person like Joel makes that same indecisiveness seem so mature, healthy, and well considered. Unconnectedness can result from a highly developed perspective on the world that rejects established academic and career patterns.

These active rejectionists, who were "marching to the beat of a different drummer," were critical of what they saw around them. They were perturbed by the materialistic aspirations and lack of social consciousness characteristic of the late 1970s. Said one, "*Selfish* is a pejorative term, and I don't want to put people down, but the values I see reinforced here are for people to act primarily for themselves. The major and unquestioned assumption is 'Pursue what you want without concern for others.'"[16]

Some of these students speak to the ideals of the institution, calling attention to the discrepancy between what it preaches and what it practices. In charging that higher education has itself become disconnected from its central mission, they may be addressing issues from a higher moral plane than those who teach them.

> Education should be a part of a way of life rather than something you do for the exam. . . . A lot of people put off until after college decisions about what sort of a person they want to be and what sort of life they want to lead. There is more to life than studying. My goal is learning to think critically. I've been more and more frustrated by the whole approach to education. They praise the methods of Socrates but use the method of the Sophists he denounced. I've heeded the advice not to let school get in the way of my education.[17]

The Unconnected are such a diverse group that their background characteristics do not reveal consistent patterns. Men are only marginally more likely to be unconnected than women. Ethnicity makes no difference. Their socioeconomic backgrounds are bimodal in that both families of very high social status and families of relatively low social status produce many members of the Unconnected. Hence, sizable proportions of the children of lawyers, professors, and corporate executives are of this type, but so are many of the children of minor professionals and the owners of small businesses.

Being less competent to cope with classroom demands is clearly not the general explanation for this orientation. The Unconnected have higher than average SAT scores; women are especially strong in verbal ability, and men have the highest overall SAT scores of the four types. In this respect, Unconnected men are the counterparts of Intellectual women. Neither does their unconnectedness prevent them from using their abilities: their grades are at the mean for all students, and they are no less likely than other students to make Phi Beta Kappa or graduate with distinction. Their academic strengths make their unconnectedness all the more perplexing.

While the Strivers are influenced by everyone, the Unconnected seem to be influenced by no one. Parents, faculty, fellow students, job market considerations—none of these seem to have much impact on them. They go through college as impervious as ducks shedding water. Some, as we have seen, deliberately choose to ignore outside influences; they insulate themselves so they can make their own choices. Others, more universally disengaged, are no more disconnected to the university than to other aspects of their lives.

Further, the parents of the Unconnected seem to make little effort to influence their children. Some purposely restrain themselves so that their children can make their own decisions; others seem to have concluded that it is futile to try to steer them. When parents do try to exert control, the Unconnected often resist (in sharp contrast to Careerists). To retain their independence, the Unconnected often keep their parents in the dark about what they are doing. ("I choose the courses I want to take and write home after the quarter to tell my parents what I took and how I did.")

Nevertheless, these students are not rebels; they have generally cordial relationships with their parents. Representative comments include, "I have been blessed with wonderful parents and I love them deeply," and, "My family is very supportive; I spend at least an hour a week on the phone with them." The independence and skepticism of the Unconnected about institutional purposes are not conducive to engagement with the faculty. They have little use for advisers. ("I did not have an adviser, and I didn't care about having one.") But is unconnectedness the cause of the lack of closeness between students and faculty, or is it the result? There is evidence for both. When the Unconnected avoid faculty, the faculty are unlikely to seek them out. Professors do better with students who know what they want, to whom they can act as mentors in their specialized fields. Faculty are less willing to take the time to counsel students who do not know what they want. So those who most need guidance are least likely to get it.

Turning to the choices that the Unconnected cannot avoid, such as declaring a major, we find that their majors are more evenly distributed across departments than those of any other type. They major in the humanities almost as often as Intellectuals do but also are almost as likely to major in the natural sciences and engineering as Careerists. This reflects their diversity, but it also indicates that many make their choices passively. ("It's a major you can decide on without really deciding.")

Their career choices are likewise quite varied, but they feel less certain of their career choices than do other types, and they vacillate between their options more than other types. They are second only to Intellectuals in avoiding mainline professions and are least likely to choose business. Many end up in communications, the arts, and teaching. They are most likely to come up with fanciful choices. ("My secret dream is to be a cocktail pianist on a cruise ship to Tahiti.")

Most important, the Unconnected tend to postpone making career decisions. By the spring of their senior year, only one-third of them had reasonably certain career plans, compared with two-thirds of the Intellectuals and virtually all of the Careerists and Strivers. One was not sure she wanted a career; if she was to have any career at all, she wanted many careers. ("I can't see doing something forever.") Another was vague about his future career and not a bit worried about being vague. A third said, "My friends want financial security and are drifting toward business. I am not afraid of being poor and don't see it as connected to happiness or self-fulfillment." The attitudes of the Unconnected toward liberal education are also hard to pin down. The latent Intellectuals among them show their colors ("I dearly love to read and write"), but others are disdainful and see college as a pointless game that must be played.

Not surprisingly, in evaluating their undergraduate experience, the Unconnected are consistently less satisfied than other students. They are dissatisfied with both their liberal education and their career preparation. They also attach less importance to most aspects of their education; nothing seems to matter much to them. When they rate their own abilities at graduation, they consistently see themselves as less able than other types see themselves. The Unconnected reveal themselves, however, in attitude rather than performance; they do at least as well as others.

CAUSES AND CONSEQUENCES

Reduced to the briefest of summaries, careerism provides clear, ready-made access to safe and respectable professions, often at the cost of forgoing a broad liberal education; intellectualism nurtures the love of learning but may exact a price when it comes to career preparation; reaching for the best of both worlds, Strivers tend to spread themselves too thin; unconnectedness is a more idiosyncratic and diverse path that allows a greater measure of self-determination but carries the risk of dissipation of purpose—a higher risk and higher gain proposition.

While the outcomes of our typology during the college years are fairly clear, the process by which these types are established is a puzzle. When we pressed our participants during the interviews to reflect on their motivations for their choices and behaviors, the ultimate reply seemed always to be, "Because that is who I am." We assume that these four orientations are deeply rooted (as confirmed by one kindergarten teacher who claimed to recognize the childhood version of our four types among her students!). Yet a systematic search for the antecedents of our four types would require a complex developmental study going back to their childhoods. This is a monumental task that we could not undertake. Instead, we have chosen to explore the long-range consequences of these four orientations—hence, the follow-up study.

The questions we have pursued go in many directions. How does belonging to one or another group influence the consolidation of the educational elite's career choices? How does it affect the trajectory of their early careers? How do these orientations intersect with their personal lives—in the establishment of intimate ties, marriage, parenthood, and alternatives to marriage? What is the impact on career success, on developing mentor relations, on the level of satisfaction in personal relationships? How are the life of the mind, social concerns, and matters of faith and meaning affected by these orientations?

As we explore the coming of age of the educational elite, we differentiate them in three ways: by typology, gender, and ethnicity. We recognize that our typology may not be applicable to all college students. Strong, non-career related intellectual interests and commitments are relatively rare outside the educational elite, so the Intellectual and Striver types are not likely to be common among the general population of higher education students. But our research indicates that, for the educational elite, the typological pathway pursued in college has important implications for adult life.

Our second major axis of differentiation, gender, is an obvious choice. As we mentioned in chapter 1, sweeping changes in women's place in society have been effected in recent decades. In our study, the importance of gender differentiation lies more in the absence of differences than in their presence: women and men of the educational elite look much less different from each other as they come of age than we would have predicted.

Although larger differences may appear as our participants move into later stages of their careers, it is important to highlight the relative sexual equality that has been achieved so far in this select group. Finally, while ethnic differences are also not marked, they, too, require special attention.

STABILITY OF THE TYPOLOGY

One of the key questions raised by our earlier book is the stability of the typology. Is a Careerist or Intellectual in college locked into that orientation for life (or at least the next ten years)? Recalling the basic developmental processes of constancy and change (chapter 1), to what extent do these four types change or remain the same over the decade after college?

A considerable degree of change in typology was already evident during the college years. We found that the freshman intellectualism score correlated quite well (.60) with the junior intellectualism score, as did the corresponding careerism scores (.58). These figures attest to a strong persistence of the typology even as it shows considerable change. Such change was more limited within the core groups, which retained three out of four students so categorized through the college years. Yet, within each category, one-fifth to one-quarter of the students changed to another type by the junior year. However, all of these were shifts into a contiguous category, owing to a score change on either the careerism or intellectualism scale (but never both). A Careerist could become a Striver (with a higher score in intellectualism) or Unconnected (with a lower score in careerism; the intellectualism score being already low), but a Careerist would never become an Intellectual. And vice versa. The same was true for all types. Considering the substantial number of people in the more amorphous group in the center (figure 1.1), what may have looked like a shift in type for these individuals was more often a case of their late differentiation into a type.

Similar changes in typology affected our participants over the decade after college. Until we discuss these changes in chapter 10, we must bear this fact in mind as we follow the unfolding of their careers and personal lives. Hence, some individuals may not retain their type identity a decade later, including those in our profile group. Yet we identify them throughout the book by their original classification; to do otherwise would prove highly confusing, and our interest lies in assessing the long-term consequences of elite education.

We also need to track the life changes experienced by each group during the decade—that is, the patterns of interaction between typology, aspect of life (such as career and family), and time period (different segments of the decade). For example, do Careerists experience more changes in their personal lives? Do Intellectuals show greater shifts in their career patterns? Do Strivers experience significant changes, in either the career or family realm, earlier in the decade than the Unconnected? In short, what is the range of stability and change for each type, for a given area, and in what time schedule do changes occur?

Since this descriptive study is not geared toward testing hypotheses, we did not start the follow-up study with specific predictions. Nonetheless, we did have some general expectations. The most obvious, for all the participants, centered on the predictable changes between the early twenties and early thirties having to do with settling down in careers and family lives.

More specifically, we expected Careerists to broaden their intellectual horizons once they consolidated their careers. And given their more conventional bent, we anticipated that they would marry and become parents sooner than others. We predicted that the necessity of making a living would divert more of the Intellectuals' attention to career matters. We were uncertain how they would behave on the family front.

We thought Strivers would have to rein in their tendency to go in all directions. We expected their career inclinations to get ahead of their intellectual interests, hence, that they would become more like Careerists. Given their gregarious nature, we thought they, too, like the Careerists, would settle down sooner in their personal lives.

We felt least confident in making predictions about the Unconnected. We were confident that the developmentally less mature subgroup would catch up and be more or less indistinguishable from their peers; perhaps some would show careerist leanings. The "social critic" contingent, we thought, would continue to go their own way. Thus, even though they would spread out into a variety of professions, they would be more selective in what they did within them and not follow the common herd. And we feared that the truly Unconnected, especially those beset by serious psychological problems and social alienation, would remain at sea. On the personal front, we anticipated that the Unconnected would be late in making commitments to marriage and parenthood. The next seven chapters reveal what actually happened.

CHAPTER 3

Education for Success

"You shall gain your bread by the sweat of your brow," says the Book of Genesis (3:19). The burden of work that began as a curse on Adam had been recast by the sixth century as a blessing, at least for the Benedictine monks who followed the rule, "To work is to pray." The idea that work is spiritually fulfilling was carried from England to the New World as the Puritan work ethic, which saw the accumulation of wealth and material success as signs of God's favor.[1]

These two conflicting currents still permeate the attitudes of Americans toward work. On the one hand, work is a virtue beyond necessity, something worth doing for its own sake or for personal development and expression. On the other hand, work is drudgery. It is what you must do to obtain the means to enjoy life.

At its most basic, work is the labor whose remuneration ensures the survival of individuals and society through the provision of food, clothing, and shelter. But our economic system is hardly "basic." A bewilderingly complex array of occupations confronts the young adult seeking a place in our modern, highly specialized economy. The first formal list of occupational titles issued by the U.S. Department of Labor in 1939 already contained 17,500 entries. Over the next fifty years, that list expanded to fill two volumes of some 1,500 pages.[2]

Every adult is expected to fit somewhere in the occupational mosaic, but there is enormous latitude as to when a person makes the transition from economic dependence to self-support. For the educational elite, nearly all of whom are headed for professional careers, the transition is delayed until well into the third decade of life. Their career goals typically require that they obtain graduate education, a long-term investment in what economists call "human capital." The perceived payoffs of such investment impel individuals, their families, and society (through scholarships, grants, fellowships, and the like) to devote time, money, and effort to developing the knowledge and skills that will enable them to join the highest vocational layer—the professional, technical, and managerial occupations.[3]

Higher education is critically important to those who aspire to this top crust because most of these professions require advanced credentials; one simply cannot practice without proper certification, whether it be law, medicine, engineering, or business. The "self-made" person with a high school diploma who builds a fortune is a vanishing breed. What is striking about the educational elite is that nearly all of them (four out of five of our participants) obtain advanced degrees. They know that advanced education is the gateway to occupational success and higher income (see chapter 5) and many use their elite undergraduate credentials and strong academic abilities as springboards for obtaining good graduate training.

Graduate degrees alone do not constitute the transition to economic independence. The proud holder of a shiny new diploma still must find a job and build a career. In this respect, the educational elite are no different from their less privileged peers, except that their prospects for finding good jobs and building successful careers are exceptionally strong. Few and far between are those in this group who end up in occupations that cannot be turned into upwardly mobile careers.

PROFILE GROUP

As members of our profile group left college, their choices of career ranged from the highly certain to the rather uncertain. Careerists Martin MacMillan and Cynthia Eastwood knew what they wanted to do. Martin also knew how to do it; Cynthia was less clear. Intellectual Kirsten Buchanan thought she knew what career to pursue; Christopher Luce was far less certain. Striver George Mehta had a very clear career objective, and Geraldine Jones thought she did. Unconnected David Levy was very uncertain about where he was headed. Katherine Johnson knew what to do for the short run.

Despite their differences, the experiences of the profile group exemplify the importance of graduate study in launching careers. All but one of them went on to spend two or more years in graduate study: two got doctorates (one M.D., one Ph.D.); two, law degrees; two, business degrees; and one did graduate work in drama. They took a variety of paths to these ends. Careerist Martin MacMillan took an extra year of college courses to get into the medical school of his choice. Careerist Cynthia Eastwood considered getting an M.B.A. after working for a few years but never got around to it. She says, "Though I carried the thought at the back of my mind, I was doing so well, I didn't see the point of becoming a student again." "Actually," she adds with a smile, "I wouldn't mind going to business school someday if they will let me teach!"

Intellectual Kirsten Buchanan spent the summer after college working and traveling in Europe, then entered business school to get an M.B.A. Intellectual Christopher Luce took a longer route to graduate school. On finishing college, he could look back with much satisfaction on the breadth and depth of his liberal education, but he had little to show by way of career preparation. His parents expected him to go to law school. Christopher considered it, but he was more drawn to academics. So he decided to take a year off to travel and to "sort things out," availing himself of what Erik Erikson calls a "psychosocial moratorium" during which "the young adult through free role experimentation may find a niche in some section of society, a niche which is firmly defined and yet seems to be uniquely made for him."[4]

In college, Christopher had had a wonderful experience traveling in England. He thought he would do the same in his own country by going through various regions and working at jobs distinctive to each. So he laid railroad tracks in the West, worked on the crew of a tugboat in the South, lived on a dairy farm in the Midwest, and unloaded fish in the Northeast. What better preparation for someone who went on to get a Ph.D. in American cultural history? At the end of his year of travel, Christopher was still not ready to settle down. So he got a job for a year as the administrator of a small humanities program at a select college and spent another year reading scripts for a motion picture company. All this time he kept a law school application at hand, but he never mailed it. Instead, he finally took the plunge and applied to the Ph.D. program in history at Yale.

Strivers George Mehta and Geraldine Jones both went to graduate school right after college, he to study business administration, she to study drama in New York. Our two Unconnected profiles, on the other hand, each took a more circuitous path that eventually led them to law school. During the summer of her junior year, Katherine Johnson had lived in a poor black neighborhood where she worked at a supermarket and taught children organic gardening. Though she found the experience initially "forbidding," she gradually overcame her "latent fear of black people." In fact, she felt so drawn to them that after graduation she got a job in the same community teaching disadvantaged teenagers who had been in trouble with the law. Katherine worked hard for a meager salary, but she found the job very fulfilling. She began to envision a permanent career as a teacher or social worker. But when the government funding for the program was cut off, Katherine lost her job. She spent the next six months looking for similar work, without success. Frustrated and feeling a little guilty, she gave up and went to law school. "I did it reluctantly," says Katherine. "I was deeply committed to those kids. But I finally lost hope."

David Levy spent three years after college at a variety of odd jobs. He was a teller at an airport exchange bank, he worked on a kibbutz in Israel, and he held down a clerical job in an insurance company. Concurrently, he contemplated becoming a lawyer and spoke to a number of attorneys about various aspects of legal careers. David was neither interested in the money nor attracted by the courtroom drama that enticed so many of his peers. His vision was more service-oriented. "Ultimately, I thought there were some things that could be accomplished positively through going to law school," he says. "I talked to some people who were making positive changes and helping people who might otherwise not get help. So I decided to do likewise."

CHOOSING A CAREER

Careers are commonly thought of as professions, such as law and medicine, that require specialized training and become permanent vocations. Even when the term is extended to occupations in business or public life, it has a sense of progressive achievement. *Career* is derived from the Latin *carrus,* "wagon," by way of Old French *carier,* "to pull by wagon"—indicating a journey on a road. Choosing a career is thus choosing a road to follow, perhaps for our entire working lives.

Choosing a career entails much more than simply picking an occupation (a general type of work, like engineering or teaching), let alone a job (a specific position with a particular employer at a given time). An occupation is a way of earning a living in a job; a career is a way of life. Our careers, even more than our occupations, define us—the type of person we are supposed to be, the style of life we are likely to lead, even the kind of person we are likely to marry. When Americans ask their favorite question at social gatherings—"What do you do?"—they are really asking, "Who are you?"

While all useful occupations deserve respect, we value some occupations more than others. Generally, the most highly valued are the professions that demand a basic body of abstract knowledge and a dedication to service. The higher income, influence, and prestige of professions like law and medicine are dependent on the ability of their practitioners to exercise group cohesiveness, commitment to high standards of service, selective membership through certification, and control over professional violations. That some professions (like medicine) are more highly valued than others in the same general field (like dentistry, pharmacy, or nursing) is generally taken for granted, but such distinctions can also lead to occupational discrimination (what psychologist John Krumboltz calls "occupationism").[5]

In earlier periods in Western history, and in many contemporary cultures, family background, regional character, religious affiliation, and other forms of collective identity have been the primary determinants of individual identity. In much of the contemporary world, however, and especially in the United States, the work we do and the careers we build supersede all other considerations in defining our selves, both private and public. Gender, ethnicity, and family background play important roles, but often only indirectly; our identities are mediated by the careers that such characteristics lead us to choose or make it possible for us to consider. The link between who we are and what we do thus works both ways: who we are helps determine what line of work we do; our work, in turn, molds us into people who more or less fit the career roles we have chosen. Our occupational role is both central to our sense of personal identity and the anchor that secures our place in society.

The decision to follow a particular career is the outcome of a long process of choice and chance that in some ways is never finished. Like all other human behaviors, its roots are buried deep in our biological heritage, psychological development, and social environment. The interaction of these factors results in three basic determinants of career decisions: opportunity, aptitude, and interest.

Opportunity is often the critical determinant for most people, since select occupational openings are highly restricted. For the educational elite, however, opportunity is maximized. Limitations are certainly present; not even the United States needs or can afford an infinite number of lawyers and doctors. But the peaks and valleys of general economic activity (the expansive 1980s, the more restrictive 1990s) have less effect on the educational elite than on any other segment of the young adult population.

Given the choice, we prefer to work at something we are good at. Although our perceptions of our aptitudes and competencies are fairly well set by the time we come to college, they are by no means immutably fixed. The process of self-discovery, an integral part of the college experience, often entails profound changes in self-perceptions.

The issue of interest or motivation is closely linked to aptitude: if you are good at something, you are more likely to be interested in it, and having an interest makes it more likely that you will be good at it. Nonetheless, aptitude and interest are neither inevitably linked nor always sustainable. Striver George Mehta and Intellectual Kirsten Buchanan were both good science students interested in medicine. Yet, their experience with premed courses snuffed out that interest. Dan aspired to be an actor even though he did not have much talent for it. His stubborn pursuit of this ill-matched interest has become a burden that he carries to this day.

For most of the educational elite, the many opportunities open to them, combined with their confidence in their aptitudes, make career choice mainly a matter of following their interests. To rephrase Kirsten Buchanan, the key question for them is not "What can I do?" but "What do I want to do?"

A fair number of our students, like Philip Genochio and Martin MacMillan, came to college with a firm conviction about what they wanted to do, and did exactly that. Such career clairvoyance is relatively more common among college men. (It can be called "career foreclosure" if it amounts to premature decision-making based on early beliefs.) Women are likely to start with a more general idea about their career future. Cynthia Eastwood did have a firm objective—becoming a successful business-woman—but she was not decided about which path to choose to achieve that goal. Martha came to college "wanting to be a writer" but was not clear about what that entailed. There are, of course, exceptions in either case.

Not surprisingly, many students come to college knowing more about what they do not want to do than about what they want to do. High school graduates, even those on their way into the educational elite, often know little about the day-to-day lives of people in various professions. Many college graduates are no more knowledgeable. As a result, career choices often tend to be quite uninformed.

College provides the opportunity to make more informed choices. Jane came to college with a strong science background and a keen determination to get a broad liberal arts education, an objective supported by her mother. ("She wants me to take lots of arts and humanities and become well rounded.") Jane became interested in both earth sciences and archaeology. To test her inclinations, she worked on archaeological digs supervised by one of her professors during the summers. Consequently, she concluded that applied earth sciences rather than archaeology would be the better career choice. So she went on to get a master's degree in geology and a Ph.D. in hydrology.

The single most common shift in career aspirations for the educational elite is from medicine to some other area. Medicine appeals to many as an altruistic and socially useful profession that is also quite prestigious and lucrative. Moreover, since everyone has been to a doctor, the field seems familiar. Hence, over one-third of our entering class professed some interest in medicine, but only 13 percent became doctors. Many of the rest could not hack their way through the premed jungle. Others who were equal to the task became disenchanted or developed other interests.

The experience of going through college, the need to earn a living, and parental expectations combine to help undergraduates settle on career choices. Yet, not everyone who lacks clear interests is able to develop them in college. The story of Alicia Turner (chapter 1)—"I didn't know what to do when I came, and I didn't know what to do when I left"—is a prime example.

DETERMINANTS OF CAREER CHOICE

In most times and places, people have not chosen their occupations; their occupations have been chosen for them. Young people simply followed in their parents' occupational footsteps. This generational duplication was considered not only normal but inevitable. As the economic role of the family has declined, children are in principle no longer locked into this pattern, especially in the United States, with its extraordinarily diverse occupational structure, its social environment of purportedly boundless opportunities, and its cultural championing of the importance of individual choice.

Despite all this, there are systematic and severe limitations on access to careers for many people. The most important limitation is socioeconomic status, or social class, which has an enormous effect on the career options of young adults. For the great majority of Americans, the occupations they enter are not very different from those of their parents. The social class they are born into is the one they will die in. Another important factor is gender, which still steers large numbers of women and men into gender-distinctive occupations.

Young people's occupational aspirations are shaped long before actual choices have to be made. Thus, many teenagers of a given social class cannot even conceive of entering occupations inconsistent with their class identity. The notion of becoming a factory worker or police officer would not cross the minds of most children of the upper middle class, just as becoming a top-level corporate manager or judge is unthinkable for most children of the lower class. This is not to say that a lower-class background poses an impassable barrier to entering high-status professions, but it does make such a choice less likely.

Yet, as we shall see, by joining the educational elite, many of our own participants were able to overcome their relatively modest family circumstances to attain levels of career success beyond their parents' fondest dreams. This is one of the more remarkable features of the educational elite: lower-class children who enter it are able to override background disadvantages. Attendance at a select educational institution may be no guarantee of high career status, but it greatly improves the chances of upward social mobility (see chapter 5).

Numerous psychological and sociological theories attempt to explain the process of career choice and development.[6] While none are definitive, they do offer some insights into the choices of the educational elite. One well-known effort is the psychologist Donald Super's model of occupational choice, which focuses on the development of a self-concept—the "who am I?" question. In this model, internal aspirations ("who I want to be") and external capacities ("who I can be") determine the sequence of decisions that culminate in career choice.[7]

Super distinguishes four stages in the process. First, ideas about work are "crystallized" during adolescence; they are then "specified" to one or a few occupations in young adulthood, especially during the college years. Decisions about these occupational leads are "implemented" by getting the necessary education and work experience, partly during the specification phase. Finally, usually between the ages of twenty-five and thirty, occupational choices become "stabilized."

By this schedule, our participants should have completed by the time of the follow-up study the process of stabilization. Many of them in fact have done so. When we asked them what they thought they would be doing in their careers in another ten years, over 40 percent said they would essentially be doing more of the same. But an almost equal proportion expected major changes. (The balance were unsure about the future.) Super's model allows for such instability by acknowledging that many individuals experience repeated subcycles of these stages while refraining from committing themselves to a particular career. Sometimes changed circumstances in the workplace may force even a committed person to go back and start over again in some other field.

In our discussion of the career trajectories of our participants in the next chapter, we examine in more detail the patterns of their career shifts and the reluctance of some to settle on a stable career choice until late in the decade after college. A major factor involved, unique to the educational elite, is the problem of "overchoice." Without the narrowing effects of lower social-class background, which allows only scant parental support, and with strong personal capacities, the educational elite face an often overwhelming array of alternatives.

An alternative approach to career choice has been developed by educational psychologist John Krumboltz on the basis of social learning theory. His assumption is that individual personalities and behavioral patterns arise primarily from unique learning experiences rather than from innate developmental or psychic processes. Krumboltz explains what he sees as the four sets of factors that influence the process of making career choices.

> To begin with, genetic endowment (the individual's sex, race, physical appearance, and the like, as well as any talents which may have a genetic basis) sets a framework that facilitates, or inhibits, the chances that an individual will be successful at any given activity. Environmental conditions and events (job opportunities, an inspiring teacher, a nearby library, and the like) make available, or make inaccessible, a unique set of learning opportunities. In this context, learning experiences occur which give people feedback about their competencies and satisfactions in a limited array of activities. People observe their own successes and failures and form generalizations (sometimes accurate, sometimes not) about what they are good at and what they enjoy. They also learn "task approach skills" (work habits, knowledge about the world of work and its relation to their self-defined characteristics) that guide them toward, or away from, various occupational challenges.[8]

Given the broad range of capacities of the educational elite and their generally privileged family backgrounds, the key variable in their choices is usually learning experiences. The educational elite are not as limited as other young adults by the wide array of social factors that determine career choice. Nevertheless, certain factors—such as family background, gender, and personality, as well as the broader social factors that lead to career "fashions" in a given period—still play a considerable role in their career choices.

Family Background

Family background affects career choice most substantially through the educational system. In study after study, the best predictor of how well children do in school is the social class of their families.[9] Family class background is also the best predictor of occupational choice and attainment.[10] It affects both the practical learning opportunities available to the child and the child's self-image as reflected in self-esteem, sense of competence, and vision of the future—all crucial determinants of both career aspirations and success in obtaining the qualifications needed to fulfill those aspirations.

Socioeconomic status is associated with intelligence test scores, academic skills, grades, attitudes toward school, and plans for college. These associations persist at the college level, and the likelihood of attending college is increased by higher class background even when grades and test scores are taken into account. Students from more affluent families have the role models, parental encouragement, self-confidence, high self-expectations, and, not least, the money to attend and excel in select educational institutions.

For the educational elite, many but not all of whom come from upper-middle- and upper-class backgrounds, the peak of the occupational pyramid is within their reach. Despite the wide range of career opportunities available to them, however, they behave very much like traditional peasants—they follow in their parents' occupational footsteps. Those who come from modest economic backgrounds, including many members of ethnic minorities, are less likely to follow that path, since they are often the first in their families to go to college, much less a select institution. Otherwise, many of our doctors and lawyers are the children of doctors and lawyers. This pattern of succession even holds in occupations that are more unusual for this group. For example, Fred entered the casino business, like his father. Melissa helps manage her father's orchards.

Even when the chosen occupation is not exactly the same as the parental model, it is often in the same general area. Rebecca, a hospital administrator, is the daughter of a physician. Philip, the son of an accountant, is a businessman. Shawn worked for a bank until two years ago, when he and his father (a retired executive) bought a cabinet manufacturing company that Shawn now manages.

Overall, about one-quarter of our participants picked a career that was the same or very similar to the occupation of one or another parent. Sons are more likely than daughters to emulate their fathers, but we have numerous cases of daughters doing so. Their mothers were far less likely to serve as career role models because relatively few of them had careers outside the home, although 62 percent were college graduates (as against 82 percent of fathers, half of whom also had advanced degrees). One notable exception is education: the daughters of women teachers and professors were especially likely to enter teaching as well.

We can ascribe the tendency to follow in parental footsteps to both practical and psychological considerations. Watching parents at close range gives a child a pretty good idea of what a particular occupation entails. Psychologically, there is a natural tendency to identify with a parent. Given the long history of children emulating parents and the powerful effect of parental models, the more significant finding is that three out of four of our participants did *not* emulate a parent. Some students struggle to reconcile the differing career expectations held for them by their fathers and mothers. Even more commonly, they must come to terms with what they want to do as opposed to what their parents want them to do.

Parental models and expectations sometimes backfire. A number of our participants made the deliberate choice not to do as their parents had done. "After watching my father neglect his family to care for his patients," said one woman, "I had no interest in becoming a doctor." And in line with the current cultural value placed on paid employment outside the home, most educational elite women have no desire to adopt the full-time homemaker role filled by so many of their mothers on a permanent basis. Thus, although almost half of our participants' mothers were full-time homemakers, only 15 percent of the women and only two of the men had settled in that role, and most of them only on a temporary basis. Some of the women were quite adamant about rejecting this choice. As one put it, "The last thing I want to do is to be stuck at home with a bunch of kids all day." But other women in the group value full-time child rearing so highly that they have given up successful careers to bring up their young children. "Motherhood is by far my most challenging job yet," said one. "There are days when nine-to-five sounds like heaven. But nothing compares to watching the unfolding of a little mind."

Following a parent's occupational footsteps is not a simple process of imitation or rejection. Though they were well aware of the power of parental modeling, many of our participants wanted to be certain that their parentally influenced choices coincided with their own independent inclinations. Douglas, the son and grandson of lawyers, had more or less decided, while in college, to become a lawyer himself. Yet he wanted to subject his decision to the test of time. "I was exposed to lawyers from an early age, so I knew what it was all about," he said. "I just needed to make sure that it really was what I wanted to do." He took a job with an accounting firm and worked for three years. Only then did he go to law school with the conviction that a legal career was what he really wanted.

Gender

Historically, gender and social class have combined as the two major determinants of career choice. But the traditional division of labor—women in the house, men in the marketplace—is in fact only a century old and mainly a middle-class phenomenon. The great majority of women around the world have always worked outside the home to meet basic needs while also taking primary responsibility for the household and children.

Nonetheless, a gender-based division of labor of some sort has been almost universal. In studies of traditional societies, anthropologists have found that some types of work are predominantly done by men in most cultures, including hunting, herding, woodworking, metalworking, weapon making, and warfare. Other types of work—horticulture, cooking, basket weaving, pot making, and cloth manufacture—are mainly carried out by women. Still other tasks are as likely to be done by women as by men, such as growing food and manufacturing ornaments.[11]

The basis for the gender specialization of occupations is sometimes self-evident. Men dig ditches because of their generally higher capacity for heavy manual labor. But do women care for children because they are more "nurturant" by nature or because they have been delegated this task and have by necessity become more nurturant? The extent to which such divisions of labor are due to physical and biological as opposed to psychological and social factors is the subject of much debate, the details of which need not occupy us here. Suffice it to say that, in principle, there is no longer as much support for assigning occupations primarily on the basis of gender, even for such traditionally male roles as soldier, airline pilot, and mechanic, or female roles as secretary, nurse, and kindergarten teacher. Segregation of workers into "male" and "female" jobs persists, but it is now seen as essentially determined by social factors rather than innate ability.

Nationally, women now account for 45 percent of the labor force. They can be found in virtually all occupations, but not in the same proportions as men. High-status professional positions are still held mainly by men; women predominate in lower-status, lower-paying positions, especially in education, child care, the health industry, clerical work, and table waiting. These are often not careers but simply occupations.

Against this background, one of the most striking findings in our study is that gender differences in career choice are quite small in the educational elite. Coming from families with highly educated parents, blessed with strong academic capacities, and full of the confidence that comes from impressive records of achievement not only in academics but across the board, the young women in our study have not hesitated to cross the occupational gender barrier. The question they pose to themselves is no longer whether they can be doctors or lawyers—they know they can—but what sort of medicine or law they want to practice.

The difficult issue for these women is the potential impact that careers will have on their lives as mates and especially mothers, and vice versa. In chapter 6 we discuss the narrowing of opportunities for women in the educational elite as they enter their thirties and begin to bear and rear children. Nevertheless, their gender generally does not lead them to choose professions different from those of men.

Personality

The role of personality in career selection is fascinating but frustratingly complex to pin down. One approach that is pertinent to our work is that of the psychologist John Holland.[12] Holland proposes that most Americans can be classified into six personality types: realistic, investigative, artistic, social, enterprising, and conventional. Individuals tend to choose occupations or work environments that match their personality orientations. Thus, an investigative type who is intellectually curious, analytical, methodical, and precise seeks a work setting that not only has compatible characteristics but will attract others who are similarly oriented. One strong option for the investigative type is to be a scientist in a laboratory, where the type of work required and the type of person likely to work there are closely matched.

This approach is complicated by the fact that many occupations have elements of more than one type of environment, and most individuals combine characteristics of two or more personality types. For example, medicine involves investigative, social, and conventional elements; doctors score very high on the investigative scale but also achieve at least moderate scores on several other scales. In addition, social factors can give the same occupation variable meaning: male police officers have strong profiles as realistic types, but women police officers are more the social type.

Vocational personality tests (like the Strong-Campbell interest inventory) based on Holland's theory and others like it have some predictive value with respect to the success and satisfaction a certain type of person is likely to experience in a given occupation. They are useful in vocational counseling, but most of us do not choose occupations on the basis of vocational tests alone. We usually rely on our intuition and aspirations to figure out what we want, along with family and peer influences. When, as happens frequently, we realize that our ideal job is unattainable, we settle for what we can get. What distinguishes the educational elite is that they rarely need to settle for less than what they want.

Does Holland's model help explain the career choices of our four types? Because our types represent orientations to academic and career pursuits rather than personality profiles, we would not expect a direct correspondence. Though Holland's model and our typology share some common elements, the connections should not be stretched. Careerists, for instance, bear some resemblance to Holland's conventional type, who are attracted to financial transactions and data manipulation and avoid artistic activities. Accordingly, we do find many Careerists choosing careers in business and engineering. Strivers have traits that fit the social type, who enjoy working with and helping people but are weak on scientific ability. Intellectuals share some features with the artistic (expressive, original, introspective) and investigative types, and some of the Unconnected fit the enterprising type (self-reliant). Consequently, we find that the Unconnected start their own businesses more than other types, that Intellectuals are especially likely to choose humanistic careers, that Strivers more often see themselves headed for public service careers.

Researchers like Holland approach vocational choice as a rational, cognitive process. Others, like Donald Super, see it as part of a less conscious developmental pattern that proceeds through a set of stages or cumulative steps. Adolescent career fantasies gradually yield to reality considerations; choices made earlier progressively narrow as the effects of past performance make themselves felt.[13] Thus, while 65 percent of high school students want to become professionals, only 14 percent actually do so. Yet the educational elite come from a segment of youth for whom options narrow the least and whose past performances serve mostly to open doors closed to others.

Family background, gender, personality, and other similar variables no doubt play important roles in determining career choices. Yet we must not underestimate the role of chance. As one man put it, an opportunity opens up and "something clicks." Life decisions are not random, but neither are they always explicable through some orderly causal chain of events.

GRADUATE STUDY

Graduation from college for middle-class youth is usually seen as the watershed between adolescence and adulthood. The college graduate is expected to enter the world of work, establish an independent life, and build a family. For young persons aiming at professional careers, however, graduation represents a decision point more than a turning point: Should I go on to graduate school to prepare for my professional career? Or should I find a job now, even though it may not be in the career that interests me?

To study or to work is the basic question. But the more fundamental issue underlying this deceptively clear-cut choice is, Am I ready to be an adult yet? Graduate school is not only a means of preparing for a high-powered career but a comfortable way of avoiding the exigencies of adult life, of delaying the moment of taking full responsibility for long-term self-support.[14] By the same token, going to work can also be a refuge from making—or even formulating—a definitive career choice if the job is unrelated to a young person's ultimate career objectives.

Unlike college, graduate school has one primary aim: career training. A general education is no longer on the agenda, whatever a student's field or intellectual orientation. Graduate study is the specialized learning of certain areas of knowledge with distinct vocabularies, ways of thinking, concepts, and technologies. Students can go to college to explore their vaguely defined interests, but if they have set no definitive goal before entering a graduate program, they will be like fish out of water.

In practice, of course, quite a few people do enter graduate programs with only a hazy notion of their future careers. Even going through graduate school does not fully prepare a person for the practice of his or her profession. As one man put it, "I didn't realize until later that going to law school is not the same thing as practicing law." Before taking this plunge, a student needs to answer three questions: Should I go to graduate school? When shall I go? Where shall I go?

SHOULD I GO?

The answer to the first question depends largely on career goals. For professions like medicine and law that require specialized training and certification, graduate training is mandatory. (In the past people entered even these occupations as apprentices to an established practitioner, as in any other trade.)[15]

For other fields, graduate study is optional. A bachelor's degree in engineering qualifies you as an engineer; a degree in economics makes you eligible for numerous entry-level jobs in business. But even in these areas, high-level positions impose additional educational demands. Without a master's degree, the young engineer has difficulty entering the ranks of management. It is very difficult to become a senior corporate economist without a master's or doctoral degree in economics.

Yet, for entry-level jobs, the match between education and occupation is not very strict. One woman majored in philosophy and became a bank teller; another studied classics and became a loan officer. Some entrepreneurs manage to go quite far even without a college degree, and highly lucrative careers are open to professional athletes regardless of their college majors, as exemplified by two of our participants, one of whom became a highly paid professional football player and another a successful professional tennis player.

Nonetheless, the increasing importance of educational credentialing is especially clear to the educational elite; 81 percent of our participants went on to do graduate work, for an average of almost three years of study. The undergraduate premedical studies of future doctors, the courses in political science and sociology taken by future lawyers, the economics and accounting courses taken by future businesspeople—these are only the beginning of professional training for the educational elite.

WHEN SHALL I GO?

There is no set answer to the question of when to go to graduate school. Business schools encourage applicants to work for a few years after college before starting graduate work; some law schools are beginning to do the same. In other fields, like medicine, the longer you wait, the tougher it is to get admitted. While it is true that some people (more often women) are now starting graduate school as late as midlife, they are the exceptions rather than the rule.

Figure 3.1 presents the timeline for full-time and part-time graduate study, showing the proportion of our participants in advanced education for each of the ten years. After graduation in June 1981, almost 30 percent were back in school full-time the following fall. This proportion increased steadily to a peak of 42 percent three years after graduation. Including those who were studying part-time, nearly half of the participants were in school by the third year. The numbers then gradually declined, but even at the end of the decade more than 10 percent were in graduate school (including those studying part-time). At that time they consisted mostly of

FIGURE 3.1

Graduate Study (*percentages engaged in full- and part-time study*)

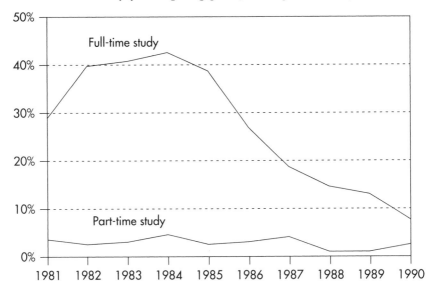

those who had entered graduate programs late, but for many pursuing a Ph.D. or medical specialty, their period of schooling actually stretched over the entire decade.

A much smaller segment chose to study part-time, at most only 5 percent of the participants in any year. Part-time study is not a desirable alternative for most people since it is incompatible with the pursuit of mainstream professions in major institutions and it greatly lengthens the advanced education period. Financial constraints and family responsibilities are the usual reasons for settling for this option.

Why do more than half of the educational elite delay graduate study for a year or more? The primary reason is financial. Graduate study is often very expensive. (In 1993–94, tuition at Stanford Law School was $20,186 a year; at the medical school, $23,000 a year.) Parents are generally unwilling or unable to subsidize their children's advanced training, and many young adults no longer want such help. A substantial number of students leave their undergraduate institutions with some debt. (On average, the 1981 Stanford graduates who had taken loans owed $6,000 at the time of graduation.) Before shouldering additional economic burdens, they want to go to work to clean the slate. To that end, one person worked as a foreign exchange trader for several years in New York before he went to law school. Before heading to business school, one got a job in the Department of Commerce; another worked for a bank.

Money is not the only consideration. A sizable group delayed graduate study to get some respite and have time for renewal. Many is the time we heard seniors complain that they were "sick of school" and could not face another year of professors, textbooks, and exams. Others questioned the motives, interests, and ambitions that had seemed so self-evident to them during their undergraduate years. They felt compelled to stop the carousel for a time, to get off onto more solid ground and make sure things were spinning in the right direction.

Taking a break often involves either a move to a different city or extended travel. About one in twelve of our participants traveled extensively at some point during the decade; men were moderately more likely than women to do so, and the travel break was most likely to occur in the first two years after graduation. Future teachers and humanists were much more likely than other groups to take a travel break (21 percent); future doctors were second (11 percent), but this was the only sort of break they took; those headed for business were least likely to go off track (2 percent).

Some of the activities chosen by those who took time off from the straight-and-narrow pursuit of a career were sharply at odds with their background and capabilities. Mark, the scion of a wealthy family and eventually an investment banker, spent part of his first year after college working as a bike messenger in New York. It was not clear whether he was risking life and limb as a lark, to prove his toughness, to experience the life of downtrodden youth, or as penance for the privileged life he was headed for.

The interval between college and graduate school can also be a remarkably calming experience. To say that Craig was on the wild side in college would be an understatement. As a freshman, he came across as a stereotypical surfer, down to the sandals on his feet. By his senior year, not much had changed: "He communicates anything but a serious approach to life—tan skin, uncombed sun-bleached hair in winter, and very bloodshot eyes suggest dissipation rather than studiousness," his file noted. He spent part of his junior year at an overseas campus, never letting his studies interfere with skiing at seventeen resorts, scuba diving in the Red Sea, crossing Italy by motor scooter, camping on Crete, viewing the French Grande Prix in Monaco, and coming close to having his car bombed in Belfast. On returning to the United States, he drove across the country on a motorcycle.

After graduation, Craig went to Washington "to get acquainted with the capital." The job he got as an unpaid staff member on a congressional committee led to a paid job as a legislative assistant to a congressman. He took another year to decide whether to go to business school or law school. From what he had seen in Washington, Craig decided that the practice of law was not for him. He completed an M.B.A. program and went into real estate. He now looks like the epitome of the settled, sober, civic-minded young executive; only an occasional glint in his eyes reveals his former self.

Like Craig, Eric also spent time in Washington. But he knew what he wanted—a career in law, with an eye on politics—so he sought some experience in politics first. He worked as an aide to a congressman (a position arranged through a family friend) and then worked on the congressman's election campaign. The congressman lost and left Washington, but Eric stayed on, spending three years in the capital before going to law school.

Although the decision to go to graduate school is usually settled within a few years after graduation, for some it drags on indefinitely. Linda worked for a nonprofit organization after college. Then she switched to IBM, worked a stint in a public library, returned to IBM as a community officer, was laid off, and got a job with a foundation doing surveys of community-based organizations. A decade after college, she was considering graduate work in public policy but had yet to enroll. Linda's journey after college, however, is not as aimless as it may sound. In most of her jobs, she was involved in facilitating public access to the use of computers. Her interest in studying public policy was thus an extension of her work experience. Yet it is also true that people like Linda are in no hurry to settle on

FIGURE 3.2
Graduate Study, by Sex (*percentages engaged in full- and part-time study*)

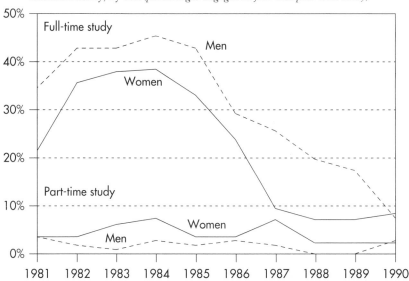

a final career. As another woman put it, "I am one of those people who reaches forty before deciding what to do."

Figure 3.2 shows the timelines for graduate study to be largely similar for men and women, especially during the first half of the decade after graduation. Overall, however, more men go to graduate school than do women: by the end of the decade, 80 percent of men as against 66 percent of women had been full-time graduate students. And they are more likely to do so, throughout the decade, on a full-time basis. By contrast, almost twice as high a proportion of women (20 percent) as men have been part-time graduate students at some point.

In the aggregate, 84 percent of men and 74 percent of women ended up working for a graduate degree either full- or part-time. Men also spent more time in their advanced degree programs. This difference partly reflects the different occupational choices of men and women. Men are more likely than women to pursue Ph.D. degrees and, to a lesser extent, medical degrees—the programs of longest duration.

There are several additional reasons women are somewhat less determined than men to obtain advanced education. Women are overrepresented among Intellectuals, who (as we shall see) are least likely to go into the major professions requiring graduate degrees. Other women are not sure that graduate study is worthwhile. They have lingering doubts about the compatibility of such careers with their interests and their prospects of thriving in fields that have typically been male bastions of privilege. And most important, family obligations, particularly the birth of a child or the decision to have a child, make graduate study difficult. This is the main reason for the greater discrepancy between the female and male curves in the second half of the decade. Six years after graduation from college, one-quarter of the men were in school full-time, but the figure for women had dropped below 10 percent. Though these gender differences are significant, on balance the remarkable similarity of female and male patterns of graduate study is by far the more important finding.

Another striking result is the virtual absence of ethnic differences in graduate study among our participants. Asian-Americans, African-Americans, and Hispanic Americans, taken as a group, attended graduate school at the same rate as whites and for just about the same length of time. However, the proportion of Asian-Americans who went to graduate school was much higher than that for other minority groups. Nonetheless, whatever the level of institutional discrimination against minorities at lower levels of the educational system, there is no evidence for it at this very high level. In fact, graduate schools are especially eager to recruit highly qualified minority students as part of their affirmative action programs.

The lack of large gender or ethnic differences in graduate study patterns is thus an important characteristic of the educational elite. Having made it into highly selective undergraduate programs, these young people come of age in an exceptionally egalitarian social space—a space quite distant from that occupied by most of the population, one more insulated from the discriminatory processes that operate in the larger society. The modest gender difference in advanced education experiences in 1990 simply could not have been predicted a generation ago; even less could the lack of ethnic differences have been foreseen.

Typology differences are at first glance quite baffling. Careerists and Strivers are most likely to go to graduate school, in almost identical proportions (85 percent); Intellectuals (68 percent) are least likely to do so. Do we not expect Intellectuals to be the most ardent pursuers of advanced education? If love of learning were the main motivation to pursue advanced study, this would be the case. But graduate school is first and foremost devoted to career preparation. Since Intellectuals are least likely to pursue mainline professions, they are least likely to go to graduate school. The sharpest contrast in this regard is between male Careerists, 95 percent of whom went to graduate school, and male Intellectuals, of whom only 62 percent did so.

Careerists and Strivers are also more apt to go to graduate school right after college. By the second year after graduation, almost twice as many Careerists were in graduate school as compared to Intellectuals. By the middle of the decade, most of the Careerists and Strivers had completed their formal schooling. By contrast, attendance rates for Intellectuals and the Unconnected were spread far more evenly over the decade. The Unconnected stand out as the group most likely to attend only part-time; six years after graduation, almost one in ten were still part-timers, while none of the Careerists were. Thus, the tendency of the Unconnected to delay choosing a career continues after college even for those who eventually settle down.

Looking at graduate specialties, we find that medical and law students are more likely than other groups to attend graduate school right after college. Over 80 percent of future doctors and 60 percent of future lawyers were in professional schools by the second year, but only 31 percent of future engineers and technicians and 21 percent of other groups. Since applicants to schools of business and management are encouraged to get a few years of work experience before going for the M.B.A., we find them most frequently enrolled five years after graduation.

At the other end of the decade, by the ninth year more than one-third of future doctors were still full-time students. Once enrolled, they kept their noses to the grindstone; only three of our twenty-three future doctors took a breather to work or travel. Teachers and humanists were also likely to be in graduate school late in the decade. With the exception of a few Ph.D. candidates, however, these are people who started graduate school after changing their initial career direction.

WHERE SHALL I GO?

Because they are graduates of a highly select institution, we expected our participants to go on to a small number of equally select graduate programs. They did not. The 160 participants who eventually obtained graduate degrees attended a variety of 89 institutions. They did, however, concentrate in select institutions—almost 60 percent went to elite COFHE or public Ivy institutions or their foreign equivalents.[16]

The most common institution our graduates went to for further study was Stanford itself. It attracted just over one-quarter of those who went to graduate school (with the Stanford School of Medicine accounting for a large majority of these students). Other prominent programs included the schools of medicine, law, and business of Harvard, Yale, Columbia, and the University of Chicago; engineering programs at MIT and Cal Tech; and Ph.D. programs at Princeton and Duke. Two attended Oxford University, one went to the London School of Economics, another to the Sorbonne in Paris. Still, some 40 percent of our sample were scattered among a wide variety of other schools, including some with quite modest reputations.

Several factors account for this dispersal of students to graduate programs with a wider range of selectivity. One is the relative scarcity of places. The graduate programs and professional schools of elite institutions can admit far fewer applicants than the numbers of college graduates they produce. For instance, Stanford grants about 1,600 undergraduate degrees a year but admits only about 86 students to its medical school, 180 to the law school, and 350 to its business school. Furthermore, the elite liberal arts colleges have no graduate programs themselves and must feed their own graduates into this stream, as do some of the top universities that lack one or another of the professional schools. (Princeton, for instance, has neither a medical nor a law school.) This makes entry into graduate programs in the top universities extremely competitive even for the educational elite.

A second consideration is financial. Select private universities are expensive. Less prestigious private institutions are cheaper; state universities are cheaper still, especially for state residents. Many who could have entered more prestigious programs opt for less expensive alternatives.

Additional considerations include the desire to be close to home, to live in an area that is attractive for long-term residence, or to stay with a partner. Where both members of a couple are pursuing graduate studies, one usually has to compromise by attending an institution that is not her or his first choice. When such conflicts arose in previous decades, women usually followed their husbands, as did several of our women. But in a departure from the traditional pattern, a number of our men followed their wives or domestic partners. And some women took advantage of the situation they were placed in. One woman left her job when her husband decided to enter a doctoral program. Though pregnant with their first child, she decided to work toward a Ph.D. herself when they were established in their new academic location.

FORGOING GRADUATE STUDY

One out of five of our participants entered the world of work soon after graduation and stayed there; whether by choice or happenstance, further education never made it onto their agenda. Women (26 percent) were more likely to be in this group than men (16 percent), and Intellectuals most likely of the four types (34 percent).

For some, forgoing graduate study was a conscious decision. Fred, for example, was disenchanted with the academic process. He had hated school since childhood and saw education as "nothing but a game," or a "ticket to career success." His ideal college education would have been to get all "A"s without going to class, an ideal he came close to achieving. He took a class in economics because of his interest in a business career, but then he took a very similar class in which he learned not much more because, as he said, "I am paying for the grades, not the classes." On graduation from college, Fred was not about to go back to school. He had worked in casinos in Atlantic City (where his father managed a large hotel) during summer breaks from college. He got a job as a blackjack dealer and rose to assistant manager.

More typically, the decision not to get an advanced degree is based on the assessment that the time and cost are not justified. Tony was interested in business. He entered an insurance company training program, which he thought would be more useful than getting an M.B.A. After two years, he got restless and joined a small start-up company as vice president. The business did not survive, but Tony had no trouble getting another job with a large consulting firm, where, he says, "I have been delighted with my work."

Linda had majored in applied earth sciences but had no interest in a career in that field. She got a job in personnel at an electronics company. Following her marriage, she and her husband moved to another area, where she got a job as a stockbroker. She has no regrets about not getting an advanced degree. Others started working with the intention of going to graduate school later but never made it.

Financial considerations often get in the way. Clint had ambitious career plans in college. He would get an M.B.A. and then become "a vice president of a firm in southern California, driving a blue Mercedes and living in a nice house with a view of the ocean." But when his father lost his job right after Clint graduated, Clint had to go to work. He has worked hard for a succession of oil companies and done well enough, but the blue Mercedes still lies in the future. He now has a family and reckons he will have to make the rest of his way without a graduate degree.

As Clint's example indicates, those who plan to go back to school usually feel they must do so before they are encumbered with family responsibilities. Otherwise, it gets much harder. One man was willing to endure a period of poverty in his late twenties by going back to school, but he had two young children and his wife would not hear of it. The only way another man could have done it would have been by asking his wife to go back to work, but she wanted to stay home to care for their child. One woman's husband had just started a new business and they needed her income, so she had to give up the idea of obtaining the M.B.A. degree she had long planned for.

A few of our participants still regret not having obtained a graduate degree, but the majority have come to terms with it. The possibility remains open for those who feel they are not yet settled in their ultimate careers.

DEGREES RECEIVED

Nearly all of those who attended graduate school received an advanced degree; only about 8 percent left before completing graduate studies. A somewhat larger proportion began graduate study at one school but completed their studies at another. The proportions of women and men who completed their degrees were about equal, but because a higher proportion of men than women went to graduate school, more men (79 percent) than women (67 percent) ended up with graduate degrees.

Figure 3.3 shows the distribution of graduate degrees received (see also table 1, appendix A). The most popular fields are law and business, accounting for half of all degrees. Next in order are master of science and M.D. degrees. (Included in this group is one who received the doctor of veterinary medicine degree.) Law is the most popular choice among both men (30 percent) and women (26 percent). In second place for both genders is the business degree, earned by 18 percent of men and 25 percent of women. Medicine comes third for men (tied with the M.S. degree) and fourth for women, slightly below the M.S. degree.

Overall, about four out of five of the graduate students were clustered

FIGURE 3.3
Graduate Degrees Earned, by Sex (*percentages*)

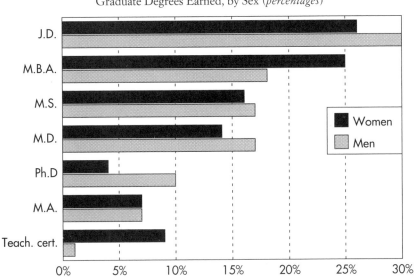

in these mainstream career programs. The 1980s was a period of pronounced careerism among young adults, as reflected in their graduate school choices. They headed for graduate programs that would lead to "sure bet" careers with high incomes, secure employment, and considerable prestige. Fields of study less directly linked to major occupations, or leading to careers with less certain prospects—humanistic, academic, and basic research programs—were far less popular. Only about one in seven students pursued master of arts or Ph.D. degrees.

An equally remarkable aspect of figure 3.3 is the great similarity between men and women in their advanced degree choices. Women got slightly more M.B.A.s and slightly fewer law and medicine degrees; men got more Ph.D.s and were notably reluctant to pursue teaching credentials. But these are rather minor variations on a largely common theme.

The information on ethnic minorities is harder to interpret, given their relatively small numbers. Yet some findings stand out. Taken as a whole, they obtained graduate degrees in almost the same proportion as whites. Asian-Americans as a group, however, have the highest percentage of graduate degrees (85 percent). Not only is this proportion much higher than that for other minorities (65 percent), but it exceeds the figures for the white majority as well (73 percent).

A number of differences are also evident in the degrees received by the four types in figure 3.4 (see also table 2, appendix A). Intellectuals went

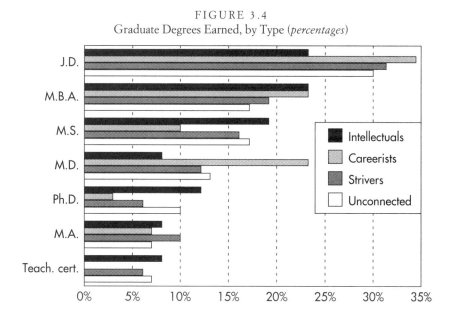

FIGURE 3.4
Graduate Degrees Earned, by Type (*percentages*)

for law and business in equal proportions (almost one-fourth each), with the master of science degree coming in third. But true to form, Intellectuals had the highest proportion of Ph.D.s (12 percent) and teaching certificates (8 percent) and the lowest proportion of M.D.s.

Of all the groups, Careerists concentrated most in law, medicine, and business, which together account for 80 percent of all Careerist degrees. They have the lowest rate of Ph.D.s, and none obtained a teaching certificate. Strivers differ from Careerists in that only half as many obtained M.D. degrees, somewhat more got Ph.D.s, and they account for the highest proportion of master of arts recipients. The Unconnected, finally, reveal a distribution similar to that of Strivers, ironically their polar opposites otherwise.

Although some large differences among the types are apparent, the overall distributions are less different than we expected. Careerists stand out for their concentration in law and medicine, Intellectuals for their engagement in programs leading to research and teaching (although the same proportion of Intellectuals got M.B.A.s as did Careerists). Strivers and the Unconnected are in between these extremes. Our typology thus goes some way toward accounting for the graduate field choices of the educational elite, but it leaves much to be explained. Thus, as we shall see later, the motivations behind the choice of graduate study field are quite different for the four types, even if the overall distributions are not radically dissimilar. For example, Careerists who go to law school are motivated more by the anticipated income and job security than are Intellectuals, who more often pursue law out of intellectual curiosity. Strivers and the Unconnected who obtain law degrees are more apt to see the law as a vehicle for social change and public service. These motivations, of course, are rarely "pure"; Careerist lawyers may have a secondary social agenda, and non-Careerist lawyers welcome the hefty income as a benefit of their work. This mix of devotion to service and self-interest is especially common among physicians.

Of those completing graduate degrees, 13 percent obtained more than one degree, women (16 percent) somewhat more than men (12 percent). (We have omitted double degrees from figures 3.3 and 3.4 for the sake of simplicity, since they do not materially change the percentages.) The most common combination is law and business degrees. Others combined a master's degree in engineering with a business degree. In both examples, the purpose was to combine specialized training in a field with expertise in business, a potent combination for reaching high-level organizational positions.

In a more unusual pairing, Arnold got a master's degree in computer science, entered medical school for the first two years of basic course work, returned to graduate school to complete a Ph.D., then finished his M.D. degree. The transition back and forth was fairly smooth until the last stage. By the time Arnold got his Ph.D., he had gained considerable recognition as a computer scientist. After presenting papers at conferences and being treated as a professional, it was tough to return to medical school as a lowly student to complete his clinical work. Arnold is finishing his residency training in pediatrics and considering various ways to use his two specialties in a synergistic manner.

TRENDS IN GRADUATE STUDY

As figures 3.3 and 3.4 show, both sexes and all four types are quite consistent in selecting law and business as their top degree choice (sometimes tied with a third field). The rush to get into these two fields is fairly new. As Ernest Boyer describes it, "During the 1960s, new law schools were spreading almost like McDonald's franchises. Applications soared and enrollment just about doubled. There was an enrollment gain of another 50 percent in the 1970s. Graduate business schools shared a similar pattern, with the M.B.A. degrees conferred in 1984 soaring to thirteen times their number in 1960."[17]

Our participants were very much a part of these career trends, which influenced a far greater segment of the population than the educational elite alone. Many factors shaped these trends, including, at the most basic level, the state of the national economy and job prospects in given fields. College students generally monitor these developments and try to anticipate the future, aided and abetted by parents, peers, counselors, and the media. Once set in motion, a bandwagon effect exaggerates these trends, turning them into "fashions." When law and business management became the "hot" career choices of the 1970s, many students chose to enter these fields simply because they were fashionable, not because they felt particularly suited for them or attracted by the type of work they offered. Through the 1980s, law and business lost some of their gloss while medicine (a perennial favorite) became more of a fashionable choice. Our 1981 graduates were on the tail end of the law and business wave and on the early crest of the move into medicine. In chapter 10, we have more to say about how current trends in career choice differ from the time our participants were entering their careers.

Undergraduates at a select institution like Stanford might be expected to comprise a high percentage of the next generation of academics. Of the 80 percent of our participants who obtained graduate degrees, less than 8 percent got doctorates. Our Stanford graduates are typical in this respect. Less than 8 percent of Ivy League graduates obtain Ph.D.s, and just over 8 percent of select liberal arts college graduates follow suit.[18] (The ten largest state universities come in considerably lower, at 4.3 percent.)[19] Thus it is still the select institutions that produce the next generation of college and university professors. The rather small number of Ph.D.s among their graduates is more likely a reflection of the limited job market in the American universities that have now stopped expanding. Moreover, a surplus of highly trained scientists is competing in a shrinking industrial market for their services.

Who are the unusual men and women who buck the trend of going headlong into a mainstream profession, taking the narrow and higher road to the Ph.D. degree instead? One prime example is Keith, an Intellectual who received a Ph.D. in political science and went into university teaching. He is as pure an academic type as they come; he has "always wanted to be a college professor." With a father who was a professor of art, Keith was imbued with academic values from an early age, and everything he has done has been oriented toward academia.

Despite their greater proclivities toward the humanities, most of our women Ph.D.s obtained their graduate degrees in scientific and technical fields, such as engineering and geology. For example, Rebecca took her doctorate in computer science and is now employed as a theorist in the computer industry. (Her father is a mathematician, and she majored in mathematics in college.)

Two exceptions to this pattern are Jill and Debbie, both of whom belong to ethnic minorities. Part Hispanic and part Native American, Jill majored in Spanish and set out to become a writer. She supported herself by working as a librarian, travel agent, and secretary, at times living with her parents to stretch her money. She then went to law school but became disenchanted almost as soon as she began practicing law. "I don't think of myself as being eccentric, but I suppose I was too unconventional to fit in," she says. She remained interested in writing. Another job in a law school proved more congenial and led to her work on a doctorate in legal history, a field that brought together her humanistic interests and legal training. A teaching career in law was the next logical step, and the special support of her dean landed her a faculty appointment. Debbie followed a more direct path from studying law in one school to teaching legal writing in another law school.

None of the ethnic minority members in our sample obtained a Ph.D. degree; all of their graduate degrees were from professional schools. Of the eleven Asian-Americans, four became doctors, four got M.S. degrees, two became lawyers, and one got a teaching certificate. Of the eleven who constituted the rest of the minority members, four became lawyers, three got M.A.s, two got M.B.A.s, only one became a doctor, and one got an M.S. Thus, the great majority of our minority women and men who pursued graduate degrees went into the mainstream professions. This is quite consistent with national figures.[20] Members of ethnic minorities often come from less affluent families and many of them are in the first generation to go to college. There is an understandable tendency for them to go into lucrative mainstream professions, just as other disadvantaged and immigrant groups have done before them. Yet the scarcity of minority faculty in universities is a matter of serious concern; their presence is essential, especially in light of the highly successful efforts of some institutions, like Stanford, to increase the proportion of undergraduate minority students. Without a greater supply of minority Ph.D.s in the academic pipeline, this imbalance will not be corrected, no matter how actively affirmative action programs are pursued.

WHAT THE EDUCATIONAL ELITE WANT IN A CAREER

We explored further the issue of graduate training and career choice by asking our participants what characteristics they sought in choosing their occupations. The single most desirable quality they identified was intellectual challenge, rated by over 90 percent as of great importance (a mean score of 4.6 on our five-point scale). In second place was creativity (mean of 4.3). These two characteristics were considerably more important than any others. Next in order were being able to work independently (4.0) and having the opportunity to work with people (3.9). More materialistic and status-related criteria, such as high income, job security, and prestige, were rated as being of only moderate importance (means of 3.4 and below).

This emphasis on the intrinsic merits of occupations is found equally among women and men. Both genders put intellectual challenge, creativity, independence, and working with people at the top of their lists. Both rate considerations like potential income and prestige much lower. The only notable difference is that women are more interested in working with people, and men are more concerned about finding an outlet for their creativity. These differences may be in line with traditional role expectations, but on the whole, gender, again, simply does not matter much.

Ethnicity makes more of a difference, but only in one area. Disadvantaged minority group members (African-American, Hispanic, and Native American) put greater emphasis on material concerns than do other groups. This is especially true of two items, job security and high income.

Once again, this priority is hardly surprising given their disadvantaged background.

On the other hand, Asian-Americans, contrary to some stereotypes, are if anything less materialistic than average. They see high income, job security, and prestige as less important than does the majority white group, despite coming from less affluent families than the latter. Nevertheless, many go into lucrative professions.

These occupational criteria form interesting clusters in the various professions. Physicians are especially interested in serving others in secure jobs and not as concerned about creativity as are other groups. Lawyers want to make money and shape events, but they care less about working independently. Businesspeople want money and leadership but care less about working independently or serving others; the odd thing here is that they also care less than other groups about job security, suggesting that they plan to jump from organization to organization as they work their way up. Engineers are about average in most areas but definitely less people-oriented than other groups. Humanists are especially interested in having creative jobs that allow for independence, even at the cost of lower income.

These response patterns—rating the intrinsic merits of occupations over their external rewards—are surprising in light of the strong careerist bent evident in the career choices of many of our participants. How do we reconcile this apparent contradiction between saying one thing while doing something else? Is this merely a case of research subjects saying what they think investigators want to hear? Or are they underplaying the conventional aspects of career success because they take them for granted? After all, the educational elite can be virtually certain of conventional success, and by age thirty many of them already occupy high-income positions with considerable prestige and job security. Hence, do they simply feel that they can afford the luxury of stressing the intrinsic characteristics of their work rather than its materialistic rewards? Life experience has already taught some, much to their regret, that simply following the smell of success can result in a bad taste in the mouth. Even Careerists are finding that their single-minded pursuit of conventional career success does not give them everything they want out of their jobs. We return to these questions in subsequent chapters.

While gender and race are linked to only modest differences in the desired characteristics of occupations, our typology generates many more significant differences. These differences are partly redundant because some of the characteristics were used to generate the typology in the first place. Hence, the fact that Careerists and Strivers see high income and prestige as more important than do Intellectuals and the Unconnected is inevitable because that is how we defined them in the first place.

More revealing is the finding that some characteristics are not affected by type differences, in particular, the desire for intellectually challenging work. All four types rated this characteristic as their utmost concern; it is simply a must for almost everyone. In fact, Intellectuals and Careerists, our two polar types, gave exactly the same average ratings to this item, and the Unconnected rated it as of only slightly less importance than did the other groups. Such findings caution us not to exaggerate the differences in intellectual outlook between these groups.

Occupational characteristics that are not clearly linked to intellectualism and careerism—providing service to others, having the opportunity to shape events, and being in a position to exercise leadership—appeal especially to Strivers: they want to serve, shape, and lead more than other types. This group leads the others in ambition, measured not so much by conventional measures of career success as by the desire to make a difference in the world. They see themselves as movers and shakers. In turn, they also stress obtaining public recognition through their work more than do other groups.

We should note that the list of occupational characteristics rated in our follow-up questionnaire is identical to the list of items used during our participants' senior year in college. Comparing the results, we find that the overall importance attributed to the various items changed only marginally over the ten years. Intellectual challenge and creativity led the list at both times, and materialistic concerns like income and job security were seen as secondary at both times. The only significant (though still modest) changes were increases in the importance of high income and a flexible work schedule and a decrease in the importance of working with people.

As in most long-term studies of attitudes, however, we find that individual ratings of the importance of the various occupational characteristics are quite variable. Typically, only 35 to 45 percent of our participants rated any given item the same ten years later as they did when leaving college. For some items, senior-year responses were only very weakly related to follow-up responses, especially for job security, working independently, and being able to shape events. Sometimes attitudes changed dramatically—for example, some people felt that shaping events was very important when they were seniors but not at all important ten years later.

Nevertheless, the overall patterns are extraordinarily similar. Individuals change, sometimes quite remarkably, but our participants as a whole have almost exactly the same priorities and outlooks about what they want out of their careers now as when they were leaving college. We are faced again with the seeming contradiction between the occupational values they espouse and the career patterns they follow. The educational elite choose careers virtually dripping with money, status, and security, but they say that such concerns are entirely secondary to creativity, intellectual challenge, and independence. They said this when they were seniors, still largely ignorant about the realities they would face when they entered the professions that beckoned to them, and they repeated themselves ten years later even after many had learned that their jobs hardly matched their earlier ideals. Perhaps they are still looking for those ideal positions. Perhaps, as they grow older and become more fully established, they will be able to transform their careers into something more closely matching the ideal.

CHAPTER 4

Launching Careers

The economist Victor Fuchs calls the years between twenty-five and forty "a time to sow."[1] This is the stage of life when men and women invest in their careers in order to reap the rewards later. For most of them, career decisions made in college, or in the first few years thereafter, are consolidated during this period. Launching a career after graduate training involves more than merely finding and holding a job. Though some know what type of job they want and have no problem finding it, others are less certain and go through a period of testing their inclinations. Still others know what they want but cannot find it.

The educational elite are no exception. They, too, search and experiment, perhaps even more than most of their peers, because they have so many more options. What distinguishes them most is the range of high-level entry positions that are open to them. Many begin their careers in positions with more responsibility, higher pay, and better prospects of advancement than their less favored peers will ever obtain in their working lives. Elite educational credentials naturally lead into elite occupational positions, even though some of the roads traveled to reach those positions may be winding or rocky.

THE PROFILE GROUP

The journeys that led the men and women of the profile group to the consolidation of their careers were quite varied. Nonetheless, since their careers are closely linked to, and usually dependent on, graduate study, we can predict in most cases the next phase of their career development. For instance, it will hardly come as a surprise that Careerist Martin MacMillan made a seamless transition from medical school to specialty training to clinical practice. Martin is now a board-certified specialist in two medical fields and has joined a group practice in a suburban community in southern California.

Whereas Martin only recently launched his medical career, his fellow Careerist Cynthia Eastwood, who did not go to graduate school, has been pursuing her business career for a decade. Ten years after college, still energetic, ambitious, and confident, she is an even more charged-up version of her younger self. Upon graduation from college, Cynthia joined a finance company in Boston. She went through its accelerated management training program but grew disenchanted soon thereafter. "I did not like the finance industry; it was extremely staid, conservative, really boring to me," she says. "I also found the Boston environment very oppressive and very provincial." So she quit, backed by her parents, who agreed to help her make the transition back to the West Coast.

The rest of Cynthia's career has consisted of four two-year segments. The first involved working for a woman who was only a few years older and had started her own company. Cynthia's performance was spectacular: she was promoted four times in two years. But then she took issue with her employer over a matter of principle and left. The next three jobs were at computer companies. Cynthia's strategy was the same: "Always start in a job at a level that stretches your abilities and experience. Then push the envelope." In one instance, she says, "I sold myself into a selling job."

Her specific roles have varied, but typically she has functioned as a computer-software problem solver. There is a consistent pattern to Cynthia's performance. After she takes over, sales soar under her management (from $18 million to $80 million in one relatively small company); her salary keeps pace (over $100,000); promotion follows promotion; then she leaves to start over again. She left her third job in a Japanese-owned company because she felt discriminated against as a woman. ("I didn't like their style of management, and I felt there was greater opportunity for a bright young woman at a smaller non-Japanese company.") Then she got into her next job:

> I started looking around and decided I did not like working for a huge company. I wanted an opportunity to be part of the management team and really make some of the decisions. And if I screwed up I screwed up, but at least I tried it. I called a friend of mine who was a year ahead of me at Stanford. She and her brother had started a

company. I suggested we have lunch—not to ask her for a job, I was just networking, finding out what is out there. I said, "This is what I want to do, this is what I am good at. Do you have any ideas?" She said, "We need someone with good managerial skills, why don't you work with us?" So I decided to take the job. There were so many things that needed to be done. They were so naive. I needed to get them focused. My first ten months, we doubled sales. I felt great about my impact. But I had taken a 50 percent salary cut in taking the job, and I was getting nowhere. I kept telling my friend, "Look, you bring in good people, you get good results, you have to pay." It was no use.

Through another friend, Cynthia was recruited by a venture capital company. She is now "extremely excited" about her new job, the details of which she is still negotiating. Her title will be vice president for North American sales, her salary between $100,000 and $130,000. She will have equity in the company, which is poised for accelerated growth—as is Cynthia. What especially pleases her is the man she will be working for. "One of my problems so far is that I have always been smarter than the people I have worked for," she explains with disarming candor. "This man is incredibly intelligent, someone I can truly respect."

Despite sharp differences in their career orientations, Intellectual Christopher Luce entered his field in much the same way the Careerist Martin MacMillan entered his. After getting his Ph.D., Christopher started his first year as an assistant professor of history at a well-known university. Like Martin, Christopher made a seamless transition from being an advanced graduate student to a faculty member, in both his research and teaching.

There is a similar parallel between the launching of the careers of Intellectual Kirsten Buchanan and Careerist Cynthia Eastwood—once again, despite basic differences in their attitudes toward their careers. Except for the fact that Kirsten went to graduate school and Cynthia did not, both of them moved through the decade after college working very successfully at a succession of jobs. To a large extent, some professional tracks impose their own rhythm on career trajectories more or less irrespective of other considerations. Yet, as we shall see, this does not mean that everyone marches in lockstep to the same tune.

On graduating from business school, Kirsten had hoped to enter a career in international business, but there were no jobs to be found. She worked briefly for a pharmaceutical firm before joining a large company based in New York City. For the next four years, she was caught up in a fast-paced career, working relentless eighty-hour weeks. "I spent inordinate amounts of time at the office," recalls Kirsten. "If I had to do it again, I would spend a little more time socially and not put so many hours in at work." Though Kirsten performed very well, she was not happy in her job.

Then Kirsten's brother was killed when a drunk driver struck his bike. They were only a year apart and she had been very close to him. The tragedy jolted her out of her frenetic routine. ("I wanted to get balance into my life. Find what my priorities were.") She left New York to be closer to her parents in this very difficult period for all of them. Back in her hometown, she got a job in product design that provided more scope for her creativity and her interest in international business. Sales in her division rose from $35,000 to $3 million that year, making her "very proud." She was now thirty and still unattached. But soon after, she met her future husband, a physician. After their marriage, she quit her job and moved with him to a smaller city with few job opportunities for her. She took on part-time jobs for a while, but her unexpected (but not unwanted) pregnancy put an end to her business career.

At this point, Kirsten's career path deviates sharply from that of Cynthia Eastwood. Though Cynthia had married two years earlier, she did not move to follow her husband and did not have a child. So her marriage did not disrupt her career. On the contrary, Cynthia's husband is also a very successful business executive, and their careers have nicely meshed together. The very different outcomes of these ostensibly similar business careers point to a basic dissimilarity between Careerist and Intellectual perspectives on work, as we elaborate later.

There is also a marked contrast between the career trajectories of our two Strivers. George Mehta's work life unfolded in the same thoughtful, balanced, and steady manner that had characterized his college and graduate school career. He first worked for a pharmaceutical firm for a year, because it was the first reasonable job available. Then he switched to a start-up biotechnology company more in keeping with his interests. It turned out to be a troubled association because of conflicts over ethical issues and mismanagement. George says, "I am a very loyal person and have been fully committed to whatever position I have held. So I stuck it out as long as I could." When the company finally went out of business, he moved to an environmental lab where he is currently vice president for business operations. This position brought together George's interests in biology, business, and socially responsible work.

The consolidation of George Mehta's career illustrates the ability of some Strivers to meet their diverse objectives. Geraldine Jones provides a contrasting example of how a Striver may be pulled in different directions. Ten years after graduation, we would have expected to see Geraldine on the stage in New York or Los Angeles. Instead, her interview took place in a roadside diner in a remote hamlet nestled in the mountains of Vermont. After graduation, Geraldine had gone to New York to study acting. She spent two grueling years at it. ("The method of instruction seemed geared to destroy my self-esteem.") Then, with several friends, she started a small acting company. Geraldine recalls, "The professional acting scene was very tough and frustrating. Part of the problem was the environment. New York is a wonderful city but a dreadful place to live without a steady job. Running around all day, doing auditions with thousands of people was very stressful. After two years of this, I decided I was not going to be a successful actress under these circumstances."

When Geraldine's father died, her stepmother moved to a remote town in Vermont. Geraldine went to visit her, took one look at the idyllic setting, and decided to stay. Her father had left her some money to provide a modest income, which she supplemented by working in a variety of temporary jobs. It was important for her to "always work for a paycheck," not just live off her inheritance. She continued to do some acting in a nearby town, became a volunteer paramedic, and set up an environmental education program for which she is still trying to find funding. Geraldine then enrolled in a training program for paramedics, from which she will soon graduate. She finds the work fascinating. "Paramedicine serves a lot of purposes for me. First of all, it is incredibly intellectually challenging. It is also wonderful to be able to do something for people in crisis. It takes a lot of skills. You have to be very creative and very calm under incredible circumstances. And I am good at it."

Geraldine is aware that she is "still pursuing multiple goals that are not necessarily linked." Are Geraldine's multiple and conflicting career trails a reflection of her lingering identification with her chemist father (interest in the environment), her actress mother (interest in acting), and her physician stepfather (interest in paramedicine)? Or, at an even deeper level, by trying to be like both her father and mother at the same time, has she been attempting to bring her parents together within herself, thus healing the rift in her childhood? In any event, Geraldine brings a lot of energy and determination to her current task. She has earned straight "A"s in the paramedical courses. ("At Stanford I learned how to learn.") She tries to excel at whatever she does. Despite the bucolic setting in which she lives, Geraldine's life is still full of striving.

Geraldine recognizes the strains in her life. "I realize I may have overextended myself," she says, and she is not sure how it is all going to work out. Yet, she is determined to pursue whatever appeals to her rather than narrow her options. Her immediate objectives are fairly clear. As for the rest, "I don't make any rest-of-my-life plans. Circumstances change, people change. Realities in this life are such that you need to be flexible."

The big shift in Unconnected Katherine Johnson's life was her decision to go to law school after despairing of finding employment teaching disadvantaged children. From then on, her career propelled itself. Following graduate school, Katherine joined a large law firm in Los Angeles and thrived, under the tutelage of a mentor who helped her hone her professional skills. "He taught me how to become a trial lawyer," she recalls. What she learned from him was "more important than any formal education." He also looked after Katherine's interests in the complicated politics of the firm. In her finely tailored suit, poised and self-assured, Katherine now looks like the model of a successful young attorney, a far cry from the struggling young woman teaching impoverished children how to grow organic farm produce.

When our second Unconnected profile, David Levy, was an undergraduate, the last thing we would have expected him to become was a lawyer. But David had not exactly become your standard attorney. At his interview his sports shirt and baggy pants were informal, yet stylish. He was gentle and soft-spoken, choosing his words carefully. He neither postured nor strained for effect and seemed very much like a man at peace with himself.

In law school David became interested in immigration law because he was deeply concerned about the plight of illegal immigrants, especially those seeking political asylum. It set the direction of his career.

> It seemed to me that there were two things others were after. A lot of them wanted to earn a lot of money, and certainly that's one way to do it. Then, there was the prospect of becoming partner and wielding a lot of authority. When I went to law school, I knew I didn't want any part of that. I spoke to a number of attorneys and attended presentations where lawyers said what they were doing. I actually stacked the cards by going to a lot of public-interest seminars. That made a big impression on me. So I thought about the positive things you could do with a law degree rather than make a lot of money.

After graduation, David went to work for an immigration lawyer in an agricultural region in the Southwest. He was making $30,000 a year, but he lived in an inexpensive area, his needs were modest, so "it felt right." It was not long before David became disillusioned with his employer. He says, "The man's emphasis was on bringing in as much business as possible and making as much money as possible, often at the expense of the quality of work for your client. I was the only other attorney, so if a promise was made to a client, I was often the one to do the work."

David quit and went to work at a legal aid office in a small neighboring town. His salary dropped to $23,000, a fraction of what he could make in a commercial law firm. He had to struggle financially, yet he was much more content. David changed jobs once again in order to be closer to his fiancée, Judith, who is getting her Ph.D. in Philadelphia. Since he could no longer practice the same kind of immigration law, he got a position with a legal publisher writing and editing legal texts. He is ready to move again when Judith gets an academic job, wherever that may be.

Both of our Unconnected profiles demonstrate a key feature of their type. Their choices are entirely their own and they are inner-directed. The progress of their careers is not predictable. In Katherine Johnson, yesterday's social activist has become today's corporate lawyer, while law has become the vehicle for David Levy's social activism.

WORK AND SELF-WORTH

By necessity or choice, work constitutes the primary activity for most of us throughout our adult lives, consuming one-third to one-half of our waking hours.[2] Our occupations and job performance are major determinants of our social position, which in turn has a profound impact on our personal lives—whom we marry, the lifestyles we adopt, even how long we live.[3] The definition of work as the activity performed by individuals to produce goods and services of value to others describes only its economic dimension. For many people, and especially for the educational elite, work is a key definer of individual identity and a major source of psychological fulfillment.

The majority of people work primarily to obtain the basics of a decent standard of living, but the educational elite takes making a living largely for granted. The characteristics they desire in their careers show that they care most about rewards and satisfactions outside the economic sphere. Careers are not only means to an end, such as ample money for a comfortable life, they are also arenas for self-development and self-expression. This view is reflected in the response of almost all of our participants (88 percent) that they would still work even if they had no financial reason to do so. Moreover, the median income for those who would not work if they did not need to is exactly the same as that of the great majority who would continue to work.

There are many who look forward to shifts in their careers, but only few and far between are those who aim to make a quick bundle and retire young. For instance, Philip Genochio wants to help a Third World country manage its economy after he becomes financially independent. Katherine Johnson wants to get off the brutal treadmill of fast-paced legal practice and shift to a more sensible and rewarding career track that will also allow more time for her family. Yet one way or another, the educational elite sees work as central to life, for much of the meaning they get out of life is derived from their work.

Here again, women are only moderately different from men. Some 89 percent of men, compared with 78 percent of women, say they would work without needing to. Paid employment is crucial to the sense of self-worth and independence of both sexes, though it still appears to be slightly more important for men than for women. This small difference is due mostly to the presence in the sample of women who are simultaneously working and taking the major responsibility for child rearing; many of them would choose to scale back their demanding lives by not working outside the house, or working less, while their children are young.

Contrary to what one might expect, Careerists are most likely to insist that working should not be dependent only on financial need: 89 percent say they would work no matter what. This suggests that their intense dedication to careers has deeper psychological roots than the desire for money and security alone. Intellectuals come next; the men in this group say unanimously that they would work even if they did not need the money, but only 80 percent of Intellectual women agree with them. The group least committed to work for its own sake are the Unconnected women, even though their percentage (69 percent) is still quite high.

In developmental terms, work is one of the primary means for young adults to attain independence and self-sufficiency—in short, to become fully adult. The psychologist Daniel Levinson calls this period of transition to adulthood the "novice phase" and locates it between the ages of seventeen and thirty-three (give or take a year or two at either end).[4] This is almost precisely the period of our study, from entry to college to ten years following graduation. The novice phase has three segments. It begins with "early adult transition" (roughly ages seventeen to twenty-two), during which the person moves out of adolescence and begins to create a basis for adult life without being fully within it. For the educational elite, this means getting into and making it through a select college. The process is then followed by the period of "entering the adult world" between the ages of about twenty-two and twenty-eight. The task is "to explore the possibilities of this world, to test some initial choices, and to build a first provisional life structure." This allows a shift in "the center of gravity" away from the family of origin to a home base of one's own. It calls for the accomplishment of two seemingly antithetical tasks. A young adult must first explore the diverse possibilities for adult living (especially career choices), "keep options open, avoid stormy courses of events, and maximize the alternatives."[5] The second, and contrasting, task is to create a stable life structure. These are the issues that have faced our participants during much of the decade after college. The third and last phase of the "age thirty transition" provides an opportunity for revising the initial structure and becoming a full-fledged adult.

This balancing act between change and stability on the road to adulthood characterizes faithfully the career (and personal) lives of our participants in the decade after college. The transition to the adult world accelerates when parents stop supporting their children after college. ("My parents had always made it clear that once I graduated from Stanford, I would be on my own.") In fact, quite a few of our less affluent participants had already attained their independence by paying (and borrowing) their own way through college.

For others, the process of separation from parents takes longer. Some parents continue to help their adult children by giving them money, inviting them to move back home, or offering loans that somehow never have to be repaid. But most would rather not need such help. Alicia Turner lived at home on and off until her late twenties while working at odd jobs. It was the only way she could make ends meet. When she finally was able to manage on her own, it was a source of much satisfaction ("I was proud of myself").

A few participants have not yet attained financial independence, and the effect on their self-esteem is quite marked. Bill is one of the few men whose careers have not yet panned out. His family still supports him indirectly by employing his wife in the family business. He is grateful and resentful in equal measure. ("I can't wait to get on my own two feet.")

WORK, HOUSEWORK, AND PARENTHOOD

The relative merits and values of work inside and outside the home constitute one of the more difficult and contentious issues facing young couples. This issue is especially important for women, who still carry the greater share of the burden of housework. It is an issue with serious implications for both their careers and their sense of self-worth.

What is considered work has undergone important changes in American society. With the development of exchange economies in the eighteenth and nineteenth centuries, the definition of work gradually narrowed to include only productive labor outside the home. Housework, child care, and care of the elderly in the home—unpaid tasks—were no longer acknowledged as work. Since women were largely responsible for these tasks, the valuation of their economic "worth" became less than that of

men. The recent response to this situation, driven by the women's movement as well as by the trend of women's increased participation in the
exchange economy, is twofold.

First, the proportion of adult women working outside the home has
increased dramatically, from 34 percent in 1950 to 43 percent in 1970 and
58 percent in 1990.[6] The largest increase has been among married women
living with their husbands and young children (from less than 2 percent in
1960 to almost 60 percent in 1988). Among adult married women younger
than forty-four who have no children, 80 percent are now in the labor
force.[7] The change among women who are separated or divorced has been
less marked, since many of these women had been working outside the
home for decades.

Second, a movement has been under way for some time to bring household work more fully into the exchange economy as a way of increasing
homemakers' sense of self-worth and self-esteem. Proposals to pay homemakers, the great majority of whom are women, are paralleled by the
increasing use of service workers to perform household tasks, though not
necessarily in the home (for example, dry cleaning, preparing food, fast-
food restaurants, diaper services). The latter trend is relevant to the educational elite, since they have the money to buy a wide range of services, but
paid homemaking is not an issue for them. Most women of the educational
elite either work outside the home or intend to return to such employment
as soon as they feel their children are old enough for professional child
care. Full-time housework (apart from child rearing) is simply not an
option for the women in our sample. The issue of managing a household is
nonetheless very important for women and men of the educational elite
who are trying to combine careers and families, and we discuss it in chapter 8.

We received an irate response from one woman participant because she
thought our questionnaire made it impossible for her to adequately convey
the nature of her work as a full-time mother. She said she was currently
employed "by my two kids," listed her income as "$0," and added, "I
don't get paid in my profession." To the question "Do you plan to take
time out of the work force to be a parent or homemaker?" she responded,
"Stupid question?" She then further unburdened herself:

> I found myself becoming increasingly angry as I worked on this sur-
> vey—as you may be able to tell by my answers. My Stanford experi-
> ence was a very positive one. I loved my classes, professors, class-
> mates, and the environment. However, I felt tremendous pressure to
> succeed in the workplace, from my classmates and the Stanford envi-
> ronment. The survey furthers that pressure in making a person feel

less successful if they don't have a high-powered career. I have chosen not to work. I have chosen to be a full-time mother to my two boys. This survey all but ignores parenthood and the importance of influencing our future generations. This is a fault that should be examined by your study. Perhaps the emphasis on "careers" and money has become too important and the importance of family has been lost. A sad statement for a great university!

It was a cry from the heart. We heard it, and we return to it later in this chapter.

WORKING TIMELINES

Going to graduate school and going to work are almost mutually exclusive activities for the educational elite. Only the relative few who studied part-time tried to combine the two. Generally, graduate programs are so demanding that they do not allow much opportunity for holding a job except as part of the training process, such as Ph.D. programs in which fellowships include teaching or research duties.

Thus, patterns of work are generally the inverse of patterns of study. Future doctors study hard but work only as part of their training before age thirty; future business managers work, study for the M.B.A. for a couple of years, then work again. Future lawyers most often study first and work the rest of the first decade. As we discussed in chapter 3, a variety of factors enter into these decisions, ranging from financial considerations to the nature of the occupation and personal preferences.

Following a direct path from college to career may seem the most efficient course, but it is not always the optimal one. Larry waited five years after college before getting into a J.D.-M.B.A. program. Although the start of his legal career was delayed until the end of the decade, he has no regrets about the years he spent as a foreign exchange trader, congressional aide, and legislative assistant. He says, "I matured during these years and got much more out of my schooling than I would have otherwise."

Figure 4.1 shows timelines of work experience during the decade after graduation. The curves for men and women are quite similar. At the outset, close to 40 percent of men and 50 percent of women worked full-time (more men were in graduate school). The proportion of men working full-time increased to parity with women after four years, but women moved ahead once more as more men returned to graduate programs. By the seventh year, 75 percent of both sexes were employed full-time. This was the high point of women's employment, marking the age at which an apprecia-

FIGURE 4.1
Full-Time and Part-Time Work, by Sex

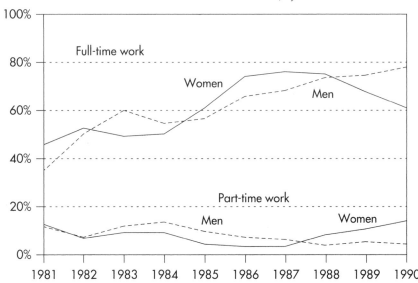

ble portion began leaving paid employment to care for children. The male curve, on the other hand, continued to climb. By the end of the decade, 78 percent of men and 61 percent of women were engaged in full-time work.

The big difference between male and female work patterns at the present time has to do with continuity of work. Men typically stay in the labor force except when laid off. Women go in and out of the work force as they bear and rear children. Thus, no more than one-quarter of American women work continuously and full-time through their adult lives; 54 percent of women with no children work full-time, but only 11 percent of those with at least one preschool child.[8] Discounting the impact of children, the women likeliest to work without interruption are those who are from disadvantaged minorities (the "necessity" factor), in nontraditional or "masculine" jobs, strongly committed to their careers, or married to men who strongly approve of their employment.[9]

All of these characteristics, except for ethnicity, apply to the women of the educational elite in their first decade out of college. The majority of them have no children; many are in nontraditional professions for women; almost all are committed to having their own careers and are married to men who expect their wives to be independent earners. Therefore, we expect most of our women participants to take relatively short breaks from work to give birth to and raise their young children.

On the other hand, we also know that women with high-income husbands are more often homemakers because they do not need to work.

How much this factor will make long-term homemakers of our career-oriented women remains to be seen, but we suspect that at least some who indicated they would work even if they had no need for the income will change their minds as they enter their thirties and learn how complicated two-career, multichild family life can be.

For the different professions, doctors start working late (only 54 percent were working full-time even by the tenth year), and lawyers are rather late (46 percent by the fifth year). In contrast, by the second year nearly three-fourths of the business-finance and teaching-humanistic groups worked full-time. In the latter group (most of whom are women), the full-time working rate dropped more sharply toward the end of the decade than for other professions as rates of childbearing began to rise.

Part-time work (the lower portion of figure 4.1) is not particularly common; a maximum of 14 percent of our participants pursue it in any year. Men worked part-time somewhat more than women until the latter part of the decade, when part-time work by women increased rapidly. Here we see one clear effect of women's attempts to juggle careers and child rearing by reducing their working hours. For men, on the other hand, part-time work was at its lowest point of the decade in the tenth year. Rare indeed is the father who cuts back on working time to be with his children, even though some say they would like to.

Ten years after graduation, 94 percent of our participants were working full- or part-time outside the home—96 percent of the men and 90 percent of the women. Most of the women who were not employed were engaged in child rearing; of the few nonemployed men, nearly all were involved in career preparation or retraining. In the interview sample there was only one man, a scriptwriter, who was actually unemployed. But even he could have been employed if he were willing to take another job, a move he was considering at the time.

Relatively small differences characterize the working patterns of the four types. Because Careerists and Strivers attended graduate school earlier, they started to work later than the other types; after the fifth year, however, all groups were equally likely to be working. But at the end of the decade an intriguing difference emerged: women Intellectuals were much more likely than women of any other type to have traded working for child rearing. The interviews suggest a number of reasons for this finding. Some Intellectual women are not as strongly committed to careers as other women, or they have chosen careers that can be interrupted or modified without serious penalty. Hence, given a choice between full-time child care and working, they opt for the former. Other Intellectual women seem to find motherhood especially rewarding. Even if they have been actively developing their outside careers, motherhood evokes in them such strong feelings that they change their life course. Intellectual Kirsten Buchanan is an excellent example (see chapter 8).

We should also note that the Unconnected worked as much as other types; their lack of "connection" in conventional terms did not mean they avoided employment. Indeed, in all aspects of the career launch process, the Unconnected do not look particularly unconnected. The bulk of them, including our two Unconnected profiles, went on to business, law, or medical school like everyone else. Even though they have exhibited a greater unwillingness to follow the standard process of career development, they usually end up falling into line.

But not always. We found that a hard-core group among the Unconnected have remained unconnected late into the decade. These individuals are usually single, since those who have not settled into a career are less likely to marry (especially if male). Moreover, various psychological factors (not necessarily negative ones) may underlie their unwillingness to commit to either a line of work or a relationship.

Naomi's whirlwind life is a good illustration. Bright, articulate, and sophisticated, Naomi was admitted to half a dozen select colleges, but, she says, "I chose Stanford because of its laid-back reputation." After she got in, however, Naomi spent the next four years "fighting the system." Her undergraduate years were punctuated by many nonacademic activities: working in boatyards, waitressing in exotic places, qualifying for her Coast Guard license. By her senior year, she appeared to have settled down somewhat, but not for long.

The next decade proved even richer in experience. She traveled extensively, lived in the Middle East, and earned a master's degree in political science in Europe. Back in the United States, she vacillated between law and business, finally chose business, and won admission to the Harvard Business School. She promptly deferred admission for a year and went to Africa to take charge of the renovation of an old temple. Finally, she went through the M.B.A. program, "hating every minute of it." The end of the decade found her poised for her first major job in international business.

Naomi's career pattern may look erratic to others, but to her, it was part of a long-term, two-part plan—to gain expertise about one geographic area of the world, and to get a graduate degree in law or business. And that is precisely what she has done. Unconnected participants like Naomi are, in fact, very connected, but their connection is to their own game plans, not to standard assumptions about how careers are launched and pursued.

On the whole we find that the striking differences among our four types while they were in college shrink considerably as the decade after college unfolds. Can we explain this convergence by saying that even the Unconnected finally "find themselves" and "grow up"? However simplistic, there may be some truth to this idea. The Unconnected may not necessarily be "immature" in a normative sense; perhaps theirs is simply a different maturational schedule. Their relative unwillingness to make career commitments in college may have seemed problematic at the time, but in hindsight, such delays may be advantageous in the long run if they lead to a better fit between who they are and what they wish to do with their lives.

At any rate, as individuals are gradually channeled into the responsibilities, demands, and restraints of young adult life, options narrow. Like a variety of feeder roads converging into a freeway, diverse career paths merge into a few lanes headed in the same direction.

CAREER STAGES

Career choices and development are often thought of as a continuous process that unfolds smoothly during our working years. The prescription for career success is seemingly simple: we choose the occupation that suits us, we apply ourselves with diligence, and we stay the course until we retire. Plenty of our participants have followed this prescription, Careerist Martin MacMillan and most of his fellow physicians among them. Yet this career pattern is no longer the general norm. Initial choice and eventual career are no longer seen as so closely linked, particularly for more broadly trained professionals. For example, Ray graduated with a degree in engineering, but his subsequent career went through several discrete phases. He worked for a public accounting firm, then for a computer software company. A subsequent stint on the editorial staff of an engineering magazine led to his becoming managing editor of a consumer magazine.

Although Ray may be a rather extreme case, his career exemplifies a pattern that has become more common: career jumps, project-oriented moves, retraining, and other discontinuous modes of career development. Only about 10 percent of college undergraduates in a national sample believe that their occupation must be consistent with their training and that they must maintain a consistent career path.[10] Even if a person stays within the same occupation, his or her career path may branch sharply several times. Jim went to work right after college. He got into the corporate training program of an insurance company but lost interest after two years. He was recruited by a fledgling high-tech company that subsequently folded. He switched fields, taking a job in a large consulting firm. Under the mentorship of his new boss, Jim flourished. When his mentor retired, Jim joined another consulting firm, this time as a partner.

The conceptual distinctions between career choice and career development are exaggerated by the fact that these two areas have been studied by two different sets of social scientists. Questions about career choice have typically occupied vocational psychologists, who try to understand and facilitate the occupational choices of high school and college students. They look at the effects on career choice of factors like personality characteristics, childhood experiences, parental models, and decision-making processes. A key practical objective of their work is to determine how a person fits with his or her chosen occupation. To that end, they have devised vocational tests to provide guidance for making appropriate choices.[11]

By contrast, sociologists and experts in organizational behavior have focused on the institutional settings in which people work and the ways in which they interact with one another.[12] Their interest lies in understanding the career patterns that emerge during adult working life as they are shaped by situational factors and varied work environments. Their practical concerns include occupational adjustments, levels of performance, job mobility, commitment to jobs, and work-family interaction. Despite differences in focus and methods of investigation, these two approaches to the study of careers deal with two sides of the same coin. Attempts to integrate these two perspectives, however, are still not very successful.[13]

Life-cycle theorists, like Erik Erikson, who rely on the concept of life stages do not specifically delineate these stages as they relate to career development. Hence, after the acquisition of the sense of ego identity, the adolescent moves on to the establishment of intimate relationships in young adulthood and then on to the "generativity" of the next phase.[14] Though Erikson is keenly aware of the importance of work during adult development, he does not describe with any specificity how careers are shaped. George Vaillant and Eva Milofsky, however, have identified a "well-defined career consolidation phase that falls between Erikson's stages of intimacy and generativity."[15] It is exactly this intermediate stage that our participants have been negotiating during the decade after college.

The most ambitious attempt to provide a life-span perspective on career development is psychologist Donald Super's synthesis of these various perspectives. Super envisages careers developing through discrete stages, each with its own characteristic tasks. These tasks are embedded in life stages: growth belongs to childhood; exploration is part of adolescence; establishment takes place in young adulthood; maintenance is the task of middle adulthood; and decline (or disengagement) characterizes the older years.[16] Career stages consist of phases of rapid transition punctuating periods of relative stability (like Levinson's stepladder sequence of the life cycle). Moreover, developmental tasks are recycled in successive periods of life: the sequence of exploration, establishment, maintenance, and disengagement occurs not just once on a grand scale but repeatedly, within several career stages. Such repetitions normally occur in successive phases of adulthood (early, middle, and late) but may cluster in one or more particularly turbulent or expansive phases.[17]

John Van Maanen and Edgar Schein add another dimension to this model with the idea that we are always traveling two career paths, an external path and an internal path. The external path consists of the jobs, positions, promotions, and other outwardly visible indicators of career progress. The internal path includes our more private plans, hopes, and expectations, known only within a narrow circle. Another view is to see a career as attached to two anchors: one anchor represents the institutional requirements of the job (what we are supposed to do), the other, the needs and motives that we are trying to fulfill through our work.[18]

To place our participants in the context of these models, the fourteen-year period during which we have studied them (from their freshman year to ten years after graduation) covers two of Super's stages: exploration and establishment. The stage of exploration includes the search for career direction in college and, for many, the career training period afterwards, when they try out one or more career options but do not always find them suitable (chapter 3). On the external path of this journey are strewn the tentative images of working environments and career identities that were picked up and discarded as a function of the courses they took, the grades they got, their assessments of their chances of being admitted to graduate programs, and so on. The internal path is characterized by their more private thoughts: dreams of who they are and what they want to be, goals and ambitions that may seem impossibly out of reach, perceptions of the models they wish to emulate.

The establishment stage, following formal schooling, starts with the intense, anxiety-filled process of getting a job. To launch their careers, they seek jobs and work situations that meet their internal criteria, but they have to adjust their expectations to enhance their attractiveness to prospective employers, who set quite stringent standards for the high-level positions they have to offer. Once the match is made, entry to the profession involves carving out a niche in the organization, learning to deal with its hierarchical structure, and absorbing the organizational culture in a constant process of assessment, self-reflection, and adjustment—or lack of adjustment, if the match turns out not to be a good one.

For most of the educational elite, these external aspects of the career launch process seem easy. They make smooth transitions, rapid adjustments, and self-confident forays into difficult situations. But rare indeed are the young adults, even of the educational elite, who make the transition from school to work without moments of self-doubt, nervousness, or hesitation. Alicia Turner was jumping for joy on her first day in the classroom, but many of our participants found themselves asking, "What have I gotten myself into?" The first job assignment felt like the first day in college. Coming from the top of the educational staircase, they were now at the lowest rung of the career ladder. From being somebody, they had become nobody.

Thus, mixed emotions are the order of the day. There is the satisfaction of having arrived, the sense of starting a decisive journey, but also the apprehension of moving from the didactic approach of the classroom to the practical reality of the office. The formal change in status is often a great help. As an intern, Martin MacMillan's duties were little different from those he had as a final-year medical student, but now he was called "Doctor" and his signature on hospital charts was worth something. That made a huge difference to his sense of identity and professional confidence as a physician.

The period of establishment—the ascent to cruising speed, as it were— has no fixed length. Though out of medical school for five years and certified in two medical specialties, Martin still does not feel fully squared in the saddle. Cynthia Eastwood has been through the process of getting settled in a job several times already, but she found the position that holds the promise of launching her career on a definitive trajectory only a few months before we interviewed her in the tenth year. For some of our participants, the period of establishment has yet to be entered.

The last two stages of Super's model, maintenance and disengagement, are still in the future for our participants. Nonetheless, they are quite relevant to the way their careers are currently shaping up because they look ahead as well as back when making choices. The past, present, and future are all intermingled in their lives: who they are now is a reflection of who they have been and who they expect to become.

CAREER SHIFTS

While many of our participants seem to be steadily moving through the phases of career exploration and establishment, others have already gone through several shifts in their careers. These shifts can be modest, such as changing employers, but not infrequently they involve embarking on a new career direction altogether. Ted's story is a good example. Ted was a varsity athlete who after graduation became a professional baseball player. Through a series of career shifts that were partly forced and partly chosen, he has since become a developer of low-cost housing for a highly disadvantaged community. He sums up the journey:

> I left college with a baseball mitt and a degree. I've used the mitt more, although the work underlying the degree is paying off. My path

has been anything but linear. I've generally gone in a given direction until I ran into a wall. I then went in a different direction until I ran into another wall. I now know I acted a little like a rat in a maze. It is only recently that I've figured out how to get above the maze, kind of like a helicopter, so I can see a bigger picture and therefore make more efficient and satisfying decisions. Without question, hitting a couple of walls helps one begin to look for different approaches. Only now have I begun to piece together a long-term plan.

CHANGING EMPLOYERS

The general pattern of career progress for our participants is one of frequent shifts: over two-thirds of our participants changed employers at least once, and on average they stayed in a job for only about three years. Of those working full-time, be they men or women, 17 percent changed employers, on average, in any given year.

The dominant motive for changing employers is to enhance career opportunities. Thus, it is not surprising that Careerists changed employers more than any other type. Most of the time, our participants were the ones deciding to move on, but a number of them lost their jobs when companies went under. Being young, ambitious, and self-confident, they had joined start-up companies on the technological cutting edge. As the downturn in the computer and related industries took hold from the mid-1980s onward, such high-risk, high-gain ventures proved highly vulnerable.

Very few were fired outright. In these rare cases, the problem typically was personality conflict rather than lack of professional competence. Jasper is a good example. He was a blustery character in college whose claim in his senior year to have become more "polished and mellow" rang hollow. Ten years later he was as contentious as ever. ("I am a polarizing person.") He had been fired from his last job yet was unwilling to provide details.

CHANGING CAREERS

Career changes are far more drastic and less common than changes of employer, but they are hardly rare. About 5 percent of our participants reported such changes each year, some more than once. Over the decade, fully 35 percent changed careers at least once. Again, women were as likely as men to change careers, and variation among the four types was minimal. Career changing is thus a general phenomenon among the educational elite, not the peculiarity of one gender or type. Nonetheless, patterns of career change are not entirely unsystematic. They are far more common among those in business (49 percent) than in medicine (11 percent), with lawyers in between (24 percent).

When people move from one field to another closely related, the principle of changing careers becomes more nebulous. M.B.A. programs have many engineers who want to shift to business careers in consulting or marketing. Such a move is clearly an occupational shift, but nothing like a petroleum engineer becoming a poet. Some career changes may not seem very striking externally, but they may be personally experienced as enormous. Dimitri worked as an engineer for six years. He was fairly content except for his nagging fears that the particular area he was in was headed for obsolescence. On a trial basis, his father offered him a job in the family business. Dimitri liked it and went back to school to get an M.B.A. He then began his current work as a financial consultant, a career he sees as entirely different from engineering. Dimitri's story is quite different from the more typical path of engineers, who often get business degrees to enhance their careers as managers but retain a strong engineering connection. His shift is so marked that he has revised his professional identity.

Some changes in career direction are more drastic. A particularly unusual path from college to graduate school was traveled by Arturo, who had searched earnestly during college for a career direction and finally decided to become a psychologist. In his senior year, a dramatic spiritual conversion experience led him to enter a Catholic seminary to become a priest. His first two years in seminary seemed to confirm his commitment to the priesthood, but the behavior of his fellow seminarians gradually led to his disenchantment. He left before he was ordained, and after teaching at a parochial school for a year, he got his teaching certificate and then a master's degree in education. He is now an assistant school principal, married, and the father of two children. Kiwon also took a turn at a religious career. First he studied engineering, but then he worked as a missionary overseas for four years on behalf of his small evangelical church. Then he, too, had a falling-out, in his case with the autocratic leader of the church. So he left and returned to engineering.

Some career changes involve principled commitments that become unsustainable. We related earlier how Katherine Johnson lost her job teaching underprivileged children, failed to find a similar position, and went to law school. A similar example is Gail. A fine student, varsity swimmer, and highly idealistic, Gail became a high school teacher and swimming coach. Her day started at 6:00 in the morning and ended twelve hours later, with swim practices sandwiched between classes. She drove herself relentlessly for four years, on a modest salary, with hardly a life of her own outside of work. Each modest yearly raise was grudgingly doled out by the school board. When a member of the board told her, "You teachers do not deserve so many raises since you work such short hours," Gail quit and went to law school.

Changing employers is often motivated by the offer of a better job or large salary increase. Changing careers almost necessitates a change of employers: 60 percent of those who changed careers in a given year also changed employers, and most of the rest left employment for graduate training. But most employer changes do not involve career change; only 21 percent of those changing employers in a given year also changed careers. Remarkably enough, some people—as many as 5 percent of those employed in a given year—managed to change careers without changing employers.

That competent and ambitious men and women should change employers during the formative years of their careers is to be expected. But why do so many of them change the direction of their careers? The main reason, of course, is that many college students make career choices without knowing what they are getting into. Even going through a graduate program may not be sufficiently eye-opening; to paraphrase one lawyer we quoted earlier, law school is not the same as practicing law. The educational elite also change careers at least in part because of their relatively privileged social backgrounds and exceptional degree of self-confidence. They know they can always make a living; they feel little risk in making changes because they know they have the ability and character to adapt to, and thrive in, new circumstances.

We have described these variations in career patterns independent of the broader life context, which is often crucial to career development decisions, particularly among couples. The needs of a spouse or partner have a major impact on decisions to change employers, even on decisions to change careers.

Most often, men's work requirements influence the career development of their women partners; for instance, women move with their husbands. One woman left her job with a large salary to become a stockbroker working on commission (earning only $24,000 annually) when her husband made a career advancement change that required their move to a new city. Such moves, even among the educational elite, are usually detrimental to the woman's career.

Nevertheless, the men in our sample are generally quite sensitive to the impact of a move on their partners' careers and lives. They always seek their partners' consent, and if it is not forthcoming, some forgo the move. For instance, one man refused a highly lucrative offer that required transferring to another city to avoid "the marriage strain that would be likely to occur" if they relocated. Beyond that, some men actually followed their women to new work locations. As we noted, David Levy left his job to be near his girlfriend's university, and he plans to go wherever she gets a teaching job. We provide further examples in chapter 8.

Some of these more accommodating men are decidedly liberal in their political and social views, but even more traditional men have bent their careers to their partners' needs. Edward is politically as conservative as they come, but he is leaving his coveted job at the Justice Department to start teaching in a second-rate law school in a small town. Why? Because his wife, also a lawyer, got an appointment there that is a key step toward a judgeship, her ultimate goal—in emulation of her father.

CAREER CONCEPTS
AND CAREER DEVELOPMENT

Michael Driver's model of "career concepts" offers an instructive approach to studying the development of career patterns over time. Like other theorists, Driver conceives of a career as much more than an occupation or a job. It includes "one's avocations, hobbies, and social activities. It is deeply rooted in the issue of family and particularly the 'identity-career patterns' of the spouse."[19] Seen in this context, puzzling or seemingly aimless career patterns begin to make more sense. For example, some people in dead-end jobs can be quite content because they primarily value the rewards of family life or avidly pursued leisure activities rather than the rewards of their work, which simply sustains them.

Driver's premise is that individuals develop about their careers relatively stable "concepts" that provide a framework within which they make sense of their work. The framework includes career commitment and direction, markers of success, and turning points for making career choices. These career concepts are derived from basic decision-making styles based on how people process information and reach decisions.[20]

Driver's career concepts and their underlying decision-making styles resolve into four basic career patterns (figure 4.2). The first is the linear pattern (a), a steady progression up the career ladder. The pace of advancement varies from the "fast track" to more moderate rates of advancement; upward movement need not be rapid, but it must be steady over the long run. This pattern is most readily seen in managerial careers in hierarchical organizations.

The central motives of the linear concept are achievement and power. Its decision-making style is hierarchic. It relies on extensive use of information in generating a long-term career game plan. Career directions are set

FIGURE 4.2
Michael Driver's Career Concepts

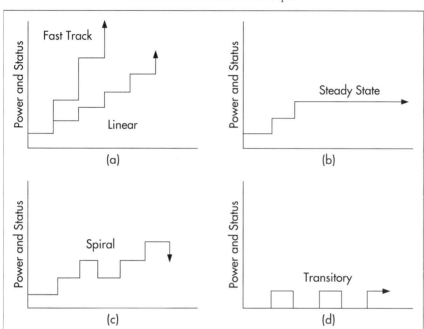

From James G. Clawson and David D. Ward, *An M.B.A.'s Guide to Self-Assessment and Career Development* (Englewood Cliffs, N.J.: Prentice-Hall, 1985), 18.

early, during youth, and have a single objective that dominates the individual's life: career advancement.

Many of the educational elite, particularly Careerists, appear to fit the linear concept, though it is too early to tell whether it represents a lifelong pattern for them. The fast track is epitomized by Philip Genochio, who, after only five years of employment, is already poised for the final push into senior management. A more moderate pace characterizes another Careerist's progress in business. A black woman, Lenora entered Stanford at sixteen, breezed through, and went straight to Stanford Business School. She then got a job with a large utilities company and steadily rose through the ranks. Her peers at work are now mostly white middle-aged men. Top-level management is in sight. Cynthia Eastwood's career, by contrast, looks far less steady, but it is no less linear in terms of its steady climb upward.

Linear careers are also common among lawyers. Ralph went to law school right after college, clerked for a judge and a Supreme Court justice, then got his present job in the U.S. attorney's office. Peter is an electrical engineer who went to school and specialized in patent law. He became a partner in a prestigious law firm at the age of thirty.

Driver's second career concept is the "steady state" (b), which begins as a linear pattern but slows down after a period of rapid advancement. Individuals with this career concept typically make an early commitment to a career and hold fast to it, making no major shifts for the rest of their working lives and reaching a plateau beyond which they never advance. This style is typical among skilled professionals—engineers remaining engineers rather than becoming managers, physicians going into private practice and never setting their sights on academic or administrative positions. Like priests, once they find their calling, they stay with it. The central steady state motives are security and competence.

Though the distinction is not always easy to make, the steady state differs from the "slow-track" version of the linear pattern in that lack of advancement is more a matter of choice. The decision-making style typical of the steady state (the decisive style) is characterized by the confidence to rely on even a small amount of information to reach a decision. Career choice is made early (often during late adolescence in response to the expectations or the advice of parents, teachers, or counselors), and alternatives are never seriously considered thereafter.

A good example of an engineer with a steady state career pattern is Edward. He is a highly competent, hands-on professional whose interests have always been in the technical aspects of engineering. He thinks he got all the formal education he needs at Stanford, and he continues to develop his skills on the job. Edward has no interest in management and disdains "white-shirt-and-tie types, who are not particularly creative." Physicians in private practice are especially likely to follow this pattern—all but two of the physicians in our interview sample readily fit this category, with Martin MacMillan one of the prime examples. Martin feels so well settled in his career at age thirty-one that he is certain he will be doing more of the same ten years from now. In fact, his first job may well see him through the rest of his medical career, and he is pleased with it.

The same steady career pattern is typical of some of our teachers. Heather majored in economics in college, thinking she would go to law school. Her father and two of her siblings, including her twin sister, are lawyers. But by graduation she had changed her mind; teaching beckoned. Her mother (also a teacher) first discouraged, then supported her decision. For the past eight years, except for time taken off to have her three children, she has taught second grade. Now she shares her position with another teacher. She is blissfully happy at her work and cannot imagine doing anything else.

In all of these examples, the individual began a career expecting it to follow a steady, stable course. Others started on a linear pattern and switched to steady state. Geoffrey is the son and grandson of small-town lawyers. His first job was with a large law firm in Chicago where for three years he worked hard and began the ascent up the career ladder. He tired, however, of "being a small cog in a big machine." He says, "I was always involved in the small pieces of large lawsuits. I never became fully involved in any one case and never got to represent real people." Meanwhile, he married and became a father. "A large city," he thought, "is not a fit place to raise a child, any more than a large law firm is a fit place for me to spend the rest of my working life." So he found a position in a law office with three partners in a small town in Oregon, not unlike the town in which his father and grandfather practiced. His office is in a quaint, renovated building on the town square. He expects to be made partner next year. "I am not one of the exciting people that you must be encountering," he said at the start of the interview, with a gentle smile. He certainly was one of the most contented.

Geoffrey took a significant cut in pay when he made the move, and the disparity in income between two such positions is bound to increase over time. But the $70,000 a year he now makes is ample for where they live. Moreover, he works just as hard as he did in Chicago, and he is fully committed to his work. He may handle as many as forty files at a time, but he welcomes the load because "they are my cases." Where will he be in ten years? "Right here," he says. "This is what I wanted to do, and this is what I will be doing."

The remaining two career concepts, both nonlinear, are characterized not by a steady progression—either on an upward trajectory or leveling to a plateau—but by sharper breaks and more radical changes in career direction. One variant is the spiral career concept (c). Driver describes it as a cyclical pattern; major changes are made every five to seven years. During these periods, the person stays long enough in a career to become well established but then seeks a new challenge and moves on. The central motive is personal growth through career exploration; the decision-making style is integrative, using maximal information but developing a more complex multidimensional plan that incorporates into the career a wide variety of life concerns. It remains open to change based on new information and subsequent life experiences. On the face of it, Careerist Cynthia Eastwood's career history would seem to fit this pattern because of its frequent shifts. But her shifts have been mostly strategic, intended to accelerate progress on the fast track. Geoffrey's career move took him off the fast track and into a work setting more compatible with a leisurely lifestyle. But he was not looking for personal growth, and he continued to practice law. So neither Cynthia nor Geoffrey fit the spiral concept.

Elaine's shift from being an accountant to a high school teacher is more typical of the spiral pattern. Right after graduation from college, Elaine went to work for a large engineering firm. She liked her job and thought she would stay in it for the rest of her career. After eight years, however, she started getting restless. She says, "I had the perfect desk job but began to lose interest. I didn't feel I was contributing enough to the community. I knew my job was not going to keep me happy for the rest of my life." She managed to win a fellowship for a teacher training program and was just about to start teaching high school math at the time of her interview.

The metamorphosis undergone by Marty was more dramatic still. Marty was accepted by the M.B.A. program at the University of Chicago but not at Harvard, his first choice. He decided to work instead and landed a computer job at an investment bank bulging with M.B.A.s. The experience convinced him he did not want a business degree. ("I did not enjoy working with that sort of individual.") Two years later, he switched to a start-up computer company. "It was a dream job in many ways," he recalls, "challenging, fun, with the promise of making everyone rich." After nine months, neither the company nor Marty was rich; he was back at square one. With some misgivings, he went into his father's real estate business, though working largely independently. He earned good money and got to know his father better; they got along well. Marty's father had also shifted careers. A high school teacher for fourteen years, he had quit to go into business for himself. Marty's mother had gone back to school in midlife.

Marty's dream had been "to make a million by age thirty," but gradual disenchantment at work slowly turned the dream into a nightmare. Making money lost its allure. Marty became fascinated by psychology. He wanted to help people and was mostly "looking for peace within myself." At age twenty-seven, Marty decided to make a clean break. He quit his job and entered an accelerated program in social work that led to a job as a drug counselor in an inner-city school in Chicago. He likes what he does, but the school bureaucracy rankles him. He has already switched schools once. He makes $36,000 instead of his former base salary of $150,000 plus other income. But he is happy. "I like myself and being who I am."

Given Driver's estimate that the typical spiral cycle should last five to seven years, it is not clear how closely it applies to young adults, like our participants, who have been out of graduate school for only the length of one cycle. Whether the examples we have given exemplify a true spiral pattern will be clear only in another decade or so.

The fourth career concept is the transitory pattern (d): an individual makes a succession of major career shifts every few years for no apparent rhyme or reason. These shifts are not intended for advancement; they are usually lateral, not vertical, moves. For some, this mode reflects an inability to hold a steady job (a rare condition for the educational elite). For others, like some entrepreneurs, it is a deliberate strategy involving a search for that one venture that finally "hits it big." The central motives are challenge, variety, and exploration of identity. The characteristic decision-making mode is the flexible style. The transitory concept shares with the steady state model a reliance on minimal amounts of information to reach decisions, but in the service of provisional decisions only. New information and the lessons of ongoing experience lead to further career shifts. As a result, the career choice period extends throughout an individual's working life.

Unlike the other three categories, transitory careers are rare among the educational elite. At most, half a dozen of our participants could conceivably fit this pattern. Given the relatively short period of career time that has passed, they may get out of this pattern in due time. Disjointed as some of these participants' careers may seem, their thoughts on the future point to stable career establishment rather than a long-term series of career flip-flops.

Let us consider the cases of two possibly transitory women, both Intellectuals. Tara walked through the graduation ceremony even though she had not completed the remaining few courses required for graduation. She had started college with the idea of going into medicine but soon scaled down her hopes to physical therapy. Then she abandoned that idea, too. She had broad intellectual interests but no career focus. For the first five years after college, Tara did "a bit of everything." Then she began to look for jobs more befitting her capabilities. A position as a receptionist with a manufacturing firm in San Diego eventually led to her current position as the supervisor of a small staff in the shipping department. Where will she be in ten years? "I have not planned things that far ahead," replies Tara.

Janice's work history is a dizzying tale of movement between New York, London, and Los Angeles. After college, she went to New York and worked in the theater as a scriptwriter, literary manager, stage manager, and production manager. Along the way she got a master's degree in English. None of her theater ventures paid off financially, but she was kept afloat by a modest trust fund. Finally, she unburdened herself of the theater and has now entered a clinical psychology program to become a therapist.

Janice's case illustrates an important principle. Externally, her career may look chaotic, but internally her goals have been quite consistent so far as she is concerned. Even while in the theater she was primarily concerned with "spiritual stuff." She wrote regularly, partly "as an attempt to heal myself." Some find the transitory style very satisfying because of the opportunities it offers for fulfilling emotional needs. Different types of work fill different needs at different times, and no one job or career offers everything sought by the transitory individual. As needs change, so must the jobs.

Based on their characteristics as undergraduates (rather than their subsequent performance), we would have expected to find a close connection between the transitory pattern and our Unconnected group. Those individuals whose careers have not taken a linear, steady state, or spiral direction are indeed all Unconnected—yet we could hardly label them transitory this early in their careers. It is possible that their careers simply have not yet taken off.

For example, after graduating from Stanford, Tom has mainly worked as a waiter in Los Angeles to support himself while studying and trying to make it as a dancer, a career he has been desperately hoping to develop. Tom had his first ballet lesson when he was already twenty-two, and he got into it "with my heart rather than my head." He has worked hard at dance, but so far without much success. Though for a while he felt like he was "in a quagmire," he is neither bitter nor resigned to his fate. "I have come farther than I hoped to come, and in terms of the career ladder, I am probably somewhere—I would say halfway toward my goal. Performance has not been a consistent thing, but I have managed to reach a certain level of professionalism. And now the next step is to perform on a regular basis."

We referred to Bill earlier as unemployed. His pleasant, boyish features make him look much younger than his age. With his low-key, shy manner, he conveys a sense of thoughtful melancholy. Bill lists his occupation for most of the past decade as "story analyst," a line of work that has consisted of reviewing film scripts for an agent. Since he majored in English and then got a master's degree in writing, his career on paper looks consistently steady state. In reality, Bill has been gainfully employed only fitfully. He lists his current income as "zero." He ranks himself low in all aspects of career evaluation. He says, "I don't care about what I do," and denies having ambitions to become a writer. But Bill's responses are so heavily laced with irony that it is hard to interpret what he says. To get out of his predicament, he is considering going back to school to get a teaching credential.

Stephanie has a lot in common with Bill. Like him, she is neither dressed for success nor possessed of the "I have it made" look so typical of their classmates. With an expression of concern and apprehension, she was one of the few persons who was clearly ill at ease during the entire interview. It was hard to listen to her story without becoming uneasy in turn.

The daughter of an emotionally abusive mother, Stephanie was already wracked by health problems with psychological overtones in college.

Nonetheless, she was bright and persistent enough to graduate from Stanford, albeit two years behind schedule. She left college with no clear career plans or prospects. She worked as a secretary, administrative assistant, and technical writer. An impulsive marriage to a man who turned out to be mentally ill further disrupted her life. Under the circumstances, it is not surprising that Stephanie's career has been erratic until recently.

> My life has taken me to unforeseeable emotional and mental extremes, as well as a physical life-and-death crisis. I have been forced to seek out opportunities to come to terms with estrangement from my birth family, complete loss of health, poverty, and many other less sudden and overwhelming changes.
>
> Working has had to fit in with other aspects of my life that have been more extraordinary and irrevocable. I have fit my working life into other circumstances that were much more compelling. So I worked as I was able, in whatever capacity I was able to do. But I have not yet experienced myself as being in a position of having much control over my work conditions and opportunities. I have never perceived myself as being a decision maker about my career. Today I feel lucky that I graduated Phi Beta Kappa from Stanford University and even more fortunate still to claim that I have survived the years since with my sanity relatively (I hope!) intact.

Stephanie felt frustrated during the interview because the questions made little sense in view of her own life experiences. She simply did not fit any of the molds into which we seemed to be trying to squeeze her. At one point, when asked about her career accomplishments, she cut the question off by saying, "My greatest accomplishment is that I am alive."

During the last year or so, Stephanie has settled into a steady and productive job. She can look at the future with much greater optimism and is thinking of going back to school to get a degree in nutrition. "Since I have had a lot of personal experience with eating problems, I may be particularly helpful to others in similar situations," she says. She also hopes to be a published writer, make a decent living, and "even drive a Volvo someday."

To explore further the links between Driver's concepts and our typology, we combined his linear and steady state concepts into a common linear pattern, and the spiral and transitory modes into a nonlinear alternative. We then determined the linearity of the careers of our own participants by looking at the degree of continuity between what they studied, their first job, and subsequent work experience. Assuming that the first half of the decade after college is largely exploratory, we paid more attention to career continuities in the second half of the decade. Our expectation was that those with linear careers should more or less be on course by the midtwenties, but we did not require that they show complete linearity from the moment of graduation.

At the time of our "snapshot" taken a decade after college, our interview group was almost evenly divided between linear careers (52 percent) and nonlinear careers (48 percent). Hence, just over half of our segment of the educational elite have followed the standard pattern of attending graduate school (perhaps after working for a year or two), entering a profession, getting one or more jobs in that profession, and staying the course. On the other hand, almost half of the respondents have not done so. They have changed career fields, interrupted already launched careers to go to graduate school, taken a year off to "find themselves" or ponder their long-term interests. Since the majority of the educational elite establish themselves in their chosen professions and are generally successful in whatever work they do (chapter 5), it is remarkable how many got to their destinations without staying on the straight and narrow paths of linear career progression. Yet there is a price to pay for meandering: those with linear careers earn considerably more at this stage of their lives, as we discuss in chapter 5.

Men are moderately more likely (58 percent) to pursue linear career tracks than women (46 percent). Given that just over one-third of the women had a child by the time of our study, and that the most common cause of nonlinearity in women's careers is having children, we cannot interpret this finding as reflecting a gender difference related to actual career concepts or styles. What it does show, however, is the clear impact of child rearing on women's career development.

Our typology has some apparent links with Driver's categories. Careerists pursue mostly linear paths (80 percent), some branching to steady state. Intellectuals and the Unconnected are half as likely to go linear, while Strivers (52 percent) occupy an intermediate position. That Careerists follow the linear path hardly needs elaboration; many of them have been linear since high school. But nonlinearity has many causes. Intellectuals are often nonlinear because they are looking for careers that suit them, or they are trying to reconcile conflicts between their intellectual interests and the demands of mainstream career building. The Unconnected are nonlinear either because they are searching for an appropriate career as they march to the beat of that different drummer or because they feel no strong pull toward any particular career. Strivers are in the middle because, as usual, they are pulled in both directions.

On a more qualitative basis, we find a reasonable fit between our types and the decision styles Driver identifies. Most of the Careerists have used the decisive style, making early career choices without much information under the influence of authority figures (parents in particular) and sticking with the decisions once made. The outcome sought is simple career success uncomplicated by other considerations.

Strivers go for a more hierarchic style based on a broader set of considerations (including intellectual concerns and the intrinsic nature of their work). The Unconnected favor the flexible style, which allows a continually open career concept and maximum autonomy. (Though they risk being so flexible that getting a long-term career under way is delayed.) Intellectuals use the integrative style, combining a greater commitment for the duration of any particular career segment with cyclical change to explore new horizons.

Of course, many of our participants represent exceptions to these generalizations. Overall, the interviews suggest that Careerists are the most homogeneous group; not only do they overwhelmingly pursue linear careers but a high proportion of them seem to use the decisive style of decision-making. Intellectuals also seem to be mostly integrative in their approach. Our less sharply distinguished groups, Strivers and the Unconnected, are, again, more eclectic.

THE MENTOR RELATIONSHIP

An important factor in the progress of a career is the presence of a mentor. *Mentoring* became a buzzword just as our participants were embarking on their careers in the 1980s. Earlier, mentors were more likely to be called advisers or role models or simply older friends. Mentors have been crucial to the career development of many of our participants, and mentoring is now recognized widely as a key factor for career advancement, especially among young professionals.

The concept of mentoring is very old, and the word has been around since the eighteenth century. The original Mentor was a friend of Odysseus who was entrusted with the education of Telemachus, Odysseus's son.[21] Currently, the mentor-protégé ("the protected one") relationship is often situated in a work setting where the mentor is a teacher, boss, or senior colleague. The role may also evolve informally if the mentor is a friend, neighbor, or relative. Mentoring is defined not in terms of formal roles but in terms of the character of the relationship and the functions it serves.

As a teacher, the mentor fosters the protégé's skills and professional development. Serving as sponsor, the mentor facilitates the protégé's career advancement and acts as a protector and guide, welcoming the initiate into a new occupational and social world and acquainting him or her with its values, customs, resources, and cast of characters. Daniel Levinson identifies the mentor as typically older than the protégé by a half-generation, roughly eight to fifteen years—enough to be seen by the protégé as an older and wiser sibling. A greater age difference tends to cast the mentor in a parental role, while a smaller age difference makes the two individuals too much like peers. Mentors are usually more than friends but less than authority figures. As a role model with professional skills, achievements, and a distinct way of life, the mentor may be an exemplar that the protégé can admire and seek to emulate in the fulfillment of his or her vocational "dream." And the mentor may provide counsel and moral support in times of stress.[22]

Our participants reported extensive experience with mentors; indeed, mentors are almost a requisite feature of career building for many of the educational elite. Thus, 62 percent indicated they have had a mentor, and many spoke of the crucial role mentors have played in their lives. Many of those whose careers have so far failed to gel have had no mentors, a lack some still regret. As one put it, "If I had only had a mentor, my career decisions would not have been made in a vacuum."

In the Striver George Mehta's case, the mentor was the vice president for administration who hired him. George says: "He was extremely bright. He had the chance to hire people with much more experience, but he saw me as a bright person who was willing to work hard. So he gave me that chance to start with. Then when working with him, he spent time with me, promoted me, and gave me a raise soon after. He then left the company, but I have kept in touch with him as an interesting person to talk to and get advice from. It was not a long relationship, but it was enough to get me started."

Most mentors of our participants have been men. Though the increasing number of women in the major occupations is now producing more women mentors, they are still rare. Most young men and women end up with male mentors, sometimes with more than one (like Philip Genochio's "council of elders"). There are exceptions, of course; all of Alicia Turner's mentors were women.

Normally, mixed-gender mentor relationships are unproblematic, but the possibility of sexual involvement can complicate matters. None of the women or men in our interview group complained of unwanted sexual overtures complicating a mentor relationship (which is not to say that such experiences never took place). But, once again, what may often be a problem for working women in general turns out to be less of an issue for the educational elite. Many of the women in our sample were eloquent in their praise of the men who had been their mentors. "He made me what I am," said one. The fact that her mentor was "an incredibly impressive man" was of special significance to another. Other characterizations, by women as well as men, included:

- A guardian angel.
- A very important influence in my life.
- He bet on me, pushed me, and promoted me.
- He was very influential in shaping my career.
- Taught me the ropes, gave me support and a sense of belonging.
- Fantastic—gave me my first job and taught me all I know.
- Through him, I gained a broad picture of the profession.
- Trained, encouraged, and sustained me.
- You can't become a good attorney without a mentor.

Occasionally, a member of the family doubles as a mentor, usually when the protégé is following the same career path. Examples include Martin MacMillan and his father (medicine), Heather and her mother (teaching), and Kathy and her husband (business). The combination of the family tie and the mentoring relationship can create an especially strong bond. By the same token, Alicia Turner's black female supervisor was a particularly influential mentor since she provided Alicia with a compelling model of a professional black woman.

There were no significant differences among the four types with respect to mentors—a surprising finding given the far stronger ties of Intellectuals and Strivers with their college teachers and advisers than was the case for Careerists and the Unconnected. Perhaps mentoring takes different forms for different types. In the interviews, Intellectuals portrayed mentors more in terms of their role in shaping the substantive content of their work; Careerists saw mentors more as allies who help in their career progression.

CURRENT OCCUPATIONS

To what occupations have the career paths taken by these men and women led them a decade after college? From what we have already seen, the general answer is obvious: they have become well-placed and highly paid professionals. Excluding homemakers and those who were still graduate students at the end of the decade, about one-third were in managerial positions in the private business sector, almost 20 percent were practicing law, 13 percent were physicians, and 13 percent were in engineering or scientific fields (see table 3, appendix A). These four categories account for the careers of three-fourths of our participants. Most of the remainder were professionals in teaching, public administration, health, and other areas. We find few professors, artists, actors, authors, or musicians. Only one in twenty is in an occupation that would not be considered on a professional career track. Careers that do not offer fairly immediate prospects of steady employment, high status, and good pay have certainly not been popular among our segment of the educational elite.

Clearly, these career choices are not representative of the American population as a whole. Less than 1 percent of working Americans are lawyers, only half of 1 percent are doctors, less than 2 percent are engineers. Even with the broadest of definitions, well under 20 percent of Americans hold professional positions.[23] By these measures, the educational elite is overrepresented in high-level professions by factors of five to twenty. The educational elite are ensured access to high-level positions through the "certifying" effects of selective schools; their high ability, which gained them admission to those schools; and their typically advantaged social backgrounds.[24]

To a considerable extent, this pattern of career choice is due to the wave of careerism among college students in the late 1970s and 1980s, made possible by the expanding economy and plentiful job opportunities at the time they were launching their careers. As we shall see, even the Intellectuals among our sample made largely careerist choices; no group of students was immune to the larger social trends, although some types made more purely careerist choices than others.

Most of the choices that eventually led to current careers are predictable from graduate school training. For example, nearly all of those who went to medical school ended up practicing medicine (twenty of the twenty-three holding M.D. degrees). Of the three who are not doctors, two are in related health fields and one has gone back to graduate school as part of a career shift. Other professional degrees allow more freedom. For men with law degrees, for example, twenty-two of twenty-seven gave their current occupation as attorney or judge; of the remainder, one each was in business, teaching, and a humanistic profession, and the other two were graduate students. For women with J.D. degrees, ten of fifteen were attorneys or judges; the rest were in business, teaching, or homemaking.

GENDER DIFFERENCES

Table 3, appendix A, shows men to be more likely than women to practice law and medicine or enter technical and scientific fields; women are more likely to enter teaching and health professions other than medicine. The largest gender difference is among homemakers, all of whom are women; this difference reduces the proportions of women in the other categories, thereby exaggerating the differences relative to men. Two men in the interview sample had taken over primary responsibility for the household and child rearing, but both of them also worked outside the home and did not describe themselves as homemakers.

Clearly, some traditional occupational differences for men and women still persist even among the educational elite. The gender differential is minor in the educational process, but at the occupational level it becomes more marked. Women graduates of selective colleges are generally more likely to choose sex-atypical majors and careers; this tendency is especially strong in the educational elite, even if it has not led to complete sex parity.[25] Sex differences, however, are by no means as pronounced as in earlier generations. Two professions that historically have been male preserves, medicine and law, have now clearly been opened up to women. In our sample, the percentages of women in these professions are at least two-thirds the percentages of men (excluding women homemakers with degrees in these fields, nearly all of whom intend to resume their full-time careers outside the home). Technical and scientific fields are also less clearly male domains now, though there are still only half as many women as men in them.

The increasing parity of men and women in these fields is a nationwide phenomenon; in 1990 women earned 42 percent of all law degrees, 34 percent of all medical degrees, and 34 percent of M.B.A.s, contrasted with less than 5 percent of any of these degrees in 1960.[26] In the class that entered the Stanford Medical School in 1993, 43 percent of the students are women.

In the largest cluster of occupations, business management and administration, our women and men are equally represented; in the smaller category of administrators in public or educational organizations, women actually outnumber men. Women have thus clearly moved into positions of leadership in these areas. At this stage in their lives, however, these young professionals are still in middle-level managerial positions. Whether women will continue to rise in executive hierarchies as quickly as men do is an important question that obviously cannot be answered yet. We consider this issue further in the next chapter, as well as when we look at our participants' visions of the next ten years (chapter 10).

Finally, we need to address the prospect of homemaking and child rearing as an occupation, not with respect to their impact on careers outside the home (chapter 8) but as careers in their own right. This raises a definitional problem with ideological and practical implications. No one disagrees about the critical importance of child rearing. But should it be paid work to be truly validated? And should payment be a condition for defining the activity as an occupation (which is the case now) or should the definition be changed? Even before these questions are answered, one thing is clear: what has turned the issue into a problem is the gender asymmetry. Whether such work is called a "burden" or a "blessing," the great majority of full-time parents within the educational elite are women, a fact that has enormous implications for their careers as well as for their lives.

As shown in table 3, appendix A, 15 percent of the women and none of the men are currently homemakers (defined as staying home to care for children, and usually manage the household as well). In addition, five more women, and two men, have been homemakers sometime during the decade after college but are now back at work. Why have these individuals gone against the current pattern among the educational elite and become full-time homemakers? Only one woman, Kimberly, has never worked after college, a situation she ascribes to "self-inflicted problems, that is, lack of focus and commitment in years prior to having children." She adds, "I have put career frustrations on hold for the time being." She is raising her two children with the help of a "live-in babysitter five days a week." She also has a "once-a-week cleaning woman" but "ideally would prefer more domestic help." The family is obviously affluent, although she declines to reveal the level of their income ("no comment"). Kimberly spends the rest of her time as a "class mother" in her daughter's nursery school. She has taken "interior design classes" and "extensive cooking lessons" and has "always enjoyed reading." She is involved in volunteer and fund-raising activities, attends a health club regularly to "work out with a trainer once a week," and plays tennis.

"I would have done everything differently, with hindsight," says Kimberly. She graduated from college with the feeling that "I got one-tenth of what Stanford has to offer." She was not ready to come to college when she did, and her education was further disrupted at the outset by the untimely death of her father, to whom she was close. Her mother's subsequent remarriage and move to another country contributed further to her being "all alone." She got precious little help or guidance from anyone and "would have benefited from a mentor." Instead of majoring in art history, Kimberly wishes she had picked political science and gone to law school.

Kimberly is a full-time mother more by default than by choice. This contrasts sharply with the experience of someone like Kirsten Buchanan (chapter 6). Moreover, though a few more of the women may also have opted for full-time motherhood, by virtue of circumstances the majority had established careers first and then chose to interrupt them to care for their children. The majority of these women worked in business. One is a lawyer, and another had an exciting career as an overseas correspondent. Several of the women are writers, and the majority plan to go to work outside the home when their children get older. We have more to say about them (as well as the two men who have been homemakers in the past) in chapter 8.

TYPOLOGY DIFFERENCES

Large differences emerge among the four types with respect to current careers (see table 4, appendix A). One out of two Careerists has entered law or medicine, but only one in six of the Intellectuals. The proportion of lawyers among Careerists (25 percent) is double the figure for Intellectuals (12 percent); in medicine the proportion is almost ten times larger (19 percent versus 2 percent). Intellectuals are much more likely to enter teaching, health professions other than medicine, and nonstandard "miscellaneous" careers. Indeed, not a single Careerist has ended up in any of these latter three categories. Overall, Intellectuals have much more frequently chosen intellectual or helping occupations, and Careerists strongly favor the highest-paid professions. These two types clearly live up to their labels.

The Striver occupational pattern is largely the same as that for Careerists. Though somewhat fewer went into medicine (10 percent), the proportion for law is about the same (22 percent), and very few are in the fields of teaching and health or the nonstandard professions. Hence, with the passage of time, the careerist element of striverhood seems to overwhelm the intellectual element. The Unconnected, on the other hand, display quite diverse occupational choices. They are the most likely of all four types, including the Intellectuals, to enter two of the most "intellectual" occupational categories: teaching (17 percent) and humanistic pursuits in art, writing, acting, and the like (4 percent). They also lead the way in the natural sciences and computer-related occupations. The "different drummer" effect is still at work—many of the Unconnected have made unconventional choices, even though the majority landed in prestigious professions or business management.

ENTREPRENEURSHIP

Most people start their careers by working for an organization, but many dream of the day when they will own their own business. Entrepreneurship fires the blood of the ambitious because it promises the biggest rewards. Others are attracted by the independence it offers ("I want to be my own boss"). Women in particular like the flexible work schedule, freedom from male domination, and freedom from the relentlessly competitive work atmosphere men seem to foster.

About one in eight participants had opened a business by the end of the decade. Men (16 percent) were more than twice as entrepreneurial as women (7 percent), and 19 percent of men as against 9 percent of women expect to be working for themselves in ten years. Some of this difference is due to the fact that more men are in professions, such as medicine, in which having a private practice, hence working for yourself, is common. Even apart from this factor, however, men seem more likely to work for themselves.

Of the four types, the most entrepreneurial groups turned out to be the Unconnected and the Intellectuals (15 percent and 17 percent, respectively, about twice the level for other groups). Their entrepreneurship rate reflects the diverse nature of the Unconnected; many of them are full of initiative and willing to work hard but simply not oriented to the institutional values and goals set forth by societal norms. This is especially true of the men in this group, who were by far the most entrepreneurial of all. Intellectual men have the advantage of receiving the highest nonwage income (chapter 5), which some have used to start up a business.

The relatively weak entrepreneurship of Careerists and Strivers reflects their general conservatism. These are "organization" men and women who seek security and guaranteed affluence more than do the other types. They are less willing to take the risk of striking out on their own. Moreover, their low levels of nonwage income (one-sixth that of Intellectual men) may not provide them with as many opportunities.

For some, the incentive to own a business is primarily financial. Tim went to business school and worked for a bank before becoming a stock market analyst. His decision to move into the investment world subsequently led him to start his own business. Already making more money than he needs, Tim is very content with the move and sees it as the best route to financial independence.

By contrast, Matthew's independent business is far more modest. For the past two years, he has done desktop publishing out of his home. He produces programs and brochures for arts organizations, building on his previous work as a marketer for ballet companies. That work had proved too stressful for him and provided little opportunity to pursue his ambition of becoming a writer. In his current arrangement, he spends several hours a day reading for pleasure and preparing to write. Working no more than twenty hours a week, he makes enough money to support himself comfortably.

WORKING HOURS

The life of a professional may appear to others to be one of ease and leisure. Advertisers portray affluent yuppies jetting to exotic places to sip drinks on pristine beaches and dance the night away in glamorous discos. The reality is quite different: professionals work harder for longer hours than salaried employees with fixed time schedules. Indeed, part of the core ethos of being a professional is that one does not separate "work" from "life" to the same extent as nonprofessionals do. For professionals, it is not unusual to have work take over life.

Thus, our participants reported an average of more than fifty hours of working time per week; sixty- and seventy-hour weeks are not unusual. Men reported longer working hours outside the home than women, by an average of over six hours per week. Still, women were working much more (over forty-seven hours) than the standard forty-hour week while also carrying much larger burdens on the home front. Predictably enough, the longest working hours were reported by Strivers, the shortest hours (but still almost forty-six hours per week) by Intellectuals.

These differences by type apply primarily to women; among men, differences are small. Among women, however, Strivers put in much longer hours than any other type. In fact, women Strivers worked more than any category of men except their male Striver counterparts. We see the consequences of these long working hours in their personal lives in the next chapter.

One lesson that emerges here is that careerism as such is not always reflected in working hours. Careerist men worked only as much as men in general; Careerist women worked less than any other type except Intellectuals. The really devoted professionals are clearly the Strivers. It is also worth pointing out that the Unconnected averaged just about as many working hours as other types. Even when they do not pursue careers in a conventional sense, they still apply themselves fully to their professions.

When a career demands long hours devoted to highly demanding tasks, as is almost uniformly the case for the educational elite, the question is whether the effort and commitment result in sufficient rewards. This issue—career satisfaction and its central component, career success—constitutes the topic of the next chapter.

CHAPTER 5

Making It

The educational elite earn a lot of money. Yet work provides for them more subjective satisfactions that cannot be reduced to dollars and cents. Career satisfaction, though a highly individual matter, is that deep feeling of fulfillment that results from compiling a record of accomplishments that match one's needs, desires, and expectations. Differentiating needs from desires and reconciling both with accomplishments and rewards is how career contentment accounts are balanced. Some people may follow Thoreau's maxim, "I make myself rich by making my wants few," but this is hardly the way the educational elite see it. The Puritan work ethic, finding rewards in hard work itself, is also foreign to our young adults.

Instead, they want it all: money, status, and comfort, as well as interesting, challenging, independent work, preferably involving close interaction with others. Collectively, they are, as it were, the Strivers of their generation; even the most Unconnected of them are more committed to a broad range of life goals than the average person.

THE PROFILE GROUP

Careerist Martin MacMillan is now a highly trained medical specialist in dual fields; these qualifications will eventually place him in the top echelon of physicians in clinical practice. His earned annual income of $72,500 is above average for his cohort study peers but still relatively low for his field.

As a salaried member of a health maintenance organization, he earns less than he expected, but he has regular hours and a reasonable on-call schedule. With greater seniority, he expects to have a larger income and a greater say in the running of the group practice. His wife contributes $10,000 to the family income through part-time work as a nurse. At the high point of his career, Martin would like to be medical director of a group practice. He hopes to earn $200,000 a year but expects to make $150,000. Coming from an upper-middle-class family he has already attained the social status of his parents. He expresses the highest level of contentment and commitment to his profession. He is now doing what he hoped he would be doing when he entered Stanford fourteen years ago. He may still lack the experience to make him feel like a seasoned expert, but it is simply a matter of time before that happens. In addition to his clarity of vision, determination, and hard work, Martin credits his father for being his chief formative influence and mentor in his professional life. "My goal," says Martin, "has been not to just make money through a medical career, but to be like him, the person I most admire."

Our earlier description of Cynthia Eastwood's career development is eloquent testimony to her resounding success. Her $60,000 salary combined with a similar amount in nonwage income, and her husband's $100,000 earnings are well above average. She is highly content with her career and "almost too committed to it." She considers herself "smarter than all the bosses" she has worked for and "more competent than 99 percent of the people I meet." She too has already attained her parents' upper-middle-class status.

Intellectual Kirsten Buchanan's career in business was also highly successful, but marked by lower levels of contentment. Motherhood ultimately derailed Kirsten's business career, but she was already unhappy in it. She earns $27,000 a year working part-time out of her home. Her husband, a medical resident, does not make much more, but he will, of course, do so once he is out of specialty training. Eventually, Kirsten expects to go back to work, but it is unlikely that she will go back to her business career.

Kirsten is highly content, committed, and competent in her current role as a full-time mother, but her new vocation cannot be assessed by external measures like income. This is a situation that currently only women in our group face, and it raises important issues we address later on.

It is still too early to assess Intellectual Christopher Luce's career, but from all indications, he shows great promise. As a graduate student, he won an award for academic excellence and another for the best scholarly essay of the year at Yale, followed by a prestigious fellowship. His starting salary is $32,000, but as a full professor, he will probably make somewhere between $60,000 and $90,000 per year. Christopher's career will not be measured by whether he gets tenure (he will), or by how many books he writes (he will write many), but by whether he emerges among the foremost scholars in his field. At the high point of his career, Christopher could imagine being a dean, a provost, or perhaps even a university president. "I don't know if I will make good on these ambitions. But they strike me as worthwhile. Even if I fall short, I will have the satisfaction of knowing that I was able to make a living with my mind—or rather, by pushing my mind as far as my abilities would allow. That's very important to me."

Both Kirsten Buchanan and Christopher Luce come from upper-middle-class families. They currently consider themselves only middle-class, no doubt because of their modest incomes at the moment. Christopher has ambivalent feelings about that. "I don't expect to attain the same standard of living I enjoyed growing up. That's a choice I made when I followed this sort of profession. Sometimes it bothers me. Especially when I know that there are many entry-level jobs out there that require far less education, but pay as much or more than I am making now. There are moments—whole days—when I wonder whether I should be doing something else." Kirsten is more certain to attain her own family's status.

Striver Geraldine Jones is less likely to regain her parents' upper-middle-class status in the near future, while her fellow Striver George Mehta has already moved up from his middle-class origins to upper-middle status. George and Geraldine have the highest and lowest incomes, respectively, among the profile group. George earns $80,000 in salary and receives $70,000 in nonwage income. His wife's $50,000 salary raises their family income to $200,000 a year. Geraldine's inheritance yields about $20,000, which she supplements by part-time work. Once she finishes her training as a paramedic, she will earn more.

George Mehta's career easily qualifies as a success by any reasonable criterion. He has attained a highly responsible position and enjoys what he does; he is very good at his work and highly committed to it. His work not only meets his personal needs but clearly serves a useful social purpose.

Evaluating Geraldine Jones's career is tougher because, for one thing, she has had more than one career. Considering her current work as a paramedic, she expresses "pretty high" contentment and "very high commitment and competence." ("I am good.") Moreover, she is living where she wants and doing what she wants to do. Would we consider her career to have been more successful if she had become a movie star or a physician? Most people may say so, but she does not. Nor do her current commitments preclude her going back to school and becoming a doctor one day.

Unconnected Katherine Johnson combines all the conventional measures of success with high levels of personal contentment, commitment, and competence. Her earned income is $80,000 a year, and her husband earns $65,000, raising the family income to $145,000, one-third higher than the sample average. Moreover, it is only a matter of time before she is made partner if she stays in corporate law. But Katherine's commitment to her family may hold back her corporate legal career. Soon after law school, she turned down a prestigious fellowship "because of the effect moving would have had on my husband's career." Right now what she wants more than anything else is more time to spend with her family.

If Katherine Johnson is a somewhat reluctant player in the arena of corporate law, David Levy has steadfastly refused to get into the game altogether. One consequence of David's following the beat of another drummer is his $32,000 yearly salary, a paltry sum for a lawyer of his competence. Yet, David has no problems with it. "Money has never been an incentive for me to go after a certain job. I don't agree with much of what some attorneys do, and I certainly wouldn't want to do those things for more money. It is much more important that I do what is worthwhile to me. So far, that hasn't included jobs that make a lot of money, but that doesn't bother me." David is fairly content with his present job. He likes the research and writing as well as the flexible work schedule. He does miss contact with clients, although he still gets some of that through his volunteer work with immigrants. How committed is he to the legal profession? "Certainly, I am committed for the time being to the law. There are important things to accomplish. I intend to stay in the profession for the foreseeable future. But I can't say what I will be doing in fifteen or twenty years. I may go back to practicing law, but I may also do something else, like teach English. I'll stay in the legal profession as long as it's rewarding—not monetarily but emotionally."

As the lives of our profile group demonstrate, there is more to career success than meets the eye. There are many ways of "making it," and it is to these various manifestations of success that we now turn for more detailed consideration.

INCOME

"The business of America is business," said President Calvin Coolidge. And the business of business is to make money, he could have added. The criterion of income as a measure of success is not as automatically used for careers outside of business; nonetheless, no other measure is as universal or as easily assessed. Hence, the success of lawyers, doctors, and engineers, even that of authors, artists, and teachers, is often measured in terms of income. The converse notion—the more money people make, the better they are at their work—is obviously less true but widely assumed, as epito-mized in the phrase, "If you're so smart, why aren't you rich?"

Equating money with success makes people uneasy, not least because competence and diligence are less than perfectly correlated with income. For our participants, this equation is accepted eagerly by a few, implicitly by most, and not at all by a sizable minority. In response to a question about what her income would be at the high point of her career, one woman wrote, "The 'high point' of my career may not mean the highest salary of my career. That is not how I measure achievement or success." Yet even those who reject this formula on principle cannot help using income as at least one measure of their own success relative to that of their peers.

Despite the relative homogeneity of the educational elite, their incomes vary tremendously, even among those who are working full-time outside the home. We will look at income from three sources: the participant's per-sonal income from employment (salaries and bonuses); employment income earned by a spouse or domestic partner; and combined nonwage income from investments and the like (figure 5.1).

The median earned income of our participants ten years after college was $54,000. By comparison, the national median income in 1991 for all

FIGURE 5.1
Median Incomes, by Sex

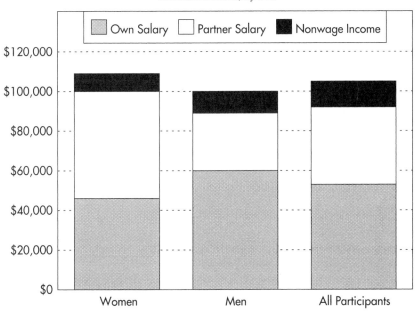

adults was $15,010; for all adults with five or more years of higher educa-
tion it was $34,277.¹ The median income of our participants' partners was
substantially lower, as shown in figure 5.1. Median nonwage household
income was $10,000. Thus, the median annual household income for those
living with a partner was $104,000.² Total income for those employed out-
side the home ranged from a low of $22,000 to a high of $550,000 a year.

These are extremely high figures. The educational elite just past age
thirty have already attained an income level that most of the population
will never reach at any point in their lives. College graduates not only have
considerably higher incomes than the general population, the incomes of
graduates of select colleges and universities are the highest of all.³ And
since the average adult earner has been working much longer than our
men and women, we can expect the disparity between their incomes and
the national averages to grow much wider over time.

The importance of graduate education for high income is further
attested by the fact that those of our participants who obtained advanced
degrees had median incomes 35 percent higher than those with only bachelor's degrees. Differences by profession are also substantial. Attorneys
have the highest median incomes ($78,500), followed by those in medicine
and business or finance (about $66,000 each). The earnings of doctors,
however, are still relatively low because some of them are in specialty training and others have just entered practice. Engineers earned median salaries
of $52,000; the lowest salaries were earned by those in teaching and
humanistic professions ($38,500).

Because most of our participants are married or living with a domestic
partner, and almost all of the partners work outside the home, total household incomes are much higher still. Topping the list are businesspeople
(about $130,000 a year) and lawyers (just over $120,000). Those with
careers in humanistic professions are at the bottom, with a median household income of about $63,000. But even they earn more than double the
national average ($29,943 for all households).⁴

Several other career factors are linked to higher earnings. Linear career
paths lead to greater income (medians of $70,000 for those with linear
careers, $41,000 for nonlinear careers). This fact may be at least partly due
to the later start that nonlinear persons have made in their current careers;
in due time, they may catch up with their more linear counterparts. Similarly, those who never changed careers during the decade made 26 percent
more than those who changed careers at least once. Those who had
worked full-time for seven or more years earned 16 percent more than
those who had worked for six or fewer years.

So far, entrepreneurship has not proved to be a financial advantage for
the educational elite (though it may offer other rewards). The median

yearly income of our self-employed participants is slightly higher than the overall median ($61,000 versus $54,000), but it is somewhat below that of businesspeople employed by others.

Attitudinal factors have moderate effects on income: the more impor-tance participants attributed to high income in their choice of occupation, the higher their actual earned income. Concern for financial security and income are similarly related. But larger differences emerge only when we compare participants at the extremes on attitude scales. Those who rated high income as very important had median incomes of $65,000, while those who rated high income as only somewhat important had median incomes of only $26,000. In other words, those who put greater emphasis on income and financial security in their choice of occupation do indeed make more money than those who see income and security as relatively unimportant. It is possible that those who make less money downplay its importance to make themselves feel better. This does not, however, seem to be what most of our participants are doing.

THE TOP AND THE BOTTOM

Of the top ten earners (over $150,000 per year), eight are white, one is African-American, and one is Asian-American; seven are men, three are women; Strivers and the Unconnected account for three each. These pat-terns of differences are close enough to our sample characteristics to sug-gest that very high income is not systematically related to ethnicity, sex, or type.

Sometimes families have helped pave the way to affluence. Mark comes from a wealthy family in Chicago; his father is a successful lawyer, and his mother is independently wealthy and heads the family foundation. In col-lege, he was interested in the humanities and showed little career ambition. Following graduation, he traveled for a while with his girlfriend (and future wife), working at odd jobs. Mark then joined the training program of an investment bank with connections to his family. Two years later, he went to Harvard to get an M.B.A. After a stint with another major bank, he put together a group of investors to acquire a publishing company, of which he is now the chief executive.

By contrast, the group includes men, like Philip Genochio (a lawyer and businessman) and a professional athlete, who have made it entirely on their own. Among the women, we have a gynecologist in private practice and a professional athlete, each of whom earns $250,000; neither has depended on family money to get where they are.

At the low end of the income range, one-quarter of the participants made less than $33,000 per year. The lowest-paid persons holding full-time jobs were teachers (including Alicia Turner), most of whom earned less than $30,000 annually. Yet even these figures are, as we noted before, higher than the average American salary. In other words, even the financially worst off of our participants are better off than most people in the country.

A number of our participants are in this low-income group only temporarily, typically because they are still finishing their professional training or just settling into their careers. For instance, Arnold is in his last year of residency training in pediatrics; he has taken longer to graduate from medical school because he concurrently got a Ph.D. in computer science. Very soon he will be making a great deal more money. As another physician who is also finishing his training, in orthopedic surgery, put it, "I don't yet make as much money as my Stanford friends, but give me a little more time." This group also includes Stephanie and Bill, whose problematic careers we discussed earlier. They, too, hope to do better, but their prospects are not as bright.

As with the top ten earners, a review of background variables finds little systematic commonality among those in the lower-income group. Hence, neither sex, ethnicity, parental social class, nor typology appears particularly relevant at either end of the scale. Once a person becomes part of the educational elite, what really seems to matter most in earning power is the drive to make money, and choosing a profession that offers good earning potential.

GENDER AND ETHNIC DIFFERENCES

As we see in figure 5.1, the earned incomes of the men among our participants ($60,000) are 27 percent higher than those of women ($47,000) (see also table 5, appendix A). The top quarter among men earned at least $75,000; for women this figure was $65,000. Given that the proportions of women in the highest-paid professions are lower than those of men, these differences are substantial but not great. Nevertheless, within each occupational category, differences between the two sexes generally favor men. In the two largest groups, law and business-finance, men clearly earn more than women: 15 percent more in business-finance, about 20 percent more in law. In other groups, women made as much as men—or even, in medicine, somewhat more than men—but the number of cases in these latter groups is often too small to draw definite conclusions.

Therefore, we find that even among the educational elite, women overall make somewhat less than men in the high-income professions. They nevertheless have very high salaries compared with national averages. The median income for all women over age twenty-four working full-time in 1990 was under $23,000, only a little over one-third of what the women in the educational elite make.[5]

The fact that men on average earned more than women is offset by the much higher incomes of the partners (spouses and domestic partners) of women compared with those of men ($53,000 as against $30,000). Since the nonwage household income of women is very close to that of the men ($9,000 versus $10,000), women come out ahead of men by 9 percent with respect to total household income ($109,000 as against $100,000). Men in the educational elite tend to marry women with considerably less earning power than their elite female peers. By contrast, our elite women have partners who earn very nearly as much as our male participants. To the extent that economic equality is being achieved among these high-powered young professionals, it is the women who appear to be most responsible for it.

By contrast to gender, ethnicity has no bearing on income in our group: ethnic minorities earn about the same as whites (the personal earnings of blacks and whites are identical). The only exception are the two Native Americans in our sample, both of whom earned considerably less than the median figure. While we have too few individuals to do systematic comparisons of spouse and household income of minorities, the general pattern is consistent: singly or as couples, minority group members are earning at least as much as whites.

TYPOLOGY DIFFERENCES

Careerists have the highest median earned incomes ($69,000), followed by Strivers; the Unconnected and Intellectuals are well below (see figure 5.2). Since women and men are not evenly distributed across types, gender is a confounding factor here, but both men and women Careerists have the highest earned incomes, while both Unconnected men and women have the lowest. The two extremes are Careerist men ($70,000) and Unconnected women ($40,000) (see table 6, appendix A).

These typology differences clearly demonstrate the impact of academic and career orientations on subsequent income: how much emphasis a young person puts on career success really does make a difference. The two types that emphasize careers most, Careerists and Strivers, make a good deal more than the types with lower career emphasis. Careerists in business or finance make almost 20 percent more than any other type in these fields.

FIGURE 5.2
Median Incomes, by Type

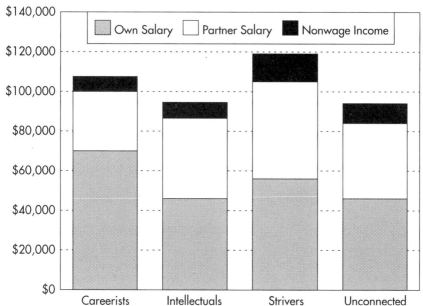

With respect to partner income, Striver partners are in the lead ($48,000), and Careerist partners rank last. Strivers also lead in nonwage income, with the Unconnected second. The result is that Strivers lead in total household income, with a median of $119,000, followed by Careerists at $106,500, and the Unconnected and Intellectuals tied at $93,000.

There is a sharp and revealing contrast in partner income between women and men Careerists. The husbands of Careerist women have a median income of $93,500—the highest single figure among partner groups—and the wives of Careerist men have the lowest income of all partner groups ($20,000). This enormous difference strongly reinforces our impression from the interviews that Careerist men are the most conventional in their choice of partners; they are most likely to choose wives who either subordinate their own career interests or are not career-minded at all.

Putting all this together, Careerist women emerge as the group with the highest household income of all eight sex-type groups ($165,000 a year), owing to the very high income of their partners combined with their own high earning capacity. Striver women rank second, combining good personal and partner salaries boosted by the highest nonwage incomes among women. Last among women are the Unconnected ($93,000); they are the lowest wage earners and have partners with the lowest partner incomes.

Among men, Intellectuals come first in total income ($113,000), even though they personally make less than other men and less than Careerist and Striver women. This is due to their very high nonwage income ($31,000 a year), which we suspect is somehow linked to their affluent parents. By contrast, despite being the highest wage earners of all sex-type groups, Careerist men rank sixth overall in household income, barely edging out Unconnected women, because their partners make the least money. At the very bottom are Unconnected men ($85,500), whose household incomes are only a little more than half that of the top group, Careerist women. Despite these differences, no segment of the educational elite is at any risk of financial strain.

ASPIRATIONS AND EXPECTATIONS

We asked our participants to indicate the highest incomes they hope to receive, as well as the highest incomes they actually expect to earn, in the course of their careers. Their aspirations are very high. Quite a few hope to be making a million dollars a year or more at the peak of their careers; one man put it at five million.

Overall, aspirations and expectations are moderately related to actual incomes: the higher the current income, the more a participant hopes to make in the future and the more he or she actually expects to make. Hence, attitudes, actual income, and aspirations are all tied together: those who want to make more do so, and they aspire to even more.

Income aspirations reveal much the same patterns as actual incomes with respect to occupation and gender. The highest aspirations are held by those in law (median of $200,000 per year), followed by business-finance and medicine; at the low end, those in teaching and humanistic professions aspire to much less ($70,000). The educational elite clearly have a good hold on economic reality.

Gender differences are consistent: men almost uniformly aspire to higher incomes than do women, regardless of profession or type, and some of these differences are very large. For example, men in law aspire to a median income of $400,000, but their women counterparts have their sights set on only $150,000; men in business-finance are aiming for $300,000, women for $150,000. In only one area, teaching and humanistic professions, are women's aspirations greater than those of men ($70,000 versus just over $50,000).

Expectations about the highest incomes they will ever actually receive, though usually lower than aspirations, follow the same patterns as the latter. (The two variables are correlated .90.) Women have lower expectations, as well as lower aspirations, than men, and the differences are greatest when the most money is involved—in law and business-finance ($300,000 for men in both these areas, $125,000 for women lawyers, and $100,000 for women business executives). But in areas where women may feel more on their own turf (in teaching and humanistic professions), the differences are much smaller or even reversed.

These differences indicate the persistence among the educational elite of lower career aspirations on the part of women. Several factors play a part in this phenomenon. Many women know they will take (or already have taken) time out from their careers to have and rear children, and they know this interruption will set back their earnings. They are also aware of the potential limits on women's access to top-level management and partnership positions in large organizations. In this respect, women are simply being realistic; they appear to adjust their aspirations according to current realities, unfair as those may be.

Moreover, an additional factor operates here in the form of a more diffuse social construct: even within the educational elite, women seem to find it more difficult than men to believe that they could be "worth" salaries of several hundred thousand dollars, under any circumstances. In other words, women's self-conceptions of their economic worth appear to be less expanded (or less exaggerated) than those of men. As a result, women's lower career aspirations may become a self-fulfilling prophecy. Women are also more likely to be concerned about social equity when incomes reach such extreme levels. Whether they are worth such money or not, they are more likely than men to question the fairness of enormous income differentials among people.

Career factors affect aspirations and expectations in the same way they affect actual incomes: those with graduate degrees have higher aspirations and expectations than those without; those who have worked longer are higher on both variables; and those who have never changed careers are higher than those who have changed. Attitudinal factors follow suit: the more emphasis placed on income and financial security in choice of occupation, the higher the income aspirations and expectations. The self-employed both hope and expect to make considerably less than the salaried, even though their current incomes are above the overall median.

In sum, three findings are of greatest significance in terms of income. First, the educational elite already "have it made" financially. They have very high incomes, their partners have very high incomes, and most of them see their future incomes increasing greatly. Second, while women are generally close to parity with men in current income, they lag behind in the two largest professional groups (law and business), and their aspirations and expectations for the long run are considerably below those of men. Third, careerism is a clear aid in making money, but it is hardly essential. Even Intellectuals and the Unconnected are strong earners, with very high incomes by national standards. This would not be true of course at all times, irrespective of general economic conditions. Being part of the educational elite does not confer immunity to financial hardship, but it does seem to make one far less vulnerable (chapter 10).

CAREER ACCOMPLISHMENTS

Accomplishments other than income are more idiosyncratic and resistant to quantification. Nonetheless, for the individual career builder, nonmonetary rewards carry great significance. They enhance self-confidence, signal important changes in status, bode well for further career success, and often lead to salary increases as well.

PROMOTIONS

Promotions depend on hierarchical structures with discrete steps of advancement. Such a structure is clearly present in large companies; many other organizations have but a few promotional steps. For example, lawyers start as associates and become full and senior partners. Physicians in private practice have no organizational ladder to climb whatsoever.

Moreover, the pace of advancement is fairly specific to given occupations. Industrial workers, for instance, are most likely to be promoted before their midthirties. Then there is a sharp drop in their rate of promotion, which falls almost to zero after age forty-five.[6] Those in the professions mature more slowly. Most young attorneys are eligible for only one promotion before age thirty, and a second some years later. Faculty members in universities do not become full professors until their forties.

The images used to analyze career advancement often rely on competitive models, as in James Rosenbaum's depiction of the employees in a large company as engaged in a "tournament."[7] Winners get promoted, losers are passed over. As long as you win, you keep moving up, but the game gets tougher as it proceeds, with each successive opponent also a multiple winner. This metaphor may convey the attitude of many competitors in the career game, but it overstates its case. Career competition is not a single-elimination contest. Those who lose in one round may make a comeback in the next, or they can leave the playing field by going to another company where they may fare better.

A major study of AT&T managers, extending over twenty years, showed that the chances of promotion are higher for some tracks than for others.[8] More active tracks have more challenging and complex jobs and are populated by those with greater ability. Conversely, challenging and complex jobs stretch an employee's capabilities, requiring that he or she acquire new skills faster than others. Thus, having what it takes to be on the fast track and being forced to cope with the demands of the fast track mutually reinforce each other—assuming, of course, that the demands can be met. When a member of the educational elite is in such a job, this assumption is rarely in error.

That the track is generally fast for the educational elite is shown by the rapidity with which they obtained job promotions. As early as the second year of work some 18 percent of our employed participants received promotions, with business-finance professionals (23 percent) leading the way. Even higher rates of promotions followed; the highest rate for any group in a single year was for engineers and technicians in the ninth year, when almost 35 percent received a promotion.

Overall, about half of our participants reported at least one job promotion. Once again, the rates for men and women were identical, at just over 49 percent each. Excluding those who did not receive any promotions at all (most of whom, like the self-employed and doctors, were not eligible for promotions), we find that Intellectuals received more promotions than any other type (averaging 1.6), and the Unconnected received the fewest (average of 1.0). This finding holds true for both sexes. Why should Intellectuals receive more job promotions than Careerists and Strivers, who are so eager to get ahead? The answer lies in part in the types of careers these different groups pursue. Careerists are especially likely to be lawyers and doctors, careers that usually do not involve promotions by age thirty. Intellectuals, on the other hand, are more often found in careers like teaching, health professions (other than medicine), and miscellaneous professional categories in which advances on the promotional ladder are expected but bring only modest increases in income.

AWARDS AND PUBLICATIONS

Awards, including graduate study fellowships, research grants, salesmanship awards, and official recognitions of service, are other measures of success. One-third of our participants had received one or more such awards. Women were as likely as men to receive awards, but Careerists were notably less likely than any other type to obtain such formal recognitions of achievement—probably for the same reasons they are less likely to get promotions.

To our amazement, the top award winners (by a slight margin) turned out to be the Unconnected. Unconnected women were by far the group most likely to win an award (50 percent), followed by men Intellectuals (38 percent). By contrast, both men and women Careerists were least likely to win awards, exactly the opposite of the income pattern.

The Unconnected stand out in another dimension of accomplishment as well—they accounted for almost half of all publications during the decade. In this respect, they were well ahead of even the Intellectuals, who produced about one-third of all publications. Following the beat of their own drummer seems to work to the advantage of the Unconnected when it comes to creativity and originality.

The publications produced ran the whole gamut from professional books to popular articles. Men were more likely to be the authors of professional books and articles; more women wrote popular articles. The Unconnected led as authors of professional books and articles and were matched only by the Intellectuals in popular articles. Careerists and Strivers published least; most of their publications were professional articles in their specialty fields.

This finding with respect to awards and publications runs counter to the income and promotion patterns we have seen: the Unconnected and Intellectuals are the high achievers. One explanation has to do with type of occupation; another may be that Careerists are not interested in awards. Their "award" is making money, and their energies and creativity are directed to that end. Moreover, many Careerists tend to channel themselves into rather narrow career lanes and succeed more by perseverance and hard work than by truly outstanding or creative performance. By contrast, Intellectuals work more with their minds and win the awards to prove it. The success of the Unconnected, in turn, is due largely to their very unconventionality and boldness of vision. It serves as a corrective to the narrow view of income as the sole criterion of accomplishment.

COMPARISONS WITH PEERS

We next turn to the educational elite's feelings about their career accomplishments in comparison with those of their peers. Some of our participants were reluctant to make such comparisons. They disliked the idea on principle, or questioned its meaningfulness. When asked how she rated her career compared with those of her peers, one woman said, "I have no idea—what an unpleasant concept." Alicia Turner's reaction was, "If you compare yourself to others, you feel either vain or bitter. So comparing myself is not uppermost in my mind." Several in the profile group had more to add. George Mehta said, "I do not compete with people. Even in school—and I happened to do very well in school—it was not in a competitive kind of way, but just my own desire to learn and to be good at what I do. So that has carried with me through my career. I have always tried to do the best I can, rather than outmaneuver others. But I suppose I have done career-wise as well as anyone and better than most people." David Levy was even more reluctant. "I am in no position to say that what I am doing is better than what somebody else is doing, or what they are doing is better. It's hard for me to do those kinds of evaluations. It is easier to do if you look at economics, in which case those people who graduated with me must be making significantly more than I am. But since that is not a priority for me, it becomes more a matter of evaluating the particular things they are doing and I am doing."

Despite such reservation, most participants went through with the comparison: 72 percent said they were on a par with their peers, 13 percent said they had done better, and 15 percent said they had done worse. Income makes a great deal of difference in these variations. The median income of those saying they were doing worse than their peers was $42,000, compared with $60,000 for those doing "about the same" and $82,500 for those saying they were doing better. But income is not everything. Businesspeople were more likely than other groups to feel they were doing better than their peers in their careers; lawyers, doctors, and engineers were about average. Humanists clearly felt they were not doing as well, with one-third saying they were doing worse than their peers and only a few saying they were outpacing them.

Women generally saw their career station in a less positive light than men. Women were twice as likely to think they were doing worse than their peers, while men were five times as likely as women to think they were doing better. These differences are partly a matter of realistic evaluations. Women are aware that they are earning less than men. To the extent that "doing well" is interpreted as a matter of income, women are reflecting the facts. Second, because women interrupt their careers for child rearing far more than men do, they feel they are falling behind their male counterparts. Third, fewer women are in the highest-level professions. If doing well means having high occupational prestige, women are, again, being objective about their status relative to that of their male counterparts.

For the four types, Careerists were the most positive when comparing themselves with their peers, Intellectuals the least positive. Strivers and the Unconnected were bimodal—they had the largest proportions saying they were doing worse, but also higher proportions saying they were doing better. The few women who said they were doing better than their peers are all Strivers, but women Strivers were also most likely to say they were doing worse. Unconnected women had the most negative view of their careers of all (just as they had the lowest incomes). By contrast, Unconnected men pull another rabbit out of the hat by being the most positive group of all: one-quarter said they were doing better than others. Showing their idiosyncratic stripes once again, they see themselves as achievers, but more on their own terms. At the other end, Intellectual men saw their careers most negatively, with almost one-fifth claiming to have done worse than their peers. Career success in conventional terms, especially in terms of making money, is clearly not where Intellectuals get their just deserts.

SOCIAL TIME

Comparisons of career achievement can be reasonably made only with reference to a given point in time. Sociologist Bernice Neugarten differentiates between chronological time, or age, and "social time." Social time is a culturally defined schedule by which people progress through life.[9] Social expectations define the ages at which young people are supposed to cross key thresholds, such as graduating from high school, going to college, entering the work force, and so on. Being "on time" means crossing these thresholds more or less at the socially expected age. Thus, students are supposed to graduate from college at about age twenty-two, give or take a year. Those who start college at age sixteen are clearly "ahead of time," while those who graduate after age twenty-five are clearly seen as "behind time."

Social time is more precisely defined for the educational elite than for other young adults. Given their family resources and academic capacities, they are expected to progress steadily and rapidly through the educational system. By contrast, social time for the general population is less restrictively defined. Financial and aptitude limits make it more common for nonelite groups to attend college later in life, as we see at nonselective state schools where many students are in their late twenties or thirties.

Career time tracks are not clearly demarcated, but expectations still exert a powerful influence. When parents fret over adult children who are procrastinating about choosing a career, they are perturbed not only by the practical consequences of being late (lower income, less prestige) but also by a more diffuse uneasiness about their children lagging behind. Failure to keep to this schedule, or violation of these expectations, can be quite disturbing; the same feelings are evoked with respect to delayed marriage and parenthood (chapter 8).

When we probed our participants' perceptions of social time during the interviews, they had no problem recognizing the concept. Once again, though, some were reluctant to make such evaluations, as a matter of principle. Others seemed to want to avoid the admission of being late.

Our quantification of the interview responses reveals that about 40 percent of our participants found their careers to be on schedule. Another 39 percent felt they were running late; only 21 percent thought they were ahead. Hence, there is a general tendency to feel pressured to "hurry up" and "get ahead" in the career chase. Note that a much larger proportion felt behind schedule than the 15 percent who felt they were doing worse than their peers.

Once again, women have a greater tendency than men to feel they are behind, and men are more likely to feel they are ahead. Intellectuals, hardly surprisingly, are much more likely to feel behind in their careers than are Careerists. But evaluations of career social time are not determined solely by career accomplishments; they depend equally on aspirations. Hence, it turns out that the most widespread concern about being behind time is felt by the ever-ambitious Strivers. This is a remarkably bimodal group, for slightly more Strivers than average feel they are ahead of the game as well. Intellectuals rarely feel they are ahead.

These findings largely replicate the patterns we noted earlier with respect to being better or worse off compared with Stanford peers. In fact, we find a very strong relationship between peer comparisons and career social time. The important difference is that the social time findings indicate a very common feeling among the educational elite of being "behind the eight ball." They may be doing as well as their peers, but many of their peers are also seen as running late. It is not simply that strong ambitions motivate their career-building efforts. They also feel a generalized pressure to succeed, based on their high levels of success in early life, the prodding of their parents, competition with colleagues, the demands of bosses, and even the urging of mentors. For the educational elite, success is an obligation.

CAREER SATISFACTION: THE FOUR C's

Of all the facets of working life, job satisfaction has been the most intensely studied. Satisfied workers are popularly presumed to be more productive, more stable, and less prone to turnover and disruption; hence, there has been a massive (but often fruitless) search for the conditions that promote job satisfaction.[10] Better documented is the finding that work satisfaction increases steadily over time, for both college-educated adults and others. Greater seniority means better pay and more job security. Experience brings a greater sense of competence and mastery, as well as more clout in the workplace. Younger workers are more restless, less committed, less certain about what they want to do, than older workers. But then, as people pass their peak, they tend to fall behind in fast-moving fields or get tired and bored. The young bring greater zest and enthusiasm to their jobs.[11]

The men and women in our group are no longer novices in their careers, but many have yet to hit full stride. They have the potential for job satisfaction that a half-dozen years in their professions, strong feelings of competence, and clarity of purpose can bring. They also have the potential for dissatisfaction that high ambition and impatience can engender when careers do not move as quickly as hoped.

We explored the issue of career satisfaction during the interviews by asking our participants to evaluate four dimensions, the "four C's": contentment, commitment, competence, and compensation.[12] As we define it, "contentment" refers to how satisfied they are with their career choice, not making a global judgment of how satisfied they are in their jobs (a judgment that would be the summary of all four measures). "Commitment" has two components: how firmly they are attached to their basic career, on the one hand, and to their current position, on the other. "Competence" refers to how they assess their professional capability on the job. Do they feel on top of it, or have to scramble to stay afloat? "Compensation" deals with financial and other rewards. Their responses were assigned to one of three categories in each dimension: high, moderate, or low.[13]

The findings are striking. Half of our participants are highly content with their career choices, and almost as many are moderately content. Only 7 percent expressed a low level of contentment. Neither gender nor typology matters here: women are as satisfied as men, and the overly critical Unconnected as much as the more easily pleased Strivers.

Measures of competence are even more positive, with 53 percent in the high category and only 5 percent in the low category. Gender differences, again, are completely absent. Among the educational elite, women not only enter high-status occupations at roughly the same rates as men but feel as confident as men in their ability to perform well professionally. Coupled with their contentment with their career choices, this finding clearly reflects the feeling among elite women that they have largely broken through the traditional gender barriers.

Type does make some difference: more Careerists are at the high end of the scale, while the Unconnected express the lowest sense of competence. Income differentials probably account for most of this difference. But we should also bear in mind that the Unconnected tend to be the most critical in general, whether assessing themselves or others.

Commitment figures show some differences, largely gender-related. Here again, almost half express high levels of commitment, but the figure for men (57 percent) is much higher than that for women (36 percent), and women are somewhat more likely to feel low commitment than are men. It must be understood that "low" commitment does not necessarily mean a serious lack of dedication or loyalty to one's career. It may also reflect a reaction to the prospects for advancement and achievement. If women see more obstacles on the path of career advancement in male-dominated professions, and they feel more conflict between their career and family obligations, one way to resolve the conflict is by investing less of themselves— even when feelings of contentment and competence are quite strong.

Among the four types, Strivers are the most committed and Intellectuals are the least committed. Intellectuals have been telling us all along that career concerns are not foremost in their minds; Strivers tend to express high commitment to everything they do, including their careers. Somewhat surprisingly, Careerists appear only slightly more committed than the Unconnected. We expected these two groups to be at the extremes in this dimension. Careerists' commitment seems to be more to themselves than to their careers as such, while a good portion of the Unconnected define commitment in their own unconventional terms.

As might be expected in a culture where everyone seems dissatisfied with the size of their paychecks, even the educational elite are less pleased with their compensation. Only 29 percent declare themselves highly satisfied with what they are earning (some twenty points lower than any of the other measures), while 21 percent indicate a low level of satisfaction. Gender differences appear here, as with commitment. The proportion of women highly satisfied with their compensation is less than half that of men (16 percent versus 39 percent); the numbers are reversed on the low end. There is no mystery here. Women make somewhat less than men, they know it, and they are not happy about it. Typology differences regarding compensation satisfaction also parallel actual incomes: the proportion of Careerists who are highly satisfied is three times that of Intellectuals. Intellectualism has its costs when it comes to career compensation, and the Intellectuals know it. Strivers and the Unconnected fall in the middle range.

One would expect the four C's to go together, yet they are only weakly related to one another. Especially for women, compensation is almost totally unrelated to contentment, commitment, and competence. For men, it is moderately related to these dimensions. Women separate issues of money from their assessments of their careers more than men do. Some women take a less instrumental view of work, looking for other sources of satisfaction; other women, having resigned themselves to lower levels of compensation, turn to other dimensions to make the most of careers that they do not see leading ever upward.

With respect to type, the most revealing finding about the interrelationship between the four C's is that compensation and contentment are completely unrelated for Intellectuals and Strivers but moderately related for Careerists and Unconnecteds. The two groups high in intellectualism are more concerned about entering occupations they find intrinsically rewarding, whether or not they receive high income. For those without this intellectual bent, contentment depends much more on income.[14]

OBSTACLES TO CAREER DEVELOPMENT

The general picture of career satisfaction we have painted is so far highly positive. But it would be a mistake to conclude that they lead charmed lives. Even in the best of cases, a lot of toil and turmoil has gone into getting them where they are. Rejections from first-choice graduate schools, failed bar exams, salary raises that were due but not forthcoming, and countless other mishaps have taken their toll. Careers that look successful on the outside may be bleak on the inside. Wrong choices, missed opportunities, and lack of meaning and purpose have troubled quite a few of our participants, at least temporarily, and acted as obstacles to their career development.

CAREER DISSATISFACTION

Unhappiness in one's work is likely to hinder career advancement. But career success is not a guarantee of work satisfaction. Their work experiences have already disillusioned some of our participants. Even Careerists are finding that their single-minded pursuit of conventional career success does not give them everything they want out of their jobs. Lawyers seem particularly vulnerable to this conflict between reaping the rewards of a lucrative profession and failing to get much personal satisfaction out of it. The practice of law makes enormous demands on their time and energy, getting in the way of their family lives and other interests. Ironically, it is the more successful lawyers who complain most. Peter, for example, who is as successful as they come, says he would choose a different career if he were to do it again: "My job is too stressful and not fulfilling enough," he complains. At age thirty-one, he is hoping for "early retirement and spending time with my family." Yet, more realistically, he says of the next ten years, "I will be working much the same as I am now."

Other lawyers complain about the drudgery of poring over judicial casebooks and preparing lengthy briefs. The intellectual excitement they thought they would find in practicing law turns out not to be there. This mismatch between expectation and reality is best illustrated by Julian. During his undergraduate years, Julian, a true Striver, had been very keen on pursuing both a liberal education ("I would like to be exposed to as many things as possible") and a successful career. He majored in political science, with the objective of either working for the State Department or becoming a lawyer.

Julian spent the spring quarter of his junior year in Washington, D.C., where he worked in the office of his congressman. With his excellent communication skills and enthusiasm, he was promoted from an intern to a legislative assistant almost immediately. Working in a town full of lawyers made him look closely at the prospect of becoming one himself. On the one hand, he resisted the idea. ("I was dead set against law school.") On the other hand, he was intrigued and challenged by the perception that "to understand a society or culture, you need to understand its laws. Laws reflect society." When Julian took the LSAT with no preparation and did very well, his choice tilted distinctly toward law, though he remained ambivalent about it.

Another important consideration at the back of Julian's mind was the financial security a legal practice would provide. He came from a modest family background; his divorced mother had raised her children in strained circumstances. Julian worked throughout college, barely scraping together enough to survive. He even turned down a job offer in Washington after his summer internship and went home to work as a housekeeping assistant in a hospital so he could save on his living costs. ("I went from nuclear energy legislation to cleaning bathrooms.")

Julian went to law school and did very well. He then joined a prestigious law firm and became a highly competent trial attorney. He has a six-figure income and anticipates making over $500,000 a year at the high point of his career. Yet Julian is not happy. While he is pleased to have achieved financial security, neither the money nor the perks and status of his job mean that much to him. His main complaint is that "the legal profession takes 90 percent of my time but provides only 10 percent of my satisfaction." Since his work is so time-consuming, it leaves little opportunity for much else. Even in his first year in law school, Julian saw this coming. To keep up with his intellectual interests, he began working simultaneously for a master's degree in international relations, but it fell by the wayside. He thought he would practice law for five years to pay his debts and then switch careers. But when his wife decided to go to law school, he had to finance her education.

Julian feels trapped. He says, "There are times when I really enjoy my work, but most of the time my heart is really not in it." Teaching part-time in a law school helps keep up his intellectual excitement, but it is not enough to satisfy him. What does he think he will be doing in another ten years? "I either will be running my own hotel or bed-and-breakfast place or will be a successful partner in a large international law firm."

Pursuing an ambitious occupation runs the risk of disaffection. But not doing so has its own drawbacks. Angela majored in economics in college but had no specific career goals as an undergraduate. She says:

> I left high school academically motivated, with a sense of direction, and very eager to learn and grow. I was also socially naive, emotionally immature, and very shy. My early experiences at Stanford left me discouraged academically, overwhelmed socially, and confused emotionally. I lost sight of my goals and sense of direction. I let social temptations and student employment totally distract me from academics. Basically, I floundered through to graduation. My senior year, my only goal was to get a job after graduation, any job, whoever would employ me. I got a job, went to work, but had no career goals. I did fairly well but was not motivated—could have gone much further. In a few years, I realized I had blown my opportunities at Stanford and that I was not doing what I really wanted to be doing professionally. The thought greatly depressed me. It took the death of a loved one and a period of financial strain for me to realize that I could still strive for something even though I missed my chances at Stanford. I became more focused at work, and my career started to take off. Then I gave birth to twins, stayed home to care for them. I decided to be primary caregiver to my kids in order to be the one who influences, shapes, and guides them. However, as they demand less of my time, I plan to reenter the work force or do volunteer work related to social or environmental issues. I regret having missed my chance to become a doctor.

INDIVIDUAL CAREER PROBLEMS

In response to an open-ended question about career problems, our participants identified more than fifty distinct issues, ranging from losing a job to having problems with office politics to conflicts with parents about career decisions. Only about one-quarter reported no career problems (or chose not to tell us about them). The most common problems (reported by over 40 percent of our participants) were job-specific: trouble with a supervisor, insufficient experience to handle the work, lack of challenge, and so on.

Second most common are problems related to the time demands of a career. Single people say they work so much they have no social life. Those who are married complain about lack of time with their spouses and children. These issues sound like the consequences of, or the price to be paid for, career success, not like obstacles to career advancement. But the competing demands of personal interests and family obligations do slow career progress. Yet another set of problems has to do with career decisions: what to do next, whether to return to school, which specialty to pursue, and so on. Financial problems, mainly having to do with graduate school, are the final category.

Women report only slightly more problems than men. But on the whole, men and women complain about very similar career problems, with job-specific issues being most common and time demands second. The only real difference is that men report more financial problems, and women much more often face the problem of choosing between careers and families. The familiar pattern thus repeats itself: by and large, women and men of the educational elite do not look very different. The major factor distinguishing them is the issue of caring for young children.

Differences among the four types are more appreciable. Though the numbers of problems reported by the four types are very similar, the Unconnected are particularly likely to report problems in coping with their work, owing to lack of experience or credentials. Encountering such problems may be part of the cost of doing things their own way. Intellectuals also report more work-related problems, typically those resulting from not being well prepared. Conversely, Careerists and Strivers have considerably more trouble making career decisions. Careerists care less about the intrinsic nature of their work and are thus less internally directed toward particular professions. Strivers have problems because their interests are so wide—they want careers that are both materially rewarding and substantively interesting, and striking the balance is not easy. Naturally, Strivers also stand out for their especially common problem dealing with time demands. Careerists, on the other hand, report very few problems in this area. These findings are consistent with the way these two types operate: Strivers are so busy trying to do it all that they are bound to feel harried and short on time; Careerists feel that their jobs are too important to allow other demands to interfere.

SOLVING CAREER PROBLEMS

In tandem with the question about career problems, we asked our participants to tell us about solutions. This open-ended question evoked about thirty different responses, a somewhat less varied array than the problems they identified. Different problems often have a common solution, for example, changing employers.

Just over one-quarter of those who identified problems were unable to come up with solutions. They "just dealt with it," "did nothing," "didn't know what to do." Equal proportions of women and men gave such responses. The Unconnected were the most likely type to say that no solution was forthcoming.

The solutions fell into five main categories, the most common one being "exit"—changing jobs, changing locations, changing occupations (40 percent of all solutions). The attractiveness of this solution is not so much a reflection of their willingness to run away from problems but a function of their having so many options. The second category is "internal" solutions—changing attitudes, seeking therapy, working harder, even getting more exercise. These two strategies account for about two-thirds of all solutions offered. Only in third place do we find efforts to change the situation at work itself. The final two categories, much less common, are obtaining monetary help (to solve financial problems, often related to graduate training) and returning to school for additional education or retraining.

The reluctance to deal directly with the problems at work is mainly due to the difficulty of bringing about organizational change. Given that they are still in the early stages of their careers, equipped with relatively few organizational resources or allies and inexperienced at handling political battles, our participants did not feel they had much influence in their workplaces. Furthermore, challenging the source of the problem was perceived to involve more risk and inconvenience than they were willing to take on. Yet, the reluctance on the part of the educational elite to rock the boat may also say something about their general reluctance to get involved (chapter 9) or deal with problems at a societal rather than individual level. There were also some unique solutions to special problems. In raising start-up capital to finance his firm for two years, one man said, "I had twelve credit cards (no shit! twelve credit cards) and many sleepless nights." The problem must have been solved, since he now earns $330,000 a year.

There is no gender difference in the types of solutions employed. Both sexes are most likely to leave the scene first, try to change themselves second, and try to deal with the work problem third. The same is generally true for the four types as well. There is, however, a moderately greater tendency by the Unconnected to express their concerns in the work situation, seeking to change it rather than leave or change themselves. This tendency fits well with their greater detachment from mainstream institutional values (going back to their college days) and their more finely honed critical sense.

INSTITUTIONAL PROBLEMS: DISCRIMINATION

Beyond such individual hurdles are more general institutional obstacles that may affect women and minority group members in particular. However, these obstacles do not appear to matter as much for the educational elite as they do for the general population. Elite women may do somewhat less well than men, but all segments of the educational elite do far better than their less highly educated contemporaries. Membership in this exclusive category thus exerts a marked homogenizing influence and creates not so much a leveling but uplifting effect.

Apart from occasional references, only a few of our interview subjects complained of their careers being compromised on the basis of their race or ethnicity. This is not to say that they were unaware of or denied the deleterious effects of insidious or overt racism. Yet so far as their own careers were concerned, they generally felt well integrated within the educational elite and hence protected by its prerogatives.

Ethnic consciousness of minorities becomes transformed through joining the educational elite. For example, Clay came to Stanford from a middle-class black family. His father is a physician. Unlike his two other brothers, who were "not doing anything," Clay wanted to be a doctor. It did not happen. By the end of his freshman year, Clay had immersed himself in the black student subculture instead. He became very critical of Stanford, especially of the "apathy" of the student population with regard to issues like apartheid. Stanford was an "elite capitalist institution" that "picked those blacks who were going for the buck like everyone else" and ended up acquiring "white people's biases and prejudices." Stanford did not want "troublemakers." ("There is only one black kid from Detroit, which is 91 percent black. Why?") As a more self-aware black man, Clay found it "draining" to be at Stanford.

Ten years later, when we met Clay again, he was an elegantly dressed young man in an exquisitely furnished office in a highly successful black law firm in Chicago. He had done very well, and he spoke with great pride about acting as counsel to a $1 billion urban renewal project. In contrast to his attitude in his student days, when being black seemed to permeate his life, Clay now seemed oblivious to his ethnicity. It was not until the questions turned to social concerns that he spoke about his political activities on behalf of the black community. Clay had not forgotten his roots, nor had he abandoned his dedication to his ethnic group. He merely had put the issue in the broader context of his life. Looked at positively, one could say that becoming part of the educational elite had integrated Clay into the mainstream power structure. Looked at more critically, it had co-opted him.

The problem of sex discrimination evoked concern from larger numbers of participants. Discrimination based on gender has become one of the central social and legal concerns in American society over the past several decades. In the workplace, it most often affects women with respect to being hired, trained, paid equally, and promoted. Despite great advances, many serious problems of sex discrimination remain.

There was no lack of awareness of the pervasiveness of sex discrimination in the workplace among either the women or men participants. They recognized it even in graduate school. "It makes me very angry," said one woman, "to see the pay discrepancies between men and women researchers and between one graduate program and another." Another complained of "gender discrimination, age discrimination, and regional discrimination ('I didn't fit in the "good ole boy" network')."

We were specifically concerned, however, with gender discrimination in their own experience. It is especially important to investigate sex discrimination within the educational elite because this stratum sets the pace and the standards within major occupations. If sex discrimination is rampant and unchecked at the top of the occupational scale, many argue, it is bound to be even worse at lower levels—and all the harder to change. If women at the top are treated equally with men, on the other hand, structural change may trickle down throughout the labor force and will be greatly facilitated. One could argue, though, that sex discrimination is most likely at the top, where it really matters—men are most determined and able to hang on to their privileged positon at the top, where they have control. At lower levels, we find more bureaucratized, formalized structures for hiring, promotion, and salary-setting, so equality is more easily built into the system.

The many factors that differentiate the work experiences and career patterns of women and men can be placed in three categories. First are the more or less free choices that men and women make about their careers and the consequences of those choices. If women do not choose to go into a given field, such as engineering, but instead go into a field like teaching (assuming both fields are equally open to them), women will make less money than men, have lower occupational status, and so on. The sticking point here is the assumption that fields are equally open; often they are not.

The second category comprises the various obstacles that are placed in the path of women who wish to pursue a given occupation. If women are not encouraged to do well in math or science in school, and then are discouraged from majoring in engineering in college and are steered instead into fields like English, they will have lower occupational prestige and income not by choice but by lack of choice. If they choose predominantly "male" careers and find that they are not given the same credence, opportunities, and respect as men, their only "choice" is to work twice as hard as men to obtain the same results.

Third, since women by necessity bear and typically rear children, motherhood has a markedly different impact on their career choices and consolidation than does fatherhood on their male counterparts, under current circumstances.

Sex discrimination operates in all three categories. The ostensibly free career choices women make are a function of how they were brought up and differentially socialized (setting aside for the moment the potential effects of biologically based gender differences, whatever they may be). Adolescent and young adult women are channeled toward certain occupations and men toward others. Likewise, although motherhood can be portrayed as a matter of free choice, the conflict between career and family does not burden men the way it does women. Biology here is not really the main factor: the impact of motherhood on women's careers is due not so much to the experiences of pregnancy and childbirth as to the time demands of rearing children, which in principle could be done by fathers as well as mothers.

Defined more narrowly, sex discrimination is limited to the second category whereby the career choices of women are limited and their career progress stymied because of their gender alone, irrespective of their performance in school or on the job. This, in fact, is the basis of the current legal definition of sex discrimination.

For the educational elite, the effect of motherhood on career is the most compelling of these factors. We consider this critical issue in chapter 8, after our discussion of pairing-up and parenthood. We shall focus here on issues of "free" occupational choice and sex discrimination, as legally defined.

Let us first compare women with Intellectuals. Both of these groups express somewhat lower levels of career commitment, have lower incomes, consider their compensation to be relatively inadequate, and more often feel behind schedule compared with their peers in the educational elite. These similarities cannot be explained solely by the fact that women are overrepresented among Intellectuals. Intellectual men reveal the same pattern, and women of the other types lag somewhat behind their male counterparts.

Under these assumptions, explaining the lower earned incomes of Intellectuals (and, to that extent, their lower career "success") is not difficult. First, they more often enter professions that do not pay spectacular salaries. Second, even if they go into more lucrative fields, they are more likely to choose the sort of occupation that appeals to them intellectually rather than the one that pays the highest salary. One can raise valid questions about the social values of a society that pays lawyers ten times as much as schoolteachers. Yet, given the society we live in, college students are quite aware of the salary levels that await them if they make one or another occupational choice. Therefore, one could argue that the lower compensation of Intellectuals does not raise questions of equity or justice within the current rules of the game. Hence, the issue becomes not a matter of "discrimination" but one of choice. The same reasoning would be applied to women.

The problem with this argument is that women of the educational elite do not look very different from the men in terms of their values, priorities, and desires. We saw this in the cohort study, and we see it once again ten years later. Probably more than any other identifiable segment of the population, the educational elite comes closest to gender equality in most of the attitudes and outlooks relevant to building careers—at least through the third decade of life. Most women in this group want what the men want with respect to their careers. So why should they not be doing just as well?

The problem of sex discrimination as legally defined is widely documented in the general population. The most commonly cited indicator is the lower earnings of women compared with men. Even among highly educated people a sex differential persists, as illustrated by the 1990 census finding that the monthly income of doctoral degree holders is $4,679 for men but only $3,162 for women (67 percent of men's incomes).[15]

The matter of income differentials is not simple, however. In addition to gender, such factors as seniority, level of responsibility, and patterns of employment are other important determinants of income. Since women have been largely excluded from the major professions until recently, they tend to lag behind in seniority and experience—hence, in pay also. Women also remain primarily responsible for child rearing and are thus more likely to interrupt their careers—hence, their salaries lag further.

But the situation is changing; the walls blocking the entry of women into male-dominated professions were definitively breached in the 1970s. Between 1967 and 1980, women's share of medical degrees rose from 5 to 26 percent, and their share of law degrees went from 4 to 22 percent.[16] Furthermore, the proportion of women managers in business and financial institutions, as well as in the public sector, is slightly higher than the figure for men (31 percent as against 28 percent). In all administration and industry, the 1990 census found that women account for 32 percent of all managers.[17] Nonetheless, serious discrepancies persist. For one thing, the proportion of women managers varies widely in different industries. For another, these figures pool managers at various levels, but women are concentrated in lower-level management; among senior executives, women are still scarce.[18]

What, then, of our women participants? We found only modest evidence of gender discrimination in their reported experience. In their questionnaire responses, only eight women listed sex discrimination as their biggest career problem. Five more said it was their second-biggest problem, making a total of 15 percent reporting gender discrimination at all. (Only one man made this complaint.) Looked at another way, gender discrimination represents only about 12 percent of all the problems women reported in their careers, well below the other main types of problems referred to earlier. Furthermore, when we asked women in the interviews about sex discrimination, it turned out to be a difficult problem to pin down. All of the women were perfectly aware of the general problem of gender discrimination in the workplace. Yet very few of them could specify how it applied to them.

We are further limited by the fact that, of the thirteen women who felt discriminated against, only four happened to be in the interview sample. And since one of the latter was African-American and another Hispanic, it was hard for them to separate the effect of ethnicity from that of gender. Moreover, both of these women had been highly successful in their careers. One of them is Alice, a manager in a large telecommunications company. She has risen rapidly in the organization yet feels that "ultimately it is not competence but politics that determines how high you rise in the hierarchy." She is fortunate to have had two excellent mentors who have protected and fostered her interests.

Cecilia is a Mexican-American lawyer who attributes the obstacles in her career to "problems stemming from prejudice against me as a woman and a minority." She has dealt with bias by "trying to ignore the obvious bigots (I can't change them) and concentrating on presenting myself as a competent individual and attorney."

The other two are white. Victoria is an engineer and ascribes the problems she has encountered to "being a woman in a primarily male profession." The last woman is Cynthia Eastwood.

It is tempting to assume that if a woman has been successful in her career, she has not been discriminated against. But that is not necessarily the case; women like Alice and Cynthia could prevail despite unfavorable odds. Conversely, the fact that a woman does not have a successful career does not necessarily mean that she was discriminated against, even though she may feel she was. These women work in highly demanding and competitive jobs and, like the men, have their limitations.

As we see, the assessment of sex discrimination is difficult in this group of women. Our general conclusion is that, given their professional qualifications and the settings in which they work, they have so far rarely come face to face with stark gender prejudice or flagrant acts of discrimination. Instead, they encounter an attitudinal problem on the part of bosses, colleagues, and clients. The "glass ceiling" they run into is indeed transparent.

Louise is director of strategic marketing at a high-tech company. She did not cite gender discrimination as a problem on her questionnaire but referred to it in her interview. "Yes, I think there is a 'glass ceiling.' The last six years I have been in a male-dominated industry, and it has slowed me down somewhat. But it is when you get into more senior positions that it gets more difficult. On the other hand, I would not want to be president of the company I work for, though I would very much like to be vice president. Part of it has to do with technical competence, but I also inherently am not interested in being president."

It was difficult to find out why Louise did not want to be president; somehow, the position simply did not "feel right" to her. Similar exchanges took place with other highly competent women. These women look at the quality of life of male senior executives and decide that the personal costs of achieving the money, prestige, and sense of power, which seem to make such jobs attractive to men, are too high. Their comments included phrases like, "I must enjoy the job," "I don't want to live on an airplane," "It is brutal," "I want to have a life of my own," "I want a family," and perhaps most telling of all, "I don't have a wife."

In light of such statements, it becomes hard to distinguish between decisions based on personal choice and those that reflect lack of choice. On the one hand, women hesitate to attempt to scale the summit because they fear the climb will be harder for them, since they lack the supports available to their fellow male climbers, both at work and at home. In addition, they do not think the view from the top is worth the effort. This combined expectation then makes the climb itself all the more difficult.

All of these considerations notwithstanding, our results in this area reveal much less gender discrimination than do most other studies, such as the recent survey of the women graduates of the Harvard schools of medicine, law, and business[19] (see chapter 8). However, we would add the cautionary note that our participants are still in the early stages of their careers. If the last push to the top really is the hardest, we may find much more widespread evidence of gender discrimination after another decade.

We did have at least one case of gender discrimination against a man—Keith, one of our Intellectual academics. Despite his high level of competence, he had a very hard time finding a teaching position because, he said, most departments of political science are now seeking to "diversify" their faculty, that is, to hire more women and minorities. Diversification is most eagerly sought in the area of political theory, which happens to be his specialty. Hence, as a white male, he faced an "atrocious job market." Yet, true liberal that he is, Keith is fully in favor of affirmative action.

Affirmative action may be seen as an officially sanctioned form of discriminatory restitution. We have no reason to suspect that the women in our sample are less competent than the men, and none of them thought they had been hired for a job they were not qualified to do. Yet just as gender discrimination can be subtle and hard to document, so, too, can affirmative action. We cannot dismiss the possibility that the careers of some of our women were enhanced because of their gender; the same would be true for members of ethnic minorities. Women and minorities in the educational elite are exactly the sort of people that are being avidly courted by many organizations. Our women were sensitive about this. One had turned down a fine academic position because she thought, "They are trying to fill their quota."

As with discrimination, however, most of our women interviewees strongly doubted this prospect. On the whole, they felt they had been on equal standing with men, neither hurt nor helped by their gender. Their Stanford diploma, certifying their membership in the educational elite, protected the great majority of them against discrimination while making it unnecessary for them to curry favor because of their gender. "As a woman in financial services," said one of them, "the Stanford degree has given me immediate acceptance by coworkers and has allowed me to penetrate circles which may have been closed to me otherwise."

ILLNESS AND MENTAL HEALTH

Considerable research demonstrates the positive impact of higher education on subsequent health, apart from such factors as income and prior health condition. This impact is due to the types of occupations filled by better educated people, the healthier environments they live in, and their relatively good information about and access to health services. Conversely, serious ill health is likely to interfere with both education and subsequent career success. Unlike the Grant Study of Harvard undergraduates, which focused on issues of adaptation and health, ours was primarily concerned with the process of academic and career choice. The effects of physical and mental illness, however, are so pervasive that we cannot ignore them. During the decade after college, fourteen individuals reported one year of serious illness each; three others had been ill for two or more years, one of whom suffered five years of illness. Men and women were equally likely to suffer a major illness. Furthermore, two of our participants, both of them women, died before the follow-up study.

The Unconnected were most likely to suffer serious illness (42 percent of all cases of illness, and 13 percent of the Unconnected group). As we noted earlier, illness does not generally explain unconnectedness, except for some individuals who are too distracted and distraught to fashion consistently rewarding careers for themselves.

On the other hand, even severe illness need not be debilitating. Indeed, our findings about the career development of those who suffered major illness suggest that, for the educational elite, illness is usually only a temporary impediment. Those who have been seriously ill do have somewhat lower incomes than those who have not (medians of $37,000 versus $54,000). But they actually express as much career satisfaction as their healthier peers and are slightly more contented with their career choices, more committed to their careers, and more positive about their competence; they are even more satisfied with their compensation than others. Perhaps their expectations have been lowered, but we also detected changes in attitude. After all, there is nothing like a close brush with death to make one take stock of one's life. Nonetheless, we think this finding also tells us something about the character of many of the educational elite. In the face of diversity, they do not collapse; they get back on their feet and surge forward. Two examples provide ample illustration. The first is none other than Striver George Mehta. Earlier in the chapter we left him well settled in his successful and socially useful career. He was happily married, and they were expecting their first child (chapter 6). All of this almost came to grief quite unexpectedly when George suffered a stroke. Late one afternoon, while alone in his office, he developed cerebral symptoms and was rushed to the hospital. An abnormal blood vessel had ruptured in his brain, paralyzing the left side of his body. George not only survived but was well enough to be out of intensive care ten days after neurosurgery to attend the birth of his son, their first child: "It was an occasion," says George, "that meant a great deal, and one that I'll never forget."

George left the hospital a month later. Life was not easy for the Mehtas for a while, but they came through. George gradually regained most of his bodily functions and went back to work in his previous job. The ordeal took away nothing from his thoughtful, serene, and finely balanced self; on the contrary, it deepened his appreciation of life.

Alan's story is even more dramatic. Alan's college goal was "to gain a well-rounded education." He was especially interested in English but also excelled in math. By contrast, his career goals were less formed. In his freshman year, Alan got all "A"s despite the fact that he spent twenty-two hours per week in practice and competition. In answer to the question put to prospective freshmen, "What will be your most troublesome concerns, if any, at Stanford?" Alan responded, "I hope to have no troublesome concerns at Stanford." And so it was, throughout his first two years. In his junior year, Alan noted: "Great start—nice room, good roommates, pretty good classes." Then disaster struck. When Alan returned his senior questionnaire, two years later, it included the following note. "This is offered as a word of explanation toward some answers that might otherwise seem a bit strange: I broke my neck during gymnastics practice on December 6, 1979, the beginning of my junior year. I spent nine months in the hospital and went back to school in the fall of 1980. I was in school for four quarters but have now stopped out because I am concerned about my health. I am undergoing physical therapy about seven hours a day, Monday through Friday."

The *Stanford Daily* ran an article at the time of the accident with a photograph of Alan. It shows a handsome young man with a thoughtful expression staring into the distance as his powerful arms hold his body perfectly balanced on the parallel bars. "Eight weeks ago he fell," the article said, "and he hasn't moved since." Actually, Alan had already learned to hold a pen in his mouth and draw pictures with it. His first drawing was of a boy in a wheelchair. One of his friends said, "He doesn't ever want pity. I know [he] will come back to school and get his degree someday. I just know it."[20]

The friend was right. With unswaying support from family and friends, Alan came back to school. Unable to move his arms and legs, he was confined to a wheelchair, traveled in a special van, and was assisted by an attendant at all times. But his mind and spirit were intact. He double majored in English and mathematical science. Friends took notes for him, and his mother typed his papers. Alan did the rest.

It took Alan an extra year as an undergraduate and then two more years in a coterminal program to get his master's degree in education. He then started working as an educational software designer and programmer. The first year on the job, he designed and wrote a computer game that sold over 100,000 copies and won the "game of the year" award and several other industry citations.

Ten years later, Alan still does not have the use of his legs and arms. His breathing is aided by a pacemaker. Attendants assist him around the clock with virtually every physical move (Alan thinks of them as his employees, not caretakers). He operates computers by himself with an ultrasound-driven headset and a metal stick he holds with his teeth. His speech and thinking are unimpaired. If one knew nothing about any of this, his follow-up questionnaire would not give the slightest hint of the incredible odds against which he has prevailed. To the question "What kinds of problems, if any, have you faced in pursuing your career?" Alan's response is: "None." He is not involved with disabled groups because he does not identify with disabled people and dislikes dwelling on his condition. Alan gives us a new perspective on the issues of career success that we have been struggling with. He sets a humbling standard of what it really means to "make it."

SOCIAL MOBILITY

Income, accomplishments, and subjective measures of satisfaction tell us about the career success of the educational elite as individuals. Comparisons with their peers give us another perspective. But since family background plays such an important role in career success, another key comparison is intergenerational social status. After all, if the educational elite simply turn out to be the children of affluent families, their achievements, however remarkable, would be only what we expect, given what we know generally about the self-perpetuation of social class. If the educational elite comes from more varied social backgrounds, however, their achievements would indicate that elite schooling plays a meritocratic role in American society, that the more gifted have a chance to get ahead regardless of their family origin.

Comparisons of social class status between generations are complicated by historically changing economic conditions. The parents of our participants became established in their careers during the prosperous 1950s; their children came of age in the economically more troubled 1980s. We cannot readily control for these variables, but we need to keep them in mind.

In the first year of the cohort study (1977), we asked our participants to identify their social class background. About 64 percent said they came from upper- or upper-middle-class backgrounds, 22 percent from the middle class, and only 14 percent from working-, lower-middle-, or lower-class backgrounds.[21] This contrasts sharply with national self-reported social class figures: 43 percent middle-class, only 9 percent upper-middle- or upper-class, and 54 percent lower-middle- or lower-class.[22]

Studies of social mobility have identified two key variables that affect occupational status: family background and level of education.[23] These two factors explain differences in occupational achievement, the most important component of social class, in almost equal measure. Each in turn subsumes several variables. Father's occupational status is the single most important influence; race, ethnicity, religion, and farm background also contribute. Educational attainment depends most on cognitive skills (aptitudes): better skills lead to more years in the educational system, which in turn lead to higher occupational status. Cognitive skills also improve occupational mobility independent of their effects through schooling. But the length of schooling, or highest degree obtained, is not the only component that improves social class chances. Of particular relevance to the educational elite is the finding that graduates of selective colleges earn 28 percent more than graduates with the same degrees from nonselective institutions. Thus, if education generally contributes to social mobility, education in elite institutions should greatly intensify this effect.

Against this background, how do our participants compare with their parents? As shown in figure 5.3 and tables 7 and 8, appendix A, there is both considerable constancy as well as change between the generations. To begin with, 58 percent report the same social class as their parents, 26 percent indicate upward mobility, and 16 percent report downward mobility. Quite strikingly, *all* of the participants in the lower-middle, working-, or lower-class groups report upward mobility. Although about one-sixth of our participants from these class backgrounds report a current status of "lower-middle" class (figure 5.3), even these individuals have moved up because they all come from lower- or working-class families. Similarly, 46 percent of those with middle-class backgrounds have moved to a higher level and only 4 percent are downwardly mobile. This self-assessment is in marked contrast to that of the general population, for whom upward mobility from the lower and middle strata ranges from 42 percent (for those of lower-class, white-collar background) to 58 percent (those of lower-, or working-class, background).[24] Further, downward mobility for the middle class at the national level is much more prevalent at about

FIGURE 5.3
Social Mobility (*movement from parents' class location*)

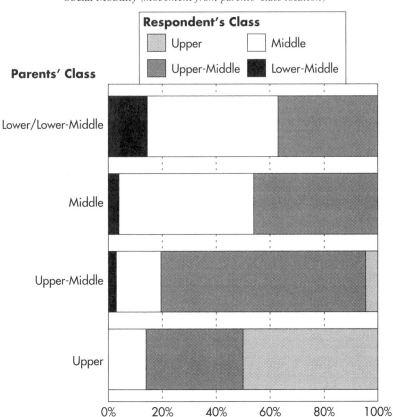

38 percent. Thus, most of the mobility is upward, and the educational elite is more upwardly mobile (or more able to maintain their already high class standing) than their less educated counterparts.[25]

The children of the upper-middle class have largely retained, or regained, their parental family status. About 20 percent of our participants from the upper-middle class report downward mobility or have yet to regain their parents' level. Upward mobility for the upper-middle class (moving into the upper class) is so far extremely rare (4 percent, or 5 of 114 individuals). The children of the upper class have the hardest time retaining their family status. Half (7 of 14) have managed to do so but half report downward mobility.

Social mobility is not just a matter of making more money, just as social status is not just a matter of having money. Martha's parents earned about $40,000 a year when she graduated, but she classified them as working-class, since her father was a truck driver and her mother a clerk. Martha is now getting a Ph.D. in psychology and sees herself as part of the upper-middle class, even though her only income is the $12,000 fellowship she gets as a doctoral student. And she has no doubts about what led to her change of class position. "Stanford has opened doors for me and will continue to do so in the future," she says. "I believe it has raised my status in the social class system. It has inspired a sense of self-confidence and entitlement in me."

Conversely, money alone seems insufficient as an indicator of social class. Michael, who has earned millions of dollars as a professional athlete, still ranks himself only in the upper-middle class. He must feel that his lower-middle-class family background, so distant from the cultural stratosphere of the upper class, will never allow him to place himself in that stratum, no matter how much money he makes.

Some of the downwardly mobile individuals have revealing histories. Gail, the idealistic teacher and swim coach of chapter 4, comes from the upper-middle class. (Her father is vice president of a manufacturing company, her mother a nurse.) Gail made a modest living toiling in the public school system and, as a law student, now has an income of only $5,000 a year. She feels she has dropped to the lower-middle class, but, of course, that will change once she finishes law school. Andrea, also the daughter of a business executive, is in engineering management making $60,000 a year, which is simply not enough for her to feel she has maintained the upper-class status of her parents. By contrast, Bill, who has never made much money and is currently unemployed, still considers himself part of the upper-middle class like his parents. (Both his father and grandfather are prominent Stanford-educated lawyers.)

These self-assessments of social class are likely to be transitory, given the relative youth of our participants. Thus, the downward trend in our findings is probably overstated, just as the upward trend is understated. Overall, it seems likely that by age forty we will find virtually no cases of downward mobility and many of those who currently see themselves as only maintaining their parents' class position will feel they have begun to surpass it.

Women indicate somewhat greater downward mobility than men (21 percent versus 11 percent), but equal upward mobility (27 percent versus 25 percent; see table 8, appendix A). This greater loss of class standing is largely due, paradoxically, to the fact that almost all of the women have careers. They base their current class status on their own accomplishments (and to a lesser extent, on those of their partners). Given that women hold somewhat fewer high-prestige jobs, and make somewhat less money than men, women of very high class background are more likely to report a decline in class position. In other words, even educational elite women from high-status families see themselves as (modestly) disadvantaged relative to comparable men, in pursuing high-status professions and high income.

The strong relationship between ethnicity and social class leads to the correlative finding that 70 percent of disadvantaged minority group students report upward mobility, compared with 23 percent of whites. Although we have only seventeen such students in our follow-up sample, this finding indicates that entry into the educational elite almost guarantees upward mobility for minority students.

Over half of the Asian-Americans in our sample came from the middle class. A small proportion of our participants were still in the middle class, the rest having moved up to the upper-middle class. Our Mexican-American and African-American participants came from more modest backgrounds. Almost half came from the lower-middle or lower working classes (compared with 1 percent of whites). Every single one of them has now moved up by at least one social-class level. Whereas less than one-quarter of these families were upper-middle class, now over half of their children are. The social mobility for disadvantaged minorities who joined the educational elite is thus tremendous.

Of our four types, three have almost identical mobility patterns. About 30 percent of Careerists, Strivers, and the Unconnected report upward mobility and 13 percent downward mobility. Intellectuals lag behind, with only 18 percent progressing upward and 22 percent downward. These latter figures partly reflect a gender effect, though they hold for Intellectual men as well as women. Many Intellectual men can go no higher, being products of the higher social classes to begin with. In addition, intellectualism leads them to choose a career for its intrinsic properties rather than its status and income. To a certain extent, then, Intellectuals are more downwardly mobile by choice. To call this a "problem" is misleading. And lest we forget, they are hardly on the edge of starvation.

With this chapter, we end our exploration of the career choice, consolidation, and success of the educational elite. Against this background, we now turn to the same issues in their personal lives.

CHAPTER 6

Pairing Up, Settling Down

The family is the hub of the societal wheel and marriage the linchpin that holds it together. The difficulties of married life in modern society, which expects so much of marriage but offers so little social support to the family, has made this conventional view questionable to many. Couples seek the comfort and satisfactions of marriage, but chafe under its limiting reins. Traditionalists uphold its virtues, and radicals call for its abolition. Heaven for some, hell for others, a bit of both for most, marriage is an institution that seems always ailing but never dead.

Despite its burdens and failures, marriage remains a key personal objective for most adults: 95 percent of American men and women still get married at least once at some point in their lives.[1] In 1992, 62 percent of the U.S. population aged eighteen and over was married; for the generation of our participants (ages thirty to thirty-four), the figure was 67 percent.[2] Families based on these marriages encompass a good deal of diversity. We may still think of the typical family as a married couple with their own children, staying together "till death do them part." That pattern may be the ideal but is no longer typical; less than half of American families currently fit it.

The educational elite find marriage as irresistible as anyone else does. Ten years after college, 63 percent of our participants had married at least once, women (68 percent) somewhat more than men (59 percent). Of those who had been married, 8 percent had divorced. As a result, just under 60 percent were currently married; another 10 percent were living with a partner. Although three in ten were still living alone at the end of the decade, almost all of them hoped to be married or living with a partner before the end of the next decade. Only one in a hundred could see themselves without a permanent relationship throughout their adult lives.

Marriage, like work, is one of the great social imperatives. Together, they constitute "settling down," through which one becomes a fully established adult. Historically, work and marriage have been inseparable economically. It was only after the Industrial Revolution that the family gradually lost its primary character as a unit of economic production, becoming instead a locus of intimacy between husband and wife. Most couples now expect marriage to provide the primary emotional gratifications of their lives.[3] Many of the traditional functions of the family persist, of course, such as rearing children, management of the household, economic support, and expansion of the kinship network. Similarly, the religious and social principles underpinning the obligations of the marital contract continue to exert a powerful influence on our ideals and expectations. Meanwhile, the institution of marriage continues to evolve dramatically—most importantly through changes in the roles of women and men in the marital relationship itself.

THE PROFILE GROUP

Five out of eight members of the profile group are married. Intellectual Christopher Luce is single. Striver Geraldine Jones is living with her domestic partner, as is David Levy, with his fiancée. Striver George Mehta was the first in the group to get married. "I guess I married at the relatively young age of twenty-six, but after meeting and getting to know my future wife, I couldn't imagine doing things any differently then or now." Intellectual Kirsten Buchanan was the last to marry, at age thirty, and she, too, would not do things differently. The rest married six years after graduating from college, when they were about twenty-seven.

Careerist Martin MacMillan would have been a one-woman man, as he has been a one-career man, if circumstances had permitted. He had a serious relationship in college until he found his girlfriend at a ski resort with someone else. He then established an intimate relationship with Vanessa, a fellow medical student, that lasted through internship but did not survive their separation as they headed for different residency programs. Martin remembers Vanessa as "the first woman who loved me for who I am." Martin is not sure why he did not marry her, but it possibly was the prospect of being married to another physician that gave him pause. He then met Jane, a nurse and someone who fit better his model of a wife.

They are now happily settled. Martin is fully committed to his family, and his marriage is "for life," as secure, solid, and certain as his career.

In getting married, Careerist Cynthia Eastwood relied on some of the same "power moves" that have propelled her career. The year after she graduated from college, she had a brief and unsatisfactory relationship with a man. Then she met Jeffrey. He was exactly what she wanted for a husband. They had been undergraduates at the same time but had never met. Now she was working; he was a second-year M.B.A. student. They began to date and Cynthia's heart caught up with her head as they rapidly grew fond of each other. There was only one problem: Jeffrey was even more ambitious and driven than Cynthia. As the increasingly long hours Jeffrey put in at work left less and less time for Cynthia, she began to have the nagging thought that maybe she did not "come first in his life." So she escalated a minor conflict over his inability to attend a family brunch into a major test of their relationship. The ultimatum she issued was a bluff, but it worked. Jeffrey panicked. He recruited their mutual friends. He told his boss to ease up on his responsibilities. ("You are ruining my personal life.") And he topped it off by asking Cynthia to marry him. She agreed.

Intellectual Kirsten Buchanan's first serious relationship after college turned out to be a mismatch. She met a man during the heyday of her business career. He, too, was heavily immersed in his work, which involved a lot of travel, so they did not see much of each other. Yet it was not the repeated separations that doomed the relationship, but his failure to live up to her standards of emotional balance and compatibility. "I was more into the relationship than he was," says Kirsten. "He very much needed me. I felt responsible for helping him realize who he was, helped him with his family issues, helped him feel good about himself. It was not a particularly healthy relationship, and it ended in a slow natural death." But it dragged on for eight years.

After her brother's death, when Kirsten moved to be with her parents, she met Tom. "I had an extra ticket to a concert," she explains, "so I asked a friend who was a medical resident to bring along anyone he wanted. It turned out to be my future husband." Tom, who was also a medical resident, happened to be an old friend of one of Kirsten's brothers. Their families lived four blocks apart. Kirsten had never met him before, but she had an almost immediate sense that he was the right man. "He was the man I had been waiting for, though it took a long time to find him. A good man. He was the best person for me." Two years of marriage have confirmed Kirsten's judgment.

Intellectual Christopher Luce is the one true bachelor in the profile group. He met his first girlfriend during freshman orientation week. For the next eight years they dated on and off until they broke it off. "It was a wonderful relationship, really wonderful. We were very close, but we both felt that we were too young to marry."

Handsome, articulate, and socially polished, Christopher then went through a succession of brief relationships until he went to Yale, where he became seriously involved with a woman for a second time. She was a "brilliant scholar" with a promising academic career ahead of her. But things "did not feel right" to Christopher. They lived together for two years before deciding to end the relationship.

Christopher is philosophical about his marital status. "My father did not marry until he had established himself in a career and knew what he wanted. It has made for a very happy marriage with my mother. I have often thought about that. I guess his example has guided my feelings about career and marriage up to this point." Marriage has a strong appeal for him, but he feels that it represents an "incredible commitment," which he is not yet willing to undertake. "It's precisely because marriage is such an important commitment—the most important commitment you can make—that I want to wait until I am ready. Right now, I enjoy being on my own."

Nonetheless, given "the right time and the right person," Christopher wants to settle down. He hopes to find someone endowed with a "sensibility" that combines "humor, gentleness, and intelligence." Since such women must be plentiful in the academic circles that Christopher moves in, it should not be hard to find one. But Christopher has additional expectations of his future wife which are harder to fulfill, as we shall relate in the next chapter.

Our two profile Strivers once again demonstrate alternative paths within their type, in some ways replicating their divergent career patterns. George Mehta's personal life mirrors his career. Well-thought-out and sensible moves have led to a happy marriage that fulfills his emotional needs and keeps his life on an even keel. Following college, George dated a few women, but his first and only serious relationship has been with his wife Claudia. He met her at an ice skating rink during a social function organized by Sierra Club Singles. It was love at first sight. Yet, despite their strong attraction to each other, George and Claudia dated for six months, lived together for another six months before getting engaged, and then waited for nine more months before they got married. As the children of divorced parents, both wanted to make quite sure they were compatible before fully committing themselves.

"It is in my personal life, more so than in my professional career, that I have had the most growing up to do," says Striver Geraldine Jones. While at Stanford, Geraldine had a number of boyfriends, and her relationship with the last one survived graduation by nine months. During her theatrical career in New York City, Geraldine had a series of relationships, but none of them were particularly meaningful. When she moved to Vermont, she met Tony, a photographer and painter who had sought refuge from a failed marriage and a problematic career. Their relationship matured as they shared their mutual interest in the environment and found that their personal needs and vocational interests were complementary. They started living together three years ago, yet their relationship is troubled and its future uncertain.

Our two Unconnected profiles live up to their propensity to fashion their lives according to their own lights. Unconnected as he may have been, David Levy has the longest uninterrupted relationship of anyone in the profile group. He met Judith in college. They started as friends, became lovers, then lived together on and off after college, and are now engaged to be married. During this span of over ten years, neither of them has been involved with anyone else. The decision to get married followed their wish to have children, but David says, "We don't expect getting married is going to change our relationship."

Unconnected Katherine Johnson also had a serious relationship in college, but it did not last much beyond graduation. She then met her husband in law school. They dated for four years, lived together for another year, and then got married when they decided to have a child. One of the more remarkable aspects of David's and Katherine's relationships with their respective mates is their willingness to go against the conventional grain. David has adapted his career to accommodate his fiancée's career aspirations, and Katherine's husband has subordinated his career to their family needs.

CHOOSING A MATE

Just as the determinants of career choice have roots that go back to childhood, the choice of a partner is strongly affected by personal biography and parental models. The decision schedule is also similar to that for career choice: a period of exploration in college is followed by a linear progression for some, a more meandering journey for others, during which choices crystallize, usually by the latter part of the third decade.

Career journeys have a different character, however, from the more personal quest for intimacy. If you do not work, someone else has to work to sustain you; if you do not marry, no one has to do it for you. It is not hard to make a case for singlehood; it is quite difficult to make a case for unemployment. Intimacy and marriage belong to the private sphere, where there is considerable leeway in making choices. Work is in the public sphere, where your business is also other people's business. Formal qualifications and training are necessary for careers. Yet there is no formal training for marriage. As we are so often told, it is easier to get a marriage certificate than a driver's license, never mind a license to practice law or medicine. Most young adults are far better prepared to enter the world of work than they are to join a partner in starting a new life as a family.

In earlier times, clear guidelines and social "scripts" defined each spouse's role, which was learned in the course of coming of age. Parents or the extended family chose the mate as well as line of work, and parental example constituted a compelling model for a young person's adult behavior. In our modern culture, however, the guidelines are fuzzy and very much in dispute.

Today's individualistic model of marriage, however, should not be exaggerated. The young person is now free in principle to choose anyone as a partner and to develop any sort of relationship. In practice, of course, partner choice is strongly influenced by class, ethnicity, occupation, religion, and a host of other largely predetermined social characteristics. Consequently, marriage relationships are still fairly standardized and predictable, even though they may allow for greater variety. What is more, the division of labor in the household stubbornly resists equalization or gender neutrality. Even among young couples who share the burden of housework, men continue to concentrate on "male" household tasks, women on "female" tasks. How much the educational elite conform to this nineteenth-century model of household management is a major issue we address in the next chapter.

If intimacy and love are at the heart of modern marriage, in principle if not always in practice, what do they represent? How are they experienced? What are their outward manifestations? Psychologists have attempted to study these issues, but the subject seems to wilt in their hands. The most eloquent and compelling depictions of love are still to be found in literature and art.

Love is equated by many with the romantic, swooning, falling-in-love experience.[4] A more analytical approach finds (in agreement with the ancient Greeks) that love is far from a unitary phenomenon. *Eros,* or passionate love, is only one of its forms. The psychologist Robert Sternberg offers a triangular model of love consisting of three basic components: intimacy (feelings of caring and closeness), passion (sexual attraction), and commitment (determination to stay in the relationship for the long haul). Different combinations of these components result in a variety of forms of love.[5] We did not explore in detail the romantic and sexual experiences of our participants, but we devoted a substantial segment of the interviews to matters of intimate relationships and marriage.

WHO HAS TOUCHED YOUR HEART?

As we switched our inquiry during the interviews from career issues to personal development, we posed a different sort of question: Who has touched your heart most over the past ten years?[6] The question took everyone by surprise. Some gave quick—sometimes almost too quick—answers. Others took a long time before coming up with a response. Still others could give no answer at all. The question was a sensitive one that could evoke embarrassment. (Offering no answer could reflect a certain poverty of emotional life.) Some answers were tinged with the painful memory of a lost love or a departed parent or sibling. Other responses were guarded and secretive—when someone other than the interviewee's spouse was in mind. A few were genuinely unwilling to choose among the many who had touched their hearts.

The most common answer was the participant's spouse or domestic partner; 60 percent of those who had a partner gave this response. Some gave this response without hesitation; other responses were tinged with tell-tale fidgeting. Some qualified their responses, making them sound obligatory: "I will have to say my wife," and, "It must be my husband."

Those with children often included them with the spouse ("the package," as one man put it). Others (12 percent) singled out the child or placed the child ahead of the spouse. Fathers did this as often as mothers but were even more emphatic about it. One man said, "My son, hands down." Another asserted, "Having a child is unlike anything I have experienced in my life." Some used the question to launch into an extended discussion of their children and would have talked about them all afternoon. Then there were a few one-of-a-kind responses: "My wife, my daughter, my dog," said one man, and in an afterthought, "We also have to put my son in there somewhere."

Nuclear family members thus accounted for more than half of all responses, and for the great majority of the responses of participants with partners. Single people cited in equal numbers a former or current lover and family members. Women were more likely than men to cite family; mothers were mentioned more often than fathers. For some, the person who touched their hearts most had died recently (usually a grandparent) or unexpectedly (an automobile accident, a suicide).

Finally, a small proportion gave a variety of other responses. "The

Ecuadorian community" was the response of a man who had spent a long time in South America. One woman gave pride of place to her psychiatrist. Only five said no one at all had touched their hearts since college.

Another window into the emotional lives of our participants was provided by their responses to questions about the high and low points in their personal lives during the past decade. The overwhelming majority cited as the high point the initiation or blossoming of a love relationship: "the start of our relationship"; "my last love affair"; "our marriage"; "the honeymoon." The birth of a child came next, followed by a sprinkling of various other events that were linked as often to career development as to personal lives.

The low points were usually the obverse of the high points. Typically, the single (and quite a few who are married as well) said, "When I broke up with my girl/boyfriend." The married ones referred to "our first year of marriage," "being tied down," "when my husband's drinking hit bottom," "my divorce," and "the suicide of my former husband." Pregnancy, too, could have troublesome associations, including "getting chicken pox when pregnant," "getting my Ph.D. when pregnant," and "postpartum depression." Much rarer were events not related to spouses, such as "brother's accidental death," "parents' divorce," and, for a gay man, "the time just before coming out."

Thus, personal high and low points very much revolved around those who had touched their hearts. Erik Erikson's view that the phase-specific task of young adulthood is to resolve the issue of intimacy-versus-distancing is well borne out here. Getting close to or getting away from love objects—attempting to define and find a life partner and learning how to develop a relationship that provides sufficient but not excessive intimacy—has clearly been the major component of our participants' emotional lives.

PATTERNS OF MARITAL CHOICE

Three separate decisions are involved in marriage: to marry or not to marry; when to marry; and whom to marry. For most of our participants, the question of whether to marry is taken for granted. The issue of when to marry is more variable and often tied to career considerations. But when to marry is also highly dependent on finding the right person. With marriage now a matter of personal choice, and romantic love prescribed as the basis of that choice, finding the right person has been the critical consideration for our participants.

Unlike much of the rest of their lives, the educational elite cannot schedule falling in love, nor can the right "chemistry" be synthesized on cue. Moreover, "looking for a spouse," let alone drawing up a shopping list of desirable qualities having to do with financial prospects, class status, and the like, is considered cheap, predatory, or demeaning. Even the admission of being in the "marriage market" is to be avoided. Hence, those who are even eagerly looking for a spouse are likely to act as if they are not.

The process of selecting a mate, like choosing a career, has been the subject of much research. Theories typically envisage it as a series of steps. For example, in psychologist Bernard Murstein's model, we evaluate prospective mates by passing them through a set of "filters."[7] We judge potential spouses first by readily visible, external characteristics—physical appearance, sexual attractiveness, dress, manners, and other behaviors that convey a sense of the candidate's social background. Those who make it through the first filter are then scrutinized for less tangible elements, such as attitudes and values concerning issues like politics and religion. Our choices so far involve mainly generic judgments of the overall "value" of the prospective mate. The next step is more personal and specific. It involves not just quality but fit. The question shifts from "Is she/he good enough?" to "Is this the person I want?" The focus here is on compatibility, of temperaments, interests, needs, and expectations. Murstein's model is more likely to operate early in courtship, with some variability in the order in which the filters are applied.

The experience of falling in love with someone you barely know makes a shambles of any orderly sequence. More typically, couples go through a cyclical rather than linear process of evaluating each other. Assets and liabilities are reevaluated repeatedly as the prospective partners learn more about each other. In real life, neither the couples themselves nor close observers are likely to detect any sort of orderly decision-making process. This is not to suggest that such decisions are haphazardly made or left entirely to chance. Rather, it is the complexity of the process and its operation largely below the surface of consciousness that accounts for its opaqueness.

Philip Genochio (chapter 1) is a good example of someone who had spelled out his expectations clearly. With his filters firmly in place, it was relatively easy for him to "process" prospective mates to find exactly what he wanted. Although everyone in our profile group had some idea of what they wanted, their "filters" were not all set in place as firmly or on the same schedule. In making their marital choices, Careerists generally know what they want, determined as much by their heads as by their hearts. They make choices compatible with career, ones that will enhance rather than impede its progress. Hence, there is a consistency and complementarity between their personal and working lives.

The two Intellectuals have taken the longest time: Kirsten found her husband the latest, after "processing" a dead-end relationship for eight years; Christopher Luce has not "activated" his filters yet, though they are in place. Striver George Mehta, who is not an impulsive man, immediately recognized what he wanted but spent a long time carefully evaluating his intended wife (and being evaluated in return). Striver Geraldine Jones's domestic partner has already jammed a couple of her filters. Unconnected David Levy chose the earliest of all but is only now taking the final step to marriage. Katherine Johnson is another early decider after one false start.

GETTING THE "BEST VALUE"

The matter of the assets and liabilities of a potential mate raises another important point in mate selection. However much men and women may yearn for love and romance, they are simultaneously looking for "best value" in a mate, in setting up the marital partnership. To a large extent, a kind of "marital market" is in operation, albeit one that is not highly formalized or explicit.[8] Thus, despite the seeming disdain for the search for a "good match," it is remarkable how regularly people marry partners whose personal assets and liabilities are roughly equivalent to their own. An unequal match is usually avoided and is liable to evoke strong objections from parents and friends close to the person who appears to be selling short or overreaching.

These tendencies have been formalized in two theories of marital choice: the theory of associative mating and the theory of social exchange. The associative mating (or "homogamy") argument maintains that similarity of background is the single most important determinant in choosing a partner, that we are likely to choose someone similar to us in age, social class, race, ethnicity, religious affiliation, and so on. The features we have in common help the candidate pass more easily through the objective "filters." Since such background features are also critical in shaping our personal attitudes, interests, and temperament, they may lead to a greater subjective sense of compatibility as well.

We have many examples of the pull of homogamy in our sample. One woman dated a number of men after college without getting seriously involved. When, at age twenty-five, her sister-in-law introduced her to her future husband, it was love at first sight. She says, "We come from the same city, our parents have known each other, we all get along very well. It has been wonderful." Paul and Jessica are both children of missionaries in Japan. They went to the same high school, then Paul started at Stanford and Jessica went to Hawaii to become a nurse. They kept in touch, and their friendship eventually blossomed into love. Melissa, who works on her father's orchard, is married to Adam, who comes from a farming family in the same area and has his own orchards nearby.

One of the important components of homogamy is propinquity, or geographical nearness. Inuits in Alaska and Bedouins in Arabia do not marry each other since their paths do not cross. Members of the educational elite marry each other because their paths cross a good deal: in college, in graduate school, at work. Being in the same place at the same time is one important element, but it is not as simple as riding on the same bus. People from even very different backgrounds can develop a wide range of commonalities by living, studying, working, or worshiping in the same location.

More typically, however, two people in the same such place are from similar backgrounds so homogamy and propinquity mutually reinforce each other. Thus, members of the educational elite often come from similar backgrounds, and at the same time, being part of the group makes one more similar to others in it. It is no wonder that college and graduate school have always been such excellent marital fishing waters. Until a few decades ago, an important motivation for going to college was to find a mate. That is no longer a primary objective for most, but it remains an important side benefit. Quite a few of the men and women who met their spouse in college viewed it as one of their main gains. Ten percent of our interview sample consists of couples who met as undergraduates at Stanford; of those married, this accounts for nearly 17 percent. An equal proportion met their spouses in graduate school. One-quarter of the doctors are married to nurses.

Not everyone, of course, marries someone similar. Several of our women are married to men who are ten or more years older; Louise's husband is twenty years older. She dated during and after college, but her husband is the only person with whom she has had a truly intimate relationship. He, too, had never married before. They dated for a year or so and got married four years ago. (Louise is blissfully happy: "My contentment is the highest it could be," she says. "Our commitment to each other is forever.")

The interviews suggest that men in the educational elite more often marry within their college or even precollege circle of friends, while women are more apt to marry within their occupational sphere. These tendencies partly account for the differentials in spousal income discussed in chapter 5: men are less apt to marry within the educational elite, particularly if they are Careerists, and women marry within the group they have joined by attending elite institutions. But really sharp discrepancies in social class, religious affiliation, and ethnicity are uncommon and tend to be problematic.

One example of lack of homogamy breaking up a marriage is Tara and her immigrant husband. "He was a wonderful man, and we were in love," says Tara. Juan was intelligent but not well educated, and he barely spoke English. His occupational prospects were meager. None of this mattered at first, but gradually Tara began to feel confined. She was ready to move out of this "love is all that matters" phase of her life, but he would not let go of her. "I had to leave him, though I still loved him," she says with sadness.

The problem in such a case usually stems not from a simple mismatch in background but from a combination of factors. Had Juan been an engineer or a doctor, his South American background would have been much less of a drawback. By the same token, Tara doubts that she would have fallen in love with an engineer or a doctor at that stage of her life, no matter where he came from; it was precisely Juan's differences from her normal milieu that may have attracted her to him. To give her the benefit of the doubt, it is also possible that she fell in love with him for who he was, regardless of his background.

Every relationship has a tolerance level for differences; when it is exceeded, trouble ensues. The level of tolerance may be quite high. One example of a successful nonhomogamous union is Bernard and Felicia's marriage. They met while he was a Stanford undergraduate and she was a student at a local community college. He came from an upper-middle-class family, she from a lower-middle-class Hispanic family. They were members of the same church but otherwise had nothing in common but their love. We will hear more about them later.

The power of homogamy is perhaps best illustrated by the statistics on interracial marriages. There are fifty-two million married couples in the United States, but less than one million are interracial. What keeps people from crossing racial lines is not just skin color but a whole slew of other characteristics that can make another person too different. Ethnicity, religion, and class constitute similar, if less exclusionary, barriers. None of these barriers is insurmountable, but they reduce the options in marital choice. Hence, it was no surprise to find that there were just a handful of interracial couples in our interview sample (usually those of Asian background married to Caucasians), even though many more interracial friendships had flourished during college. Interfaith marriages are more common, and we discuss them in chapter 8.

The main problem with the concept of homogamy as a determinant of marital choice is its lack of specificity. It makes eminent sense that similarity of background should attract people to one another. But since there are so many people with whom we share backgrounds, why is it that we choose the particular person we do from the large pool of eligible mates? Homogamy is a necessary but insufficient condition for marriage. Such concepts are better at explaining the behavior of people collectively than that of specific individuals.

Social exchange theory goes further than homogamy alone. Like the homogamy approach, it assumes that people make more or less rational choices based on at least implicit cost-benefit considerations. Thus, the potential mate is assessed according to whatever is perceived to be desirable in the marital relationship, and homogamy tends to ensure relative equity. Similar backgrounds are more likely to yield equivalent value.

The notion of equity helps to explain how homogamy can be tempered by the process of value exchange. Very few of our couples are matched asset for asset and liability for liability across the board, no matter how similar their backgrounds. Yet equity is possible because a surplus of liabilities in one area can be offset by greater assets in another. Thus, looks, intelligence, social status, accomplishments, personal style, and so on, can be mixed and matched. As long as the net balance on both ledgers is roughly equivalent, equity is obtained.

From this perspective (and frame of mind), it would seem that the "best deal" would be to find someone with the most assets and the fewest liabilities. The equity hypothesis that drives social exchange theory says otherwise. The best deal is the one with fairly equivalent value to both parties, because both can feel they are striking a good bargain. Equity is desirable not only because it is fair but because inequitable relationships cause stress: the one who gets less will feel cheated; the one who gets more will find it difficult to maintain self-esteem. This rule of equivalency generally holds true for our couples.

The problem with marriage-market models is that they reduce the search for intimacy to what Lee has called "love with a shopping list."[9] No wonder that such models offend people's sensibilities and have led to heated debate. The very examples and language they use grate on our nerves and seem to strip people of all finer feelings. Where is unconditional love in all of this? Where are the emotional subtleties that make every love relationship so unique? How do we explain the enduring loyalty of couples through better or worse, in illness or in health?

Women generally are more perturbed than men by market analogies of marital choice, partly because they focus more on the emotional than the physical or material components of relationships and find them harder to reconcile with a "bottom-line" mentality. Moreover, being well aware of women's traditional position of having less power and autonomy, women may be on guard against notions of being traded back and forth rather than being the trading partners of men. Whether we like it or not, however, denying that considerations like equity exchange influence our marital choices would be naive. We want someone who is "good enough" for us, who is "worthy" of our love—while we also want to be sure we are valued and valuable enough in the eyes of our mates.

TIMING OF MARRIAGE

Marriage for the educational elite is an after-college event; very few of our participants got married as undergraduates. Nearly 5 percent married in the first year after college, and at least 2 percent married in each year thereafter (figure 6.1). Overall, women married slightly earlier than men, but by the end of the decade after graduation there was only a very modest sex difference: 57 percent of men and 62 percent of women were married (59 percent of the sample as a whole).

As figure 6.1 shows, the timing of marriage is not uniform throughout the first decade. The first peak comes the year after graduation, representing the finalizing of relationships established in college or, in a few cases, in high school. Matthew met Jean in his freshman dorm, where she was the resident associate. They dated throughout college, married right after, and have been happily living together since. It was a very early choice but a good one. ("I am extremely happy," says Matthew. "I couldn't ask for a better family life.")

FIGURE 6.1
First Marriage, by Sex (*percentages marrying each year*)

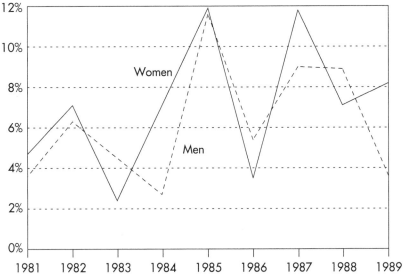

The second and major peak comes in the fifth year after graduation, at about age twenty-six, when 12 percent of our sample married. This peak follows the completion of graduate study for many of our participants. Recalling figure 3.1, this is exactly the point when the proportion engaged in graduate study drops. Others who did not go to graduate school were sufficiently settled in their jobs to contemplate marriage at that point. Others waited longer, sometimes owing to practical considerations, sometimes as an almost deliberate waiting period to allow the relationship to mature. Elizabeth met Glen when they were freshmen. They dated throughout college and started to live together after they graduated. But Elizabeth felt that marriage was too important a decision to rush into before she "really knew" Glen. They finally married four years later. The final decision is usually based on a mix of practical and emotional considerations. One woman met her boyfriend when she was a senior and he was getting his master's degree. They dated for a year and then lived together for a year. Judy then was accepted into an M.B.A. program in another city. They were forced to make a choice: marry or separate. They married.

The timing of marriage does not seem to be affected much by type of professional preparation; future doctors have the longest road to travel, but they were almost as likely (23 percent) to be married by the fifth year as the average respondent (26 percent). The same is true for other professional groups.

The third peak, in the seventh year after college, represents a second wave of participants marrying at the completion of graduate studies, which they had entered after working for a couple of years. By the end of the decade, the rate of marriage for men had dropped to its lowest point since college (4.5 percent); women were marrying at double that rate (8.2 percent). The higher figure for women at this stage may reflect the advent of age thirty, that highly symbolic year in their sense of social time. For men, age thirty does not carry similar significance; age forty is more of an anticipated marker, an issue we return to later.

These ages of first marriage are higher overall by about two years than the national average. As with entry into the labor force, the educational elite get a late start relative to the general population. The main factor, of course, is their extended period of career preparation. By and large, few of them feel ready to commit to marriage before they have finished graduate school and can support themselves financially.

With respect to the various professions, between 55 and 65 percent of each group were married by the time of our survey, except the engineers, of whom only 39 percent were married. Engineers, however, were by far the most likely to be living with a partner (26 percent, compared with no more than 10 percent of any other group), contradicting the common perception of engineers as more traditional. Combining the two rates, we find little difference among the groups.

Looked at the other way around, about 30 percent of each group had never married, except for those in teaching and humanistic professions, who paired up more than others (only 21 percent of them had never married by age thirty). Individuals in these groups pursued graduate degrees, and their careers were less likely to intrude into their personal lives.

We get further insight into patterns of marital choice by looking at the linearity of relationships. Linearity in personal relationships is more difficult to assess than in careers; even our participants expressed some uncertainty about what "being in a relationship" meant. If we allow for this uncertainty and assume that age twenty-five is when the period of experimentation ends and the settling down process starts in earnest, we find that three out of four participants had basically a linear pattern of relationships, exemplified by one primary relationship that resulted in marriage or cohabitation.

Women were somewhat more linear than men (80 percent versus 70 percent), a finding consistent with the common observation that women are more monogamous and get involved in fewer short-term intimate relationships. Careerists were likewise the most linear of the four types (86 percent), Intellectuals the least (69 percent). Once again, Careerists are more conventional. Yet we find no overall relationship between linear careers and linear personal relationships. The majority of respondents are linear in both their careers and their personal lives, but less conventional patterns of career development are not linked to unconventional relationship patterns, or vice versa.

In a few cases, the decision to marry was made even before coming to college. Edward, the engineer we met before, had a girlfriend back home when he came to college. He kept his commitment to her throughout his stay and went back to marry her after graduation. ("That's not bad," he congratulated himself.) Marie was also committed to her high school boyfriend when she came to college and actually married him during the summer after her junior year, as we discuss in the next chapter.

Marie and Edward grew up in traditional families in small towns. Both were very close to their parents. These conditions are conducive to making early commitments. Neither used college as a time for exploration and experimentation in intimate relationships; their emotional ties remained solidly anchored back home. They have now established close-knit families themselves and are deeply devoted to their spouses and especially fond of their children. Edward's wife is a schoolteacher who stopped working to take care of their two children. Marie is very much the housewife and mother, handling most of the domestic chores despite her successful career in an engineering research lab.

These early relationships sometimes are slow to mature. One couple had known each other since they were on the same swim team in high school, but they did not start dating until she was in her junior year of college. They eventually married, four years after graduation.

More typically, college is a time of multiple romantic involvements, despite the common complaint on college campuses that "students do not date any more." Yet love relationships in college are like shipboard romances; the end of the journey usually leads to a parting of the ways. Aware of the dispersion that accompanies graduation, some couples refrain from getting too close; others back off as the journey approaches its end. There is some comfort in leaving things unsettled rather than saying good-bye. Those who are too close to part easily, yet not close enough to make a firm commitment, face a more painful dilemma.

Even for those who want a committed relationship, most college involvements do not survive the separation at graduation. One man and his girlfriend were seriously discussing marriage in their senior year. But when he went off to graduate school, "our attraction for each other withered as we spent time apart," he says. Nonetheless, quite a few of these relationships do survive and culminate in marriage. As we noted earlier, about one in ten in the interview sample met their spouse in college.

Generally, the educational elite are in no rush to get married. Before the first major peak four years out of college, only 20 percent were married. This delay is not only due to the demands of graduate school or career consolidation but also to their high standards for what they want in a mate. Thus, some of the attachments they make are never meant to be permanent; others do not work out despite their potential.

Trudy had her first serious relationship when she started teaching high school a year after college. Her boyfriend was a medical student, and they became engaged after he graduated. She thought they were ready for marriage, but he procrastinated. When he went off on vacation without Trudy because she could not join him, she broke off the engagement. During the past four years, she has had a number of other relationships, but none has lasted beyond six months. She says, "I have become leery of making commitments to anyone, regardless of how much he has to offer."

Immersion in work can also inhibit marriage. That first job, especially in law or business, frequently demands seventy- or eighty-hour workweeks, effectively taking the person out of circulation. Some people become absorbed in their work in order to avoid intimacy, though this tendency does not seem to be common among our participants. One exceptionally vivacious black woman says, "I had three dates in the two years after college because I was so heavily involved in my work." Her first and only serious relationship was with a fellow Harvard M.B.A. student, whom she married two years ago.

For those who pursue their careers relentlessly, meeting their eventual mates comes as a relief. "It was like letting a gust of fresh air into my life" is how one man put it. Another was totally immersed in the study and practice of law for the first five years after college. Despite the prestige of clerking for a distinguished judge in Washington, D.C., he says, "I felt miserable and lonely. It was the unhappiest time of my life. Then I met my wife. It was very joyous and has been a lot of fun."

Occasionally, unforeseen circumstances, such as an unplanned pregnancy, push a couple into marriage, but this is quite rare among the educational elite. We identified only two such cases in our sample, both involving male participants. One man had been going out with his girlfriend for several years. Though he was less keen on getting married than she was, he asked her to move in with him. Soon after, she was pregnant. He is not sure if the pregnancy was intentional, but he says, "I married her because it was the honorable thing to do. She also refused to have an abortion. That meant her raising our child by herself. I couldn't have that happen." Since there was a lot going for the relationship anyway, it was not a hard decision to make. Yet, he says, being "cornered into it" bothered him. Another man was even more concerned that his girlfriend's pregnancy after five years of living together might have been meant to force the issue. His decision was more difficult because he had had no serious intention of marrying her until then and felt far from ready to have children. In both cases, we have only the account of the man involved. None of our women participants reported a similar experience.

Finally, we must point out that for virtually all of our participants, choosing a mate is not a single-minded pursuit. Rather, it is embedded in the larger matrix of interpersonal relationships—friendships, social interaction with business associates, sexual affairs, falling in and out of love and then starting over. Finding a spouse is thus more in the nature of a leisurely fishing expedition than a grim search for a great white whale.

GENDER DIFFERENCES

Similarities in education and career have narrowed the gap dramatically in the views of women and men of the educational elite regarding marriage. None of the women need a husband for economic support, and the men are not dependent on their working wives. Emotional considerations and the desire to have a family are the primary motivations in their search for a mate.

Despite the similarities, some traditional sex differences linger on. For instance, our men indicated greater interest in temporary sexual relationships before marriage than did our women, though some women had been through periods of sexual adventuring. ("I had a wild time after college.") The generally greater importance for women of the relational component in intimate and sexual partnerships is another indication that, while the women in our group have become very much like the men with respect to their career attitudes and values, that is not the case when it comes to intimate relationships.

Another major (and probably related) gender difference is due to the "biological clock." Our women (now in their early thirties) have as yet no immediate need to be concerned about losing their reproductive capacity. But passing thirty sounds a warning signal. As they begin to anticipate reaching their midthirties unattached or childless, apprehension rises. By contrast, men are far less concerned about passing thirty. What really gets their attention is turning forty, even though that event is in the distant future. As one man said, "If I am not married by forty, I'll start worrying." Yet, an unattached woman's reaction was, "I'll be forty, my God!"

These men and women are quite aware of the gender implications of demographic realities. Since women typically marry men who are somewhat older, there is a surplus of unattached men for women in their twenties. This relative scarcity of single women puts them at a demographic advantage until, by about age thirty, the numbers even up. Then, as women move into their midthirties, they encounter a progressive scarcity of unattached men. This phenomenon is especially true for college-educated women; census figures show that they have only a 20 percent probability of getting married if they are still single at age forty.[10] Furthermore, since sexual attractiveness has traditionally been more dependent on physical looks for women and on social status for men, the effects of age become an increasingly greater concern for women as they get older.

Career-oriented women are thus in a bind. The third decade is the critical time to pursue professional training and get established in a career, but it is also the most propitious time to find a mate. Some women may be angered by such an analysis. After all, they rightly complain, they are not like ripe fruit that must be picked before it loses its value. Nor are we suggesting that women are desperate to find husbands (any more than men are desperate to find wives). Some women may not even want to have anything to do with men in their personal lives, in which case they have nothing to worry about on this score. Nevertheless, the demographic realities are what they are and almost all the unattached women in our sample want a career as well as a family. Actually, it is not marriage as such that creates most of the problems for them, but motherhood. The choice is either not to have children or (more commonly) to try to time their arrival with the least disruptive effect on careers. We return to this major issue in the next two chapters.

Modern young women also face the problem that men have become more hesitant to commit themselves to permanent relationships. This "flight from commitment" has attracted a lot of attention. It is said to be "as significant as the more explicit feminist revolt of the last two decades."[11] For one thing, the access men now have to intimate relationships with women of their own background is less dependent on prospects of marriage. For another, changing gender roles have made marriage seem more costly for men in terms of sharing household burdens, although having a working wife has its own substantial advantages as well. A typical dilemma for a young professional woman, more often than for a man, is how to convert a satisfying provisional relationship with a desirable boyfriend or domestic partner into a more permanent commitment.

While it is not our purpose to describe strategies for "how to catch a man," we are concerned with presenting the perspectives of those women who find these conditions troublesome. One key factor is whether a woman is seen by the man she cares for in generic terms as a desirable mate, or as a unique individual. For instance, Claude sees in his girlfriend a cluster of desirable features but nothing unique. Should he lose her, he knows there are other women out there with similar assets. So he is happy to live with her but not willing to marry her. If Claude saw her not just as "very good" but as "one of a kind," the prospect of losing her would give him pause. Several of the still-single men in our sample expressed regret that they had failed to appreciate the unique value of a former girlfriend and lost her with no equivalent substitute in sight. How to get that message across to men in good time rather than in retrospect is the challenge.

ETHNICITY DIFFERENCES

The rate of marriage for ethnic minorities is generally lower than for whites among the educational elite, especially for the more disadvantaged black and Hispanic groups. The proportion of those married among Asian-Americans (54 percent) is only slightly lower than for whites (61 percent), but it is much lower for African-Americans and Mexican-Americans (35 percent). The same holds true for those in domestic partnerships. Moreover, the percentage of those separated or divorced among the more disadvantaged groups is higher (chapter 8).

When we look at gender differences within each ethnic group, further distinctions come to light. For comparison, white women are more likely to be married than white men. This contrast is even more true for Asian-Americans: four out of six of the women are married and one is living with a domestic partner; among the men, only half are married. By contrast, all of the black men are married, as against only one in four of the women (and one woman is divorced). The numbers for other ethnic minorities are too small to be meaningful. But these differences are so striking that they are unlikely to be due to chance (especially since they conform to national statistics).

The most obvious, even if not the only, explanation is the number of eligible men in each group. Assuming the role of homogamy prevails, people would be expected to marry someone within their own ethnic group and with comparable occupational and personal characteristics and "assets." For our elite participants, the numbers of men and women within these ethnic groups are highly uneven. White women account for 41 percent of their group. But black women account for 72 percent of blacks in our sample, and if black men are scarce at Stanford, it is not likely that there are more of them at Harvard or Yale. This fact places an undue burden, or a double jeopardy, on black women who want both a professional career and a husband of comparable background. We illustrate this dilemma with more examples when we discuss the unmarried group.

DIFFERENCES BY TYPE

As we move away from careers and into the personal lives of our subjects, our typology begins to lose some of its differentiating and explanatory power—mainly because issues of careerism and intellectualism have a more direct bearing on occupations than on interpersonal relationships. Moreover, as the lives of our participants become subjected over time to an increasing barrage of external events and the exigencies of their particular phase of life, the differences due to type begin to level off.

We learned to our surprise that when it comes to marriage, the Unconnected are the most likely to "connect." They have the highest rate of marriage (65 percent); their opposites, the Strivers, have the lowest (55 percent). Why should this be so? Some of the Unconnected pair up to compensate for their lack of connection in other areas. For others, personal life more often takes precedence over other concerns. As for the Strivers, they are so preoccupied with careers and other pursuits that they have less time and energy for marriage, even though they are as committed to the idea of it as any other type.

Introducing the factor of gender makes these findings even more intriguing (see table 9, appendix A). The low marriage rate among Strivers turns out to be the doing of the women in the group. Women Strivers are by far the least likely to marry of all the women; only half of them had married by the tenth year, compared with at least three-quarters of women of other types. By contrast, men Strivers were no less likely to marry than other men. Careerism as such does not interfere with marriage (Careerist women marry as much as any other type), but women who place great emphasis on both careers and their broader intellectual and other interests seem to simply spread themselves too thin. They have less room in their lives for permanent relationships. As for the low propensity of Intellectual men to marry, we suspect that it is mainly a function of their relatively slow career development. As only fourteen men are involved here, it may also be due to idiosyncratic factors.

COHABITATION

The U.S. Census Bureau defines cohabitation as "persons of opposite sex sharing living quarters."[12] We use the term "domestic partner" here with the assumption that the couple living together is not simply sharing a dwelling for convenience but is romantically or sexually involved. This would exclude, for instance, one of our gay men, who rents one of the bedrooms in his two-bedroom San Francisco apartment to a woman. They share the kitchen but do not cook or eat together. They even share the one bathroom in the house, but despite the intimacy this may suggest, they do not even pretend to be friends.

An estimated 3.3 million unmarried couples are currently living together in the United States, six times the number in 1970.[13] They are primarily young adults: almost 70 percent are younger than thirty-five, and one-quarter are under twenty-five. One-quarter of college graduates have lived with someone for some time, and twice that many say they would like to do so. In Sweden, cohabitation has become part of the social norm—90 percent of adults report having had the experience. Although over 250,000 children live with cohabiting couples in the United States, most are from previous marriages; domestic partners are generally unlikely to have children.[14]

Among our participants, 10 percent were living with a partner of the opposite sex ten years out of college (about the same proportion of men as women). In addition, about 25 percent had lived with their future spouses, or someone they did not marry, for periods ranging from several months to five years. Others had had domestic partners whom they did not marry.

Hence, about one in three of our participants cohabited with someone for some time during the decade after college—making it a much more common practice than we encounter in the general population, but not atypical of their age cohort.

As with marriage, the Unconnected lead the way. One in six was living with a partner; only one in twenty Careerists was in a "marriage-equivalent" situation. This finding is a reflection of the Unconnected being less conventional. Careerists, on the other hand, confirm once again their conventionality.

The cohabiting relationship may have legal standing only as common-law marriage, which is recognized only in some jurisdictions. But the reciprocal responsibilities and expectations of the couple are usually quite similar to those who are married. Why then do these couples live together instead of getting married? Some people object to marriage in principle as a sexist and exploitative institution, but none of our cohabiting participants was motivated by such ideological fervor. Others see practical merits in living together compared with marriage: women have greater freedom to pursue careers (familial pressure to have children is much lower if they are not married); men can avoid legal and economic obligations; both sexes enjoy a greater sense of independence and autonomy. For same-sex couples, this is the only type of relationship available under current laws.

Such considerations were also not paramount for most of our cohabiting participants. Rather, they typically fall in one of two categories. For some, living together is simply a prelude to marriage while they work out practical or external matters. Others are still scrutinizing the prospect of marriage, either generally or with respect to their specific domestic partner. The experience of living together was expected to provide those in a serious relationship greater exposure to the partner, not only in the glow of candlelight dinners but in the glare of the breakfast table. They hoped to dispel false and faulty perceptions and thus avoid subsequent disillusionment. Cohabitation was the ultimate "road test" of the relationship, a sort of trial marriage. As a result, couples living together seem to be in a holding pattern. Some are about to land in marriage; others are circling high above wondering if they should head toward another destination.

It is thus no wonder that these relationships reveal a considerable range of commitment. At one end, we have couples who are virtually married. David Levy and his partner Judith are formally engaged to be married after a long period of cohabitation. Ted is seriously interested in marrying Debra, but not quite ready to take the plunge. Prior to his relationship with her, Ted had had a succession of liaisons, starting with his college girlfriend in an on-and-off relationship during the five years she was in medical school. After she graduated, they drifted apart without a formal break.

Ted then got into a pattern of dating women for six-month periods. When the standard six months ended with Debra, he wanted to stay with her, so they moved in together. Ted says, "We are committed to each other. We are quite compatible and happy, and I especially like the sense of constancy after being on the six-month roller coaster for so long." Debra is "monitoring" the relationship and from time to time likes to talk things over "to update its emotional content and quality." Is marriage likely for Ted and Debra? "We have discussed it," says Ted, "but are concerned that formalizing our relationship may increase the potential for failure." He has consulted his married brothers, who think Debra is "terrific" and have urged him to marry her. "But," he says, "I can't take that step yet."

A more complicated situation faces Aretha. She is a lawyer, and as a highly educated black woman, she faces the serious shortage of highly educated black men we noted above. Three years ago Aretha met Thomas, several years younger and just entering law school. They started going out and then moved in together, though Thomas kept his own apartment as a place to study. Aretha and Thomas have developed a close and satisfying relationship, but it still falls short of a definitive commitment. She is ready to marry and eager to have children; he says he does not want children. She ascribes this feeling to his being an only child and is confident that "once we have children he will love them." Another complication has to do with their careers. She is already fairly well established; he is just starting. Job opportunities are limited where they live. Do they move? Who follows whom?

In at least one case, living together appears to be a substitute for, rather than a prelude to, marriage. Fernando had a four-year relationship with a social worker who was very keen on marriage. He was not, so she finally left him. He then met a woman from Argentina. They began to live together and recently bought a house. But this is no prelude to marriage. He says, "I am skeptical about marriage. . . . My mother left my dad when I was five. I have a very unstable family model." In this case, the rejection, or at least indefinite postponement, of marriage is presumably by mutual consent. Yet, under the surface, the primary obstacle is Fernando's reluctance to commit himself.

The dynamics of male hesitancy about commitment are well illustrated in Ben's life. Setting aside his many casual involvements, three women have been significant to him. The first was his Stanford girlfriend, Laura, "a woman with remarkable abilities." He says, "We fit together well and got along famously." But Ben was in no mood to settle down. In his senior year he said, "I can't think of myself as anything but a bachelor. It upsets me to see my friends getting picked off one by one."

Though Laura and Ben went their separate ways, they retained a strong sense of attachment. When Laura's father died, Ben stood by her. When her mother developed cancer, she turned to him for comfort. Late one night, she called him when Ben happened to be with another woman. As Laura poured out her grief, the other woman ("a demanding and high-maintenance type," he explains) became miffed. So Ben cut short his conversation with Laura, for which he has not forgiven himself.

Following business school, Ben met Linda, a young lawyer. Once again he established a satisfying relationship, but when she began making noises about settling down, he turned cold. Ben returned to Phoenix, his and Laura's hometown, and they resumed their relationship. Though he never explicitly admitted being in love with her, the way Ben spoke of the intensity of his "first feeling" for her leaves little doubt about how much he cared for her. Yet the familiar pattern repeated itself: she wanted to finalize their commitment, he demurred. So Laura married someone else. They have remained friends.

Ben's third and current serious relationship is with Alexis. They work in the same industry. "She is an attractive, athletic, smart woman," he says. "Everyone in Western civilization, including my mother, thinks she will make an excellent wife." Why are they not married? Ben is hard-pressed to explain. For one thing, he has become well able to look after himself. He is a good cook, keeps an orderly house, and has an active social life in the community. More important, he views marriage as "costly" to his freedom; he would have to restrict himself to one woman for life. In principle, he is committed to the idea of marriage and wants to have a family. In practice, he is not. "I don't really try to analyze these issues rationally," explains Ben. "Instead, I listen to my gut, and so far I have not heard the command, 'Do it.' I realize time is passing, but I hear no clock ticking."

Ben wants to be fair to Alexis and will not stay with her if he is "no longer adding something to her life." Marrying her would add a good deal to her life, but Ben is not sure it would add enough to his, at least not in the foreseeable future.

GAY PARTNERSHIPS

The law does not recognize marriages between same-sex couples, but some cities, like New York and San Francisco, do allow gay and lesbian couples to register as domestic partners. This provides largely symbolic satisfaction but also some practical benefits.[15] Same-sex partnerships are in many ways quite similar to those of their heterosexual counterparts.

Four men in the interview sample (4 percent) were exclusively gay, a proportion that is consistent with the more reliable current national figures.[16] A fifth man was bisexual. He has been dating women while being aware of his attraction to men. He now frequents gay bars, but his physical contact with men is restricted to dancing.

None of the women in the interview sample were self-declared lesbians. This is not to say that none of the women (or none of the men other than those mentioned) have had homosexual experiences. Homosexuality among women is reported to occur usually at about one-third the rate of men, so the fact that none surfaced in a sample of this size is not surprising. What concerns us here, in any event, is not sexual behavior as such, but the way it influences the shaping of intimate relationships. None of the women in the interview sample were cohabiting with other women.

The four exclusively gay men in our sample are not currently living with a partner, although all of them say they would like to.[17] Nonetheless, they all have been or are in close intimate relationships. Since we have too few people in this category for systematic analysis, we will let the stories of their lives speak for them. And since far less is usually known about gay members of the educational elite, we will tell their stories at some length.

Ray came to the follow-up interview dressed in jeans and a short-sleeved shirt, with a ring in his left ear. Looking like a graduate student, he was articulate and cordial, with a wry sense of humor. Ray's personal life, as well as career, had been profoundly affected by his "coming out mentally as gay." Ray had been aware of his sexual attraction to boys during adolescence. In college he tried to do the "conventional thing," making several attempts to date women. When that went poorly, he resigned himself to an "asexual life." This pattern persisted after college.

"At age twenty-four, I had an identity crisis," Ray explains. "I no longer wanted to deny my sexuality. So I had my first sexual experience with another man." The transition was traumatic. "I went through some of the darkest moments of my life. I was depressed, drinking heavily, listening to bad music, and seeking refuge in sleep." His acerbic manner had been an ongoing problem at work, and now the situation worsened. After an argument with his boss, he walked out. With his newfound gay self, Ray no longer felt he belonged in the world of business. He drew on his student experience in journalism to land a job with a publisher. Eventually he moved into his current job as the managing editor of a magazine in Los Angeles.

Ray's biggest hurdle was revealing his homosexuality to his family. His father had always been emotionally distant. "He never touched me throughout my life, except to shake my hand at Christmas," Ray recalls. "A very analytical, cerebral sort of man." After the initial shock of Ray's revelation, his father tried to be understanding, but their relationship remains strained. The situation is somewhat better with his mother, who nonetheless mourns the loss of prospective grandchildren.

Ray's first, and so far only, close relationship has been with an older gay man in a stable relationship with another man. Though this put Ray in a marginal position, he says, "It was the first time I was truly in love. It helped me grow from an emotionally immature adolescent to an adult. I had always felt enormously maladapted but now could see myself as someone who could be liked and loved by others." He adds, "My involvement in gay organizations further empowered me to believe in my ability to change things." The relationship ended after a year. At the moment, Ray would welcome another close companion, but he has no interest in living with someone. He says, "My sense of independence, feistiness, and unwillingness to compromise would create problems."

Luke's life has also been marked by considerable turmoil. The awareness of his homosexuality goes back to his youth, when he consistently fought it off. His parents worked for a religious organization, and Luke had firmly accepted their moral values, which condemned homosexuality. But by his junior year in high school, he could no longer ignore or suppress his sexual feelings. Nevertheless, it was not until his junior year in college that he came out and became active in the gay subculture. Luke says, "I went through a compulsive disclosure phase during which I was telling every waiter in every restaurant that I was gay." He confronted his parents rather abruptly, and they took it hard. A psychologist at their church helped smooth things over, but his parents remain dejected. After college, Luke went through a phase of sexual experimentation. He moved to Los Angeles, where conflicts in his personal life and trouble at work led to serious drinking problems. He returned to the San Francisco Bay Area, joined Alcoholics Anonymous, and got his drinking under control. Rather than get another job, he started his own desktop publishing business. Though Luke views his drinking as a consequence of the stresses of his life, his alcoholism itself may have been at the root of a lot of his problems.

Luke's career and emotional life are now firmly back on track. He feels settled and content. He is dating a man but still feels unsure about establishing a stable long-term relationship with him. The idea of such a relationship appeals to him, but he is leery of painful entanglements. He may go on with his rather solitary but by no means lonely life. He seems very much at peace with himself.

David characterizes his younger years as "relatively asexual" until he had his first sexual encounter with a man at age nineteen. From then on he was a confirmed homosexual; he has never felt sexually or romantically attracted to women. The second youngest child of a large and conventional

Asian-American family, David came to college with high expectations. His widowed mother hoped he would become a doctor. He obliged her by starting on the premedical track but did not do well and dropped it. He was burdened by self-doubt ("I don't know if I am good enough"), and he never settled on a definitive career. For a period of four years after college, David was involved with a bisexual man. Since then, there have been a few other men in his life but nothing as intense as that experience. He says, "I am looking for a man with that special spark who is also intelligent, loving, self-assured, and has gotten his head together."

In contrast to the rather turbulent lives and careers of these three gay men, Theodore has had a very linear career in engineering. He has done very well and now supervises a staff of over 250 people. He enjoys his work "immensely" but has a fantasy of owning and operating his own restaurant someday.

Theodore has been aware of being gay since his youth but kept it to himself, not even telling the woman therapist whom he saw for two and a half years for his problems with self-esteem. She became quite significant in his life. "She is a woman who really helped me. She helped me heal myself, helped me learn how to love myself, and helped me treat myself as an individual." He told the therapist in parting, "There is something else I need to work out on my own, and someday I will tell you about it."

Theodore came out as a gay man only in his late twenties. He has since established an intimate relationship with another man. Though his lover lives in another city, they spend most weekends together. He feels content and committed. He hopes they will live together someday, even bringing up adoptive children, since both are strongly family-oriented.

BEING SINGLE

Over the past several decades, singlehood has come to be seen more as a positive choice than as merely a failure to get married, and it is now recognized that being alone is not the same as being lonely. In the past, aging "bachelors" and "spinsters" were viewed with a mixture of pity and suspicion (and perhaps a bit of envy). These labels have now gone out of fashion, and the single life is perceived to have its own rewards. Not only does it avoid the burdens of marriage and the disillusionment of unhappy unions, it offers its own satisfactions in terms of greater independence, career options, mobility, self-fulfillment, and enjoyment of life. This is reflected in (as well as influenced by) the fact that the number of unmarried men and women doubled between the 1960s and the mid-1980s. The number of men living alone increased by 60 percent and women by 40 percent.[18]

Nevertheless, the norm in American society, despite important changes in social attitudes, is still to consider marriage and parenthood evidence of full adulthood. The never-married are still seen as outside the mainstream of society. (Imagine an unmarried man, let alone a single woman, as president of the United States.) Hence, it is not surprising that virtually all of the single men and women in our sample would rather be married or living with a partner, given the right person and circumstances.

PATTERNS OF SINGLE LIFE

Just over one in four of our participants (25 percent of women, 30 percent of men) had never married by the end of the first decade after graduation. In addition, 5 percent of the sample (8 percent of those ever married) are separated or divorced. (We deal with the divorced group in chapter 8.)

The lives of the thirty-one single men and women in the interview sample reveal a variety of relational patterns. Some are, or have been, in intimate relationships that are as close as those of cohabiting or married couples. Others have had few or no intimate ties whatsoever.

Rebecca is an example of a single woman who has had a rich emotional life. "I have been seriously in love three times," she says, "while also having had several less intense relationships." Her first love was a musician. "He opened up a new realm of musical experience for me," explains Rebecca, who still plays in a "garage-type band." The relationship ended after two years because she found him intellectually limited (she is a brilliant scientist). Her next relationship, with a graduate student in history, opened up further intellectual vistas for her. This "minor" relationship was followed by her second "major" love. "It was rather bizarre," she says. "He was unhappily married but would not leave his wife because of his two children. Had he left his family, I would have married him." This man was able to meet Rebecca's demanding emotional and intellectual expectations. Nonetheless, "in retrospect, it would have been a big mistake." Her third "major" and current love is "wonderful in all respects." He is a few years younger and has just finished his Ph.D. in physics. The son of a prominent family in South America, he is eager to return home, but Rebecca has no wish to relocate. The relationship is strong enough that she thinks they will work something out.

Others in the singles group nearly married but their relationships collapsed. We already related Gail's experience with her medical student fiancé. Jason's breakup was even more traumatic. A successful, thoughtful, and likable young man, Jason is the sort of person we would have expected to marry rather early. He met Ingrid soon after graduation and became deeply attached to her. They kept in touch while she went to India with the Peace Corps and he went to graduate school to get his Ph.D. in applied physics. On her return, they got engaged, but shortly after she changed her mind and broke off the relationship. The breakup was due largely to a clash of values. Jason is a politically conservative scientist engaged in sophisticated weapons research. Ingrid is an artist and a political liberal dedicated to peace. Additional differences in their "styles of communication" made it all the more difficult to bridge the ideological gap. Jason referred to the episode as "meeting someone special and losing someone special," saying they were the best and the worst events in his personal life. He is still heartbroken.

Our men include only a few "swinging singles." Scott is a handsome young businessman with longish hair and a relaxed, self-satisfied smile. He tells the tales of his romantic adventures with relish. "The first two years after college, when I used to travel a lot, was a dry spell," explains Scott, "although there were a few cuties along the way." His first serious relationship was with a law student while he was in business school. When she began to push for marriage, Scott fled. Another "dry spell" was relieved when he began courting two women simultaneously in two different cities. Both of these relationships "crashed and burned." A succession of other relationships met the same fate. He is currently dating a college student, but that relationship also seems destined to crash and burn. Scott is simply neither willing nor ready to commit himself to any one woman indefinitely, at least not at this time.

REASONS FOR REMAINING SINGLE

All of our single participants appear to be eligible young men and women. So why have they remained single? To explore this issue, we asked them three questions: Have there been external obstacles to your getting married? Have you not found the right person? Are you not ready yet to make a commitment? Half of them ascribed their singlehood to not having found the right person. The balance split between those citing external obstacles and those not being ready for commitment.

The issue of external obstacles was the most straightforward. The opposition of Teresa's parents to Daniel is one good example. Daniel fell in love with Teresa in college, and their relationship continued for five years beyond graduation. When they decided to marry, her Catholic parents did not like his career prospects and objected to his not being Catholic. Teresa stood by Daniel, but eventually her parents prevailed; she simply could not bring herself to break with her family. It was a hard blow for Daniel; he still sighs when telling the story.

Having a married lover presented one woman with an obvious obstacle. Tseng's problem is of a different kind. He had just finished medical school when he fell in love with a fellow intern. They were considering marriage when her former boyfriend committed suicide. She blamed herself and became distraught. Tseng stood by her, but he gradually came to feel more like an emotional crutch than her lover. So he broke off the relationship.

Examples multiply rapidly when we bring career considerations into the picture. For the past five years, Araxie and her boyfriend have been working on their doctorates. She lives on the East Coast, he on the West Coast. They speak on the phone every night and will get married as soon as they graduate, but a 3,000-mile marriage makes no sense to them. Others who have avoided settling down in anticipation of career conflicts say:

- I have placed too much emphasis on job and career.
- My girlfriend was very eager to get married and have kids, but I wasn't sure how my career would combine with family obligations.
- I have put work first and then love. Now they are more even. I am dating someone now, but I wonder if he is willing to go with me wherever my job takes me.
- I don't want to marry a woman with no career aspirations. But I have no intention of interrupting my career to look after kids. I know this may sound sexist.
- It is very difficult to balance personal and professional lives. I have a colleague with an eight-year-old son who is constantly torn between her job and her home life. I don't want to be in the same situation.
- I work very hard. I don't make myself available for any social life.
- The only thing missing from my personal life is some ongoing relationship. My friends are always setting up blind dates for me, but they never work out. It takes so long to get to know someone, and I don't have time.
- My job insecurity has caused me to question marriage and child rearing.

It could be argued that career-related concerns are not external obstacles but deliberate choices. Single-minded dedication to one's career restricts the time available to meet people and cultivate relationships. It can also turn one into the sort of person who is less likely to be seen as a desirable mate. While both of these considerations apply to both sexes, they have a more compelling impact on women.

Dedication to career penalizes women more than men. Women clearly have more to worry about when it comes to the impact of marriage and parenthood on careers because by and large they are the ones who end up shouldering the primary responsibility on the home front. On the other hand, some men reject women who develop the very characteristics that are admired in successful professional men (assertiveness, decisiveness, ambition, driving oneself and others relentlessly, and so on). This double standard places ambitious career women in an obvious bind; they must be assertive on the job but adopt a very different role in personal relationships. For men, a fair measure of assertiveness both at work and in courtship is seen as normal. As one woman said,

> I have several women friends who have no marriage prospects at all. Men are put off by aggressive women. My friends who are in this category are not just assertive, they are aggressive. So for some men, especially of an older generation, this is a bit difficult. What these women want for themselves are men who are very bright and able but not very aggressive. For example, one of my friends finally got married to a man who is brilliant but kind of lazy. So she runs everything. These women don't want a man who is just as aggressive as they are because that would mean a constant battle. But these women also don't want a man who is not capable and accomplished.

How sensitive some men are to this issue is illustrated by Jennifer's experience with her husband. They are managers in different divisions of the same company. After a meeting that Jennifer had run with brisk efficiency, her husband had heard some of the men commenting on how forceful she was. This embarrassed him because he feared people would infer that if Jennifer was so assertive at work, she would be likewise at home, reflecting badly on him. So he told her, "I don't want you running meetings like that."

Some of our men tried to skirt this issue, but others were more outspoken. One man says, "I am put off by the aggressiveness of the women lawyers I work with. I don't blame them, they have tough jobs. But that doesn't help me get close to them. I want my wife to be intelligent and well-educated but also supportive, caring, not pushy and competitive. She must be fun, friendly, and easy to live with. Not a feisty woman who is into sparring."

"I have not found the right person" is not only the most commonly cited reason for not getting married, it is also the most socially acceptable.

It implies that you are thoughtful, selective, and unwilling to settle for just anyone. To admit that there are external obstacles reflects poorly on your ability to overcome them. And to say you are not ready to make a commitment suggests that you are immature. So we suspect that many of the statements about not having found the right person were smoke screens for other reasons, especially that of not wanting to make a commitment.

Sometimes the standards are set so high that they virtually ensure that a mate will never be found. One man said with a sigh, "They all look good on paper, but in actual experience they don't live up to my expectations." Sandra's very high standards compound the problems that arise from her highly successful career and forceful personality. Poised, attractive, and elegantly dressed, Sandra is a highly competent vice president of a major bank in New York. By any reasonable standard, she should be the answer to many a man's dream, yet she is unattached. She does not lack good friends, and she has had several men in her life, but none have endured. As she explains, "I am ferociously independent and very committed to my work. I also have very high standards and expectations of the men I meet. As a result, I have built a wall around myself. The man I want would have to be highly accomplished, self-confident, ambitious, and with a sense of humor. A rather sensible and conservative person who should have at the same time an open mind."

Despite her high expectations, Sandra is willing to make allowances. "With such a person," Sandra says, "I would be willing to be more flexible and make compromises. I will take primary responsibility for raising our children, and I would not even mind taking care of him as well." Other participants said:

- I want a man who would be a good companion. Someone seriously engaged in his work but not a slave to it. Someone I'll be able to share my life interests, values, and outlook with.
- The woman I am looking for should have two sides to her. On the one hand, she should be intelligent, well-educated, professionally accomplished, interested in philosophical discussions. On the other hand, there should be a frivolous and light side to her.
- Most important for me is for the woman to have spunk. I have a sarcastic wit; she should be able to tolerate it. She should certainly be intelligent. I have seen medical students marry nurses whom they then leave behind. Yet, I have no wish to marry another doctor.

As we discussed earlier, ethnic minority women of the educational elite, especially African-Americans, have an unusually difficult time finding the right man since there are relatively few men of the same ethnic and educational background to choose from. Victoria is a black physician. Her lengthy period of education and training left little opportunity to meet men. At the end of her specialty training, she felt, "I may have now priced myself out of the market." When she met an interesting black lawyer on a plane, his reaction to her was, "Wow! I could never go out with someone like you!" There is, nonetheless, a glimmer of hope. An old friend from her residency days has been recently manifesting some romantic interest. "Things are not clicking yet," says Victoria, "but there is hope."

Ruby is a bright and successful executive. Her peers at work are mainly white, middle-aged, married men—not the best marriage prospects for her. She has bought a five-bedroom house, furnished it with antiques, and is waiting for the "right man." But Ruby knows that "there are not many of them out there," and she adds, "The typical black man with a successful career would not be interested in me anyway. He would find a secretary or a receptionist who will be glad to quit her job and take care of him."

Ruby thinks she has less of a chance to marry a black man than a white man, though she is well aware of the odds on that score. Nonetheless, she recently met a man who shows promise. He is a black social worker who comes from a well-off family and is thus less likely to be intimidated by her six-figure income (which she expects to rise to $500,000 in ten years). Ruby's mother is urging her to "go after him." It is not a perfect match, but Ruby is giving it serious thought. Otherwise, she will settle for remaining single and in a few years adopt one or two children and raise them on her own.

Generally, single men are less clear about what they are looking for than single women, who know what they want but cannot find it. A much greater proportion of single women than men (71 percent versus 36 percent) said they have not found the right person, while none of the women and 36 percent of the men said they were not ready to make a commitment.

The single men who live alone are even more set in their independent ways than the cohabiting men who are reluctant to make a commitment. Sometimes this trait is part of a broader pattern. For example, one man says, "I have been on a two-year plan with jobs and a two-month plan in relationships. I am attracted to relationships with built-in expiration dates." He ascribes this preference to the difficulty he has trusting people, a lingering effect of his breakup with his college girlfriend. Yet, he is not content with his situation. "I am trying to learn to give more, adapt more, and compromise more. I expect to be married with children at some point, but I still feel I have a ways to go."

A number of these men seem to always be on the move—rolling stones that gather no moss. "I avoid getting close to women until there is something on the horizon which would necessitate my moving" is the way one of them put it. This pattern also characterizes at least one of our single women. Janice's exceptionally disjointed career has been matched by her equally uneven personal life. "No man has touched my heart," she says, although she was engaged to a man who "turned out to be wrong." He was a staid businessman who wanted a settled life; she did not. The next man was "the total opposite, a totally irresponsible and emotionally intense person who had no use for marriage." Other stillborn relationships followed. It is hard to tell whether Janice's lack of commitment both at work and in her personal life is a general problem or whether instability in one area disrupts the other as well.

In some instances, it was clear that this behavior pattern was related to specific life experiences. Perry is a good example. A youthful, pleasant, easygoing, and successful lawyer, he owns a home and for all intents and purposes seems ready to settle down. Yet, he says, "I have never been truly in love," a situation he first ascribed to his career being unsettled until recently. Then he claimed that the problem was his "inability to find the right person," and then again, his "unwillingness to be pressured into a relationship." Finally, it emerged that Perry had been overweight in his younger years and that experience had damaged his self-image. He has been told that he has a "boyish cuddly charm" that many women love. Yet he feels shy and awkward in responding to them.

Jack also happens to be a lawyer. He is an athletic, rather reserved person who nonetheless willingly explored the roots of his unattached status. Like Perry, he has never had an intense love experience. The woman he has been closest to is a friend and fellow lawyer (the wife of a colleague). They provide support and understanding to each other, but there are no romantic or erotic undercurrents in the relationship. He has dated some women, but these relationships only last a few months. ("After we break up, she becomes just a friend.")

The first explanation Jack offered was the standard "I haven't found the right person." But women have told him he is "too set in his ways for any woman to fit in." The person he is looking for should be intelligent, well-educated, and athletic. Jack himself is an avid athlete, so the commonality of interest is one factor. He also confesses to being "sexually attracted only to very athletic women." So he is looking for more than aerobic fitness. Jack lives in Washington, D.C., which is populated by a great many young women who meet these requirements, as Jack is well aware. But he has yet to find the right person.

After further probing, Jack revealed that he was brought up in a family that was closely tied to a small, highly restrictive, evangelical church. During his college years, Jack had gradually distanced himself from that community, but only with great difficulty. Since then, he has ostensibly broken loose entirely. He is no longer ruled by the moral stringency of his former church, but he has not developed an adequate substitute for it. His sense of identity is no longer anchored in his family, but he has not fashioned a new self of his own. Deep down, Jack still does not know who he is or wants to be, hence, he cannot very well find a partner who would suit him.

CHAPTER 7

Patterns of Family Life

Growing up at home and living in a college dorm are hardly a full rehearsal for setting up a household. Picking a life companion and establishing one's own residence give young adults a new measure of autonomy, as well as complex responsibilities they have never before faced. However much in love a couple may be, they are strangers to each other with respect to the everyday details of routine living until they share a household. Doing so calls for a great deal of adaptation and compromise before the gears of their lives mesh together.

Dual-career couples face an additional challenge. Neither person is willing or able to take full charge of the household. Working out a division of labor that not only matches tasks with the abilities and interests of each person but also satisfies the ideology of equality between the sexes is no easy matter. How effectively a couple works out the mundane and unromantic logistics of living together strongly influences the development of their relationship. Not only is the issue of obvious practical importance, it has a direct impact on each partner's emotional experience of the other.

The burdens as well as the joys of managing a household are greatly magnified with the arrival of children. Parenthood, more than any other aspect of personal life, has an extraordinary impact on young women and men, perhaps even more so for the educational elite than for other young couples.

THE PROFILE GROUP

All the couples in the profile group have worked out ways of sharing the burdens of managing the household. These arrangements vary considerably and have changed over time, the arrival of children necessitating the most significant shifts for four of the five married couples who are parents.

Both profile Careerists have spouses who have taken on the primary burden of managing the household. Before the arrival of their first child, Martin MacMillan and his wife (who worked full-time as a nurse) divided up the household tasks fairly evenly, though she had the ultimate responsibility. After the birth of their son and then their daughter, she stayed home to take care of the children and manage the house with the help of a housekeeper. Since then, she has gone back to work part-time. She is currently carrying their third child and will again stop work for a while. "Of course, I wouldn't consider such a drastic step for myself," says Martin, tongue in cheek.

Martin helps take care of their children in the evenings and on weekends. As a physician, he is highly qualified to care for them when they are sick. When he comes home in the evening and his wife is eager to get some relief, he says, "I sometimes feel like I am starting on a second shift at the hospital." He is a very caring father.

Careerist Cynthia Eastwood is pleased to describe her husband Jeffrey as "the perfect wife." While he has not taken overall charge of the house, Jeffrey does more than his share (while also working as hard as Cynthia). They have no children. Cynthia was ready to get pregnant, but her last business venture made motherhood "out of the question." Jeffrey is a fine cook, and on those evenings when he comes home very late, he buys his dinner and brings it home with him. So Cynthia does little cooking. Jeffrey is also a meticulous housekeeper with a keen eye for interior decoration. Cynthia does the shopping and pays the bills. She is in charge of their social life and keeps in touch with their vast network of friends. When they do have a child, they plan to hire a live-in nanny; they have no intention of interrupting their careers.

Our two Intellectuals differ sharply in their family lives. Kirsten Buchanan is more thoroughly immersed in her family than anyone else in the profile group; Christopher Luce is the least burdened by considerations of marriage and parenthood. Prior to the birth of their unplanned (but very much wanted) first child, Kirsten and her husband Tom split the household responsibilities between them, "equal all the way." But the arrival of their daughter changed all that. Kirsten says: "Tom and I agreed before we got married that someone was going to stay home full-time with our future children. Our first surprise came in the middle of Tom's fellowship, hence, I got to stay home with the baby, much to Tom's dismay. (Also, he was lousy at breast-feeding.) His great hope is that someday I will earn enough money so both of us can be home part-time." Kirsten now stays home caring for her son and his little sister. Tom helps over the weekends and on special occasions to the extent that his pressing schedule as a physician allows.

One of Intellectual Christopher Luce's reasons for remaining single is his strong desire not to become encumbered by family responsibilities. Having observed the chaos of a household with young children, he worries that he would not be able to get much work done. "Scholarship is a solitary pursuit, requiring an immense amount of concentration. I struggle with that as it is. I don't know how I would manage to get anything done with children to care for." When he does marry, Christopher hopes to delay parenthood until he has tenure.

The association between Striver Geraldine Jones and her domestic partner, Tony, is a troubled one. Some of their problems lie in the very nature of their relationship, but some have also arisen from the logistics of living together. Tony, the "pampered son of a traditional Italian mother is used to being taken care of." His housekeeping standards are not up to Geraldine's. So she ends up doing far more than her share, even though she has a great deal more to do outside the home than he does. These aggravations add to her uncertainty about their future together. Under the circumstances, Geraldine is not about to have children, even though she would dearly love to be a mother someday.

Compared with Geraldine Jones's situation, the management of Striver George Mehta's household has been a model of shared responsibility. Before they became parents, George and his wife Claudia each did a "bit of everything" and usually cooked together. George took care of the yard while Claudia paid the bills. With the coming of their first child, Claudia planned to stay home for a couple of years, but George was determined to do his share in bringing up their child. When George suffered a stroke, their carefully laid plans were disrupted. His physical limitations made it hard for him to help, but now that he can do "pretty much everything," he helps in all respects, including child care.

Unconnected David Levy's egalitarian management of the household he shares with Judith hardly comes as a surprise. "We have chosen what we like to do," says David. "It is fairly equal, both in terms of time and commitment." Judith does more of the shopping and cooking, and David does more of the housekeeping. When they have children, who does what will depend on their respective jobs. "Currently, I have a very flexible schedule," says David. "If I get into another type of job, it will be more difficult. But we will somehow work things out."

Unconnected Katherine Johnson has an unusual husband who has taken over the primary responsibility for their house and child (assisted by a housekeeper and nanny). He comes home in the afternoon and takes over when their household help leaves. When Katherine comes home from work late in the evening, dinner is ready and their son is bathed and fed. Back when they were both in law school and living together, Katherine and her husband split housekeeping chores evenly. As her work hours expanded, her husband took over more of the responsibilities. Katherine is both pleased and uneasy. She says, "When my husband gets back on a more demanding work schedule, I hope to restructure my hours so that I can do at home what he is doing now. I would prefer to contribute more to managing the house and taking care of our child."

BUYING A RESIDENCE

For young adults, purchasing their first home is not just a financial decision but a symbol of the attainment of full economic and social independence. It is a way of making clear that the new social unit they constitute is established on solid ground.

Fully 64 percent of our married participants bought a residence during the first decade after college. Only 30 percent of those who had never married had bought a residence, even though a substantial portion (about one-third) were living with a domestic partner. Parenthood pushes the home-ownership figure even higher, to 74 percent (compared with only 40 percent for those without children).

There are no gender differences in home ownership: women are as likely to be involved in a home purchase as men. But there are clear differences among types, in line with income differential: Careerists lead the way (62 percent), and Intellectuals are at the bottom (43 percent). Relatively low numbers of doctors, teachers, and those in the humanist professions own their homes. This is certain to change soon for physicians, many of whom are just launching their careers, but probably not for the latter group, whose incomes are likely to stay relatively low for some time.

We had the opportunity to see only a few of our participants' homes. Clint, a married Careerist, lives in an impressively grand (though still sparsely furnished) home in a select suburb of Los Angeles. Luke, the gay Intellectual, has a small, cozy apartment in San Francisco, with bookcases on every wall. Their homes are faithful reflections of the men and their lifestyles. At the time of his graduation from college, Clint had no trouble imagining where he would be in ten years. "I will be vice president of a firm in southern California, driving a blue Mercedes 480SL and living in a nice house with a view of the ocean. I will be financially secure, love my job, and have all the things I want. I'll be raising a family of one or two children, maintaining a spiritual standard for my family; in short, I'll be your stereotypical executive."

Except for a few details (no view of the ocean and no blue Mercedes yet), Clint is just about where he thought he would be. If Clint's abode is a monument for the world to see and conveys a sense of the material success of its owner, Luke's house is a refuge to shelter him from the world, a house in which to pursue the serene pleasures of the life of the mind. His expectation ten years ago was "to be settled on the West Coast, working in a satisfying job (not necessarily my ultimate career position though), involved in a satisfying love relationship (probably not married)." Luke, too, is just about where he thought he would be—as far away from someone like Clint as one can imagine.

We asked our participants about the importance of various factors in choosing their residential location. The most important factor overall was opportunities for employment—they move to their jobs, rather than seeking jobs where they are. Again, if not surprisingly, their careerism shows through: jobs come first. Second most important was the type of living environment—urban and full of hustle and bustle for some, more relaxed and suburban, or almost rural, for others. These two factors were far more important than any others. Most important among the subsidiary considerations were opportunities for intellectual growth, career opportunities for one's spouse, and proximity to friends.

Differences between the reasons men and women have for choosing their residential location are quite modest. The only items that show significant differences are all career-related: women put less emphasis than men on their own employment opportunities, and they put more emphasis than men on their partner's career opportunities. This finding is our first clear, albeit modest, bit of evidence that educational elite women put themselves in any sort of backseat.

Among the four types, only one result stands out: Strivers put more emphasis on the whole range of factors than does any other type, and the Unconnected put less emphasis on many of the factors than do other types. We saw a similar result in the cohort study: Strivers generally attribute greater importance to all sorts of things; the Unconnected see everything as less important. Thus, what is most interesting here is the relative lack of differences, in that career-related items are of generally greatest importance for all four types, including Intellectuals. Cultural opportunities are of only modest importance for all types; community affairs and investment opportunities are least important, a harbinger of where these issues stand in their lives (chapter 9).

MANAGING A HOUSEHOLD

Who does what in the household is one of the key issues confronting couples of the educational elite. For two-career couples, time is indeed the fundamental scarce resource.[1] At the most practical level, the extent to which partners share the burdens of housework and domestic management has a profound effect on the quality of their daily lives and their relationships.

The tasks of managing a household are closely tied to those of caring for children. Most of our couples had no difficulty working out arrangements for sharing household burdens before they became parents. The arrival of children made this negotiation much more problematic. When a woman quit her job to care for her children at home, she also took on the primary responsibility for managing the house as well. For others, it meant renegotiating the sharing of responsibilities and often hiring additional help. We will discuss the more difficult issue of child care later on; at this point we will focus on how childless couples handle the responsibilities of household management.

Whether these responsibilities were split along traditional gender lines or followed a more egalitarian, gender-indifferent model is obviously important. Yet what matters even more for the harmonious functioning of a relationship are the expectations partners have of each other in this respect. It is when these expectations are inconsistent that conflict is most likely to ensue. Let us first consider some of the more unusual cases of household responsibilities being taken over by one spouse or the other.

Randal got married two years ago, after a courtship of five years. His wife is six years older and comes from a socioeconomic background distinctly lower than that of his upper-middle-class family. Randal says they are very happy together; he especially values the fact that "we accept each other as we are." Randal's wife works full-time and is fully in charge of the house. They have no children. He explains, a bit apologetically, "I have offered to help around the house, but my wife says, 'No, honey, I'll do it, it's my responsibility.' She grew up in a very conventional family so that is the way she has been brought up." Randal has not had a demanding career to occupy him. In fact, he was unemployed at the time of the interview.

Randal's case is exceptional among our participants. Tim's household is more typical of reverting to the traditional pattern after the arrival of children. Tim is a Japanese-American engineer from a very traditional background. Initially, he and his wife both worked (she earned half as much as he) and shared household responsibilities fairly evenly. After the birth of their child, she stopped working and took over the housekeeping chores. Tim says, "I have a demanding job, so I leave early in the morning and get back home quite late. So I can't do that much to help my wife except for occasional relief duty." Tim says they are both content with this arrangement.

Louise and her husband exemplify the model of splitting chores evenly. They minimize the amount of housekeeping and cooking by rarely being home; instead, they put in long hours at work, go to the gym during their spare time, and go away almost every weekend. On those evenings when they are home, Louise does the cooking, but it is "mostly microwave stuff or a Prego spaghetti sauce–type of thing." Her husband is in charge of cleaning the house and taking care of the yard. Otherwise, she says, "we do everything together." That includes grocery shopping and running errands. "The only time I have gone shopping for myself," Louise recalls, "was to buy maternity clothes."

A similar pattern holds for James, a physician married to a nurse. He and his wife have a close and highly satisfying marriage. They eat out five times a week, partly because his hours are so unpredictable. Otherwise, she takes care of the routine housework while he does the "dirty work" of cleaning the bathroom and taking care of the yard.

Neither Louise nor James has children, but Louise is now expecting and James and his wife plan on becoming parents sometime fairly soon. It is clear to them that their current arrangements will have to be restructured after the arrival of children, but neither couple has quite figured out how to do it. Yet they feel confident that they will somehow work it out, and they expect hired help to be part of the solution, though to this point they have managed without such assistance.

A great deal has been said and written about the "housework gap"— men's contributions to running the household not keeping pace with women's increasing commitment to paid employment outside the home. Nonetheless, important changes have happened. From 1969 to 1987, the average time men spent on housework rose by 173 hours per year (the equivalent of half an hour a day) for men with no children. As a consequence, women spent 7.5 fewer hours, and men 5.2 more hours a week doing housework in 1985 than in 1965. Thus, while men currently still do less housework than women, they do more of it than their fathers did.[2] Several studies show that egalitarian sex-role attitudes increase with educational level, suggesting that the most egalitarian attitudes will be found in the educational elite.[3]

Our questionnaire data confirm this change and make it clear that the model of shared household responsibility, not the traditional division of labor or the reversed-role variant, is now the dominant one. Almost 70 percent of our participants with partners say the responsibility for household management is shared. This does not mean that housework itself is equally distributed. When it comes to such basic household tasks as cooking and cleaning, only 44 percent report equal sharing. Shared responsibility for the household thus translates into a fair degree of gender-based division of labor. Although 72 percent of men and 64 percent of women among our married participants report shared household responsibility, 34 percent of the women claim primary responsibility, and 25 percent of the men say their wives are largely responsible. (Only 3 percent of men say they are primarily responsible; only 2 percent of women say their husbands are.) Thus, in almost all cases where responsibility is not equally shared, women are the primary housekeepers. An even larger share of the burden of the basic household tasks, cooking and cleaning, falls on women: almost 60 percent of the men say their wives do more; only 6 percent say their wives do less than they do. For women, 39 percent say they do more than their husbands, half report sharing, and only 7 percent say their husbands do more. These figures indicate that egalitarian households are considerably more common among educational elite women than among their counterpart men. Among men, 36 percent of couples share; among women the figure is 54 percent. Nearly two-fifths of our participant women end up doing the bulk of the housework.

Type differences in housework responsibility are mainly due to the different proportions of women in the four types. Intellectuals report more shared responsibility than most other types, but Intellectuals are predominantly women; Careerists are more traditional, but they are mostly men. Interestingly, the men who are most likely to share household tasks are the Strivers. As a result, Strivers as a group reveal the highest proportion of shared-task households, at almost 70 percent. True to their style of trying to do it all, Striver men are willing to put more effort into home-front equality than other types. As one of them says, "We share the responsibilities and don't make an issue out of it. Each of us does a bit of everything, though we tend to do more of what comes easier. We also like doing some things like cooking together."

The issue of sharing household responsibilities is a source of ongoing discussion and frequent contention among these couples, especially early in their marital relationships. Over time the matter gets more or less settled, either when an acceptable division of household tasks is worked out or when one party, usually the woman, gives up arguing for equality and accepts a greater burden of household work.

The proposition that men should help around the house is a generally accepted principle, but the process of putting it into practice is hardly automatic. Sometimes there is easy agreement: "I cook, you clean." At other times, the arrangement is more informal—whoever gets home first, or has the time, does the job at hand. The flexible approach seems to work best if it can be made to work at all. More often than not, couples end up relying on chore lists tacked onto bulletin boards and taped to refrigerators. The initiative for this more formalized approach almost always comes from the women (after informal arrangements fail). Those women who persevere, with a mix of diplomacy and gentle coercion, eventually prevail. Yet, the problem is rarely fully settled and sometimes leads to marital conflict (chapter 8).

The assignment of specific tasks is surprisingly gender-independent in many cases, even if it is conventional in most. Some of the men are accomplished cooks; one man's wife taught him how to repair cars. But men typically are the ones who mow the lawn, fix appliances, look after the cars, and almost always dispose of the trash. The last job is sometimes elevated to the status of a major contribution. More than one man listed a long string of responsibilities carried out by his wife and then, when asked "What do you do?" declared solemnly, "I take the garbage out."

The persistence of traditional gender roles is sometimes quite astonishing. One woman has a Ph.D. in electrical engineering and is a manager in an electronics firm supervising male engineers. Who manages the family finances? "I write the checks," she replies, "then my husband balances the checkbook." On the other hand, food shopping, cooking, and cleaning are done just about as often by men as by women. Many women consider their husbands to be the better cooks. "He is the best cook I have met" was announced by several women with considerable pride and pleasure.

Two issues frequently lead to conflict. The first is a seemingly genuine gender difference in perceptions of what constitutes an acceptable level of order and cleanliness in the house, with women generally adhering to a higher standard than men. This leads to the following sample dialogue. She: "We need to clean up the house." He: "It looks clean to me." She: "Not clean enough to me." He: "Then you clean it." She gets annoyed at him for refusing to help, and he feels irritated that she is fussing over nothing. There are, of course, exceptions to this rule. Some men drive their wives to distraction with their fastidiousness. "He is very anal," explained one woman about her husband's mania for spotlessness, putting to good use what she had learned in a psychology course.

The second difference is that men are more attentive to order and women focus on cleanliness. When put in charge of cleaning the living room, a man will do a good job of tidying up but fail to dust the tabletops. When she proceeds to do the dusting herself, he says, "What is the point of my doing the work if you are going to do it over?" She replies, "What is the point of your doing it if you are not going to do it right?" As a result, women often feel they must be selective in what they ask their husbands to do. For instance, one woman and her husband had agreed that if one of them cooked, the other would do the dishes. But since she often had to redo the dishes he had washed, she now prefers that he do the cooking so she can do the dishes to her satisfaction.

As this example illustrates, women may be grateful for whatever help they can get but still feel a need to manage their husbands' housekeeping activities. They have to do this diplomatically so as not to irritate them, since men generally do not like being told what to do. But the most common grievance women express is that men have to be asked to help rather than taking the initiative themselves. Hence, the common reply to the question "Does your husband help with housework?" is "Yes, if asked." This means that the woman has to keep track of what needs to be done. And the very fact that she has to ask her husband for help implies that he is doing her a favor rather than simply doing his share. Even when tasks are fairly equally shared, these issues rankle many of the women.

EFFECTS OF INCOME

Although it is clear that women generally bear the brunt of the housework burden, the respective incomes of the two partners make a big difference. The higher the man's income, the more likely it is that his wife or partner will be responsible for managing the household and doing most household tasks. Conversely, the higher the woman's income, the more likely it is that household responsibility is shared. For example, only 47 percent of women in the bottom fourth of incomes report that responsibility for household tasks is shared equally, compared with 83 percent of women in the top fourth. And 87 percent of men in the bottom fourth of incomes report equal sharing, compared with 62 percent of men in the top fourth.

Thus, more traditional sex-role divisions are found in families with large income disparities between husband and wife. High-income men are more likely to have wives who do not work outside the home and therefore these women feel responsible for managing the house (often with hired help). High-income women are likely to have husbands who make no more and often less money than they do. This entitles them to do no more than their share at home, and if the principle of equity does not work, the high-earning woman has the leverage to enforce it. Thus, for the educational elite, women's equality in the home is heavily dependent on economic parity. We must remember, however, that most of our couples need the two incomes and only high-income earners can afford the "luxury" of one partner being a full-time homemaker. With a few exceptions, it is women who play that role.

SATISFACTION WITH THE DIVISION OF LABOR

Despite the disparities we have found, the men and women in our sample appear to be by and large satisfied with their household arrangements. Over 80 percent say they do not want a different division of household labor and responsibility, and women are only moderately more in favor of a change (26 percent) than men (16 percent). Further, income has no effect on satisfaction in this area. That is, neither high-income nor low-income individuals of either sex are especially dissatisfied with the division of labor, even though we find such clear effects of income on women's share of responsibility. Even women who are less than fully satisfied with current arrangements may have persuaded themselves that they are better off than others, or that what they have is the best they are going to get, hence there is little point in rocking the boat.

The satisfaction of our respondents with their current housekeeping arrangements may also be due in part to their ability to afford household help. Almost 40 percent of our participants employed household help (apart from child care), most often for cleaning. Significantly, more women than men have hired help (48 percent to 32 percent), at least partly owing to the higher family incomes of our married women (chapter 5). Thus, one way the educational elite mitigate the problem of the household division of labor is by reducing the amount of labor involved. Another way is the "low-maintenance" lifestyle (as exemplified by Louise and her Prego sauce).

PARENTHOOD

Having a child, an experience of just over one-third of our participants, is the single most important event in the lives of our young couples. No other experience had a more profound impact on the subsequent course of their marriages and careers. This is especially true of mothers, but it also holds for fathers.

At the most obvious level, parenthood requires serious restructuring of everyday life. With the arrival of children, the family becomes a "continuous coverage" institution and parenting "a twenty-four-hour-a-day, seven-day-a-week job with no time off for good behavior."[4] The child becomes the number-one priority. As one woman engineer put it while apologizing for being tardy in returning the questionnaire, "Sorry this is late. I am never on time for anything except my son." For conscientious parents, even being away from their child does not exempt them from feeling responsible for their child's well-being.

At a deeper level, parenthood redefines our sense of identity in two basic ways: how we perceive our own selves, and how we are perceived by others, especially with respect to gender identity (our sense of masculinity and femininity) and gender roles (social expectations of how men and women should behave). With parenthood, gender differences that have been latent (or resisted because of the ideology of gender equality) tend to become further magnified.[5]

In achieving this redefinition of their identity, young two-career couples who espouse an ethic of gender equality have few models and minimal cultural guidance. Almost half of our participants came from families in which mothers took care of the house and reared the children while fathers were the sole financial supporters. Another 20 percent have mothers who were employed outside the home only intermittently in jobs that hardly amounted to careers, spending most of the years of their children's youth as homemakers. Only one-third had mothers with employment records even remotely resembling committed, long-term careers. By the same token, few of their fathers took much responsibility for child care or housekeeping, confining their contributions largely to "men's work." Thus, how dual-career parents are supposed to work out the complexities of egalitarian parenthood is not something they have had the opportunity to observe with their own parents.

Many of our couples had developed satisfactory arrangements for household management while childless only to have these arrangements thrown off balance with the birth of their first child. Caring for a baby is obviously a far more complex matter than washing dishes. Since women bear and nurse their children, they have also cared for them through much of human history. Despite enormous changes in the lives of modern women, this process has changed little: when the baby appears on the scene, the mother takes over. Whether by the woman's choice or the man's default, whether planned or only accepted after the fact, the outcome remains the same.

Whether this gender difference is purely the result of the way women and men are socialized, owing to a biological predisposition, or a mix of the two, does not concern us here. Even among the educational elite, who are far more aware of the impact of differential gender socialization than are most members of their cohort, women are overwhelmingly more likely to take primary responsibility for their very young children.

Beyond gender roles, deep psychological changes are linked to parenthood. Parents typically refer to the birth of their first child as a turning point in their lives and the culmination of the development of their sense of adulthood. Children are one of the most important sources of family satisfaction and a "high point" of the personal lives of these men and women, as we shall detail in the next chapter. Children become important influences in the continuing development of their parents' personalities—children "bring up" their parents as they are being brought up by them.[6] Becoming a parent also redefines the relationship of the individual to his or her own parents. Erik Erikson refers to this interrelationship as the "cogwheeling" of generations.[7]

All its joys notwithstanding, parenthood also represents a normative crisis at best and a highly disruptive experience at worst. It is a period of transition for which most people are unprepared and untutored. And since parenthood is expected to be "natural," not knowing how to parent results in further feelings of confusion and incompetence. These feelings are accentuated for the educational elite, who are accustomed to being well informed and in control of their lives. Yet a crisis as such is not a disaster. In this context the word *crisis* should be taken in its original Greek meaning of "a moment of decision." Like the Chinese ideograph of the word, it represents both danger and opportunity.

BECOMING A PARENT

About one in three of our participants had one or more children in the first decade after college, slightly more women than men: 19 percent had only one child; 14 percent had two; and 2 percent had three. Men were more likely to have two children and women to have one. None had more than three. Among the married group, 56 percent had children, and only married couples had children; for the educational elite, having children out of wedlock, even when cohabiting, is not a desirable option. One man was living with a woman who had a child from a previous marriage. Otherwise, we found not a single instance of an unmarried couple or single mother with a child.

This contrasts sharply with the fact that currently one in four babies in the United States is born to an unwed mother. Most unwed mothers are very young and from disadvantaged backgrounds that have almost nothing in common with the lives of the educational elite. Some professional women now make the voluntary decision to have or adopt children without being married, but these cases are rather rare and such women are usually well into their thirties, feeling pushed by the biological clock. As we noted, only Alice, the black business executive, foresaw this possibility. Even she, however, could not envision giving birth to a child as a single woman.

Overall, the four types reveal no differences in childbearing patterns—about equal percentages of each type had children (see table 10, appendix

A). Yet when we look at married men and women separately, Striver women (88 percent) and Careerist men (74 percent) turn out to be much more likely than others to have children. Careerist men, we know, tend to have the most conventional marriages; once married, they proceed almost automatically to parenthood. Striver women, on the other hand, are the group least likely to marry but, once married, the most likely to have a child. This finding suggests that Striver women postpone marriage until they are ready to have children.

On the other hand, the two sex-by-type groups that are least likely to have children once they are married are Careerist and Unconnected women (about 40 percent for each group). Careerist women put careers first but, unlike Careerist men, they can hardly have a traditional marriage with a wife at home caring for their children. To this point, at least, if there is a conflict between career and motherhood for these women, career wins. How long they can keep this up remains to be seen. Unconnected women, meanwhile, may have fewer children because they have relatively low household incomes and therefore feel less able to afford children. Unfortunately, we have too few cases of Unconnected mothers in the interview sample to be able to discern more personal reasons for this difference.

While the experience of becoming a parent had a significant impact on all of our participants, some of the women in particular were transformed by the changes parenthood entailed.[8] We noted this with profile Intellectual Kirsten Buchanan. The example of Cindy, another Intellectual, is equally instructive because she, too, had demonstrated a high level of competence in her career by the time she became a mother.

Cindy is a Japanese-American who spent a year in Washington, D.C., after college to get her bearings because she was not quite sure of her career intentions. Her work at two different public-interest organizations brought her into close contact with numerous lawyers who were using their legal skills to effect changes in society. This kind of work appealed to her own social and intellectual concerns, so she went to law school. She liked law school and did very well, graduating near the top of her class. The political environment of the law school also raised her consciousness about her ethnic identity. As a result, she became very involved with minority women's organizations.

Following law school, Cindy clerked under a woman federal judge in Chicago and met her future husband, who worked for a bank. After their marriage, they decided to move to the West Coast. Cindy interviewed with a number of large law firms and was pleasantly surprised to find that they defied her stereotype of big-time corporate lawyers. Moreover, they were happy to accommodate her intellectual interests and allow her time for pro bono work with victims of domestic violence. Cindy joined a prestigious firm and eventually moved to the litigation section. Her career was launched, and she became a highly competent, self-assured young corporate attorney.

A year ago, Cindy had her first child. Her daughter Clara's birth coincided with the death of Cindy's grandmother, to whom she was very close, and the unexpected divorce of her parents. The combination of these events—but mostly, in Cindy's view, her becoming a mother—completely changed her "sense of connectedness." She found herself reassessing both her past and future priorities. Her interview report describes Cindy's reactions as follows:

> Cindy described the unprecedented expression of fully unconditional love from Clara and her own capacity to reciprocate. She marvels at the intense emotional bonding that has already developed between mother and daughter (she describes her own mother as her own best friend) and the fact that all this unconditional connecting occurs despite no capacity yet to communicate verbally. Clara's impact on the way Cindy will now approach the future is apparent; Cindy further indicated a desire to have another child within the next three years.
>
> Cindy is about to return to work after a five-month leave, and she is torn between not being sure about committing the required hours and her nonetheless keen desire not to be that "half-assed" about the job she enjoys so much. Cindy's new family priorities are likely to win out. She has already concluded that she will ask not to be considered in the partnership review process this year as she returns from maternity leave. More significant, she is seriously considering a departure from the law firm by the beginning of the 1992 academic year so that she might take up the teaching of law.
>
> In the short term, however, she continues to struggle with conflicting inclinations. One is "to prove something," by which she means her need to feel that she can succeed and make her mark in "the white male corporate world." She attributes this to inheriting from her Japanese father his own "chip on the shoulder" need to prove himself in the wake of WWII, during which he was interred with other Japanese-Americans. Although she and her parents never spoke of that period, and although she seemed to come late to an ethnic self-awareness, it seems clear now to Cindy that her career commitment is influenced to some degree by a lingering if subconscious family need to overcome ethnic stereotyping.
>
> On top of all this, she is also conflicted in the short term by the sense that she owes the law firm another year and a half of service in

return for their flexibility and generosity with regard to her leave and her pro bono interests. In the long run, however, her career commitment will probably change due to emerging personal priorities.

There is no reason to think that Cindy loves Clara more than Martin MacMillan loves his young son, who also occupies pride of place in his heart. Yet, when Martin became a father, the question of a major shift in his medical career never crossed his mind. This is where gender makes the difference. As a consequence of fatherhood, some men may shift the focus of their inner lives or even reorder their work priorities; but after all is said and done, they go on with the business of their careers. Not women. Whether they contemplate a major reordering of their career future, as Cindy does, or consider children mainly a logistical challenge to their work schedules, their business never goes on as usual after they become mothers. This difference between men and women was borne out in virtually every interview with our parent participants. A similar, albeit not as strong factor is the effect of our typology (itself linked to gender). Careerists are the least likely and Intellectuals the most likely to realign their career trajectories after becoming parents.

THE TIMING OF PARENTHOOD

The timing of parenthood depends not only on marriage but also, and almost as much, on the timing of graduate study and going to work (figure 7.1). Very few participants had children in the early years after graduation, during graduate study and initial career development. Even though some married early, they clearly felt that having a child would introduce too many complications into their lives.

A few men and women had a child before the fourth year after graduation, but the pace had hardly quickened until the sixth year (the peak year for marriage). Then comes the first burst of procreative activity, especially for men, 10 percent of whom became fathers in the seventh year. The next year, motherhood showed a dramatic jump. All told, one in three of our participants had become a parent by the end of the decade.

The fact that women have their children somewhat later than men, even though they marry somewhat sooner and then catch up with men, reflects two contrary factors. One is women's perception that they must time parenthood more carefully with respect to career development, especially because they consider the careers of their husbands as well as their own. This issue tends to postpone motherhood for educational elite women.

FIGURE 7.1
First Child Born, by Sex (*percentages for each year*)

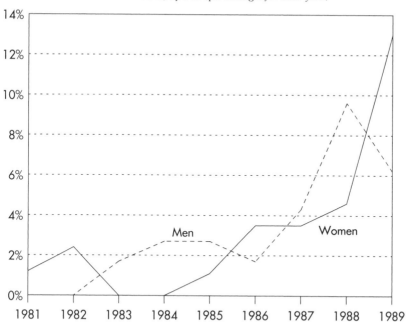

The national average age of first birth for all women has risen to age twenty-four.[9] For our participant women, it will be well over thirty. At an average age of thirty-one, two-thirds do not yet have children, though many of them plan to. Women face a difficult choice: having their children early conflicts with the establishment of their careers; having children later interrupts their careers when they are in full swing.

The second consideration has to do with the symbolism of turning thirty. As we said earlier, women think they hear the ticking of the biological clock loud and clear at age thirty, even though, of course, nothing special happens physiologically at that age. But the ticking pushes many women into having children in their late twenties, after lagging behind men most of the previous decade. For the same reason, many more are likely to follow suit over the next several years.

The only type difference in the timing of parenthood is a clear tendency of the Intellectuals to have children later than other groups, owing, in part, to the large proportion of women in this group. Also, Intellectuals as a whole marry a little later than the other groups.

We also find little difference by sex or type in the number of children our participants plan to have. Whether they already have children or not, most of them conform to the prevailing ideal of two parents, two children. Slightly more men than women intend to have three (and in very rare cases more than three) children. Overall, though, conformity to the standard family model is quite uniform within the educational elite. They want a second child for the usual reasons, but they want to stop at two to avoid too much disruption of their careers and to be able to provide well for their offspring. Hence, the logic of their family planning is the same as that used by most others.

FORGOING PARENTHOOD

Not everyone becomes a parent, and not everyone wants to (or perhaps should) become a parent. Though choosing not to have children is still unusual for couples, it is increasingly seen as socially acceptable and even, in certain circles, as a positive choice ("a child-free lifestyle"). Some 10 to 15 percent of married couples in the United States are infertile. Some of these couples adopt children; others who could have children choose not to. Childless women are more likely to have high-level jobs, work throughout their lives, and earn more money.[10]

A variety of reasons are offered by childless couples for forgoing parenthood: potentially deleterious impact of children on careers or on the marital bond, concerns about overpopulation, and reluctance to bring children into a world beset with so many problems. Most of these considerations mean very little to our participants. What does matter to them is the potential impact of parenthood on careers.

The decision not to have children is generally reached in one of two ways. Some decide early in their lives not to have children. The psychologist Jean Veevers calls them "early articulators."[11] In contrast, the "postponers" take a more passive route. They defer the decision repeatedly until the matter is settled by default when they reach a point in their lives when it is no longer feasible or sensible to have children. In Veevers's study of fifty-two childless couples, early articulators accounted for one-third of those choosing not to have children; most of them were women. Some of them ("rejecters") actively disliked the notion of having children and would not want them under any circumstances; avoiding parenthood was not a function of the particular relationship they were in. Early articulators who were not rejecters decided not to have children to avoid the negative impact on their independence and on the quality of their marital relationships and careers. Our childless couples belong with Veevers's postponers.

When we asked our participants if work had affected their decision to have children, 46 percent of the women and 26 percent of the men replied affirmatively, a large difference but one we expected to be even larger. Career concerns led them to postpone having children, either to get established in their careers first or to have more money saved up to tide them over in the period when mothers would not be working. Men expressed more concern about the loss of income by their wives; women more often said that their jobs were too time-consuming for them to have children yet. A few women objected to the wording of this question and reversed it. As one said, "While working (however you wish to define it) has not affected my decision to have children, having children has to some degree affected my decision to work outside the home." That too, of course, is an important issue, which we consider in chapter 8.

The Unconnected and Careerists see work as delaying parenthood more than do Strivers and Intellectuals. Differences are striking for women but minimal for men. Two-thirds (67 percent) of Unconnected women and 50 percent of Careerist women say work has affected their decision to have children. Unconnected women have the lowest income (chapter 5), and their career progress, already relatively slow, would be further impeded by children; thus, they most often cite financial reasons for delaying parenthood. The issue for Careerist women is their desire not to see their more successful careers handicapped by the interruption of childbearing. Less than half as many Intellectual and Striver women report work having a similar effect on the decision to have children; they are less concerned with their careers and more keen on motherhood.

Even though so many would-be parents have delayed parenthood for the sake of their careers, few of them are unhappy with the situation. Only 7 percent expressed genuine dissatisfaction, and another 20 percent said they had mixed feelings about the delay. This pattern applies equally to men and women. That so few are dissatisfied so far is not particularly surprising since they are still relatively young and not yet subject to the crucial biological changes ahead.

Some hitherto childless couples have a fairly clear plan about when to start a family. They cite most often work-related considerations. Some echo Philip Genochio's words about delaying the advent of children until working hours get better. Others are waiting for some ill-defined future when circumstances will be more propitious. Ingrid and her husband are currently so tied up in their work that often the best they can do as a couple is to "share a cup of soup and a sandwich" late in the evening. "How can we have children when we live like this?" she wonders. Ingrid is willing to take off a year to have a child, but her husband is reluctant to accept the drop in family income that would entail.

CHILD CARE

Elizabeth is a successful and ambitious financial manager. She came to the interview with a three-week-old baby in her arms, whom she nursed twice to keep quiet. She was impeccably dressed and had lavished much care on the baby as well. Throughout the interview, Elizabeth maintained her poise and tried to act as if the baby were not even there. It was a valiant effort, yet it was quite apparent that she was under tremendous stress and her resources were stretched thin. "I have six weeks of leave, of which I have used up half," she said. "I have not yet found someone to take care of the baby. Somebody better show up soon because I am determined to go back to work." Her words sounded more like a defiant declaration than a statement of intent.

We happened to catch Elizabeth at a particularly difficult time, but virtually all dual-career couples have been in similar tight spots at one time or another. This generation of parents has largely broken with previous patterns of child rearing by relying much more on others for child care. With both working in time-consuming professions, new parents have little choice. Or rather, the existing choices are difficult ones. Caring for children is almost evenly split between those who care for their own children and those who rely on others to do so.

STAYING HOME: THE FIRST YEAR

The first alternative is to do what parents have done in most societies throughout much of human history: take care of their own children. Even among the educational elite, however, it is the women who do the actual caretaking. When it comes to infant care, the traditional division of labor that was moderately present for household tasks is greatly accentuated. Thus, 57 percent of mothers in our sample spent at least a year at home caring for their infant children, but only 4 percent of fathers did likewise.

Most educational elite women do not want to interrupt their careers for long. Mothers did not usually stay home with their children for more than a year, and most of the 43 percent who stayed home less than a year were off the job for six months or less. Only one out of four have stayed home three or more years, including one who has been a homemaker since the first year after graduation. Thus far, at any rate, these long-term, full-time homemakers are exceptional, though perhaps more women will adopt that role in the next few years as they have more children or as more of them become first-time mothers.

Most men, on the other hand, took no more than a few weeks off when their children were born, experiencing no more career disruption than an extended vacation entails. The "child-care imperative" is obviously a female concern, though it is strongly supplemented by private-employee or institutional child-care arrangements. In this respect, our male participants are lagging behind the general population, among whom one father out of five cares for his children while his wife is at work.[12] The greater participation of other fathers in raising their children, however, does not necessarily reflect changed social attitudes (our participants are likely to prove more egalitarian) so much as the unaffordability of child care for most families. It is often cheaper for men who are unemployed, in part-time jobs, or on night shifts to take care of their children while their wives work outside the home. None of these conditions applies to the fathers in our group. Quality child care can be so expensive ("My sister spends $20,000 a year," said one woman) that our own lower-income women barely break even, thus basically paying for the privilege to work.

Careerist and Striver mothers were most likely (about 75 percent) to spend at least a year at home, a somewhat surprising finding given that these women are more strongly career-oriented than other types. Intellectuals were just about average, but Unconnected women were far less likely to take as much as a year off (only 19 percent), and they were less likely than other types to have children in the first place. The hesitancy on the part of Unconnected women to have children may be linked in part to economic factors. Careerist women are married to men with very high incomes, so they can more easily afford to stay home. Unconnected women have the least affluent spouses and lowest incomes, so they may find it more burdensome both to have and to raise children. Yet economic status does not explain the strong motherhood tendencies of women Strivers, who have relatively high personal incomes but spouses with only average incomes. These women suffer the greatest financial loss by interrupting their careers but, once they are married, accept that loss more readily than any other group.

The only men who spent a year or more taking care of children happen to be among the Unconnected, but because there were only two, we hesitate to make too much of this finding. Moreover, only one of the men is in the interview sample, and since he said nothing about his time at home we could not explore it further in the interview. Nonetheless, it is consistent with the characteristics of the Unconnected to find that the only men who would put child rearing above more conventional male concerns are found in this group.

CHILD-CARE ARRANGEMENTS

Child-care arrangements primarily involve having a child cared for while both parents are at work. But a child also requires care when the parents come home from work. Fully 61 percent of women say they are primarily responsible for child care during nonworking hours, compared with only 10 percent of men. When a child is sick, this same proportion of women say they are the ones who stay home, while only 3 percent of men give this response. (Taking turns and having a third party help out account for the remainder.) Like infant care during the first year, child care thus remains very much the primary responsibility of women.

Caring for one's own child has obvious advantages. At the practical level, it avoids the frustration and expense of finding competent and trustworthy caregivers. Such help is hard to come by even if one can afford to pay well for it, as our participants generally can. And even when excellent child-care facilities are available, they may be inconveniently located. More than one of our participants bemoaned the poor quality of institutional child care in the local area. Ultimately, most mothers consider themselves better able than anyone else to care for their children.

At the emotional level, the rewards of caring for one's own child can be enormous, as reflected in the joy and satisfaction expressed by many of our participants. Beyond these intrinsic rewards, there are significant social considerations. Institutional child care is still somewhat suspect as an "unnatural" way to raise children in our highly individualistic society. Many women equate raising their own children with being "good mothers."[13] Even Katherine Johnson, who has the dual advantages of both a full-time employee and her husband caring for her child, says, "I would prefer to spend more time with my child. I have so little time that I have been reluctant to have another baby." It is not that Katherine feels guilty, nor is she concerned that her child is not being well cared for. She simply feels she is missing out on the joy of being with her child for longer periods.

On the debit side, the burden of caring for small children is enormous. It is physically exhausting and emotionally draining, leaving little time or energy for much else. The impact of very young children on the marital relationship and the couple's overall quality of life is usually reported to be negative (chapter 8). It is costly for a career woman to stay home when she has been earning $50,000 or more. Long-term monetary and personal costs can be even greater if her career is slowed down or thrown off track altogether. To have years of preparation and hard work and ambition come to naught is not easy. The ultimate cost depends, of course, on a woman's particular occupation, her stage of career development, and the institutional policies and practices of her employer.

The fathers in our study, though rarely primary caregivers, always "helped out," but to a variable extent. And even under optimal career circumstances, they, too, felt the extra burden. Profile Striver George Mehta said:

> Perhaps because I have higher expectations, I find it hard to be a working dad, although working moms get more attention. I do not mean to underestimate the difficulties of being a mother, let alone a working mother. It's just that I would like to spend more time with my son. Even though I have scaled back my hours at work, I would enjoy a part-time work schedule. As for child care, it is true that families can sometimes do without one income, as could we. However, even though I have the higher income, my wife has vastly superior health benefits. So we both work. As it turns out, our son is in a really good child-care environment, and in retrospect, I am not sure what would be better for him: the increased attention that a parent could provide versus the social stimulation of a center. However, with a second child someday, we think that the case for staying at home would be clearer, and we will aim for this.

Much of what we said earlier about the division of household responsibilities also applies here. The crucial difference is that the tasks involved in caring for a child are obviously more critical and cannot be shirked. Someone has to do them, they must be done right, and they must be done on the child's schedule, not at the parent's convenience. These conditions are especially demanding for the educational elite, owing to their habit of producing "quality" work and their need to feel that they control their own destiny. When suddenly they find themselves catering to the needs of little beings who stubbornly refuse to fall in step with their careful planning and regimentation, they are thrown off balance.

THIRD-PARTY CHILD CARE

The second major option for child care, chosen by about half of our couples, is letting others do the bulk of it. These other caregivers may be household employees, babysitting cooperatives, day-care centers, schools, or relatives. From our sample, about 15 percent have paid employees at home; 30 percent rely on child-care institutions, and 4 percent rely on relatives. By contrast, working mothers in the general population with children under age five rely more evenly on so-called family day care, nonrelatives caring for children in their own homes (29 percent), followed by institutions and relatives (including the father in 15 percent of cases). About 5 percent of all mothers even look after their own children in the workplace.[14]

The relative merits and demerits of third-party child care are the obverse of those of taking care of one's own children. Typically, the mother is relieved of the burden of caring for the child during working hours and can pursue her career with less interruption (though she is hardly relieved of the sense of responsibility during the day). Parents often feel more interested in their children and more able to devote themselves wholeheartedly when they do spend "quality time" with them. And some parents strongly value the educational programs provided by many centers, which increasingly combine basic literacy and math instruction with play and games.

On the negative side there is, first, the issue of finding and paying for adequate child care. Some parents lurch from one child-care crisis to another—an *au pair* girl from Europe becomes homesick and decides to return home; a nanny from an agency turns out to be unreliable; the local day-care center personnel seem bored and unimaginative; some other alternative turns into a nightmare. Costs are usually not a serious problem for the educational elite, but some of our low-end earners felt their child-care expenses were eating up far too much of their income.

Another major concern for parents is the impact of collective child care on their youngsters' emotional and cognitive development. One of the women Intellectuals who reviewed a draft of this book (and cares for her children) had this to say:

> One of the key concerns I have after reading this book is the children of the educational elite. You state that "relatively few of our participants are unhappy with their child-care arrangements." Did someone ask the kids? Despite the fact that some can afford nannies for their children, I worry about children raised by caretakers. Forget quality time, which is a yuppie guilt-reducing term. Nothing replaces the full-time commitment of a parent—male or female. We are dealing with educated parents here. You say half of the elite's mothers stayed home with them during their formative years. Yet these well-attended children are either unwilling or unable to stay home to nurture their own children. You state that most of the elite women are back on the job within a year, and remember that we are not talking single mothers here. I find this frightening. I would have expected more of them to stay home temporarily or part-time. I'm not on a soapbox or tooting my own horn. I recognize that some women are in careers, such

as medicine, that you can't interrupt. Some women do not find motherhood fulfilling.

Face it, folks, early infancy offers very little by way of rewards. Sleep deprivation can be overwhelming. Some women need $green$ evidence of their worth. I just wish more mothers and fathers were home for their children.

This is a matter of no little controversy as a research issue and a matter of public policy. The debate is mainly over the effects of institutional care in the first year of life. With a national figure of 53 percent of children younger than one enrolled in some form of institutional care (up from 31 percent in 1976), the number of children at stake is enormous. The infants of college graduates are even more affected: 68 percent of their mothers work at least part of their first year of life.[15] A massive, federally funded research project is now attempting to assess the situation.[16] But study results are not likely to change the national trend. Whether by choice or because of economic necessity, women are not going to stop working. The real question is how to provide child-care services that are readily available, affordable, and satisfactory.

Our couples are, if anything, even more concerned than the general population about the impact of institutional child care on their children because they are better informed and can afford to worry about getting "the best" for their children. On the whole, they prefer care providers and circumstances more closely approximating parental care, but costs can be an overriding factor. Thus, we find that the lower the participant's income, the more likely the participant is to use a collective form of child care: 53 percent of parents with incomes in the lowest fourth use institutional forms, but only 8 percent of parents in the top quarter. Conversely, the higher the income, the more likely the family is to have a child-care employee: 61 percent of the top fourth of income earners but only 13 percent of lowest-fourth earners employ in-home care providers. Thus, high-income respondents solve the child-care problem by having either a full-time homemaker (almost always the mother) or an employee providing "parent-equivalent" child care. Lower-income respondents "choose" collective child care instead.

Despite the preference for personal child care that these figures indicate, relatively few of our participants are unhappy with their child-care situation. Only one in five say they would prefer different child-care arrangements, and women (15 percent) are actually less dissatisfied than men (24 percent). Two factors are at work here. First, the educational elite have the financial resources and wherewithal to find and afford high-quality child care, so they are not likely to place their children in institutions that do not meet their standards. Second, men's dissatisfaction mainly results from their desire to spend more time with their children—some of them wish they could work fewer hours and be home more of the time. Women already spend more time with their children and carry more of the responsibility for raising them, so they are less likely to express this concern. In addition, since these couples are doing the best they can, and what they have is better than what most others manage to get, they have probably made peace with the situation even if they are not delighted with it.

RELATIONSHIPS WITH PARENTS

Members of the profile group have generally maintained quite close relationships with their families. Careerist Martin MacMillan remains close to his own parents and siblings, especially to his father. Cynthia Eastwood remains close to her own family, especially her mother, whom she calls weekly, no matter how busy she is. Cynthia thinks "she is really smart" and highly enterprising. She credits her mother with instilling in her the tremendous drive that propels her life.

Intellectual Kirsten Buchanan's ties to her parents remain very strong. Christopher Luce cares deeply about his parents and intends to help care for them as they get older. "They were very devoted to my brother and me when we were growing up. I want to return that devotion in kind. I can't imagine doing anything else." Although they are quite proud of his academic accomplishments, his parents do not quite grasp the nature of what he does. For instance, when he publishes a scholarly paper, they ask him how much money it has earned him. "I have given up trying to explain it to them. Sometimes I don't understand it myself. It would be nice if they understood what I do and why it matters to me. It's such a big part of who I am. But it's inaccessible to them." Striver Geraldine Jones keeps in fairly close touch with her mother and stepfather. She also sees her stepmother, who lives nearby and was instrumental in Geraldine's move to the area. We discuss George Mehta's relationship with his parents later in this chapter. During his college years, Unconnected David Levy's relationship with his parents was at times a bit strained. But now that he is settled in his career, all is well. One of his brothers, a clinical psychologist, is married to a physician and stays home full-time to care for their young son.

Leaving one's family of origin and establishing a separate family are crucial steps in adult development for most people. As shown in the sociologist Alice Rossi's study of three-generation families, parenthood redefines the relationship between adult children and their own parents in a succession of stages.[17] Rossi finds that feelings of closeness and intimacy are stronger between parents and daughters than between parents and sons, with the closest ties those between mothers and daughters. This pattern is set by age ten, when over 45 percent of daughters describe their relationships with their mothers as very close. During adolescence, the sense of intimacy drops for all intergenerational relationships, hitting bottom at age sixteen. By age twenty-five, levels of intimacy have generally regained their preadolescent levels.

Though many of our participants in their early thirties appear to treat their parents as a unit, a closer look often reveals distinct preferences for one or the other parent. A woman lawyer who is much closer to her college-graduate mother than to her blue-collar father says she and her mother "have much more in common and more to talk about." A man claims, "I am the apple of my father's eye. He is the 'rock of Gibraltar' who was very patient with me when I was growing up." His mother has been more of a background figure in his life.

The parent-child relationship after the child passes thirty is, of course, quite different from earlier times. It involves the interaction of more or less autonomous adults with their middle-aged parents. Up to age thirty-five, feelings of closeness with both parents continue to increase moderately for daughters but decline somewhat for sons. As young adults become parents themselves, they develop a greater appreciation of their mothers and fathers and become more willing to see and accept them for who and what they are. The older generation, though less involved in supporting and managing the lives of their children, continues to have a stake in their well-being that is greatly heightened by the arrival of grandchildren. Not least, grandchildren are important for the grandparents' sense of generational continuity—a sense that young adults only begin to develop as they have children of their own.

Our findings are generally consistent with these patterns. In the interview sample, 62 percent of participants said they had close relationships with their parents. In line with Rossi's analysis, the proportion of women (68 percent) was somewhat higher than that of men (56 percent). Married participants of both sexes were more often close to their parents than were single participants, and among singles, women were more often close to their parents than were men.

The types that stand out for being on especially good terms with their parents are the Intellectuals (79 percent) and Careerists (67 percent). For Careerists, this finding is consistent with their earlier history. As undergraduates, they indicated that their parents were highly influential in steering their academic and career choices; as young adults, their parents continue to be relatively more involved with their lives. On the other hand, the Unconnected are true to form in that the lowest percentage of them feel close to their parents, only 50 percent. This may be a residue of the delayed consolidation of their sense of identity. The less clearly formed our sense of identity is, the more distance we need to maintain from those we are trying to differentiate ourselves from. Conversely, to the extent that the Unconnected tend to be more autonomous, they feel less need to be close to their parents.

For those who are in the same professions as their parents and actually work with them (Melissa caring for her father's orchards, Douglas managing the family-owned furniture business), the familial bonds are further strengthened. But even without such special circumstances, the tie between some respondents and their parents is exceptionally strong. When Maria gets home from her seventy-mile commute from work, she goes for a walk with her parents before going to her own house. Another striking example is Billy, who lives seven houses down the street from his parents' house, where he grew up. "I was a little concerned when we first moved in, that the closeness would be a challenge to my wife," recalls Billy. "But it has worked out just fine. We visit back and forth all the time. I play tennis with my dad every week. My mother is all set to be Grandma." Billy's in-laws also live close by, and he and his wife are on close terms with them as well.

Beyond the parental relationship, some participants have very close extended families. Joel, an orthopedic surgeon, lives in the same city as his parents and three siblings. In addition to holidays, they gather together each Friday night for Sabbath dinners, taking turns as host. In contrast, Naomi's family almost never gets together as a group, even though they easily could. Yet, she says, they do not feel alienated from each other. Sometimes distance takes it toll; Paul's parents live in Japan, hence, visits are few and far between. These and similar considerations lead to familial relationships that are described as "cordial but not close."

Looked at more generally, we find among the interview sample that closeness to parents is related to overall career engagement (see chapter 5, note 14). Participants who are more engaged and content with their careers are more likely to be close to their parents, and vice versa. The difference is especially noticeable for participants in the bottom third of scores on the career engagement index: only 40 percent of them are close to their parents, compared with 72 percent of those with greater career engagement. Some parents put a great deal of emphasis on the career success of their children. If the children are engaged in their careers and doing well, the parents are more accepting and content, making it easier for their children to maintain close relationships with them.

For both practical and psychological reasons, an even more powerful magnet that brings parents and their adult children closer is the arrival of grandchildren. Those who live in the same area as their parents can receive practical help in caring for their young children, as we illustrate shortly. On the psychological plane, becoming parents themselves has elevated our women and men to full adult status. Hence, they can now meet their parents on a more equal plane. Just as important, the joy they all share in the new addition to the family adds enormous affection and solidarity to the extended family unit. Even some relationships that have been seriously strained are ameliorated by grandchildren.

With few exceptions, our participants are no longer financially dependent on their parents. Conversely, only a few are involved yet in assisting their parents. One only son is the primary source of support for his widowed mother. An oldest daughter has taken charge of finding a nursing home for her father. Some parents in turn provide practical help. Jane and her husband are both well-paid engineers who could easily afford household help, but they rely instead on her parents (a retired physician and nurse), who spend one day a week thoroughly cleaning and tidying up their house, as well as taking care of their grandchildren.

Close relationships with parents are not always harmonious ones, even though persistent conflict will eventually lead to more distant relationships. For example, attempts at parental assistance become problematic if they are perceived as intrusive and controlling. One woman has a close but conflicted relationship with her parents, who are generous to a fault but use their generosity as a form of control. "Whenever I buy anything for the house," she complains, "my parents think it is either a piece of junk or that I paid too much for it. I once bought an antique dining room table, and my parents wanted to know how much it cost. When I said I would rather not tell, they wanted it to be a gift from them, which put me in a bind."

In another case, the father of a capable businesswoman with degrees in engineering and business still tries to manage her financial affairs. For instance, he wanted her to have a life insurance policy and offered to pay the premiums. Then he stopped paying them, so she is now stuck with the policy but does not dare cancel it. Another father has given a share in his business to his daughter, but he keeps the details so closely guarded that preparing her tax returns is a yearly nightmare.

Asian-Americans find it especially difficult to deal with some of the norms of their cultural heritage. "My mother still treats me like a child even though I am now a mother myself," complains Diana. Diana's mother is so fond of her grandchild that she expects Diana to follow her instructions in minute detail, down to how to cut the child's hair. "Finally, I had to tell her," says Diana, "look, Mom, she is my child, not yours."

A variety of other factors create rifts with parents. One is making the "wrong" choice in marriage by choosing someone from a different ethnic or religious group. One of the more problematic cases involves a Mexican-American man who converted to Judaism when he got married. His abandonment of the Catholic church was especially opposed by his father, a man so traditional that he still refuses to allow his wife to get a driver's license. We consider further examples in chapter 8.

A different problem is faced by a man who has "betrayed" his mother's radical political ideology by embracing the world of business. He was once very close to his mother but now has turned instead to his father, who had been quite marginal in his life earlier. His wife, on the other hand, has become more attached to his mother. Hence, family dynamics are in constant flux.

Intergenerational relationships are usually reshaped after a divorce, with children often siding with their mothers. Carol grew closer to her mother through a tragedy. Her brain-damaged younger sister went into a coma and their father, a physician, insisted that life support systems be withdrawn. Her mother's refusal broke up the marriage, and Carol thought her father had been heartless. A few years later, when her mother developed cancer, the father would do nothing to help and Carol cut off all contact with him.

Some of our participants managed to sustain good relationships with both parents after their divorce. Only rarely did they turn to their father's side. Only one woman tried to be supportive of her mother but gradually grew closer to her father instead, for reasons she could not explain.

A fascinating account of the discovery of family roots was provided by our profile Striver, George Mehta. George grew up knowing very little about his father except that he was from India (hence the family name). George's American mother had met her husband in Cyprus when he was a senior United Nations officer and she was working as a secretary for a high-ranking official. After they married, the family moved to India. Then when George was two and his sister an infant, George's mother divorced her husband and had no further contact with him. She never explained to the children why she left her husband, and they refrained from asking questions.

One day George's wife Claudia came across a book about an eminent Indian diplomat who had the same name as her husband and whose photograph bore an uncanny resemblance to him. George had never heard of the man, who turned out to be the ranking Indian official who had assisted Lord Mountbatten in drawing up the partition plans for India. When George asked his mother about him, she said, "Oh, yes, he is your grandfather. Didn't I ever tell you?" "No, mother," George replied, "you didn't."

George now joined Claudia in the quest for his father's origins. It ultimately took them to India to meet his father's illustrious family. The father had died five years earlier, but there was a half-brother, an uncle (a retired brigadier general), and assorted other relatives. Some of the old family servants remembered him as a small boy. As George learned more about his grandfather, he developed a strong sense of identification with him. Mr. Mehta had made his way in life without relying on his family fortune. His compassion and generosity had been as legendary as his distinguished career. Had he known about his grandfather, George says, he would have tried to emulate him (chapter 9).

Parental alcoholism, most often on the part of fathers, leaves scars that make young adults distance themselves from their families. Roy and his parents live on opposite coasts, and "it's just as well," he sighs. "My father still drinks, so it makes visits difficult. On top of it, my mother insists on telling us how to raise our kids. So we are not very eager to see them, even though I still care for them as my parents."

The majority of our participants seem to have had responsible and caring parents, albeit with their share of failings. But a few exceptional ones have wreaked havoc in their children's lives. The educational elite are thus by no means immune to parental abuse. Doris is a severely anorexic woman whose father was "an intelligent and a brilliant writer, but a real sicko." When she was young, he was very fond of her, but as she entered puberty he turned hostile and physically abusive. At one point, he pushed her down the stairs. Another time he hit her so hard he tore a tendon in his own arm. Doris's father also humiliated her emotionally and intellectually. She says, "He made sure to beat me in the first game of chess we played, while he was teaching me the rules of the game. When he died, I felt very little grief. I was actually relieved that no one would be kicking me around anymore." Her explanation for the father's behavior is that he hated his own mother and somehow transferred this hatred to his wife and daughters.

Doris did not fare much better with her mother. She was a clinical psychologist who had given birth to Doris at age forty and treated her "like a monster." Despite her professional background, Doris's mother gave her very little psychological support, comfort, or understanding. Her parents separated when Doris was young, so more of the abuse was suffered at the hands of the mother. After years of self-doubt and a sense of psychological inadequacy, Doris has finally been able to conclude that "it is they who were weird, not me."

Another particularly dramatic case came to our attention when Eli provided us with a written account of his life history. Having read our earlier book, Eli had been struck with how well the Unconnected label fit him. So through the story of his life, he wanted to explain why he failed to "connect" in college. The following excerpts only do partial justice to the lengthy document that tells the remarkable story of his life. It was a story that took us completely by surprise because we knew nothing about it when he was an undergraduate and a study subject for four years. It is a humbling reminder of how ignorant we can be about the deepest currents of the lives of the young men and women whom we teach, advise, and study, and how much suffering can exist under the cheery front of the most privileged students.

> I was born on October 18, 1959, the second of three sons to an upper-middle-class family. My father was a doctor and my mother was a housewife. I was (for reasons unknown) the focal point of some internal rage in my mother, apparently from the moment I was born. I was regularly beaten up with closed fists as well as whipped with belts and hit with various other objects. When I was older my father began to participate in the abuse. He would beat me while my mother held me down. By the time I was eight, my mother had split my head open twice, once with the heel of a shoe and once with a belt buckle. I was warned not to tell anyone and learned that even if I did I would not be believed. The second time my mother split my head open, I came to my father, bleeding from the scalp. He simply looked me in the eye and said "Don't get me involved between you and your mother," and walked away.

In addition to the physical abuse there was also tremendous psychological abuse. Eli was belittled, humiliated, spat upon, and given the nickname within the family of "The Filth." "Since neither of my two brothers were subjected to any of this abuse they had to find a way to deal with this situation. As a result they concluded that I was 'contaminated.' For seven years they neither touched me or allowed me to touch them. All of this left me as isolated as I believe a child can be, so I withdrew into myself. This, I believe, is what led to my 'unconnectedness.'"

To escape his circumstances, Eli excelled in academics. In addition, he found refuge in substance abuse. He began drinking at age eleven and using drugs at age thirteen. Abuse of drugs and alcohol would later become a real problem for him, but for a long time it was something that he believes helped keep him alive. "I was consciously suicidal from the time I was about eight. I kept a stash of 100 Actifed pills until I went to Stanford."

About this time Eli began running away from home. He slept in canyons or vacant houses in the hills and panhandled on the streets to get money. Eventually he would be picked up by the police and sent to juvenile hall or a home for runaways before being released to his parents.

After three years of this, Eli was sent to a co-ed boarding school for "troubled kids." He thrived at the school. He was taken in by one of the teachers at the school and lived as a member of her family. As a result, he essentially stopped using drugs and alcohol for the three years that he was at this school. By the time he graduated Eli was treasurer of the student body, earned varsity letters in cross-country running, basketball, and volleyball, had the lead in the school play, was editor of the yearbook, won awards for pottery, learned sign language and tutored at a school for the deaf, was Valedictorian, and was accepted at Stanford.

After a difficult freshman year, Eli went overseas for his sophomore year. "Socially and academically it was a wonderful experience. Unfortunately one of the reasons that it was so successful is that I discovered the double-edged joy of narcotics." When Eli returned to Stanford he found a circle of friends, and although he was now heavily involved in drug use, his academic work did not suffer: he scored 717 out of 800 on his LSAT for admission to law school.

After college Eli took a year off before law school to work and travel throughout the United States, Europe, and North Africa with his college roommate. "We originally planned on writing a book entitled *Europe on 5 Women a Day,* but it never happened." On his return, Eli started law school. "I shaved off my beard, cut my hair, and prepared to become a mainstream yuppie clone. It didn't take. By the end of the first semester I had discovered that success in law school only required the ability to memorize a lot of material and regurgitate it on the exams. So I spent law school smoking a lot of dope and cramming madly at the end of each semester. Other than clerking for a Superior Court judge the summer after my first year and studying at Oxford the summer after my second, law school was a waste of time." After passing the California Bar, Eli started working at a corporate law firm but his continuing drug use caused this to be a disaster.

After being fired from the law firm, Eli took a job as a wilderness guide in Alaska. When that job ended at the end of the summer, Eli moved to Colorado to ski. It was here that he finally got clean and sober and began teaching paralegal classes at a local junior college. After the course ended he began dating one of his students and two years later they were married.

It was a "three for the price of one" deal as she had two daughters ages three and six. The three of them are my greatest joy. The girls are now eleven and fourteen and, as their biological father is basically uninvolved, they're mine. Raising these girls has given me the childhood I never had. They are growing up to be strong, independent young women to whom evil is still something they've experienced only on television. My wife is the perfect partner for me. She also survived an abusive childhood so there is a lot of understanding between us. We have very similar goals and desires from life as well as similar ideas in regard to children and family (in our home no one hits anyone at any time for any reason) and we have a wonderfully close family life.

Several years after his marriage, Eli moved his family to Idaho to find a safe place to raise his children. He got a job at a local junior college.

Everything was perfect. That's when I fell apart. I went into a depression the like of which I had never experienced. For three months I moved into the basement and was unable even to talk to my family. Had I not had my wife and kids to think about I think I would have killed myself. I was unable to work; in fact, I was literally unable to do anything. I have never believed in psychotherapy, but it was the only game in town, so I began to see a shrink. The fact is that I had never really dealt with the things that happened to me as a child—I was too busy surviving. After we moved here, the surviving was over and I had to pay the piper.

Since this was written Eli has enrolled at the University of Idaho, working toward his teaching credential. He is planning to teach history and work with teenagers. After two years of therapy, he says, "I am finally coming out of a black hole." Eli credits his wife and children for sustaining him through the ordeal. Now, by nurturing them and the children of others, he hopes to break the cycle of abuse and violence that has marred his own life for so long.

CHAPTER 8

Is This What I Want?

"I have left my husband," says a woman to her friend.

"But why?" protests the friend. "Your husband is the most wonderful man you could possibly hope to find." And she goes on to enumerate the many fine qualities that make the man such an ideal mate. "Everything you say is true," agrees the woman. "But take a look at my shoes. They are made of the finest leather, exquisitely designed, the very best you could hope to find; but it is only I who know where they pinch my feet."

As this somewhat modified version of an ancient tale conveys, in marriage, as in many aspects of life, what ultimately counts is not quality but fit. The critical question is not "Is he (or she) good enough?" but, "Is this what I want?"

In chapter 5, we addressed the matter of career success; in this chapter, we address the corresponding issue of marital success, considering especially how the two basic dimensions of young adulthood, career and family, merge and clash. How well these two dimensions fit together is a key determinant of the overall contentment of couples at this stage in their lives.

THE PROFILE GROUP

All five married couples in the profile group have generally happy marriages despite considerable differences in how their family lives have meshed with their careers. Of the two cohabiting couples, one fits this pattern of contentment, the other does not. Our one unattached single man remains untested.

We referred earlier to Martin MacMillan's commitment "for life" to his marriage. His level of contentment is also high, although "not everything is wonderful all the time." About his competence as a spouse, Martin says, "I am still learning." As a physician, he is used to giving orders, but he realizes that his house is not a hospital. The occasional conflicts he and his wife have are mainly rooted in the demands and stresses of caring for young children. Although parenthood has cut into the time Martin and his wife have for each other, he is delighted to be a father. He says, "My son remains a profound joy in my life. My daughter similarly blesses us." Martin's affection for his children is the one thing in his life that will not take a backseat to his love of medicine. Nonetheless, neither marriage nor parenthood have had a major impact on the course of Martin's career, which probably would not have progressed so smoothly if Martin had married a physician instead of a nurse. If he were to do it again, Martin would follow the same path, though he might wait a little longer before getting into the cycle of marriage and parenthood. He has not had much of a breather between the rigors of his medical training and the onset of his family responsibilities.

Careerist Cynthia Eastwood is effusive in her expressions of satisfaction with her marriage ("wonderful") and commitment ("150 percent"). She and Jeffrey are "great spouses in a truly equal relationship in which we complement each other." She values highly the "friendship, support, love, and passion" that binds them together. Like her career, Cynthia's marriage has been "great and is getting better every year." Her mettle as a mother is yet to be tested. Yet Cynthia, who thrives on new challenges, has no fears. When the bar goes up, she jumps higher. When she has a child, she will become a "Supermom."

Intellectual Kirsten Buchanan is no Supermom, but she is a superb mother. Her keen intelligence, managerial competence, and deep maternal feelings have been channeled into the raising of her two children. "Motherhood is by far my most challenging job yet," she says. Kirsten and her husband are very happy, even though caring for two small children places a lot of strain on their daily lives. Especially when the children were younger, Kirsten felt "like a very good mother but not a very good wife. It is a difficult stage." Reflecting back on the drastic shift in her career trajectory that followed marriage and motherhood, Kirsten says,

The simple truth is this: I made an error in my choice of career. While at Stanford, two factors steered me towards business, my two summers working in Europe, and the fact that most of my international clan of friends were at business school. My friends pointed out that I had a knack for helping them with their studies and encouraged me to go into business. Two profs I respected while at biz school told me that I was one of their most insightful marketing students ever. Pretty heady stuff. The fit seemed right.

I also thought business would be something I could control better than a medical or law degree. Leave work at the office and let my private time be my own. This comes from having a father who was a dedicated physician with very little time left over for his family.

It took two years working in New York for me to realize that just because I was very good at something did not mean it was the right job. My performance reviews were stellar insofar as accomplishments, technical skills, ability to work with others, communication skills, timeliness, perseverance, etc. However, it was consistently commented that I was not happy with my job description, and that I sought more creativity. Whereas, I obviously had a multidisciplined job as an analyst, my job failed to engage my intellect sufficiently to give me a sense of fulfillment. For me, contentment is a function of the degree of intellectual engagement in my job. My job will have to be an extension of that essence. To deny it is to deny what I am.

I do not know what I will do once my children get into school. Nor does my uncertainty bother me. I recall my words as an incoming freshman, "I can do anything." I may seem to you that I am back where I started, but I am not. I am happy, confident, and wiser. Perhaps the knowledge that I am financially, emotionally, and professionally able to tackle anything is what makes it possible for me to stay home with the children. I have no regrets.

The fact that Intellectual Christopher Luce has not yet faced the same music does not mean that he has not given serious thought to the potential conflict between career and family life. As mentioned earlier, his unwillingness to settle down is only partly based on his not having yet found the right person and his reluctance to give up his freedom. There is also the real concern of how to juggle family responsibilities with his intellectual pursuits and academic career.

Christopher actually faces a tougher choice in this respect than the other men. What he really wants, deep down, is a wife who will look after their children. But unlike Philip Genochio, he is not willing to come out and say so because that would be anathema in his politically enlightened academic world, an ideological perspective he himself shares. Moreover, the only type of woman he can imagine marrying would be highly educated and an intellectually sophisticated person who is not likely to keep house for him or care for their children single-handedly. And unlike David Levy, Christopher is unwilling to bend his career to accommodate the career aspirations of such women. So he is stuck with one foot in each camp. "I recognize my own selfishness in this regard. And I know I am going to have to make concessions somewhere along the line. It's going to be a very painful process."

Some others have managed to straddle both camps. Striver George Mehta is a good example. Like the fine balance he achieved between his intellectual life and career aspirations in college, George has also integrated his career and family life. "We love each other very much," says George without affectation. "I couldn't imagine going through life without Claudia." She is a a "friend and confidante" he can count on. Their commitment, which was thoroughly tested before marriage, is fully binding. "After meeting and getting to know my wife," says George, "I couldn't imagine doing things differently than now." He acknowledges that "a child is very, very special." Yet, he says, "the primary relationship is between my wife and me. My illness has made me realize that all the more, but it was true before as well." In hindsight, George wishes he had spent less time on his career and more with his family: "I took pride in my work and wanted to work longer hours, but now I have some regret about working so hard. I have now learned that it's okay to work fewer hours, especially now that I am older and can employ experience rather than a willingness to throw raw hours at a situation."

Striver Geraldine Jones's personal life and career have been through some twists and turns, with little impact on each other. It is possible, of course, that being more settled in one area of life would have stabilized her in the other. Now that Geraldine seems to have anchored herself in her work as a paramedic, perhaps her personal life will settle down as well.

The nontraditional arrangements that our two Unconnected participants fashioned for themselves have worked out very well for each of them. During the decade that David Levy and Judith have been together, their careers have meshed along with their personal lives. "We are happy together," says David, "and very committed to each other." He values the "emotional attachment, companionship, and caring" and feels "lucky to be in a relationship like that and to be able to support each other." There have been periods when the pressure of their work has not allowed them enough time for each other, so "it gets a bit stressful at times." David wants to make sure to be in the sort of jobs that allow enough such time, which will be especially important after they have children.

Katherine Johnson is "100 percent" happy and committed to her marriage. She is also fully appreciative of having a husband whose willingness to tend the hearth has allowed her to pursue her highly successful career. The high point of her life has been the birth of her child, and the low point continues to be the brutal pace of her work. She is in the sort of law firm that "expects you to put your personal life on hold until, if successful, you are made partner and earn $500,000 a year." Katherine is successful, but she does not want to put her life on hold. Although she has already negotiated to work three-quarters time, she is still unhappy over how little time she has for her family. Neither Katherine nor her husband want to go on with their current arrangement, and they want to have another child soon. Consequently, Katherine is likely to get off her current career course sometime over the next decade. What she would really like to do instead is be a judge. But to do that, Katherine would either have to stay on course until she attains a senior position in her law firm or rely on political connections, which she does not have. The more realistic alternative for her seems to be to work for a smaller law firm, at a slower pace and for less pay. Katherine's case highlights the dilemma faced by highly successful career women even in the best of circumstances, a major issue we address in the rest of this chapter.

MARITAL SATISFACTION

Like career success, marital satisfaction is a function of right choice and proper maintenance, and it can be assessed by external as well as internal criteria. A business that loses money fails; a marriage that ends in divorce has gone bankrupt. But a marriage remaining intact in and of itself does not mean it is successful. No matter how successful a career or marriage looks from the outside, a full understanding is based on how it looks on the inside to the persons involved.

ASSESSING MARITAL SATISFACTION

Numerous studies have attempted to determine what makes for "good" or "bad" marriages. Some of the conclusions are obvious. For instance, one of the most consistent differences reported between good and bad marriages is the "niceness" or "nastiness" of daily encounters between the spouses. Good marriages are characterized by a lot more niceness, and bad marriages are full of nastiness, a conclusion that must be as true as it is self-evident.[1]

Two additional factors of great importance are compatibility and resources. Not only are couples of similar age, social background, religious outlook, and so on, more likely to marry, they are also more likely to be satisfied with their marriages. And couples with more education, higher social status, and larger incomes are insulated from many of the practical survival problems that arise and cause friction for couples with fewer resources. Communication skills and conflict resolution strategies can further improve the quality of relationships. By contrast, higher expectations, the lesser dependence of career women on their husbands, and more liberal attitudes toward divorce can have the opposite effect. In fact, college graduates have only slightly more stable marriages than nongraduates.[2]

To gauge our participants' subjective assessments of their marriages, we used the same four criteria that we applied to careers: contentment, commitment, competence, and compensation. In this case compensation refers to the rewards and satisfactions they derive from their marriages.

CONTENTMENT

If the educational elite seem highly satisfied with their careers, they are even more pleased with their marriages: 72 percent express high contentment, 86 percent indicate high commitment, and 71 percent see themselves as highly competent. By contrast, less than 2 percent fall into the low category in any of these dimensions. We get a lively sense of how positively these young men and women view their marriages through a selection of their comments on marital contentment:

- The highest it could be. He is the greatest guy, and we have the greatest time.
- I am very happy. I have a good wife. No problems.
- I am extremely happy in my marriage; I have grown up a lot in my relationship with my wife. Things have been especially great since we had our son.
- 100 percent. He is a great guy, fun, and very supportive.
- Very high. We are very comfortable. I consider myself to be very lucky.
- It has been an excellent choice. We love each other very much.
- Very high. We are especially happy with our children. If I did one thing right in my life, this is it.
- He is the best person I could be married to.
- We have a wonderful relationship and are delighted with our child.
- We consider ourselves so fortunate that at times we feel like pinching ourselves.

Given the high national divorce rate and the litany of marital woes commonly found in studies of marital satisfaction, our first reaction to these findings was skepticism. We wondered if our couples sounded so happy because they were simply too young, with too few years of marriage behind them, to have run into the rough spots and hidden incompatibilities that are bound to make a substantial portion of their marriages problematic. Given the prevalence of divorce, it is highly unlikely that this segment of the educational elite will be indefinitely exempt from the malaise and alienation that are the fate of so many marriages. So far, however, most are doing very well.

Of course, not everyone is deliriously happy. For one thing, the above ratings exclude those who are divorced (almost one in ten of those ever married), whom we discuss separately. Moreover, even among those who say they are content, some qualify or hedge their expressions of satisfaction:

- I am quite happy, though I wish he were a little more sensitive with people, including myself.
- It is better now. We have had our ups and downs.
- We are doing all right now. He is a good father to the kids.
- We get along well. My wife and I may disagree, but we don't fight.
- We are not afraid to face our problems when they come up.
- It depends. When I get home to my husband and kids after a long day at work and the house looks like it has been hit by a tornado, I don't feel very happy.
- My wife and I have had a stormy relationship. It's better now, but there are still deficiencies. There is always the possibility of our breaking up, as we almost did a couple of times.
- We have known each other since high school. I can't think of being married to anyone else. But since I am a perfectionist, something always falls short.

COMMITMENT

Religious, social, and practical considerations keep some couples together even though they are less than entirely contented. The commitment symbolized by marriage can induce couples to paint positive pictures of their marriages even when the canvas is badly frayed. Judy and her husband, both from conservative backgrounds, are a good example. Although the thought of divorce has crossed her mind during periods of severe crisis in her marriage, she has never considered it a real option because, she says, "divorce is not part of our vocabulary." When Arnold states, "We have had a lot of divorces in our family; I don't want the same thing to happen to me," the ring of determination in his voice reflects something beyond contentment.

As these examples suggest, commitment generally outpaces contentment among the educational elite: 86 percent indicate that they are highly committed, 72 percent are highly contented. This response partly arises from their highly refined sense of responsibility ("I am not about to jump over the fence for greener grass"), as well as their equally refined horror of failure. They feel a strong incentive to stick with their choices, even when they consider the alternatives. ("One does wonder what else might have been.")

These qualifications notwithstanding, the interviews provide many ringing testimonials of commitment among these couples:

- This is it.
- It's a lifelong commitment.
- I can't imagine being married to anyone else.
- 100 percent.
- Nothing is going to change. We will always be together.
- Total.
- When I first met him, I had the sense that this was it. I have never felt otherwise.
- I am committed to my wife and to fulfilling her aspirations in life.

Yet, once again, others qualify their commitment, often redirecting it from their spouse to their children.

- For the first couple of years, I had serious doubts if the marriage was going to survive. But it has gotten better since we had our daughter.
- I love my kids too much to think differently.
- Our son holds us together.

COMPETENCE

At its broadest, competence as a spouse would encompass helping one's partner live up to his or her potential, sustaining the other for better or worse, being a sensitive companion and soul mate. Perhaps because many of our participants understood these concerns to be subsumed under contentment and commitment, they often interpreted competence as doing one's share in more mundane matters. The way our participants saw it, if marriage is a partnership, how well it works largely depends on how effective each person is at performing spousal roles. As one said, "Once the bigger picture is decided, it is the little things that matter. Sharing life's small and sometimes unpleasant tasks is a key to marital happiness."

The percentage of those who claim to be highly competent spouses is almost exactly the same (71 percent) as that for those expressing high levels of contentment. But contentment, commitment, and competence are not mere synonyms. Contentment and commitment are strongly related (a correlation coefficient of .72), but neither is closely related to competence (coefficients of about .30). Contentment in marriage is thus intimately bound up with commitment, as both cause and effect, but feelings of competence may or may not be present to the same extent. In any case, at this stage in their marriages, a strong sense of competence does not seem to be required for a contented, committed feeling.

Moreover, as our participants were quick to point out, competence is a complex notion. One kind of competence relates to the practical skills of living together (earning a living, managing the household, rearing children). We bring a different kind of competence to social interaction (maintaining family and social ties, dealing effectively with people) and to intimate relationships (being affectionate, trustworthy, a good lover, loyal). Given the fairly short length of their marriages, many of our couples rightly feel that they are still new at the game but getting better at it.

We expected problems of competence in personal and intimate relationships to figure most prominently, but that was not the case. Instead, the most important area turned out to be the inability or unwillingness of partners to pitch in on more mundane matters. This complaint was voiced mainly by women in reference to their husbands' failure to help sufficiently with housework and child care (chapter 7).

Traditionally, the failure to be a good provider has been the primary form of spousal incompetence for men, but that is not the case for men in the educational elite; they do fine on that score. From a career woman's perspective, the crucial expectation is now that their husbands will pull their weight on the home front. This has set a new "standard" for the evaluation of what is desirable in a husband. One woman whose husband excels in "doing his share" said, "Women would kill to have my husband."

Most men readily acknowledge their shortcomings on the home front ("I know I should help more") and ascribe them to the pressure of work. Yet they also betray an undercurrent of resentment. They feel that what they do is not appreciated enough and that they are always found wanting, even if they are doing the best they can. By contrast, men voice few complaints about the competence of their wives. None were described as lousy cooks, sloppy housekeepers, or incompetent mothers—perhaps, in part, because of men's self-consciousness about their own failure to do more around the house.

A key distinction our participants made in this area was between being able to perform a task and being willing to do it. A man may be a good cook, but if he is not willing to cook, his partner gets very frustrated. On the other hand, since no one can be good at everything, allowances are made for shortcomings if they are accompanied by a willingness to try. Even blatant weaknesses can be tolerated if they are balanced by strengths in other areas (thus satisfying the equity principle). But a steadfast refusal to perform either the gender-specific roles of a conventional marriage or the shared roles of an egalitarian marriage is seen as the worst form of spousal incompetence, since it calls into question the person's commitment to the relationship.[3] By the same token, to have their competence and their love questioned because they are not washing enough dishes is galling to men who see themselves as hard-working and devoted husbands.[4]

COMPENSATION

Compensation refers to the rewards and satisfactions a person derives from marriage. This issue evoked a wide variety of responses, which we have grouped under a few common themes. Leading the list (54 percent of responses) were comments referring to some aspect of close friendship. Many said, "My wife/husband is my best friend." Others spoke of "companionship," "camaraderie," "having fun together." A few specified "shared interests," "values," "respect," and "acceptance." One man said, "We are happy together because we respect each other as independent entities. She knows me, understands me, and accepts me for who I am."

Children were the second most often named reward of marriage (23 percent). Bernard came to his interview on a Sunday at a small airport lounge with his wife and three children in tow. At one point during the interview, his youngest girl came and sat on her father's lap. When the question came up about compensation in marriage, Bernard looked at his daughter and said softly, "You are looking at it."

"Security" was cited as another major reward, by close to 15 percent. The term was more often used by women. Men were more likely to refer to "stability," "being grounded," and "having someone to come home to." Other terms more often used by women were "support," "acceptance," "intimacy," "emotional well-being," and "being appreciated."

Only 10 percent specified "love," and most comments suggested that a more companionate form of love, based on intimacy and commitment, characterizes the marriages of our participants. No one said, "We have great sex," though a satisfying sexual relationship seemed to be taken for granted.

If this all sounds like the description of couples in the twilight of life rather than in the full bloom of youth, we do not mean to imply that the spark of passion has already gone out of their lives. Rather, even at this fairly early stage of their marriages, they have moved past the romantic phase of happily-ever-after bliss and settled into a more enduring form of love. There are also some who are happier than they could have imagined. "I am very content. I found a person who suits me very well, who, in addition to being my wife, is also my closest friend. My commitment turned out to be more than I expected; I find I put in more energy in my relationship with my wife than I thought I would because of my work as a surgeon. But now I find it hard to spend so much time at work because I want to be with her. Our marriage is so idyllic that it almost feels like somebody has written a novel for us to act out."

Given the high overall rates of satisfaction in marriage, there is little room for gender or type differences. We see a slight tendency on the part of women to be more contented than men (79 percent versus 68 percent in the high category) and to be more committed (92 percent versus 82 percent in the high category), but not even a whisper of difference in competence.

A bit more variation is evident by type. Surprisingly, Strivers are somewhat less content (54 percent in the high category, compared with the mean of 72 percent) and less committed (69 percent, as against a mean of 86 percent). Since Strivers, particularly Striver women, are also less likely to marry than other groups, it seems likely that Strivers have exceptionally high expectations of marriage that are hard to live up to. The Unconnected see themselves as somewhat less competent spouses than others (54 percent highly competent versus a mean of 71 percent). But this finding is not accompanied by lower contentment or commitment and is most likely to be another manifestation of the Unconnected "discounting" their abilities.

SOCIAL TIME

As with career consolidation, another measure of marital satisfaction comes from our participants' perceptions of where they stand in their personal lives with respect to social time. The majority of married subjects (68 percent) consider themselves "on time"; 23 percent see themselves as ahead of schedule, and only 9 percent feel behind. By contrast, most of the unmarried (88 percent) say they are behind schedule. Marriage is thus the crucial issue: by the time they reach the age of thirty, the educational elite feel they should be married (or have a steady partner). Though having children is not the direct issue here, we suspect that, especially for women, being unmarried at age thirty creates anxiety about the prospect of not having children until their mid to late thirties—if ever.

Personal social time and career social time are closely related. Those who feel behind time personally also feel slow in their careers; most of those who feel on time personally also feel on time in their careers. Perhaps there is a true linkage in our progress along the career and family tracks. But how we view this issue, our attitude, may be as meaningful as the reality.

The one exception to this pattern is the group that feels ahead of the game in their careers. Though this group generally feels ahead of the game personally as well, a substantial portion (40 percent) feel behind in personal time.

MARITAL CONFLICT

Most couples enter the marital relationship with little expectation of facing conflicts. When conflicts arise, shock and incredulity may lead them to question the wisdom of the marriage. But over time, most couples learn how to deal with conflict more effectively. As one woman put it, "The longer you live with someone, the more you learn to argue gracefully." By the same token, a good marriage, like a healthy body, does not simply mean the absence of distress and dysfunction. If it lacks positive attributes—affection, attraction, intimacy, mutual respect and support—it will not thrive, no matter how rarely major conflicts arise.

PATTERNS OF MARITAL CONFLICT

Our couples reported a wide variety of marital conflicts, ranging from minor and transient disagreements to irreconcilable differences. The first and largest category is occasional disagreement between spouses who are otherwise quite satisfied with their marriages. As we have noted repeatedly, these disagreements are often over the sharing of housekeeping and child-rearing responsibilities. Heather is one of the most happily married women in our sample and has perfectly integrated her roles as a mother and a teacher. Yet it took some effort for her to negotiate a satisfactory working agreement with her husband, a business executive.

> Early in our marriage, when I stayed home to take care of our two children, I also took care of the house. But after I went back to work, it became very hard to do both, even though I was teaching only part-time. So my husband and I had a number of discussions and four good fights about it. Though he never said he did not want to help, he somehow never managed to do it. Then I came up with a list of "tedious tasks," and I made him apply his managerial skills in setting up a system of splitting the chores. Now I cook four dinners a week, pay the bills, and take care of the kids; he cooks three dinners, is in charge of the dogs, the recycling, and the lawn.

The problem is more acute between Elizabeth, the financial analyst who came to the interview with her three-week-old baby, and her husband Tim. She met him in college, and they lived together following graduation, marrying four years later. They are "best friends," fond of each other, and committed to their marriage. Yet they have been unable to resolve the issue of the division of labor at home. Elizabeth's work hours are as long as Tim's, and she makes as much money. Yet the primary responsibility for housekeeping falls on her shoulders. He is "in principle interested in helping," but his assistance amounts to very little in practice.

Elizabeth admits that part of the problem is her high expectations. She says, "My housekeeping standards are higher than his, so I must either push him to do a more thorough job or do it over myself." After the baby came, Tim began to do a lot more at home. Elizabeth fears, however, that he will do so only for the short run and that she will be saddled with the main child-rearing tasks ahead. If that happens, she sees more marital conflict looming on the horizon. Elizabeth not only worries about the situation but is also truly perplexed as to why a reasonable and fair man like Tim, who so genuinely cares for her, cannot seem to understand the situation.

The stresses that these situations engender are the result of what sociologists call "role conflict" and "role strain." Role conflict arises when the functions and expectations of two or more roles are incompatible. Career building and homemaking are the primary incompatible roles here: time spent on one is time taken away from the other. Another form of role conflict is the incompatible demands of spousal and parental roles, especially for the mothers of young children who find it difficult to be simultaneously a good wife and good mother. Men do not face the same dilemma, because they play a much smaller parental role.

Role strain is failure to live up to the demands of a role owing to high expectations, lack of competence, insufficient experience, or simply lack of time due to the heavy demands of the several roles to be played by one person. Elizabeth, as a career woman and first-time mother with exacting standards for herself, feels a great deal of both role conflict and role strain.

"Problems in communication" is another common complaint of these couples. For instance, Elizabeth is baffled that she and Tim are unable to deal effectively with their conflict over housekeeping chores. She says, "Though we are both skillful negotiators at work, we cannot resolve this issue in a rational, businesslike manner. I let resentment build up, then will get angry over some trivial matter and blow up."

This complaint was raised by quite a few others who also see themselves as articulate men and women with good communication skills that somehow prove ineffectual in getting through to their spouses. For instance, as a vice president for employee benefits, Alex thinks of himself as a "professional negotiator." Yet not only does that skill not seem to help at home, but on the contrary, it makes his wife Teresa feel frustrated in trying to make her views prevail against his. So she simply withdraws and lets their disagreements fester.

Some respondents attributed this problem to a basic gender difference. Edward says, "As a man and an engineer, I have a 'rational' approach to issues which my wife does not share," so he finds himself frustrated and irritated in trying to resolve their differences (a feeling she no doubt shares). Similarly, Peter is "analytic," and his wife is more "emotional" in her outlook. The idea of gender-based styles of communication seems to resonate with many people, as evidenced by the enormous popularity of books on the subject.[5]

Yet what appear to be "problems in communication" often conceal deeper and very real conflicts. For example, Alex acknowledges that many of Mary's complaints have to do with her role as the "accommodater" in their marriage, adapting herself to the demands of their family and his career. She even plays this role with her own parents when the latter retreat to her home as a refuge from their frenetic lives (her mother is an actress, her father a television producer). To top it off, as a preschool teacher Mary is "mother" to a flock of children, just as she is a "fantastic mother" to her own. As a result, "she is always giving, giving." Alex recognizes all this but still feels that he himself does not get enough of his wife's affection. Beyond their communication problems is a disparity in their needs. As he puts it, "I need a hug, while she needs a helping hand."

The second category of conflict involves marriages that have already been damaged. The problems here are more intractable and the level of conflict higher, thus putting in jeopardy the relationship itself. Most cases involve women participants. In fact, most of the instances of marital conflict that came to our attention were brought up by women, presumably because women are more willing to discuss their emotional lives and men are more hesitant to reveal anything important about their personal or intimate feelings. And, in practical terms, men may have less to complain about because most of them are not struggling with the burdens of housekeeping and child rearing in addition to their work.

Rebecca married her college boyfriend after living with him for some time. She holds an M.B.A. and is the mother of a small child. Her husband, "intelligent and loving" as he is, does very little around the house. "He comes from a traditional Orthodox Jewish family," she explains. "His mother did everything at home. So he expects me to do the same things, the same way. But I have a full-time job, and his mother didn't." Rebecca has made little headway in resolving the issue and feels stymied.

A man doing his share around the house does not solve all problems. Sarah is married to a brilliant scientist who is a good father and a helpful husband. When she met and married him, in very short order, he looked right for her. What she did not know was that he had a serious alcohol problem. Initially his drinking bouts were episodic, but when he "hit rock bottom," he had to be hospitalized. Sarah's anguish about her husband's drinking is compounded by the fact that her father is an alcoholic. Despite her husband's year of sobriety, she knows the dangers that lurk in the future. ("I can see the writing on the wall.") At the height of the crisis, her parents urged her to leave her husband. "You are still young, attractive, and talented," they argued. "You can make a fresh start." But she stuck with him. She says she loves him, but what appears to be keeping the marriage together is concern for their young son.

Linda's problem is her husband's inability to hold a job—he has lost nine in five years. The pattern is repetitive: he gets a job, begins to have problems with his performance, "blames everyone but himself," and starts drinking and using drugs ("acting like an adolescent"). Soon enough, his performance deteriorates and he quits or is fired. The cycle then repeats itself. Linda is beginning to lose patience. Her inability to depend on her husband's income is an obvious concern. Moreover, her fear that he is likely to continue this pattern leads her to take only safe and secure jobs herself. As a result, she avoids positions that might involve risk but also offer strong opportunities for advancement. Linda is also getting tired of listening to her husband's endless recriminations against his employers and his self-pitying complaints about being victimized.

Why doesn't Linda leave him? "I almost did," she says, "then boom, I got pregnant. I was very upset for several months but couldn't bring myself to get an abortion. I am actually glad I didn't because I was amazed how quickly and intensely I became attached to my baby." She is also pleased that her husband has turned out to be "an excellent father." He also cares about Linda, stands by her, and is considerate and helpful around the house. Nonetheless, Linda has served her husband an ultimatum: "From now on, it's up to you. You get your act together, or I'll move on."

Arturo's relationship with his wife was intensely romantic at the outset but soon foundered. "There was a long period of hurting, followed by one of healing, which is still going on," he remarks, with the voice of a man who is still hurting. He ascribes their difficulties to his wife's "enormous amount of suppressed anger, which she had harbored over the years, caused by being neglected and abused by her alcoholic parents, especially her father, and also her brothers." As a result, she brought to the marriage an exquisite sensitivity to any sign of neglect or abuse. Arturo says, "She was quick to react with vehemence whenever she thought I was not listening to what she was saying, and the slightest hint of criticism was taken as a put-down."

Arturo was slow to realize that "our conflicts were not necessarily a reflection of my own inadequacy as a husband." As the son of a violent, alcoholic father himself, he had his own problems with self-esteem. He says, "I wish we had married a little later, after we had sorted out our own problems." Nonetheless, by standing by each other and cooperating in bringing up their children, Arturo and his wife have developed a strong feeling of competence as parents that has helped their relationship as spouses as well. "My wife is now a tremendous friend and a source of love for me," says Arturo. "We will be together for the rest of our lives."

Another kind of family conflict, external to the relationship itself, occurs in some interfaith marriages. In a number of instances, parental objections actually prevented the marriage; Joel's rejection by his girlfriend's Catholic parents because he is Jewish is one example. Sometimes the couple married despite the objections, and then one or both sets of parents set out to make them regret it. Alejandro's problems were the obverse of Joel's: it was his fiancée's Jewish parents who objected. Alejandro and Ruth met in business school, fell in love, and wanted to marry. Her parents were "dead set against it and particularly vicious in their opposition," says Alejandro. "It was not only because I was Catholic but, even worse, because I was a Chicano. Ruth's parents told her they could possibly have relented if I had been an Irish Catholic, but they were not going to have a Mexican in the family."

Ruth stood firm. They moved in together, and she continued to argue her case with her parents, who steadfastly refused even to meet him. Finally, she stopped speaking to them. When Alejandro and Ruth got married, her parents came to the wedding reluctantly and met Alejandro face to face for the first time after four years. His acceptance of Ruth's wish that the children be brought up in the Jewish faith softened her parents somewhat. And with the arrival of the first baby, the turnabout was dramatic: Ruth's mother, Alejandro's chief antagonist, became "the most doting of grandmothers." And when Alejandro decided to convert to Judaism, at his own initiative, all was forgiven. His conversion, however, alienated Alejandro from his own devoutly Catholic parents, who had been sullenly opposed to the match all along and now were dismayed at his "betrayal of his faith and his people."

A variety of other sources of simmering resentment also came up in the interviews. The two men who felt trapped into marrying their pregnant girlfriends are still smarting over it. Some others, mostly men, lament that their spouses have not met their expectations and wonder about the opportunities they missed, either by not waiting longer to marry or by not marrying that special woman who would no longer wait for them. The sense that perhaps "I did not get as good a deal as I could," as one of them put it, gnaws at them, lowering their tolerance of any deficiencies they see in their spouses. Some women feel likewise. Others who are struggling to reconcile the competing demands of career and family wonder if they would not have been better off remaining single or marrying someone else. The passage of time, on the other hand, and the arrival of children tend to submerge these feelings among both sexes.

EFFECTS OF PARENTHOOD

Studies of marital satisfaction over the life cycle typically show couples at their most content when they are newly married. Levels of satisfaction drop noticeably when they have children but recover as the children start school and require less care and attention. As the children enter adolescence, satisfaction plummets. It then rises once more as the children enter adulthood and leave home.[6]

This pattern does not apply equally to all types of marriages. Single-child families are less subject to the above pattern than larger families in that the drop in marital satisfaction for women is minimal after the birth of the first child but much more marked after the second.[7] Marriages that are more conventional in their gender roles or marked by high levels of satisfaction before the arrival of children suffer a much smaller drop in marital satisfaction when children come on the scene than do other marriages.[8] These patterns suggest that, although children always put a lot of strain on a marriage, they need not affect a happy marriage negatively (they may in fact make it stronger), but they do intensify the strains in a less happy relationship. Moreover, though marriages suffer a decline in satisfaction when the children are born, after they grow up their parents express a higher level of marital satisfaction than do childless couples the same age. Thus, childless couples have neither the lows nor the highs experienced by those with children.[9]

Two recent longitudinal studies of the impact of the first child on marriage shed further light on these issues. One study was carried out by Jay Belsky, the other by Carolyn and Philip Cowan.[10] Both studies dealt with samples of couples from the time of first pregnancy to several years after the birth of the child. The results of these studies are fairly consistent: many, but by no means all, couples experience significant difficulties following the birth of their first child. In Belsky's group, one out of two marriages went into "decline"; in the Cowans' study, over 12 percent of the new parents had separated or divorced by the time the baby was one and a half years old. Belsky claims that what happens after the baby arrives depends not on the new child-care demands but on the nature of the couple's previous relationship, and their expectations about parenthood. Dissatisfaction comes earlier and is much greater for women. Couples who were least satisfied with their marriages before the child were most likely to suffer a further decline (which argues against the notion that having a child saves faltering marriages). Moreover, the greater the woman's attachment to her career, the more likely she is to experience a decline in marital satisfaction. Couples whose marriage improves with parenthood are those who can both include and exclude the child: if they can retain some of the exclusivity of the marital bond while also forging a new, larger unit that has much meaning for both of them, parenthood is likely to have a positive impact.

The Cowans place the experience of parenthood in the broader context of the inner life of each parent, the quality of their relationship with each other, and the quality of their relationship with their own parents. They find that declining marital satisfaction cannot be linked to any particular factor, such as conflict at work or the division of labor at home. But they can identify several conditions that increase the likelihood of dissatisfaction. These include ambivalence toward having children in the first place, women expecting their husbands to be more involved in child care than they turn out to be, differing conceptions of proper parenting methods and goals, and trouble in the couple's sexual relationship.

Our own results on the effect of children on marital satisfaction among the educational elite show that childless couples as a group are, at this stage, more content with their marriages (86 percent highly content, but only 59 percent of those with children) and more committed to their partners (93 percent versus 79 percent). As their children get older, levels of contentment are expected to rise. The only area in which children do not make a difference is personal competence. Since our study was not primarily focused on the impact of parenthood, however, we do not have systematic data on the factors leading to this apparent lower marital contentment and commitment. Nonetheless, the interview evidence suggests that the demands of parenthood underlie many of the dissatisfactions expressed. But it is also true that relationships with problems prior to the birth of the first child were more likely to develop negative parenthood patterns, making the relationship even worse, which is consistent with the findings of the above studies.

EFFECTS OF HOUSEHOLD RESPONSIBILITY

With respect to the issue of housework, we see an intriguing pattern: men in traditional households feel less content and competent in their marriages than those in shared-responsibility households. Although there are certainly happy marriages among traditional households, and consistency of expectations on the part of both spouses is a key factor in marital happiness, the tide has turned against the traditional pattern among the educational elite. This finding is a strong argument in favor of sharing household tasks, not only for the sake of women but in the interests of men as well: egalitarian marriages seem to work out better for both partners.

Commitment, however, is not at issue here. Men in traditional roles were just as committed as men in shared-labor marriages. It seems likely that women's insistence on shared housekeeping and child rearing makes sharing a part of the very definition of spousal competence. Men who do not live up to the definition feel less competent and therefore less content. In addition, their wives are less content and, by making an issue out of the division of labor, lower the man's contentment as well.

As for women, we find that those in marriages with shared responsibilities also tend to be more content than those in traditional marriages; but they feel somewhat less competent as spouses. Role conflict is clearly at work here: if women have their own careers, they devote less time and energy to the household and then feel they are not performing the homemaker role as well as they should, or as compared to more traditional housewives as exemplified by many of their mothers.

In light of these findings, if men and women are to forge a harmonious marital relationship on an equitable footing of shared responsibility both at work and at home, there should not only be a change in behavior (mostly on the part of men on the home front) but a basic change in attitude on the part of both spouses about their respective roles and responsibilities. In dual-career marriages, men need to accept a more gender-blind division of labor at home, with respect to household chores and child rearing. Women, meanwhile, would benefit from recognizing that men are still subject to traditional expectations about women's responsibility for the home and need their wives to be patient and understanding (as well as firm) as they orient themselves to a more egalitarian partnership.

Although men continue to be criticized for lack of engagement in caring for their children, or abdicating their responsibilities as fathers altogether, there is also an important trend in the emergence of the "nurturing father" who takes on his share of the responsibility, and sometimes the primary responsibility, for the care of his children.[11]

DIVORCE

The statistics on divorce are numbingly familiar: half of all marriages break up, 80 percent of those divorced eventually remarry (after an average period of three years), and one-third of these will divorce again. Divorced men are more likely to remarry than divorced women; the younger the person and the fewer the children, the higher the likelihood of remarriage.[12]

In our entire sample, we had nine failed marriages, amounting to about 8 percent of all marriages. This is a far lower figure than expected, since nationally, 28 percent of thirty- to thirty-four-year-olds who have ever been married have been divorced.[13] Our participants, however, married later than their peers in the general population, so divorce has not had as much chance to occur yet.

Four of the divorced participants were in the interview sample. Tara's marriage to her Argentinean boyfriend (chapter 6) fell victim to their violation of the principle of homogamy. As long as they worked in the same restaurant, status parity sustained their love. When she tired of being a waitress and moved on to work for a computer company, while he continued to wash dishes, the gap between them became a chasm. After three years of off-and-on separation, she left him for good. She is now living with an engineer, a far cry from the "Latin type" of her former husband. She is ready to settle down with a stable man, but she still wonders, "Will I be happy with him?"

Cecilia is Hispanic, a writer turned lawyer. She was married to a fellow lawyer and felt "hindered" by him. "Our career and life trajectories clashed," says Cecilia. With the benefit of hindsight, "I should not have married him, or anyone else, for a while." Since then, she has gone through important changes in her career and personal life and has been in psychotherapy. Currently, she cherishes her friendships but finds close relationships with men "limiting and frustrating." Yet, she adds, "I still hope to find someone who will support my career and be a life partner, and not a burden."

Tammy is a black lawyer. She had known Norton casually for some time before they started dating. They married three months later. "It was an impulsive decision," Tammy admits. "I got infatuated with the guy." Tammy comes from a middle-class family with strong religious values. She was ready to settle down and raise a family, but Norton was not. "He still wanted to act like we were in school," she says. "He was treating me more like a girlfriend than a wife." Before long she left him.

Tammy's divorce left her disillusioned, but her marriage did undercut the "social pressure" she felt to get married, since at least she had already done it. She has now recovered her interest in having a family and is "actively looking," but she knows the poor odds facing professional black women. Tammy dated a blue-collar worker for a while. It did not work. "The men I work with wear tuxedoes," she says ruefully. "This guy didn't own a suit." He could not get over the fact that Tammy was a lawyer and made a lot of money. But he was never seriously in the running; she is determined to be married to someone at her level. "The majority of my friends are not yet married," she says. "Only 20 percent are married, and 20 percent are divorced. Guys don't want to grow up," she laments. "They just don't want to grow up."

Our final divorced interviewed participant is Jeremy. His is a classic case of how personality change can undermine a marriage. Jeremy met Naomi when he was twenty-six. She was an attractive young woman from a conventional middle-class Jewish family, with very clear ideas of what she wanted in a husband. He fit the bill: she fell for him, and he fell for her. "For a while," says Jeremy, "we did the married thing. I was doing well in my business. We moved to a larger apartment, bought a bigger car. We traveled. We laughed together. We had fun together. We got along." Naomi's parents were a bit too much in the picture, and she was never quite free of their influence, but that caused only minor friction.

Then began Jeremy's metamorphosis, much to Naomi's bewilderment and eventual rage. His disenchantment with his business career was the first stage. Hints at deeper personal changes soon followed. Naomi's dreams of living a well-rehearsed life began to crumble. What had happened to the man she married? She felt "cheated." Her parents fueled the fires of her dismay. The couple entered marital counseling. Moving in different directions, they could not find one another again. "During one session," Jeremy says, "as Naomi was talking, I looked up and thought I saw my mother sitting there." That snapped the nuptial cord. There followed "a painful period of getting unmarried." He tried to become friends with Naomi. "We had become lovers fast enough but never friends," he recalls. But it was too late for that. As he tried to break loose, she clung to him for dear life. Finally, she became vindictive and fought for all she could get as compensation for his default. Following his divorce, Jeremy avoided women for a while, then started dating again. Now that he has become established in a new career and is at peace with himself, he is open to a fresh start.

BLENDING CAREER AND FAMILY LIFE

Having examined the two main trajectories of career and family development, we can now consider more systematically how they relate to each other. When we look at the sample as a whole, it may come as a surprise that personal satisfaction and career satisfaction turn out to be completely unrelated to each other. Career contentment and personal contentment are not linked: participants who are highly content in their careers are no more likely to be content with their marriages than participants who are less satisfied by their work. The same holds for career commitment and personal commitment, and for all other combinations of personal and career variables. It is as if career and personal lives operate in two separate compartments; how the educational elite feel about one aspect of their lives seems to have very little to do with how they feel about the other.

This does not mean that careers and personal lives have no impact on each other. Rather, this finding largely reflects the generally high levels of career and personal satisfaction among the educational elite, levels that leave little room for variation. A related consideration is that marriage is unrelated to most aspects of career development and satisfaction. Married participants are not significantly different from single people in terms of career contentment, commitment, competence, or compensation. What makes a difference is not marriage but parenthood—or to be more precise, motherhood.

In principle, parenthood need not seriously hamper a woman's career any more than it does that of a man. A fully engaged father can take on his share of responsibility for the children during nonworking hours, and paid child care can free up both parents to pursue their careers. In practice, this is not what happens. Women are the primary homemakers and parents, regardless of how much paid help they use, and usually adopt one or more of several strategies to try to blend careers and family life: separation, accommodation, compromise, or conflict. Ideally, and in all fairness, women should not have to confront these problems any more or less than men do. But current reality is that they do. Hence, we need to examine them in that context.

Separation between Career and Family

The most obvious way to avoid a conflict between career and family is to pursue one or the other, but not both at the same time. This seemingly simple solution is actually very difficult for women in the educational elite because most of them are not interested in being full-time homemakers and mothers on a permanent basis. By the same token, most women are unwilling to forgo the prospect of marriage and motherhood while they pursue their careers.

Nonetheless, for many women, separating career (defined as outside-the-home employment) and family remains a viable choice. About two-thirds of our participants have so far opted for careers without children. But given what we said earlier about virtually everyone hoping to have a family, we do not expect many of them to forgo family for career permanently. A few certainly will, but the great majority will eventually marry and have children.

On the other hand a minority of women have chosen families over careers. We have some fifteen women (22 percent of mothers) who are full-time mothers a decade after college (chapter 4). How long they will remain so is difficult to predict, since few indicate that homemaking is likely to be their long-term occupation. So far, these women too have effectively avoided the conflict between career and family. Most are content with their current arrangement and would not change it, even though there are drawbacks to it. As one of them put it, "I don't love housework, but I consider it part of my current career." Moreover, two of them probably speak for the group when they say, "I would prefer more domestic help," and, "I'd like my husband to do more around the house (he's getting better)."

Most of these women who stay home do more than look after their house and children. One produces brochures; another trades in oil commodities out of her home (her father is in the oil business). Even when they are not earning money, these women are actively engaged in a wide variety of volunteer, social, intellectual, and leisure activities. One has written two plays, another has published "five poems, one short story, and four book reviews." They include a marathon runner and the captain of a tennis team. Others chair committees, raise money, and engage in political activities. They can do all this because at least some of them have a great deal of help. One woman has "live-in help five days a week as baby-sitter and once a week a cleaning woman."

Although none of them would deny the rigors of raising small children and the drudgery of housework, these women hardly fit the stereotype of the full-time mother as a prisoner in her own home, her mind rusting away and her education going to waste as she yearns for the vigor and excitement of the workplace.

A few women were inclined to make motherhood a central part of their working lives even as they were leaving college. Andrea fell in love in college and got married soon after graduation. Though she claimed to be "really into a career," her vision of family life was largely traditional: her husband would be the primary breadwinner, and she would do "some sort of work" that was compatible with the needs of her family. Andrea predicted that, ten years after graduation she would be "living in a big house with lots of land, two kids in school, a dog, a station wagon for going skiing on weekends—your basic little family." A decade later, Andrea says, "it came true. We live in a big house on two acres, have three children, have an order in for a St. Bernard puppy, and I drive a four-wheel drive Suburban (which we need for going skiing on weekends)." Her next prediction? "In ten years my oldest child will be ready to move into one of the freshman dorms at Stanford and my youngest will be in junior high school. I expect to be working part-time in the field of health education, still actively involved with my children's activities and schools, doing some community volunteer work, and playing a lot of tennis. I hope this next ten-year prediction will be just as accurate."

Lest we exaggerate the joys of staying home, we must also point out the sacrifices entailed in taking time off from careers. The more immediate cost is monetary. For eight years, one woman had a highly successful career as an auditor with a big CPA firm. When her child was born, her outside income was reduced to occasional freelance commissions. She had been the primary wage earner while her husband was in graduate school for three years; now he is the main source of support. Although they still have a family income of about $150,000, she says,

> My husband and I see downward mobility as a good thing. We bought our house on one income, not two. Our short-term goal is to be debt-free within two years. Our long-term goals are to have more time to spend with family, friends, and society. Both of us see ourselves doing social/volunteer/minimal-wages work. We will never "want," but that's because we didn't get caught up in chasing the carrot in the first place and are therefore able to afford the luxury of stepping out of the rat race when we want to.

One may marvel at the prospect of "downward mobility" on $150,000 a year. Nonetheless, in her case the decision to stay home was not simply a matter of choosing between career and family. Rather, it was embedded in a larger matrix of social values and life goals.

When women interrupt their careers to stay home with their children, they experience a welter of contradictory feelings. On the one hand, they miss the excitement and rewards of their successful careers. On the other hand, having had a career, and been successful at it, they are not tormented by what-if thoughts. As we noted in chapter 4, all but two of these women were fully engaged in their careers until the birth of their children. Their choice to stay home was therefore conscious and deliberate. Moreover, most of these women are not giving up their jobs because they have failed or been unhappy at them, but because of the responsibilities they feel and the rewards they anticipate in caring for their children.

- I have chosen not to work. I have chosen to be a full-time mother. The issue for me is not one of child-care quality or costs but of not wanting to give up spending the developmental years with my young children.
- I chose to leave my career path to raise my children since I didn't feel comfortable combining the two.
- I decided that my personal commitments to my marriage and baby are more important than my career.

Only a few women were motivated to stay home by dissatisfaction at work. One of them said, "I do not like to work for people." Another elaborated further:

If I had been in the full swing of developing a standard "career" outside the home, I might have been less inclined to quit "work" and stay home to raise my child. However, the jobs I'd held were not exactly career-track-type positions, nor, to the extent that they might lead to something more interesting/challenging, were they in a field in which I wanted to develop a career or profession. In fact, my career goal of being a novelist/freelance writer is more consistent with staying at home (assuming one has time to write). And while being a full-time mother doesn't leave me as much time as I'd like to work on my writing, there's no question that if I "went back to work" outside the home, I'd have even less time to write. Would I consider going back to work as an administrative assistant? No, but I would continue trying to develop a career as a writer. The problem, of course, with such a career is that, until I start earning money from my writing, it can't be called a career or "work." But if I should manage to break into a publication large enough to pay its writers in dollars instead of contributor's copies, then my "aspirations" would magically be transformed into a "career" as a writer.

Another important feature of these mothers is that virtually all of them are planning to go back to work sometime over the next five years. Those with graduate degrees in law or business are planning to resume their previous careers; others are thinking of going back to school (one for an M.B.A., another for a nursing degree). Consequently, it makes more sense to view the interruption of the careers of educational elite women by parenthood, or the career of motherhood, as a largely transitory phase in their lives.

Given the satisfying circumstances of their lives as full-time mothers, and the staunch, almost defiant defenses they give for their choices, one wonders why none of our men have opted to be full-time fathers. Since the career patterns of many of these women prior to parenthood were virtually identical to those of many men, the answer must be sought in the social attitudes and structures that discourage men from making similar choices. Full-time parenthood can become a real option for men as well as women only if the cultural bias leveled at this choice is nullified. In particular, the substantial monetary and status penalties associated with voluntary male homemaking would have to be greatly diminished. As our findings suggest, such change is not likely to happen soon, even for the educational elite, even though there may be some movement in that direction.

ACCOMMODATION

When Kirsten Buchanan establishes herself in a new career, she will try to achieve an accommodation between work and family life, aiming for a harmonious balance between the two. Cindy's contemplated switch after the birth of her daughter from corporate law to the teaching of law is another good example. Cindy is like Kirsten in being an Intellectual and a woman. Moreover, though both women have led successful careers in mainline occupations, they sense a certain incongruence between their work and their intellectual values ("a realization," said Kirsten, "that my spirit always knew but my stubborn mind kept rejecting"). The experience of motherhood not only triggered their deep-seated parental feelings, but by making them break stride, it led them to reconsider their career objectives as well.

For these two mothers, accommodation has as much to do with being an Intellectual as it does with being a woman. Hence, this mode appeals not only to many women but to a fair number of men as well, and men who opt for accommodation are typically Intellectuals. One example cited earlier is Keith, whose academic career moves were largely shaped by his wish to accommodate the career trajectory of his domestic partner. Another example is Andrew. The son of Christian missionaries, Andrew grew up in Japan and became fully acculturated and fluent in Japanese. In college, he pursued a typically Intellectual education, and though he lacked formal business training, he went on to work for an American company as a sales representative in Japan. Andrew was highly successful at his work, earning $200,000 a year, but at the cost of a grueling work schedule. Midway through the decade, he married a nurse who had also grown up in Japan. The frenetic pace of his job put a heavy strain on their marriage. "Burned out from overexertion on the job and placing all other aspects of life on hold," Andrew decided to return to the United States to reconsider his options while his wife resumed her nursing career. They bought a farm near a small West Coast town, away from the fast pace of the big city.

Andrew still makes a more than ample income as a consultant to his former employer; he has become, in effect, financially independent. Though he expects to make about $500,000 a year at the "high point" of his career, he is not interested in rising up the corporate hierarchy. ("A title is just a means to get a job done.") More important, he expects to be a father who will help raise his children, and he wants to return to the pursuit of his intellectual interests.

Compromise

"What have you learned so far?" asked Sarah as she sat down for her interview. "Have there been many compromises?" Compromise turned out to be the operative word in Sarah's career. She was already a working journalist by the time she graduated from college. Energetic and ambitious, she threw herself wholeheartedly into her work as a reporter and for four years gave little thought to anything else. Following her marriage and the birth of her daughter, she could no longer pursue the reporter's life, which required that she drop everything at a moment's notice and rush to wherever news was being made. So she left journalism to work as a publicist at a private institution. Though she has continued to work full-time, her heart is no longer in her job. "I used to be on the other side," she says ruefully. "I am no longer the journalist asking the hard questions, but there was no way I could care for my daughter and husband and continue in my former career, so I compromised."

Compromise may seem like another version of accommodation, but there is an important difference between the two. Accommodation is the active choice to reshape one's career to bring it more into line with the demands of personal life. Compromise is yielding to circumstances less willingly. Since arrangements are made grudgingly, the compromiser is usually less satisfied with the result.

Accommodation and compromise may also be combined to steer a person through multiple goals. As one woman said, "You see your path toward personal and professional goals zigzagging with constant compromising and balancing—my career versus my husband's, my personal desires versus my professional ones, professional ambition (long hours, never eating dinner with my husband during the week, etc.) versus a 'normal' life."

Accommodation and compromise can also be combined in making career decisions, not just in choosing an occupation but in the strategies pursued in an ongoing career as well. This point was driven home by Rebecca. We had discussed her career with respect to the four C's, when she said, "There is another 'C' which you need to look at. It is Convenience. Married women with children, or those hoping to have a family, look at job opportunities with an eye to their convenience as closely as they do to other considerations. How long is the commute? How flexible are the hours? How much travel is involved? Men may also worry about these things, but they are not affected by them the same way. For a woman, these considerations are crucial."

The "fifth C" obviously narrows women's career choices. Moreover, by forgoing those options that are less convenient but also more likely to lead to advancement, some give up the career race by default, by not getting into it in the first place.

Some combination of accommodation and compromise underlies the notion of the "Mommy track." In 1989, in an article in the *Harvard Business Review,* Felice Schwartz argued for the establishment of two career tracks for women.[14] The first would be a "career primary" track for those willing and able to work long hours, take promotions and relocations as they come, and, in essence, do whatever is demanded by the job. The second would be a "career and family" track for women who are willing to accept lower pay and lesser advancement in return for a less demanding and more flexible schedule that could accommodate family needs more easily. Her critics, not Schwartz herself, labeled the latter the "Mommy track." The idea of a two-track system for women set off a furor. Some claimed that "women bristle at the notion of a 'mommy track'—even if they choose to slow their careers or reduce their hours—because it is founded on assumptions determined solely by gender and labeled to define only one aspect of a woman's complex identity. Moreover, the assumptions are dangerous because any kind of tracking assumes uniformity among the group. No such uniformity exists."[15] Those in favor of a two-track system argued that whatever we call it, it simply describes the current practice of many women, allows more flexibility for those who choose it, and would save money for employers by reducing the turnover rate among women managers who leave because of childbirth or child-care obligations. Several of our women participants have made such choices even though none of them said that they were on a "mommy track."

The problem here is not with the concept itself but with the gender asymmetry. If dual-career couples are going to have a personal hand in raising their children, it is hard to see how they can avoid adjusting their careers accordingly. Forcing women alone into such choices is discriminatory. But if a two-track system were offered and accepted by men as well as women (hence, a "parent track"), then discrimination would no longer be the issue. However feasible and promising the idea of a "parent track" may be, it is currently rather conjectural, given the massive evidence that most men would not currently choose such an option nearly as often as women would.

CONFLICT

Push comes to shove when women reject the modes discussed so far and press on at full throttle on both career and family trajectories. Two problems emerge. The first is the acute shortage of time and the overload of work—hurried lives and harried families. The second is the barrier to career advancement that results from giving time and attention to children and home life. In a phrase, the "glass ceiling" becomes reinforced by the "maternal wall." As Kirsten Buchanan put it,

> There is still one field in which we all seem to get the curve ball: MOTHERHOOD. Almost every woman, from those with the most spectacular careers down to my humble self, domestic goddess that I am, will experience the upheaval and chaos that come with children. I recall the advice of one of the top-ranking females at one company: "Marriage is self-sabotage in the corporate world, but pregnancy is corporate suicide." Two vice presidents that hired me echoed these sentiments by telling me that they preferred to hire single women, because they worked like dogs, and married men, because they were more stable than single men. The more children a married man had, the better.

What employers fear, rightly or wrongly, is that when baby's interests are pitted against those of the company, baby wins. This conflict would arise much less often, of course, if the structure, policies, and values of the workplace were different, if adequate child-care facilities were readily available, and if fathers took as much responsibility for their children as mothers do. But that is not the case.

Swiss and Walker's study of 902 women graduates (classes of 1971 and 1981) of the Harvard schools of medicine, business, and law is revealing in this regard. The statistics and personal accounts obtained from these women paint a rather grim picture of the problems in reconciling the demands of career and family. Some 85 percent of these women believed that reducing their work hours would be detrimental to their careers, but 70 percent of mothers had done so, and 53 percent had changed jobs, because of family responsibilities. Though 96 percent of the mothers went back to work before their first child was a year old, 39 percent believed that having children had nonetheless slowed their careers. Yet, in spite of all, 85 percent said they had been able to combine career and family successfully, albeit at great personal cost. They credited their husbands for playing a key role in coparenting and for supporting their careers, and they praised the accommodating policies of their companies and institutions. These women had a strong sense of their abilities and were ultraefficient and able to focus on the important tasks without getting distracted by minor ones. They had established their careers before having children and sought out companies or institutions that made allowances for family needs.[16]

The pattern that emerges from our study is more positive, even though all the problems referred to by the Harvard graduates can be identified among our women as well. Several things may account for this difference. Most important, the Harvard sample is considerably older; the women who graduated from medical school in 1971 finished college at least fourteen years before our participants left Stanford. These women were part of the earlier wave who entered mainline professions in large numbers, so they had to hack their way through unexplored and rough territory. Though gender equality still is not firmly established among the professional elite, much has improved since then, and the young women in our sample are beneficiaries of the earlier pioneers' efforts. Moreover, our women also have not yet moved along in their careers far enough to generate as much of a clash between career advancement and family.[17]

Finally, most of our women have not yet produced that second or third child that makes parenting so much more demanding and so much more difficult to blend with a career. We must remember that only about one-third of them have had a child by age thirty. Hence, the full impact of childbearing and child rearing has yet to be felt. Since the proportion of women working full-time dropped sharply after the eighth year, we can expect that in their third decade of adulthood even larger proportions of women will interrupt their careers for the sake of children. It may well be that gender differences in career conflicts will become much larger by the time our participants reach their mid- to late thirties—unless, of course, workplace culture changes concurrently.

HAVING IT ALL?

As large numbers of married career women began to enter the mainstream professions, the "Superwoman" or "Supermom" who "has it all" became a much-touted figure in the popular media. Yet this image has come to be seen as a myth, if not a cruel hoax.[18] The fact of the matter is that there are no Superwomen or Supermen who effortlessly meet the demands of a fast-track career while being a loving wife/husband, devoted mother/father, gracious homemaker, and so forth, all at one and the same time.[19]

There has to be some measure of accommodation even in the best of circumstances, but as the authors of the Harvard study correctly point out, pushing the "work/family dilemma into an either-or choice" allows little room for it. One woman surgeon estimated that trying to combine career and family allowed her to attain "about 80 percent" of what she would have liked to achieve in each role. As she put it, "(1) I'm a worse mother because I am not at home; (2) I'm a worse doctor because I'm a mom; (3) I wouldn't have it any other way."[20] In these judgments, the frame of comparison here is the woman's own self-assessment. Thus, although the combination of career and motherhood takes its toll on both counts, it may well be that she is still a better surgeon than others who are not parents, and a better parent than others who have no career outside the home.

Within reason, the majority of our Stanford women without children, and about half of those with children, seem to manage amazingly well on both fronts. They are competent and hard-working professionals who have managed to combine the demands of career and family, making some accommodation but no major compromise on either front. Like the Harvard women, their lives are not easy, yet they are satisfying. These women do not have all the benefits of full-time motherhood, nor are they unhampered in the pursuit of their careers. Yet the major elements of both are integrated in their lives.

Ideally, career and family are not only complementary but synergistic—they mutually reinforce each other. Heather, described earlier, comes from a family of lawyers, including her father and three of her siblings. Her mother is a schoolteacher. Heather considered becoming a lawyer herself but instead went into elementary school teaching, against her mother's advice but with her eventual support.

After getting her teaching credential, Heather started teaching second grade. She married shortly thereafter and had two children. She continued working and now splits a teaching position with another woman. She carries the major responsibility for child care and shares household chores with her husband. As far as she is concerned, her career and family responsibilities mesh perfectly. "I love it," says Heather. "The better teacher I am, the better mother I become. The better mother I am, the better teacher I become."

Could Heather make the same claim if she were a full-time lawyer or doctor? In fact, Martin MacMillan does make the very same claim. ("Having children made me a much better doctor.") But, of course, becoming a father did not alter the course of Martin's career; he did not, for instance, cut back his work to half-time, as did Heather. There is nothing inherently incompatible between parenthood and the practice of law or medicine. Practically, however, the enormous demands of these professions, as currently practiced, make the combined tasks much more difficult.

Does this mean that only women in careers like elementary school teaching can "have it all"? We already know from the examples of Katherine Johnson and others that it is certainly possible to be a devoted mother and a fast-track corporate lawyer or respected engineer. But it is a hard row to hoe. Just how hard it can sometimes be is shown by the experience of Maria.

Maria is the electrical engineer who married her high school boyfriend in college and got pregnant in her senior year. She spent the first three years after graduation having two more children and being a full-time wife and mother in an isolated rural community. She then decided to launch her engineering career, taking a job in a government lab seventy miles from home. For the first two years, she made little headway at a dead-end job. Then she switched to the space research division (despite her lack of a graduate degree) with the help of a manager who was willing to take a chance on her. Her career rapidly blossomed, and she became a full-fledged research scientist.

Yet back at home she remained very much the wife and mother. Her husband, who never went to college, was proud but bewildered by her career success. Since his work was carried on at home, he was willing to look after their youngest child, who was not yet in school. But he adamantly refused to cook or clean, activities he felt would have cost him tremendous loss of face in their highly traditional community.

Marie's workday starts and ends with her long commute. When she gets back home, she first visits her parents and then goes home and starts cooking dinner. When she is traveling (often to Washington), her husband takes the children to his mother's for their meals. At night and on weekends, she takes care of the house and children. If there is anyone in our group who can lay claim to the title of "Supermom," it is surely Maria.

With this chapter, we conclude our account of the parallel tracks of the career and personal lives of our participants. At this stage in their lives, the twin demands of work and love absorb most of their time and energies. Yet there is more to the life of the educational elite, extending beyond their immediate selves and relationships, and it is these areas to which we turn next.

CHAPTER 9

Beyond the Self

What happens to the liberal educational ideal after college? What is left of it a decade later? Much of today's debate on the purposes of college education focuses on the content and importance of this "common core" component of the curriculum—the courses in the liberal arts, natural sciences, and social sciences that make up the general education of students, quite apart from courses in their majors more directly related to career preparation and training.[1]

The Yale Report of 1828, assessing the purposes and direction of the undergraduate curriculum, defined liberal learning as the provision of "the discipline and the furniture of the mind."[2] Well into the nineteenth century, courses in the humanities dominated the substance of this curriculum, and they still provide the most central—and controversial—elements.[3] In contrast to mere vocational training, liberal education is expected to produce an educated person. The key question, of course, is what is meant by an "educated person." When we asked our cohort study participants to give us their views in their last year as undergraduates (by which time they had presumably become "educated"), we received many thoughtful responses. One student said:

> An educated person should have an understanding of the world, philosophy, history, the arts, science, math, and literature. I feel that an educated person is a kind of Renaissance person. He or she should be well rounded. Yet, I also feel that being educated means one should know at least one of these areas well. Of course, there are cer-

tain skills that an educated person must have, such as the ability to think, analyze, and write clearly, but I think that there is a difference between an educated person and one who simply knows a skill. Educated implies a greater cultivation of the individual.[4]

How much does this liberal educational experience affect the lives of students after they leave college? This issue is especially pertinent to the educational elite because the institutions they attend set the tone of the entire system of higher education and are charged with the task of defining and transmitting this indispensable core of higher education. Hence, if anyone receives the type of education posite ˙ by the liberal arts tradition, it is the educational elite. Correspondingly, the educational elite is generally expected to keep that tradition alive as they mature and grow older. In fact, higher education is a well-known factor associated with increased adult participation in cultural and civic activities, though its effects at different adult ages have not been well studied.[5] Through their engagement in ideas and activities related to the arts, politics, literature, philosophy, and the like, we expect the educated elite to be not only participants in but active contributors to the life of the mind.

In select institutions, whether by choice or institutional compulsion, liberal education occupies a substantial portion of time. Institutional requirements in this regard vary widely, as do individual interests. For some, like our Intellectuals, it is their dominant academic concern; for others, it is not. After students leave college, the building of careers, intimate relationships, and families comes to dominate their lives, as we have described in the preceding chapters. When you work sixty hours a week and have a family to look after, there is little time for anything else. As the fashion designer Coco Chanel put it, "There is time for work. And time for love. That leaves no other time."[6] The economist Juliet Schor, referring to the decline of leisure time among "overworked Americans," says "they have only sixteen and a half hours of leisure time a week, after the obligations of job and household are taken care of."[7]

Does this mean that the liberal educational ethos acquired in college dies on the vine? Do college graduates lose the inclination to learn for the love of it, to engage in philosophical discourse, to ponder the course of history and the meaning of politics, to explore new areas of knowledge, to experience the insights and pleasures of literature and art? Does lack of time make it impossible to engage in these activities even when they wish they could?

To answer these questions, we inquired about the intellectual interests that animate our segment of the educational elite ten years after college. We asked them about what they read, the music they listen to, their interest in art. We inquired into their social and political involvements and their links to community or associational activities outside their work and family. And we delved into the philosophical and religious dimensions of their lives, asking them about what meaning beyond their immediate selves they find in the world.

There is a troublesome tendency to relegate liberal learning to the periphery of the college curriculum and cast it as a leisure-time activity later on. Thus for most of our participants, intellectual and cultural pursuits, social and political activities, and religious and philosophical concerns have become matters that are attended to after the demands of careers and families are met, if there is time and energy left to spare. And in our attempt to describe those activities, we have followed the same pattern, thus reinforcing it. The very fact that we have segregated these areas and discuss them at the end of the book contributes further to their "add-on" quality. In contrast, one could argue that liberal learning should not be treated as a thing apart, but should inform all aspects of one's life, including career and family. But that is easier said than done.

LIFE OF THE MIND

In trying to assess the scope and substance of intellectual pursuits beyond the college years, we ran into some of the same questions we had encountered earlier in the cohort study: What exactly is intellectualism? Can we arrive at a definition of intellectualism that is widely shared and not unduly bound by a particular conception of the nature and purpose of intellectual activity?

The intellects of these professional men and women are obviously heavily engaged in their work—they make their livings by using their minds. But we are concerned with intellectualism here in a broader sense, beyond the highly focused, technical, analytical use of the intellect required in the professions. We are looking for cultural and social activities the educational elite pursue that are intellectually stimulating, provide aesthetic satisfaction, and expand their mental and moral horizons.

This distinction between intellectual engagement in professional activity and the pursuit of the life of the mind for its own sake is bound to be somewhat arbitrary. For assembly-line workers who toil with their hands during the day and read novels in the evening or go to the opera, the separation between work and intellectual pursuits may be self-evident. Yet that is not the case in the many professions that demand a high degree of intellectual engagement.

Those in scientific fields like medicine and engineering tend to feel slighted by the traditional association of intellectualism with the humanities. As one of them asked, "Why should writing a book about engineering be just a technical rather than an intellectual accomplishment? Why is it any less intellectual than literary criticism?"

The point is well taken. Nonetheless, as we hear our participants talk about their jobs and the way they use their minds professionally, we think it is fair to say that relatively few are involved in work that is predominantly intellectual in the expanded (and classic) sense of the term. Their own opinions generally support this judgment. Few and far between are the participants who see intellectualism at the core of their professional lives.

We have two central questions: How do the educational elite keep their minds alive outside the workplace? And to what extent do intellectual concerns inform their occupational perspective?

THE PROFILE GROUP

Everyone in the profile group is awfully busy. The demands of the phase of life they are in dominate their schedules and have a leveling effect on their choices. Nonetheless, important differences persist among these men and women in the ways they reach out to fulfill their needs and interests beyond their immediate selves.

Careerist Martin MacMillan provides a good example of a man whose life is fully occupied by his career and family. What leisure time he has he spends playing tennis (his passion from college days) or golf, which he has just picked up. Martin regrets the lack of a more "intellectual dimension" in his life outside of work, just as he did back in college. "I would like to read more history and acquire the intellectual tools for understanding what people are thinking about," he says. Yet such regrets are tempered by what really matters to him. "If I am faced with a sick child," he asks, "would I be able to take better care of that child if I had read Shakespeare the night before?"

Careerist Cynthia Eastwood presents a different picture. The issue for her is not the amount of intellectual activity but its nature and quality. Cynthia pursues her cultural life with the same relentless zeal she brings to her career. She describes her leisure reading as "eclectic." "There are twenty books piled up next to my bed," she explains. "My husband is constantly moving them about since they take up so much room. I am usually reading one while browsing through the others. I pick them up in used-book stores." But that is not all. Cynthia listens to novels on tape when traveling and reads whatever is around during the hours she spends on the station-

ary bicycle. She cared only for "popular music" until her husband introduced her to classical music, and now they have season tickets to the symphony. "We have great seats that I got through a friend," says Cynthia, as
pleased with this further proof of her networking skills as with the superior
acoustics of their choice seats. They go to plays every month and have the
beginnings of an art collection. So Cynthia is soaked in "culture" but does
not seem to be deeply engaged in it.

The Intellectuals stand in sharp contrast. Christopher Luce is, of
course, a special case. After all, as a university professor, he is an intellectual by profession. Yet his intellectual hunger is such that Christopher still
thinks he is falling short.

> Intellectual pleasure has never been separate for me from intellectual
> work, even while I was at Stanford. Everything I see and hear is grist
> for the mill in my field, but I wish I had time to read books really
> outside my field, like, say, about the Roman Empire or the Middle
> Ages. Actually, one of the points of the collapsing of the disciplines is
> that now I read as much history, sociology, and philosophy as I do lit-
> erature. I have also kept my biology textbooks from college, and I
> wish I could go back or just go through them, since they provide a
> way of entering the world that is so alien to the humanities. What I
> would really like to do is read a book a week on any subjects outside
> my field that interest me. I manage to do that for a month or two,
> then something happens.

Christopher complains that he does not have a "well-developed musical
taste." He listens mainly to popular music. On the other hand, he is highly
informed about art because part of his graduate work involved the visual
arts. Here again, his intellectual and career interests merge.

A more typical picture of the life of the mind of an Intellectual is provided by Kirsten Buchanan. Unlike Christopher, Kirsten is not an academic; nonetheless, she maintained an active intellectual life throughout her
fast-paced career. It sustained her at a time when her business career failed
to engage her intellect sufficiently to give her a sense of fulfillment. "I had
no trouble finding intellectual fulfillment in New York City. I spent all my
nonwork hours compensating for the lack of stimulation in my job. I read
voraciously, went to the theater, explored the city neighborhoods, and
devoured the museums."

The move to a cultural backwater after her marriage and the arrival of
her first child took away from Kirsten even the option of culture-after-
hours. "I think intellectualism is what is lacking right now," says Kirsten.
"Before, I did a fairly good job. But you begin to lose your vocabulary

being with a baby twenty-four hours a day. And intellectual concerns seem incongruous when compared with 'Sesame Street,' advanced finger painting, and Curious George." Kirsten now mainly reads books on child development, but she also keeps "a volume of Shakespeare at hand, even if it is mostly for rereading." She is accumulating books (by the armful, she gestures) that she will read one day when she has more time. Judging by the number of books she reads, Kirsten currently is no more engaged than Martin MacMillan, and far less than Cynthia Eastwood. But in her perspective on life she remains a true Intellectual.

Striver George Mehta's situation before becoming a father was quite similar to Kirsten's prior to becoming a mother. George, too, was able to maintain an active intellectual life despite the pressures of his business career.

> I have just started taking piano lessons. I used to play the clarinet in high school, but I have always wanted to learn how to play the piano. I taught myself some over the years, but now I want to do it right. I have not painted much the past few years, but I keep up with art in our area. We also have season tickets to the symphony. So music and art are my main interests. I wish I had more time for reading. I do read magazines, but don't count that. I particularly enjoy the *Economist*—it has broader scope than anything published here. I use it to keep up with the world. After I became a father, I have definitely had less time for intellectual and community pursuits with the arrival of our son. We have entered a phase of life during which raising a child is very important to us, and it is a time-consuming task! We are consciously devoting time to him so that we can foster his care and development; we are not developing ourselves as much, but the other rewards are worth it.

The intellectual life of Striver Geraldine Jones has had two distinct phases very much linked to her career. During the years when she was working in the theater in New York, she was professionally and personally immersed in culture. Since moving to rural Vermont, she has been largely cut off from similar cultural activities. She is spread thin between her job and her environmental activities. Yet whenever she has an opportunity to travel, she will go to the theater or the opera. Hence, her intellectual interests are quite alive even if not as active as before.

Unconnected David Levy has developed a keen intellectual orientation to life. Before he took his present job, he read a lot of autobiography and fiction for pleasure. But now that he spends his days writing and editing, it is harder for him to keep reading after-hours. David is also very interested in music. He still plays the piano and the guitar and listens to classical and folk music. Since David's fiancée is in the field of literature, they share many intellectual interests. Perhaps even more important, his intellectual perspective permeates his approach to the practice of law, placing it in broader conceptual, historical, and social contexts.

Katherine Johnson is no stranger to the life of the mind, but she very much regrets that lack of time has made it impossible for her to read as actively as she used to do. Until she started her present job, she went "through five to six books a week." Now she is restricted to reading the *New Yorker* and an occasional novel. She has tried to keep up her interest in art, although of late there has been little of that, too. Formerly an avid follower of the avant-garde theater, she has not been to a play for a while. She attended two ballets over the last two years and the symphony five times. Katherine is also interested in science and regrets that she did not pay more attention to it while she was an undergraduate.

WHY BOTHER?

As products of the same university culture, neither we nor our participants question the importance of the life of the mind. One could ask, nonetheless, why people should bother to read literature, visit museums, challenge their beliefs in a perpetual search for meaning, or engage in any of the myriad other cultural activities deemed "intellectual." Do such activities provide lofty pleasure? Do they make us better persons? Do they give us insights into who we are? Or make us more responsible citizens? Do these activities lead to a more just and equitable society? Or is intellectualism, after all, just an elitist exercise, a reinforcement of class boundaries with the appearance of refinement, a way to bolster snobbish aspirations? And does not intellectualism ultimately lead to the estrangement of the educational elite from the larger society?

Two conflicts fuel this long-standing controversy in American culture. One is the clash between defenders of the traditional canon, who champion an authoritative list of "great works" of literature and the arts, and the advocates of multiculturalism. The former put their faith in the enduring value of the works of high culture that constitute the intellectual heritage of Western culture. In their view, exposure to these works is a central purpose of liberal education in college. The detractors see the traditional canon as a self-serving and exclusionary tool of dominant groups (caricatured by some as "dead white males") to perpetuate their control while denying the inclusion of the worthwhile works of lesser-known figures, particularly women and ethnic minorities. Those who decry the abandonment of the canon equate it with the "closing of the American mind."[8] Those who welcome such abandonment may be said to see it as the opening of the American mind.

When our participants were undergraduates, Stanford instituted a new set of distribution requirements to ensure exposure to broad fields of knowledge within the humanities, natural sciences, and social sciences. It also revamped its Western culture program, a yearlong set of courses taken by all freshmen. The undergraduate experience of our segment of the educational elite was thus more traditional. The impact of multiculturalism was evident only in the subsidiary requirement that students take at least one course focusing on a non-Western culture and another on gender issues. In communicating on how their liberal education enhanced their college experience, our participants noted:

- Because of my exposure to other fields, I think I'm a more well-rounded engineer than many of my peers. I mean, I'm a nerd, but at least I'm familiar with literature, anthropology, and foreign languages.[9]
- Higher quality of life—love of reading, of new information, of broad-based interests (music, literature, architecture, politics), all came through liberal arts education.
- I did enjoy the nontechnological classes that I took at Stanford, and I believe that they have helped make me more well-rounded. Some of my breadth courses have created interests that I have pursued outside of the classroom, such as an appreciation of art.

The second source of contention is the rift in American culture between the theoretical and the practical, the intellectual and the occupational. When we educate our youth to prepare them for adult life, we give abstract, theoretical, cognitive thought pride of place. Once young adults enter the world of work, however, concrete, practical, applied knowledge and activities come to dominate their lives. Intellectuals are both revered, at one level, and despised as eggheads, at another.[10] This tension is present within the university itself. Its twin purposes of intellectual development and vocational training are often competing rather than complementary aims.

This is hardly a new or uniquely American problem. In ancient Greece, the more utilitarian purposes of education advocated by the Sophists were in conflict with the pursuit of pure truth by Plato's academy. In the United States, advocates of practical training have been at odds with the champions of liberal education since the eighteenth century.

What is the solution? In a typically ambitious way, the approach favored by American higher education has been to aim for the best of both worlds. In our terms, the system urges all college students, especially the educational elite, to be Strivers. For the early American college, this effort translated into three primary aims. One was vocational—training young men for the clergy or political leadership; the second was moral—developing the ethical and religious habits appropriate to cultivated gentlemen (and a small number of ladies); the third was social—maintaining a small educated elite in a predominantly agricultural society through induction into the traditions of classical culture by way of humanistic studies.[11]

Since then, the vocational dimension of college education has expanded enormously while its moral purposes have become more diffuse. Yet the cultivation of an educated elite remains an important purpose, even though the very notion of an elite is continually under fire. The graduates of select institutions like Stanford are thus heirs to a long tradition, but with a difference. What was once the exclusive prerogative of the children of the privileged classes has now become available to the sons and daughters of the middle class and, to a growing extent, the children of the disadvantaged classes as well.

As a consequence, whatever its intrinsic value in sustaining the life of the mind, liberal learning is now an integral part of the education of the professional elite. It is no wonder that the more successful people are professionally, the more likely they are to be engaged in the arts as patrons or active participants—for two different reasons. On the one hand, members of the elite are likely to have a genuine interest in intellectual and cultural endeavors. On the other hand, they know that engagement in the arts is a sure enhancer of prestige and social legitimacy. Hence, it is not just the feeding and care of the mind that is at stake here. The educational elite also uses liberal learning to put a cultural gloss on its careerist face.

THE SCORECARD

At this stage in their lives, the careers of our participants are driven mainly by external demands. They must compete in the workplace to excel in their professions, regardless of the degree of personal satisfaction they derive from their work. By contrast, the life of the mind is sustained mostly by intrinsic rewards. External pressure to maintain intellectual interests is almost nonexistent. The books they read, the music they listen to, the artistic interests they pursue, all these interests are restricted to their private lives, and they are held accountable to no one for them. What they do in the intellectual realm outside of their work is thus essentially optional and typically becomes part of their leisure life.

We were aware that the life of the mind was likely to be seen as optional before conducting this study. Nonetheless, we were still taken aback to discover how relatively little time and effort many (but not all) of our participants devoted to intellectual and cultural pursuits. No more than 21 percent of our interviewees demonstrated a high level of engagement in intellectual pursuits, and almost one-third freely admitted having little or no serious involvement at all. This distribution is far lower than that of any of the dimensions of career and personal engagement we have discussed in previous chapters.

On two counts there was near-unanimous agreement: almost everyone testified to the value of a rich intellectual life, in principle, and almost everyone pleaded lack of time to pursue it in practice. Moreover, most of our participants endorse the value of liberal learning. This claim that they lack time is valid. But lack of time is hardly the whole story, because their range of other involvement is very large and even the busiest people manage to find time for leisure activities like sports and travel. One spectacularly successful business executive with graduate degrees from two top universities says openly, "To be honest with you, I have not read anything outside of my work for a long time. When I get the time, I'd rather go camping with my wife." At the other extreme another man works out of his book-filled apartment as a desktop publisher. He keeps his working hours low and his income pegged to a level sufficient only for sustenance (earning about one-tenth of what the first man makes). This schedule allows him to spend two hours every morning reading literature for pleasure.

Most of our participants fall between these extremes. As we noted with the profile group, they feel a tension between the desire and the ability to be intellectually engaged. Others expressed similar thoughts:

- My interests in art, theater, and music are on hold until my situation at work and at home changes a bit.
- My intellectual activities are now limited to vacations, when I read avidly, and to the occasional weekend trips to San Francisco, where we may see a play or go to a museum.
- I am embarrassed to say that I hardly manage to finish the books that I start. We used to go to the theater, to the symphony, but can no longer do that with any regularity. Even though my husband continues to get season tickets, we just don't have the time and the energy.
- I don't read enough of what I want to. I would like to read novels and

other books for pure enjoyment, but my work and family take up all my time. It took me a year and a half to get through one Ken Kesey book.

- I pick up a novel during vacations, and that is about it. I have lost touch with history and archaeology, which were my big interests in college. Before the children, I kept up my interest in art, theater, and classical music, but not during the last five years. Working full-time as an engineer and being the mother of two does not leave much time.

- I come home from the office at seven. My husband and I have dinner and put the children to bed. Then all I can do is lie down and look at the headlines in the paper.

We expected unmarried respondents to be more engaged in the life of the mind, given that they are free of family responsibilities. This may be true in some cases, but overall we find no difference between married and single participants. Singles simply fill up more of their time with work (which also lowers their chances of getting married) or devote their free time to sports and other leisure activities.

When faced with someone like Elizabeth, with her three-week-old baby fidgeting in her arms, it felt rather foolish to ask what books she has read lately or what concerts she has attended. Although time is clearly of the essence in a situation like hers, other considerations affect the way marriage can tilt the balance toward greater or lesser intellectual involvement. If a spouse has a strong intellectual or cultural bent, it can stimulate or revive his or her partner's interests. "I had never cared much about classical music," said one woman, "until I got married. My husband started taking me to the symphony and taught me a lot about music. Now I enjoy it, and music has become a common interest for us." But another said, "I love going to concerts, but my husband doesn't. Whenever I drag him to one, he falls asleep. I have tried to go with a friend instead, but it's not the same."

GENDER AND TYPOLOGY DIFFERENCES

Despite the much greater impact of parenthood on women than on men, gender is not significantly related to engagement in intellectual pursuits. The demands of building careers and families are inhibiting for both sexes, though in different ways. Women put more of their time and energy into child rearing, men into career development. The end result is the same: the life of the mind takes a backseat.

The leveling effect of career and family concerns is much weaker with respect to the four types. True to their outlooks on life, and as exemplified by our profile group, Intellectuals have the greatest intellectual and cultural engagement (44 percent demonstrating high engagement), Careerists the least (8 percent). The figures for Strivers and the Unconnected are also low (18 percent and 12 percent, respectively). Among Intellectuals, women come across as more seriously engaged. For instance, a considerably higher proportion of women than men report having been engaged in some type of fine arts activity during the past decade.

The interviews shed further light on the breadth and quality of the intellectual pursuits of the four types. On the whole, Intellectuals and a portion of the Strivers seemed more deeply engaged in the life of the mind. Jill, an Intellectual who is a lawyer and writer, devotes a great deal of time to literature; she reads biographies, short stories, poetry, and science fiction. Listening to music (both classical and popular) is also a part of her daily life, and she even finds that running provides her with an "intellectual and spiritual high." When we look at the intellectual interests of Careerists, on the other hand, not only are they quite limited but they also seem more superficial. For example, one Careerist engineer describes how he goes through an art exhibit: "I read every label, top to bottom, under each painting. It drives my wife up the wall." Another says with pride, "I only read nonfiction. I am a nuts-and-bolts man."

Something of the same mentality characterizes one of our Careerist businesswomen who subscribes to a lot of magazines—twenty-three to be exact. They are mainly in the self-improvement and how-to categories. To handle the constant flow, she places the incoming magazines in a large basket and works her way through them. As a single career woman with little social life, she seems to live vicariously through these magazines while enjoying the feeling that she is also doing something instructional and useful.

The differences among the four groups are, of course, not always cut and dried. Even a professional intellectual like the academic Keith spends much of his free time hiking and backpacking. Lately, he and his wife have become folk-dancing buffs. Mark, ostensibly Unconnected, majored in classics. His mother is a patron of the arts, his wife an art teacher. Mark has been surrounded by high culture for so long that he could barely escape it even if he tried. Though he does not see it as an integral part of his life, he is intellectually knowledgeable about it. ("I have the vocabulary to discuss it," he says blithely.)

It may well be, as they are wont to claim, that the languishing of the life of the mind among the educational elite is simply a function of their phase of life. Yet many of them made exactly the same argument ten years ago in college, when some were compromising their chances of obtaining a broad liberal education in favor of career concerns; they saw that focus as only a temporary condition. "Once I get settled in my career, I'll have plenty of time to read and expand my horizons." So far, for most of them, that is not what has happened. As one Intellectual observed, "It is hard to postpone the mind. It stagnates or gets too comfortable with reading only sufficient for cocktail conversations."

Those who demonstrated strong intellectual commitments while in college but have been unable to sustain them truly regret it. They are the ones most likely to reengage their intellects as circumstances become more favorable. Listen to what one Intellectual has to say on this matter: "It's amazing how quickly all the liberal arts aspects were squelched in the face of a career. Now I'd like to revive the impact of the liberal arts, reawaken that renaissance spirit Stanford imbibed me with. In effect, I'd like to pick up my Stanford education where I left it off, though I never thought I'd let that happen. Shame on me."

LIFE GOALS

When asked to rate the importance of each of a set of items dealing with goals and objectives in life, our participants painted a highly consistent and somewhat surprising picture that differs in some ways from their behavior described so far.

The goals cited as most important all relate to personal relationships; those considered least important have to do with career success and materialistic rewards. The most important goal, for both women and men, is "having a satisfying relationship with a mate/partner" (rated an average of 4.8 on a scale of 1 to 5). Rated almost as high are "being a good parent" and "spending time with my children." The three other objectives rated over 4.0 are "expanding intellectual horizons," "developing ethical and moral values," and "making friends." Except for the last item, which women find more important than men, there are no gender differences in these responses.

The goal that is deemed least important, again by both sexes, is "having the best things money can buy." "Attaining social status and prestige" does not fare much better. "Advancing in your career" and items that pertain to broad intellectual and social concerns (such as "developing artistic taste" and "solving social problems") are deemed of moderate importance (average ratings between 3.0 and 4.0). These patterns hold for both sexes and all four types (although Intellectuals rate career-related items lower than average). The life of the mind thus fares reasonably well in this context, although not as well as personal relationships.

Other questions related to goals elicited their views on why young people should go to college. With remarkable consistency, all of the items at the top of their ratings had to do with obtaining a broad liberal education, led by "learning to think" (an average rating of 4.6). Career-related objectives were all ranked lower than intellectual items, and the item ranked lowest was finding a marriage partner. The responses of both sexes fit this general pattern, though women's absolute ratings of liberal education items were somewhat higher than those of men. The same pattern applies to each of the four types: all placed liberal education goals at the top of the list and relegated career preparation to second rank. Even the Careerists placed career preparation items below intellectual and social concerns, though they gave higher absolute ratings than other groups to career concerns.

These are not exactly the responses one would expect of yuppies hell-bent on career advancement. Whether the topic is personal goals in life, or reasons to attend college, career concerns play not merely second but third fiddle to personal relationships and intellectual growth. Moreover, this downplaying of career concerns in favor of intellectual and relationship goals has characterized our participants ever since they were freshmen in college (and perhaps before that). In each of the four questionnaires they completed during the cohort study, precisely this pattern emerged. There is nothing new in their responses; they have been remarkably consistent. The difference is that we now have ten years of postcollege life experience against which to interpret the meaning of these attitudes.

The high value placed on personal relationships (with spouses, domestic partners, children, and friends) is quite consistent with the way our respondents live their lives. The deemphasis on career-related goals, however, especially the denigration of materialistic concerns, is sharply contradicted by the behavior of most of them. They are, in fact, intensely engaged in their careers, often to the exclusion even of the personal dimension. Many of them are acquisitive and aspire to climb to the upper reaches of the economic ladder, and they work long, hard hours in pursuit of that aim.

Are these men and women of the educational elite deluding themselves? Do they praise the life of the mind, while largely ignoring it, simply to make themselves look good? Do they conceal their basically careerist orientation to legitimate lives that are less meaningful and intrinsically rewarding than they would like? Is what they say perhaps a reaction to the career excesses of their generation, a yearning for something more than the self-orientation of the stereotypical yuppie—even though that yearning is not often matched by efforts to satisfy it? Or, having achieved their career aims and material success, do they now take these gains for granted and find themselves reaching out for more intellectual and less tangible rewards? Given "world enough and time," will their actions catch up with their ideals?

SOCIAL INVOLVEMENT

One of the traditional purposes of college education is to help students in their "preparation for life"; as Nevitt Sanford put it, college should promote "the development of the individual as a whole."[12] This presumably should include preparation for citizenship and public service.

Social functions in college are typically subsumed under the heading of "extracurricular" activities, typically not involving the faculty. Whether undertaken individually or within an organizational setting, they cover a broad spectrum, from athletics to voluntary service to political engagement to partying. Fun and games have always been part of college, but during the 1960s, the issue of the social "relevance" of the educational process gained much prominence and social engagement beyond the self came to be seen as its vehicle.[13]

In the late 1980s and early 1990s, women's issues and multicultural concerns replaced the earlier antiwar and countercultural emphases as the focal points of social engagement. Attending college from 1977 to 1982, our participants were too late for the latter wave of social engagement and too early for the former. Nevertheless, we found in our earlier study that sizable proportions of our students were very actively engaged in more general social causes, volunteer work, charitable fund-raising, and the like.

As the educational elite become mature adults, what happens to the idealism of their youth? How involved are they in community service or political issues? Are their leisure activities motivated purely by the desire for fun and recreation, or are they also directed at socially useful purposes?

THE PROFILE GROUP

Our profile group exemplifies a range of social interests that in many ways parallel what we found about the life of the mind. Our two Careerists have the least to show in terms of involvement in political activities or service-oriented activities outside their work. Though Martin MacMillan describes himself as a "conservative Republican," he is not politically active. His views are still conservative, as they were in his student days, although the passage of time has softened them somewhat.

Martin does not see himself as "socially uninvolved." Rather, his social concerns are embodied in being a "competent and caring physician" like his father, "whose good qualities are manifest especially through his work, which is where I spend most of my 'caring,' too," says Martin. Then he adds somewhat defensively, "I'm concerned about others but don't have (or take) time to act on that concern outside my practice. After twelve years of higher education, I'm just beginning to learn to help in my little corner of the world—give me a few more years to figure out how to save the whole planet!"

Though also an avowed Republican, Cynthia Eastwood has liberal views in some areas. For instance, she was disenchanted with the Bush administration's domestic policies. ("The President's opposition to abortion makes my blood boil.") Overall, she has little use or time for politics of any kind. Having been brought up with a strong sense of public service, however, she thinks she does not do enough. "I just send some money and recycle," she says. She would like to do more, but at present her career and marriage fully occupy her.

Intellectual Kirsten Buchanan has not had any more time than Cynthia, but before she became a mother, she was active in United Way, alumni fund-raising, and volunteer translating at the local hospital. Christopher Luce, in turn, works in a soup kitchen run by a Catholic organization (with which he has been associated since high school). Kirsten and Christopher both have a strong sense of social justice, even though neither of them is an activist of the more demonstrative sort. "I am sometimes doubtful of the value of public demonstrations," says Christopher, "although I recognize that for some people they may serve as rituals of affirmation."

Both of our Strivers have focused their social concerns on environmental issues. George Mehta's career has been significantly shaped by these concerns since his college days. Geraldine Jones had a serious interest in college in environmental engineering, but then her career followed a very different path. For the last several years, she and her domestic partner have been heavily engaged in setting up an environmental program; Geraldine has invested large amounts of time and some of her own resources. So there is a strong streak of social responsibility in both of our Strivers and a sense of "not doing quite enough," which George expresses as follows:

> Like everyone, I am concerned about the quality of education, the growing inequities among people and so on. But I don't consider that enough. It is true what I am doing in my job is related to social concerns, perhaps more so than what my friends from school are doing. In that sense, I am pretty true to my values. But it is limited. I don't feel quite comfortable with that. Everybody would be involved in

some social issue if they could make a comfortable living at it. In that sense, I am taking the fairly easy way out. I would like to do something less selfish.

When it comes down to making a commitment to public service at a significant cost to material career rewards (exactly the point George is making above), our two Unconnected profiles carry the day, once again making a mockery of their label. David Levy says, "I try to stay as well informed as I can; I guess that's the starting point. I have sort of tried to make my work address certain things I am not happy about, like people not being treated fairly. So that was one reason for going into the law, so that I might be able to help some of those people."

David's social concerns were not only instrumental in his choice of a legal career but have been an integral part of the way he pursues it. His interest in immigration law has led him to low-paying but socially useful jobs. And he has put in much time in his pro bono work with refugees, "people who have suffered horribly in their countries and are in danger of being sent back there." (He has been assisted in this by Judith, whose knowledge of Spanish is invaluable.) David says, "It is difficult, time-consuming work which can take amazing numbers of hours, consuming entire weekends." Addressing the question of the social responsibilities of his generation, David says:

> Those who graduate from Stanford have a great many options and opportunities, whether they earned them or they were just given them. And they are very talented people. To me, what's so important for that group is to use some of these options, abilities, and opportunities to put something back, because not everybody has these opportunities. Many of the people I know have done that. But everybody also has a temptation to use so many resources and opportunities to one's best advantage and to make things as comfortable as they can for their own close circle. I think it's important to go beyond that, and not everybody does it.

Katherine Johnson established her credentials as a socially concerned person when she set out to devote her working life to teaching troubled children in a disadvantaged minority community. But that opportunity for service was taken away from her. Though Katherine now inhabits a very different world, she has not forgotten her earlier loyalties (or the strained circumstances of her own upbringing). She remains keenly interested in social and educational issues. If she were to become a judge, she would be more actively involved in them. Currently, she gives money to support worthwhile causes. She would also like to give her time, but time is the one thing she does not have.

SOCIAL ACTIVITIES

Almost 90 percent of our participants have been engaged in some form of organized social activity. Gender makes no difference here, and the four types are only marginally dissimilar. Intellectuals are a bit low, with 74 percent reporting significant social activity, while the Unconnected are the highest at an astounding 98 percent. This finding also puts in a new perspective all the wailing about lack of time to pursue intellectual interests we heard in the interviews. Time is obviously not the only issue; priorities in the use of time also matter.

On average, respondents reported about three and a half significant social involvements. Participation in sports and exercise leads the list, followed by hobbies, work in service organizations, and (a distant last for both sexes) political activity. The prominence of sports and hobbies implies that over two-thirds of our participants' involvements are self-oriented, though usually still social (team sports, club hobbies, and so on). Less than one-third of their leisure-time engagements center on helping others or political action. This lack of service-oriented social involvement fits with the relatively low engagement of their intellectual lives.

Sex differences in social and service activities are rather small. For both men and women, athletics and hobbies are the main pursuits, and beyond-the-self engagements are relatively rare. The relative parity of women and men in terms of education and career activity seems to be accompanied by parity in nonwork activity outside the home as well. Women are active to about the same extent as men in the same types of social and recreational pursuits, and they do not appear to be more heavily engaged than men in helping others. At this stage in their lives, at any rate, educational elite women are no longer the mainstays of voluntary organizations—unlike earlier generations of women of similar background.

VOLUNTARY ASSOCIATIONS

Over two-thirds (69 percent) of our participants have been members of voluntary associations, and most of them currently hold such memberships. These figures are quite consistent with the findings of a

Stanford/Harvard alumni survey conducted in 1986, which showed 70 percent of respondents involved, on some level, with cultural or charitable organizations.[14]

Although the majority are members of some organization, on average our respondents list only one association each. Within these organizations, however, they tend to be quite active; more than one-fourth have held an office. The associations run the full gamut of American society, from professional groups like the American Medical Association to the Girl Scouts, local coaching associations, and the National Organization for Women. They are dispersed in literally hundreds of different organizations. As a result, only two associations have attracted more than 1 percent of our participants—the Stanford Alumni Association and the American Bar Association.

Women are somewhat more likely than men to belong to voluntary associations and to hold office in those associations, but this difference is not large. The four types vary considerably more, in surprising ways. For one thing, Intellectuals were notably less engaged in voluntary associations than other types. Second, the Unconnected were as active in associations as any other group, and they had a modestly higher rate of association leadership than other groups. Careerists are at the high end of association membership but least often fill leadership roles; the Strivers are only average in both dimensions. In other words, neither of the more career-oriented groups is especially likely to assume "take-charge" positions. Careerism does not seem to lessen off-the-job activities, but it also does not correspond with the exercise of leadership in the voluntary sector.

LEISURE ACTIVITIES

As already indicated, involvement in sports and athletics is the most common social activity of the educational elite, involving half of the women and slightly more than half of the men. Strivers and Careerists play sports more than other types, a pattern consistent with their undergraduate days. By comparison, the Intellectuals and the Unconnected are less keen on sports.

The quest for physical fitness is obviously a major motive for sports activities, as are plain fun and relaxation. But something more is operative as well: for the educational elite, a trim, attractive body is deemed practically obligatory and is an integral part of their self-image. This is one of the most distinctive features of their generation.

Hobbies range over the usual gamut: crafts, photography, playing music (quite a few are in bands), gardening, cooking. Some pursuits are more idiosyncratic. One woman trains Arabian horses; one man breeds reptiles. ("Anyone else in the cohort group breeding reptiles?" he asks.) Another man has a collection of over ten thousand records and compact discs. Overall, hobbies involve somewhat fewer people (44 percent) than do sports, but somewhat more engage in hobbies than in service activities. Women pursue hobbies as much as men do, but the hobbies chosen by women and men split along fairly traditional gender lines.

Though we did not inquire about it systematically, travel was often mentioned in the interviews as a major recreational activity. Especially before the arrival of children, the educational elite have the means and the interest to travel far and wide—to relax, to explore the world, to find the "perfect spot" for whatever they like to do. Travel is a way to enjoy the fruits of their burgeoning affluence and, again, an almost obligatory activity if they are to maintain their credentials as bona fide members of the professional elite.

SERVICE AND POLITICAL ENGAGEMENT

Charities, environmental groups, and legal aid societies were among the public-service involvements of some 42 percent of our participants. Again, women and men participated equally. Intellectuals turned out to be the least engaged in this area, owing mainly to the relative lack of involvement by Intellectual men. By contrast, the Unconnected were more active than other types, led by the men in this group. The percentage of Unconnected men reporting public-service engagement (55 percent) is over twice as large as the figure for Intellectual men.

The area of social involvement that shows the lowest level of engagement is political activity—working for political parties or political action committees, lobbying organizations, and so on. Only 13 percent of our participants reported any involvement in this area: 17 percent of men and 8 percent of women.

This is not to suggest, however, that most of our women participants are politically passive. On the contrary, quite a few are engaged in "women's issues," such as abortion rights and equal employment efforts. By the same token, members of minority groups often work in organizations promoting minority rights and advancement. We do not have sufficient information to confirm our suspicion that many of them reported these activities not as political engagements but as service organization activities.

One important factor affecting political engagement is marriage. Among all participants, almost twice the proportion of those never married (18 percent) had been involved in significant political activity than those married or living with a partner (10 percent). Among interviewees, an even higher proportion (38 percent) of unmarried participants indicated a "high level of engagement" in social or political issues, compared with those married (16 percent). Does marriage thus foster political complacency? Not according to our participants. Rather, it takes time, and parenthood takes even more time. Many, especially women, say they would like to be more active but simply cannot. The fact is that marriage definitely lowers the priority given to political activity. Perhaps parenthood also drains away some of the fervor that otherwise would be channeled into political activity. But becoming a parent also forces our participants to be more concerned with certain issues, such as the quality of schools, violence on television, and the like.

With respect to the typology, Strivers are by far the most active politically. Their level of political engagement, though still rather low (20 percent), is twice the rate for other groups. This finding is consistent with the greater social engagement of Strivers in college, and it helps account for the fact that, of the three participants who entered careers in public administration, two of them are Strivers.

Our interviewees attributed their lack of involvement in social causes and political issues not only to the competing demands of career and family but also, in many cases, to a certain sense of futility about making a difference. Some felt genuinely apathetic, evincing an almost devil-may-care attitude. A few expressed genuine regret about not being more involved and expressed the hope that they would be able to get politically involved in the future. The following comments capture some of these sentiments:

- I am not a one-issue man. I have broad social concerns, but I am pessimistic about solving any social problems. So I read and think about them but don't do anything.
- I am interested in the environment and recycle. As a teacher, I am concerned about public education, but I am not a union person and don't feel comfortable about political activities like strikes.
- I give several thousand dollars a year to organizations like Amnesty International and Planned Parenthood, but it is not enough, I should do more.
- I wish I had more social involvements. *Time* magazine is my link to the outside world.
- I am pretty lax in that department. I am worried about the quality of public education, and I fret about financing my children's college education.
- I was a volunteer for the Red Cross and active with the Girl Scouts.

Then I had a baby. I still try to help people on an individual basis. But I no longer keep up with global issues, over which I have no control. I barely read the headlines during the Gulf War.

• I am an armchair liberal. As a lawyer in Washington, it is hard for me not to be involved in social issues, but my interest in them is mainly career-related.

• My wife and two kids are my social concern.

Beyond apathy and regrets, we also encountered a more active disenchantment with politics, social institutions, and public policies. Some plainly expressed repugnance toward any sort of political involvement. Keith has a professional interest in political theory, but the more he learns about political life, the more discouraged he becomes. "I see a trend toward simplifying and labeling politics that is detrimental to our democracy," he says. "During the summer I spent in Washington, I found politics to be distasteful."

Mark, who calls his wealthy parents "limousine liberals," was himself part of the politically liberal "granola crowd" in college. Over the decade, his views have become much more conservative, to the dismay of his wife, who has retained her liberal perspective. He is disillusioned with the welfare system ("an abysmal failure") and says, "I changed my views as I became personally exposed to the problems of Chicago."

One man was already quite cynical in college about social issues, and his life in Las Vegas has hardened him further. "What is one supposed to do," he wonders, "when a local election has a professional baseball player running against a bimbo?" His strategy is to stay aloof and play ball with whomever is in power.

The Stanford/Harvard survey found alumni to be socially and politically more liberal than the general population on most issues, manifesting a genuine tolerance for dissenting ideas and variant lifestyles while leading fairly conventional lives themselves. This characterization fits our participants as well. Most of these upper-middle-class young men and women fall somewhere in the middle of the political spectrum. Extreme positions are rare but more common on the conservative right than the liberal left. Almost none of them embrace truly radical political views.

One example of a staunch political conservative is Steven. As assistant attorney general in a small southern city, Steven calls himself a "Reagan Republican." He is fed up with the direction taken by mainstream American society and feels beleaguered by "liberals" and "phony conservatives." He still bridles at the memory of the political "liberals" who dominated the faculty at Stanford and at his law school, allowing little expression for conservative views. Steven views all the talk about "diversity" on campus as a sham. As a white male, he feels vulnerable to affirmative action (though he appreciates its potential help to his wife's career). Despite the fervor of his convictions, Steven is not actively involved in politics. He attributes his noninvolvement in part to his sense of being beleaguered to the point where he can do nothing. He says, "You can't even openly discuss issues like race anymore."

Those on the left end of the political spectrum are usually feminists, members of ethnic minorities, or both. Jill, whose major concerns are civil rights, abortion, and the environment, is of mixed Hispanic and Native American heritage. She says, "I have a strong sense of solidarity with people who have basically an oral tradition and are land-based. It matters little how you label such people." One Mexican-American focuses his political engagement on improving the position of his own ethnic group by getting involved in political campaigns and contributing money to various organizations. A black lawyer in Texas is keenly sensitive to the political issues that affect his ethnic community and served as county precinct chairman during the 1990 elections. A woman with a strongly feminist outlook feels frustrated "watching men set the social agenda." Even her intellectual interests are frustrated by "male cultural dominance." She complains, "Books are written by men whose voices predominate in the lives of their characters. Or, if they are written by women, I still don't hear female voices in them." Yet, outside of such individually focused interests, there is no evidence among our participants of a more general commitment to, or genuine involvement in, a democratically and culturally evolving world.

In summary, outside of work and family life, the educational elite is highly active socially, but most of their activity is self-oriented, reflecting what Christopher Lasch labeled in 1978 the "culture of narcissism"; relatively few are engaged in political or social change and improvement. Hence, much of what we said about the life of the mind is also applicable here. We may be surprised that the educational elite, the future leaders of the country, are not more actively engaged in social and political issues. If we explain it in terms of the time crunch in their lives, we would expect that, as their life circumstances change, so will their priorities. It nevertheless remains the case that these young adults, the "best and brightest" of their generation, are by and large quite narrow in their outlook and engagements. They are genuine representatives of the "me-first" tenor of modern life.

Perhaps the most positive aspect of all this is that, just as some have managed to integrate intellectual concerns into their careers, those with a serious sense of social responsibility have also merged social commitments with their working lives. Martin MacMillan sees his dedication to medicine as a way of being a good citizen. Alicia Turner teaches her disadvantaged students with a sense of mission, hoping to do her small part to end the cycle of poverty and failure that dominates their lives. David Levy spent years doing legal work among migrant workers as an expression of his commitment to social justice. George Mehta works in a biological lab because of his concern for the environment.

What these cases also demonstrate is a long-term characteristic of American culture, not just a peculiarity of the 1980s: social engagement need not be, and indeed usually is not, predicated on grand visions of reform and utopia. Rather, individuals act largely in what they see as their own interests—but choose to do so in a context in which their actions can lead to collective improvements and solutions that work for the good of the whole, not just for their own benefit.

The most dramatic example of the way social concerns shape careers is Marty's switch from being a realtor to a drug counselor, discussed earlier. He grew up in an "apolitical household"; his parents, second-generation immigrants, were primarily concerned with their own welfare. ("My father has not voted in the last fifteen years.") After he left his lucrative career in real estate, Marty committed himself fully to helping resolve the enormous problems facing society, especially those involving young people. As he puts it, "Economic inequality is wasting the lives of an entire generation." He has passionate views about how to deal with health care, education, hunger, and homelessness.

Perhaps intellectual and social concerns thrive at this stage in the elite's lives only when they become synergistic with careers. But if we look beyond this meshing of private and public interest, to what extent is the relative lack of engagement of our participants in political action and public service a reflection of their educational experience at Stanford? At the time our participants were undergraduates, there were a number of avenues for public service engagements on and off campus, but there was no centralized focus for such activities. In view of this, president Donald Kennedy established the Haas Center for Public Service in 1984, to provide students with meaningful ways to serve society. In opening the first conference sponsored by the Center, he said:

> There is a vision: of a public service sector that mixes public and private elements, professional and volunteer elements; that has a highly responsive and highly differentiated structure; that offers a variety of niches in which individual initiative and imagination can work effectively. They knew what they were talking about when they said, very carefully, government for and by the people.
>
> The worst feature, it seems to me, of the decay in regard for government has been the tendency to fall into the conclusion that the public

motive is inherently ineffectual—that there is somehow a negative correlation between compassion and efficiency. That is a politically convenient
position for those who would like to weaken or dismantle government
programs for the less fortunate in this society, but it is wrong. It is one of
those deadly wrongs, however, that has the potential for becoming a self-
fulfilling prophesy. Restoration of faith in the capacity of public service is
thus doubly important, and I would like Stanford to be a leader in that
process of restoration.[15]

Currently, the center has its own building, which houses over forty university programs and student organizations. It serves as a focal point for a
wide variety of voluntary efforts, which now engage three out of four Stanford undergraduates in some form of public service at some time during
their college years. Their activities may range from almost casual efforts to
serious involvement in projects that call for high levels of commitment and
leadership.

In addition to whatever concrete accomplishments such engagements
may achieve in helping others, they also engender substantive discussion
and understanding of social issues, fitting them closely with the institution's educational mission. Perhaps most important, the very act of engagement may become transformed into a lifelong commitment to public service. Through such experiences, the leaders of tomorrow may learn that
somewhere between taking on the impossible task of saving the world by
sheer passion, and the irresponsible alternative of dispassionately watching
it flounder, lie the opportunities for each individual to make a difference.
And to that end, one needs not only knowledge and expertise but also
compassion and commitment. It is not enough to know—one must also
act. For as the sixteenth-century Chinese philosopher Wang Yang-Ming
has said, "Those who are supposed to know but do not act simply do not
yet know."[16]

THE SEARCH FOR MEANING

The life of the mind and social concerns are related to our core values.
They reflect not only a sense of who we are but also who we should be.
They deal not so much with questions of "What?" and "Why?" but "What
for?" This question is central to the search for meaning that guides the
actions of our participants. Integral parts of this quest are our religious
beliefs, philosophical concerns, and life goals.

In our exploration of the ways our participants searched for meaning,
our method fell short of the task, as it did with respect to the life of the

mind. Instead of an in-depth exploration of the guiding principles that govern and guide all aspects of life, we ended up mainly with an account of their religious affiliations and life goals.

THE PROFILE GROUP

Two of our profile group are devout Christians. Careerist Martin MacMillan was actively engaged with the Campus Crusade for Christ in college. A decade later, he retains his Christian faith but has been only "somewhat involved" in the Presbyterian church to which his family belongs. The fact that Martin's wife did not belong to a church before they married also enters the picture: "The motivation to go to church comes from me, but the decision comes from her." Nonetheless, Martin now often takes the children to church with or without his wife. Apart from church attendance, is there a spiritual dimension to his life? "Absolutely," says Martin. Once again, the matter is linked to his experience as a physician. "I marvel at how the body works and how things are too complex to be a matter of chance. An extension of that is how people react to each other in the face of disease. I see much good coming from ordinary people doing extraordinary things in dealing with their illnesses or their kids' illnesses. What all this conveys to me is a combination of a belief in God and a belief in the basic strength, kindness, and goodness of the human spirit. Whether that comes directly from God or some collective force that drives folks is hard to tell."

Intellectual Kirsten Buchanan is a Catholic married to a Methodist who is the son of Protestant missionaries. So they alternately attend each other's churches and often get into doctrinal debates. Kirsten and her husband are going to expose their children to the teachings of both denominations so that they can eventually make their own informed choices.

For the rest of the profile group, religion plays a less significant role in their lives. Careerist Cynthia Eastwood considers herself a Christian in a vague sort of way, but being married to a man "who has no faith whatsoever" weakens her own feeble inclination to be more actively engaged. Strivers George Mehta and Geraldine Jones have no religious affiliations, but each is endowed with a strong ethical sense.

Intellectual Christopher Luce was raised a Catholic but lost his faith in the theological tenets of the church while at Stanford. He says, "I now consider myself to be an atheist. Although it may be more tempting to use the term 'agnostic,' that would be weak-minded." As for secular values, he thinks of himself as an "aesthete." He finds the amorality of that perspective "seductive," but he is not entirely comfortable with it. Though Christopher's intellectual life and social concerns have supplanted his Catholicism, he continues to admire the morals and the social commitments of the Catholic church, and those of the Jesuits in particular. When in Mexico, he was "very struck by the intensity of the faith of the Mexican people." Christopher is still close to his college mentor, a devout Catholic, and goes to church with him when he is visiting.

Unconnected David Levy shares this intellectual perspective on religion. He was brought up in the Jewish faith. In high school and especially in college, he gradually moved away from those religious beliefs, but now they are becoming more important to him again. He says, "I feel a strong cultural tie with the Jewish people, so it is something I want to maintain." His fiancée's father is Jewish, but her mother is not. "However," says David, "since we have been together, she has developed a strong identification with Judaism and is happy to celebrate various holidays with me." They expect to bring up their children in the Jewish faith.

Katherine Johnson was brought up as a Catholic and took a lot of courses on religious and philosophical issues while in college. Over the decade, however, her interests have moved away from those areas. She now rarely goes to church. Nonetheless, she intends to send her daughter to a Catholic school so that she will be exposed to ethical values.

RELIGIOUS FAITH

Individualism is a distinctive feature of American culture. Yet when it comes to finding answers to philosophical and spiritual questions, Americans usually fall back on the answers provided by collective religious bodies and their secular alternatives—or they react against them.

In the Stanford/Harvard alumni survey, the researchers found that, in their control group from the general population, 94 percent professed a belief in God or a supreme being; 53 percent claimed religion was an important part of their lives; and 34 percent said they were "born-again" Christians. For the Stanford/Harvard alumni, only 73 percent professed a belief in God, 24 percent felt religion was important in their lives, and 9 percent considered themselves "born-again."[17] This finding is consistent with the general secularizing effect of higher education, as shown in various studies.[18]

Formal religion thus appears to be less central to the lives of the educational elite than to those of the general population. The survey also found that, whatever their religious beliefs, most of the alumni regard their beliefs as essentially personal, not collective, in nature.[19] Collective institutions may thus provide the answers (or at least approaches) to life's ultimate questions, but these individuals tend to sift through those answers for the ones that make sense to them.

These same attitudes characterize our participants. As we noted for the profile group, though religious belief and practice are central to the lives of some, and others are firmly agnostic, the majority profess a vague sort of faith. In the interview sample, only 15 percent showed a high degree of concern with religious issues; the balance was divided between those with lukewarm interest and those with practically no interest at all. No gender or typology differences were evident.

Parenthood is a major factor related to reli ious involvement. Over three times as many participants with children (25 percent) felt highly engaged with religion, compared to 8 percent of those without children (whether single or married). One mother's explanation is typical: "Even though we have not been particularly active, we do not want our children to grow up in a moral vacuum." For the educational elite, as for the general population, religion is seen as a strong source of morality. But morality can be espoused through rather minimal religious engagement—hence, 75 percent of our sample of parents are not highly engaged religiously. Rather few are engaged in a serious quest for faith, salvation, and spiritual growth.

Interfaith marriages also thrust religion into prominence because of the need in such a relationship to negotiate and compromise. One woman attends her husband's Catholic church but sends money to her own Lutheran church, even though she has not attended its services for years. One man's Jewish wife has insisted that their children be brought up in her faith. His attitude again reflects the dominant concern with morality, not faith: "I don't mind as long as the children become good people."

When we asked our participants about what they wanted for their children, they were generally in favor of nonmaterial values, and their responses remained equally uniform for women, men, and the four types. They want their children to develop moral values and a personal philosophy; to be concerned with social issues; to get along well with others; to feel close to their parents. Far less concern is expressed about seeing their children enter lucrative professions, become outstanding professionals, or "have the best that money can buy."

Sometimes one member of a couple is a believer and the other is not, a situation that, once again, calls for accommodation. A woman who was brought up as an Episcopalian is married to a man who has never belonged to a church. Her own personal faith has stayed strong, but she feels something is awry every time she takes the children to church without their father, a feeling that can dampen her own motivation to go to church. Another views her interest in Christianity in college as "just a phase," one she has since replaced with interest in political and social issues. Nonetheless, her daughter was baptized a Catholic, in line with her husband's Irish heritage.

Religious beliefs range from traditional faith in God to at least one case of a self-proclaimed "white witch." (She was rather secretive about what this meant because "people tend to misunderstand what it is all about.") The majority feel there is a "spiritual dimension" to their inner selves that is only vaguely associated with a religious belief system. "True believers" among Christians are concentrated in Catholic and evangelical churches; most of the rest attend religious services sporadically, if at all. They often celebrate religious holidays to please their parents, for sentimental reasons, or out of ethnic solidarity, but give the religious content of the holidays little attention. This vague religious faith with no firm institutional grounding comes through in many comments:

- I have no interest in going to church, but I believe in a power greater than myself and sometimes pray.
- I was brought up as a Catholic, but now I am a spiritual person more on my own (with reference to vegetarianism, yoga, running, and holistic medicine).
- I was brought up as a Presbyterian, but now I believe in universal values like treating people well. If anything, I would be a Unitarian now.
- I have a personal faith but cannot find the right church.
- I am a Catholic, but I no longer want to spend two hours in church every Sunday. I pray at home with my rosary.

Among Jews, religious faith is hard to separate from ethnic identity. As one woman put it, "I am not the least bit religious, but I have a strong cultural and ethnic affinity to Judaism." A man says, "I admire the humane tenets of Judaism, but I have no use for the rituals and rigid beliefs of Orthodoxy." Another woman was brought up with the teachings of Judaism even though her parents did not belong to a temple, and she plans to repeat the pattern. "It is important to retain some generational continuity," she explains.

Only a few of our participants have made religious belief the central organizing principle of their lives. One man spent four years as a lay preacher for his evangelical church until the autocratic and self-serving ways of the leader of the sect drove him away. He remains, however, very much a believer. We already referred to Arturo, who entered a Catholic seminary to prepare for the priesthood but decided against it before ordination. Religion, nonetheless, continues to be central to his life.

Others approach religion in a purely intellectual way. Keith's extended family includes several clergymen, but his interest in the Bible is based on the importance of biblical writings for political theory.

Finally, religious concerns affect some almost not at all, or are rejected outright.

- I am Christian, but it is not tangible to my life.
- I consider myself to be largely deficient in spiritual matters. As a gay activist, I put all ideologies through a political filter. As a result, I have a deep visceral distrust of organized religion because of its treatment of gays.
- There is no spiritual dimension in my life. Philosophical and religious issues don't interest me.
- In college, I claimed to believe "anything, everything, and nothing." I have now settled on "nothing."

This wide variety of experiences of religious faith, or the lack of it, speaks to some extent to the fluidity of the lives of these young adults. At this point, many devote as little time and energy to religious matters as they do to intellectual and social concerns. They have largely moved out of the idealistic phase of their youth but have not yet confronted the existential dilemmas that come with advancing years. Where they stand on these issues is not only an open question; it is a question most hardly feel compelled to consider.

One of our interviewers recalled, "One evening in a Wall Street watering hole talking with maybe a dozen Stanford alums of the class of '81 or thereabouts, I remember one of them saying of the group: 'Well, none of us is in jail, nobody's been indicted; a few of us have been investigated, but we're OK.' I gathered some of their senior colleagues and mentors had been jailed or indicted, and some worked for firms that were fined. It occurred to me that evening that none of us could have imagined in 1980, it might be said a decade later that success would consist of doing well while avoiding indictment or jail."

This vignette, along with other comments we heard from our participants along the same lines, raises a serious question: how well does Stanford prepare its students to deal with ethical problems in their working and personal lives?

Stanford's imposing non-denominational Memorial Church dominates the inner quad, the heart of the campus. Its dean and staff support the activities of a variety of religious traditions. Yet Stanford is a determinedly secular institution. Students may be exposed to many facets of ethical and moral issues through courses in the humanities and the social sciences, but there is no integrated attempt to make moral development a salient part of the undergraduate curriculum. Should Stanford, and other institutions like it, make such an attempt?

One group of educators, the Wingspread Group on Higher Education, thinks they should:

> From the founding of the first American colleges 300 years ago, higher education viewed the development of student character and the transmission of the values supporting that character as an essential responsibility of faculty and administration. The importance of higher education's role in the transmission of values is, if anything, even greater today than it was 300 or even 50 years ago. The weakening of the role of family and religious institutions in the lives of young people, the increase in the number of people seeking the benefits of higher education, and what appears to be the larger erosion of core values in our society makes this traditional role all the more important.[20]
>
> ... [A]n increasingly diverse society, battered by accelerating change, requires more than workplace competence. It also requires that we do a better job of passing on to the next generation a sense of the value of diversity and the critical importance of honesty, decency, integrity, compassion, and personal responsibility in a democratic society. Above all, we must get across the idea that the individual flourishes best in a genuine community to which the individual in turn has an obligation to contribute.[21]

No one would argue against the merits of students having such values. But should students not have already acquired these values by the time they come to college? One could argue that regardless, college should enhance further their moral development. But whether or not higher education should even attempt to transmit a basic set of formally defined moral values remains a highly controversial matter. American culture champions the autonomous, self-directed individual whose values are to derive from reason and personal faculties and experience alone. Contrarily, American culture also insists on the importance of the family, religious institutions, and the nation as sources of moral guidance and virtue. Education is charged with aiding these collective sources of virtue and, where necessary, making up for deficient or absent parents, faith, or patriotism. As historian David Tyack has noted in his analysis of the early days of the republic, American education was founded with the aim of producing both *free* and *uniform* citizens.[22] The obvious contradiction involved has lain at the heart of the controversy ever since: How can we foster free thinkers who simultaneously share a common set of core values about which disputes will not arise?

In *Beyond the Ivory Tower,* Derek Bok, former president of Harvard (and a Stanford alumnus) addresses these issues as they pertain to the modern university.[23] He describes the certitudes of the nineteenth-century moral philosophers giving way to the relativistic perspectives of social scientists which reject normative judgments and moral teaching, shifting such moral issues from center stage to the periphery of the undergraduate curriculum. During the 1970s, there was a resurgence of ethical debate on college campuses, focusing on the problems of war, government secrecy, race relations, and related concerns. Schools of law, medicine, and business have meanwhile placed greater emphasis on professional ethics. The purpose of these efforts is to inform students an ' heighten their awareness of ethical dilemmas, as well as to foster their capacity to reason through ethical issues and clarify their own moral values.

Bok's view is that though the objectives of these new approaches to moral education may be laudable, "the enterprise itself is beset with the gravest difficulty." Serious concerns relate to the potential for indoctrination, the limits of reason in resolving moral dilemmas, and the qualifications of instructors who deal with these sensitive issues. Nonetheless, Bok concludes:

> It does seem plausible to suppose that such classes will help students become more alert in perceiving ethical issues, more aware of the reasons underlying moral principles, and more equipped to reason carefully in applying these principles to concrete cases. Will they behave more ethically? One would suppose so, provided we assume that most students have a desire to lead ethical lives and share the basic moral values common to our society. Granted, we cannot prove that such results will be achieved. Even so, the prospects are surely great enough to warrant a determined effort, not only because the subject matter is interesting and the problems intellectually challenging but also because the goal is so important to the quality of the society in which we live.[24]

CHAPTER 10

Looking Back and Looking Forward

Time present and time past
Are both perhaps present in time future
And time future contained in time past.
T. S. Eliot, *Four Quartets*

The present is a gateway where past and future meet. In this study, our participants stand in the gateway, Janus figures seeing past and future as extensions of the present. This last chapter will look with them, both back and forward, to review the first decade after college and contemplate the second. After presenting an overview of what we have learned of the educational elite, we turn to the matter of stability and change in the typology over the ten years. This sets the stage for considering a key question: Was it worth it? Do they feel that the immense effort and expense involved in obtaining an elite education and preparing to enter the ranks of the elite professions are justified? We present their responses to these questions by listening to their voices tell us about the impact of elite education on various aspects of their lives and the role of the faculty. We then turn toward the future, seeing their vision of the anticipated time-that-is-to-come.

THE PROFILE GROUP

By the end of the decade after college, Martin MacMillan's orientation has shifted from Careerist to Striver. In hindsight, he would do things quite differently with his undergraduate education. "I truly regret not having been more 'intellectual' at Stanford. Perhaps a more active faculty could have identified my narrowness and helped avoid these regrets. Despite graduating 'with distinction,' my two deepest emotions about Stanford are regret and embarrassment. Regret, in missing out on the full potential of the Stanford educational experience; embarrassment, in my narrow immaturity that at the time prevented me from seizing the opportunity to do more."

He now wishes he had majored in history or English, since "I still would have done the sciences to be a doctor, but I'll never get another chance to study the liberal arts." He especially would have liked to attend an overseas campus (an option his father discouraged, "the one piece of bad advice" Martin says he received from him). Yet there is no question that Martin would again choose medicine as a career. On balance, he is quite pleased with the overall quality of his undergraduate education and the broadening effect Stanford has had on his l. ⁼. He says, "Stanford taught me to look up, down, backward, all around, not just straight ahead along the way. I still ended up going pretty much the same direction I started, but the trip was much more vivid, '3-D.'"

In ten years Martin expects his life to be largely an extension of his current one. He will still be part of a group practice but in a more senior role. He will have "the same wife and kids, just older." He hopes to have more time to pursue other interests, including leisure activities. He anticipates no major changes. "Why should I search for new directions?" he asks, "when I am quite happy with what I've got."

Cynthia Eastwood has remained a Careerist on the fast track. She aspires to ever higher positions in business but has no interest in being the CEO of a major company partly because she thinks she will be held back as a woman. Instead, she would rather own and run her own business. The more significant changes in Cynthia's life are likely to come on the personal front when, as she expects, she has one or two children by the end of the decade. If anyone can reconcile the demands of a high-powered career with motherhood, Cynthia Eastwood will. With respect to the impact of Stanford, Cynthia says, "Tremendous impact in all areas—career, friends, family life. The name Stanford opens many, many doors (of course you have to 'knock' on those doors and prove yourself). My closest friends are from Stanford, and I am very proud of their accomplishments, as they are of mine. Although I didn't meet my husband while we were both undergrads at Stanford, he has several degrees from Stanford so, of course, ties are there as well."

Where Martin MacMillan erred in shortchanging his liberal education, Intellectual Kirsten Buchanan's mistake was choosing the wrong career (chapter 8). But she has no regrets and remains highly satisfied with the quality of her educational experience. Ten years later, she remains an Intellectual (and she always will be).

About the overall impact of her Stanford experience Kirsten says:

I am convinced that a serious student can receive a good education anywhere if she is committed and diligent. An excellent education, however, requires an institution that can support, stimulate, and challenge a bright student. When I graduated from Stanford, I felt I had the best college experience possible. . . . If I have learned anything over the past ten years, it is the knowledge that I can do almost anything I choose to, thanks to an excellent education, adequate intellectual abilities, and willfulness. Now I am ready to experiment a bit more with my life and explore new fields. I will be spending the next decade raising my children. What an excellent time to be adventuresome!

Christopher Luce also remains very much an Intellectual. If he were to do it again, instead of majoring in English he would pursue a more ambitious course of study in the humanities, because "English came too easily, it didn't cast the net widely enough. I would pursue the development of Western civilization more broadly, taking courses that are more difficult." He would choose the same career. Yet given "world enough and time" he can also contemplate having become a movie director, investment banker, or carpenter. In ten years, Christopher expects to be a tenured professor in a major university, an accomplishment that is virtually a done deed. About Stanford's impact, he says,

Stanford changed everything. I cannot describe the exhilaration I felt while I was there. It awakened me to the world and everything in it. Perhaps that would have happened elsewhere. But I doubt if it would have happened to the same degree and with the same intensity.

From the beginning, Stanford struck me as a very human and humane institution. I became friendly with several administrators and professors there. I admired them for the breadth of their understanding as well as their capacity to think critically about a variety of issues. These men and women not only cared passionately about the life of the mind, they lived it—or so it seemed to me then.

A couple years after graduation, I confided to a Stanford professor that I was thinking of becoming one myself. He surprised me by saying that he didn't think that was much of an ambition. Anyone, he told me, could become a professor. The real challenge was to become an intellectual, someone for whom ideas mattered. I never forgot that. You could say that Stanford helped me appreciate the full measure of that challenge.

George Mehta remains the best sort of Striver. Whereas the assessments the Careerists and Intellectuals in the group make of their skills and accomplishments are very up and down, Mehta's gains have been spread more evenly. Evaluating Stanford's impact on his life, he says: "It developed my critical thinking and analytical skills. Exposed me to art and greatly increased my aesthetic sense. Gave me a tremendous opportunity to develop my social skills, which were lacking in high school. I became interested in economics and business, which formed the basis for my current career choice. Introduced me to California and the Bay Area in particular, which is where I decided to live."

George Mehta has made an amazing recovery from his stroke, but the experience left a lasting impression about the unpredictability of life. He faces the future with equanimity and hopes to pursue his work, family life, and wide array of other interests with renewed vigor.

Geraldine Jones remains very much a Striver. She is getting ready to settle down, yet she still finds it difficult to make long-term predictions. She says, "Since I keep changing, it is hard for me to look beyond two or three years." After she settles in her job as a paramedic, Geraldine will work for a while, then reconsider her options, including the possibility of going to medical school. On the personal front, Geraldine is "ready to be a mom," but her current relationship and life circumstances are not yet right for it. Hence, the future remains very open.

Unconnected David Levy has been transformed into a keen Intellectual. But true to his Unconnected past, he expresses a somewhat lower sense of satisfaction with his liberal education and his training for graduate school. His more positive gains during college were on the social front. "Living in a group setting with my peers, first in a freshman dorm, then a co-op, and then in a house off-campus with four other students, had the greatest impact on me. It exposed me to many points of view that I otherwise wouldn't have learned about, and it forced me to accommodate quickly to living with a number of persons beyond my immediate family. While classes, instructors, events, and activities were all a part of my experience, the longest-lasting impact came from living with and learning about my fellow students."

As we noted earlier, David is quite open about the future of his career. He may go back to practicing law or switch to some other field, like teaching high school. What he does will be determined to some extent by his wife's career choices and opportunities. They expect to have children, and David will no doubt be a highly involved father.

Unconnected Katherine Johnson has turned into a Striver. Though her highly successful career dominates her life, she is ambivalent about corporate law; it leaves too little time to spend with her family, to which Katherine is strongly attached. It is the same dilemma she faced ten years ago: "Teaching is too ill paid, and law is too demanding in terms of time." Though Katherine is "presently vacillating and considering switching careers," her expectation is that in ten years she will be "practicing law in some capacity, but not in a private firm that demands consistent fifty hours plus per week. I will be spending more time with my family and devoting more time to public-interest issues."

THE EDUCATIONAL ELITE: A SUMMARY

Although we have tried to be selective in presenting our findings, we have nonetheless offered a large assortment of facts and figures on a wide variety of topics. We will summarize our key findings and conclusions at this point, stripped of details and qualifications—in other words, look at the forest rather than the trees.

The educational elite consists of academically high-achieving students, many (but not all) from privileged family backgrounds, who attend prestigious public and private universities and go on to join the ranks of the professional elite. These men and women are fully aware of the importance of educational credentials for entry into high-status occupations. Correspondingly, four out of five go to graduate school, and nearly all complete their degrees. Most go to law school, business school, or medical school; others obtain advanced degrees in engineering or other technical fields; small proportions are trained in humanistic or social scientific graduate programs. They obtain their graduate education in a wide variety of institutions, many of them prestigious ones.

In choosing their careers, they say they value intellectual challenge, creativity, and independence above all else. Material considerations, such as high income and financial security, are deemed relatively unimportant. The apparent contradiction between their attitudes and the high-status, high-paying careers they end up in is partly explained by the fact that these professions offer intellectually challenging and creative work environments. Conveniently enough, these mainline professions also bring great material rewards. In this respect, the educational elite can have their cake and eat it too, without feeling like crass materialists.

Most members of the educational elite enter professions closely linked to their graduate degrees—business, law, engineering, medicine—and the rest enter a wide variety of other professions. During the decade after college, they are consolidating careers, not simply holding jobs or trying to make a living. This is most evident in the long hours they work, the tremendous commitment they bring to their careers, and their high level of competence. As a consequence, most say they would still work even if they did not need the money.

The economic rewards these men and women reap are spectacular. By age thirty, their family earnings average over $100,000, already surpassing the levels that most people, including many graduates of nonelite colleges, will reach in their entire lives. This monetary success is matched by plentiful job promotions, but many participants have also changed employers frequently, and, indeed, careers. Even those who have essentially linear careers make such changes, to get ahead.

Despite the generally high levels of satisfaction they express with specific aspects of their careers, many feel they are behind schedule in their career development. Their standards and expectations are so high that only a small minority feel ahead of the game at this point.

One of the most compelling consequences of their career success is their strong upward social mobility. Those of lower than middle-class backgrounds have already surpassed the socioeconomic status of their parents; most of those from more affluent backgrounds have already regained their parents' status. Rare are the individuals who feel they have dropped below the social position of their parents, and most of them are likely to rise to higher class position as they move into their late thirties.

If they are exceptional in their career development, the educational elite are far more ordinary in their personal lives. Six of ten are married, and one of ten is living with a domestic partner. One of three is a parent. Spouses are normally chosen from within their social and educational stratum; those who make different choices are likely to experience tension, especially with parents.

They marry and begin having children in their late twenties—later than their age cohort in the general population. Almost all of them see marriage and children as essential to their lives; if they are not yet married, they feel behind schedule. About one in ten have gotten divorced by age thirty-one, and seeds of discord are lurking in quite a few marriages.

Nonetheless, they are by and large highly satisfied with their marriages and other primary relationships. They feel strongly committed to their partners, with whom they have begun to settle into stable lives. Levels of marital contentment drop somewhat when children enter the scene, but as parents they express no regrets. By and large, whether parents or not, they feel content with their spouses and competent about their own marital roles. Areas of contention primarily relate to the sharing of housekeeping burdens and caring for their children. Reconciling the demands of career and family is the central challenge of their lives and affects women much more than men.

Outside of work and family, their main forms of activity are sports and hobbies. Many express the desire to have a rich intellectual and cultural life, but few actually do. Social and political interests are not lacking, but actual involvements are scarce. Time is always short, and leisure time goes to taking care of the body and having fun rather than to pursuing intellectual interests or social concerns. Religion is important for some, especially those raised in devout households, and it becomes important as a source of morality to others as they become parents, but it remains a peripheral concern for most. What seems to matter to them most outside of their careers is having good relationships with their spouses, children, parents, and friends and living comfortable and enjoyable lives.

GENDER

Perhaps the most striking thing about the educational elite in the first decade after college is the similarity, rather than the differences, between women and men. In terms of graduate education, women and men look alike. Women want much the same out of occupations as men do. Women are not fully represented among the most prestigious occupations, and they make somewhat less money than men, but the differences at this point are mainly due to women interrupting their careers to have children. These career women are certainly close to parity with men, and they intend to keep pushing for greater equality. Very few plan to be full-time homemakers permanently.

On the personal side, gender similarities are also marked in terms of propensity to marry, the timing of children, and settling in as homeowners. It is only in managing the home that gender differences become a real issue. Women are more often responsible for housekeeping; women stay home with infants; women provide or arrange for child care far more than men do. Many of the problems creating tension among couples revolve precisely around the division of labor in the household. Nevertheless, women and men seem equally satisfied with their primary relationships, and neither sex longs for radical changes on the home front. Perhaps the women are resigned to the situation and unwilling to complain too much, consoling themselves with the realization that their partners are far more egalitarian than their fathers were. On the other hand, their responsibility for child rearing slows their career development significantly.

Gender matters little in the use of leisure time. In their intellectual and social concerns, women are no more engaged than men. Contrary to historical patterns, women are also no more religious than men, and their life goals do not differ significantly from those of men. Looking ahead, however, gender probably will make more of a difference in the next decade as they have more children, their lives become more complicated to manage, and more families have the economic means to permit one spouse to be a full-time homemaker.

ETHNICITY

As with gender, our most important finding is the lack of significant differences between the minority groups and the white majority. Within the educational elite, ethnic minorities are just as likely to attend graduate school and complete their degrees. They are just as likely to enter prestigious professions and to have high incomes. Hence, they experience strong upward mobility—even more than whites, because more minorities come from less privileged backgrounds and have greater room to move up.

Neither are ethnic minority members different in the personal realm. With the notable exception of African-American women, they are no less likely to marry, and no less likely to have children. Their attitudes and outlooks differ only modestly from those of whites; they are somewhat more concerned about income and job security in choosing professions, probably owing to the less advantaged backgrounds of many of them, but overall they have the same priorities for themselves and their children.

This is not to say that ethnic minority members have as smooth and certain a passage as whites to the upper ranks of the occupational structure. They may be helped by affirmative action to some extent, but they constantly feel the burdens of past and present discrimination and are driven by the sense that they must do a better job than whites simply to be seen as equally competent. They feel less acceptance as "natural" members of the elite ranks they have entered, and they know that marrying or even socializing outside their own respective group is often problematic. But these lingering burdens are less striking than the parity they have gained with whites in most dimensions we have studied. It indicates both the drive and capacity of these minority group members, as well as the power of elite educational credentials to propel them up the status structure.

TYPOLOGY

Our four types show significant differences over the decade after college, although the effects of the typology become gradually attenuated over time. Careerists are conventional and conservative in such things as choice of occupation, entrepreneurship, and (for Careerist men) gender roles in the household. The Unconnected, a much less homogeneous group, are often unconventional and adventuresome, entering a wider variety of occupations, opening their own businesses, joining less standard volunteer groups. Careerists have the most linear career trajectories, the Unconnected the least linear. Intellectuals and Strivers stand between these two extremes, though Intellectuals are generally less conventional and linear than Strivers.

Choice of occupation does, of course, have decided effects. Concentrated in law, medicine, and business, Careerists earn more money than others, but their family incomes are not as high because many have spouses who earn less than those of other types. Intellectuals are not as single-mindedly committed to their careers as Careerists and Strivers are. By pursuing careers more for their intrinsic interest than for material rewards, Intellectuals make less money and are less upwardly mobile. Because of their more delayed and individualistic career choices, the Unconnected fit this pattern as well.

Intellectuals are much more engaged in the life of the mind; Careerists are rarely so engaged. Differences in type are small regarding career development, use of leisure time, involvement in voluntary associations, life goals, and self-evaluations of marriages.

CHANGES IN THE TYPOLOGY

In chapter 1, we discussed the interplay of the two fundamental processes in human development—constancy and change—and applied it to our typology during the college years. The stability of the typology is significant because it reflects on its predictive value. The more stable the typology, the more we can anticipate how a given type is likely to behave in the future. By the same token, to the extent that change occurs, it allows individuals to feel that they are not locked into these patterns for life.

In college, although there was considerable change between the freshman and junior years for the sample as a whole, only one out of four students in each type's more sharply defined core groups changed types. Moreover, all of these shifts occurred between contiguous categories, not polar opposite groups; in other words, while a Careerist may become a Striver or Unconnected, no Careerist turned into an Intellectual or vice versa, and no Striver became Unconnected, or vice versa.

Since the decade after college is a much longer stretch of time than the college years, we might expect even greater change to occur then. But since late adolescence is a more fluid and formative period than young adulthood, we would expect less change after college. Two factors are simultaneously at work here: the effect of personality development (which presumably incorporates changes in our typology) and the effect of the social environment, which becomes far more varied after college. As our participants get pulled and pushed by these internal and external changes, what does in fact happen to their typological orientations?

In the follow-up study questionnaire, we included many of the same items that had been used in constructing the original cohort study typology—questions about characteristics desired in an occupation, reasons for going to college, life goals, goals for their children, and so on. We then re-created the careerism and intellectualism scales we had used earlier to generate a new version of the typology for the follow-up study (see details in appendix B).

Responses on the individual items used in the intellectualism and careerism scales reveal considerable continuity. If, as a senior student, a participant said that "high income" was a "very important" job feature, there was a high probability that he or she felt that high income was either "very important" or "important" a decade later. Extremely few participants changed their views radically—say, from indicating that job security was not at all important to saying that job security was very important. Another indicator of stability is the fact that the mean scores on individual items in the follow-up study questionnaire were very similar to those in the cohort study questionnaires. Items considered very important by most students, such as occupational creativity and originality, were still evaluated highly by most of our young adults; items seen as relatively unimportant earlier, such as gaining a position to shape public events, were still at the bottom of the list. One important implication of this pattern is that, by and large, we do not detect any noticeable shifts in the overall degree of intellectual or career commitment among the educational elite. We have encountered this finding at several points previously—despite the careerism they display in their dedication to work, their attitudes and avowed values champion noncareerist criteria and goals above monetary and professional success.

The stability we found in responses to individual scale items augurs well for the stability of the typology as a whole. But scales combining many disparate items have a way of not behaving like the items that make them up—like a herd of individually placid, well-behaved cattle, a scale can stampede in unexpected directions. Our "stampede" is not as unexpected as it seems at first glance. Just over 40 percent of our participants were the same type ten years after graduation as they had been as college students. Thus, nearly 60 percent moved from one type to another during the ten years. As in college, these shifts typically entailed a change in the careerism or intellectualism scale, but not both at the same time. Thus an Unconnected participant could become an Intellectual or a Careerist, but not a

Striver. Only 7 percent of our participants did a complete about-face by a change in both scales (Intellectuals becoming Careerists, or Strivers becoming Unconnected, for example), and there were no shifts at all from Careerists to Intellectuals.

The types most likely to change are Careerists and the Unconnected— the most and least rigidly structured groups, respectively (see figure 10.1, as well as table 11 in appendix A). Careerists were especially likely to change to Strivers; more than half of them did so. Some were Careerists with latent intellectual interests that blossomed fully after college. Others became disillusioned with the narrowness of the Careerist orientation and made a deliberate effort to broaden their interests. Rarely, however, did this tendency lead them to abandon their strong dedication to career building in actual practice.

As for the Unconnected, most of them became more fully engaged in either intellectual or career pursuits as they matured: 37 percent became Careerists, 21 percent Intellectuals, and a few (two of twenty-eight) underwent the complete transformation from Unconnected to Striver. The major change probably involves the developmental-lag subgroup in college. Like

FIGURE 10.1
Typology Stability and Change over Ten Years

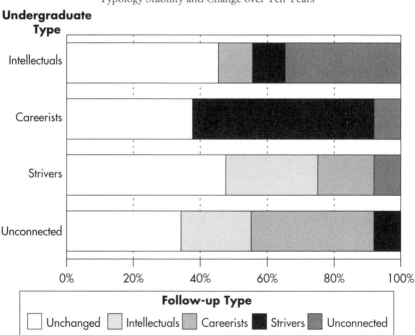

late developers in puberty, time simply took care of their lack of connectedness. Like most everybody else, they went to graduate school, became professionals, worked long hours, became active in associations, and so on. They actually were more likely than other types to win awards, publish, and occupy leadership positions in associations.

About one-third of the original Unconnected, however, remain so. These are the independent-minded social dissenters who are still following the beat of a different drummer. Just as during college they had reservations about the institutional culture and rejected many of its values, now they have similar reservations about mainstream society and its values, including those espoused by the educational elite. Others who persist in being Unconnected are the few with severe psychological problems who have not yet been able to overcome the consequences of their earlier Unconnectedness, though they may have made much progress.

Ironically, the depleted ranks of the Unconnected group are replenished by former Intellectuals, more than one-third of whom now exhibit the attitudes of Unconnectedness. Why should this be so? Intellectuals are a rather diffuse group. It is not uncommon for a student who lacks direction to gravitate to a humanistic field like English or history. (Hardly anyone majors in physics or electrical engineering out of uncertainty.) Hence, some of the original Intellectuals who switched must have been rather marginally Intellectual to begin with. For others, their intellectual ambitions have been frustrated by the necessity of earning a living in jobs not suited to their interests and inclinations. Finally, although about half the Strivers held their ground, the other half found that maintaining strong commitments to both intellectual and career pursuits was simply too demanding. Over one-quarter became Intellectuals and one-sixth became Careerists, along with a few who threw in the towel and turned Unconnected.

Not all these changes can be taken at face value, however. As we noted earlier, there is an amorphous center in our typological scheme consisting of participants who are not well differentiated; both their intellectualism and careerism scores are close to average values. Many participants who changed from one type to another were among these more amorphous members of the original types—for example, Intellectuals whose intellectualism scores were barely above the median in the cohort study but had fallen below the median by the time of the follow-up, rendering them Unconnected. Thus, the slightest breeze pushed them over in one or another direction. When we eliminate the participants whose scale scores were near the median values, we find greater typology stability—upwards of 50 percent of the same type in college and ten years after—and no about-face changes. In sum, given the normal amount of attitudinal change during these ten crucial years in personal development, the degree of stability in our typology is quite remarkable.

How do these changes match our expectations at the outset of the follow-up study? We thought Careerists would broaden their intellectual horizons. Their large-scale shift to striverhood suggests that they have done so, yet this shift is so far more by way of attitude and intention than actual practice. The change does, however, bode well for the future, which may bring out a greater engagement in areas other than career and family for this group of dedicated professionals. Our anticipation that Careerists would follow a more conventional pattern of settling down turns out to be true—for Careerist women, as well as Careerist men.

We expected Intellectuals to respond to the realities of having to make a living by becoming more career-oriented. They have done so to a certain extent, although only a few have turned into Careerists or Strivers. The larger shift of Intellectuals turning Unconnected is a complete surprise.

We thought Strivers would have to rein in their tendency to go in all directions, and they have indeed done so; almost half have become Intellectuals or Careerists. But as with Careerists, these shifts are more in attitude and perspective than in actual behavior. The low marriage rate among Strivers, especially the women, flatly contradicts our anticipation that given their gregarious nature, members of this group would be most likely to get married and would do so sooner than others.

Given the special, more varied character of the Unconnected, we felt least confident making predictions about them. Nonetheless, our expectation that the developmentally lagging subgroup would catch up has been fulfilled, as evidenced by their massive shift into the ranks of Careerists and, to a lesser extent, Intellectuals. We are not surprised that a substantial minority of the Unconnected have not changed and perhaps never will. With respect to their personal lives, the Unconnected, true to form, brought us up short: contrary to our expectations, they turned out to be the group most likely to connect.

WITHERING OF THE AMERICAN DREAM?

There is a parallel issue to the stability of the typology involving changes in the social environment, including the economy, that are likely to affect the choices that the educational elite make during and after college.

We have dealt in this book with the educational elite in a particular period in American history. Our sample was part of the "boomers' tail," the last cohorts of children born in the demographic bulge from the end of

World War II to the mid-1960s. They came of age in the economically expansive 1980s, when job opportunities were plentiful and the world seemed wide open to young professionals who were striving to establish themselves in the upper reaches of the social structure. What are the prospects of their successors just entering or leaving elite educational institutions today? Will they more or less replicate the experience of our participants, or will their lives be radically different?

Prevailing opinion takes a gloomy view of the economic future of today's young. "Low Pay and Closed Doors Greet Young in Job Market," declares a front-page article in the *New York Times*.[1] In a *Time*/CNN poll, 66 percent of Americans consider job security to be worse now compared to two years ago.[2] The job market is tighter even for professionals. Firms are recruiting less, consulting businesses that rely on bright young holders of M.B.A.s are dwindling, there is a surfeit of medical specialists, lawyers are a dime a dozen, and the academic job market fails to improve. According to a U.S. Labor Department study released in 1993, 30 percent of each crop of college graduates between now and the year 2005 "will march straight into the ranks of the jobless or the underemployed."[3] Bellboys with B.A.s.

Surely, none of this would affect the academic elite? Wrong. Even the "Harvard Man," the quintessential representative of this group, is said to have been humbled. Over the past decade at least 10 percent (possibly 20 percent) of the members of the Harvard Class of 1958 have lost their jobs. Men in their late fifties who felt securely entrenched in their business careers are out of work.[4] (Physicians and other professionals do not seem to be similarly affected.)

For the younger generation, the problem is seen as deeper than a temporary stagnation in the economy; the gloomy prospects are longer term. The boomers are said to have occupied all the high-level positions in society; they are an impediment to the prospects for advancement of the young; their self-centered lifestyle leaves no room for the next generation to find its place in the sun. They occupy the presidency, they will soon be a majority in Congress, they have filled up all the top law firms and medical clinics and corporate executive suites. The boomers may be better off than their parents were, but the next generation can never hope to reach that level because boomer consumption power has driven up prices out of sight, especially in housing. They are borrowing the country into a hole of debt from which it can never climb out. They are ruining the environment and leaving the mess for their children to clean up. They are failing to compete successfully in the global economy, leaving the way open for further de-industrialization. And they won't be retiring for another two or three decades, so they will always be in the way. The consequences for upcoming generations is thus the "withering of the American dream" (the subtitle of anthropologist Katherine Newman's *Declining Fortunes*).[5]

It is not for us to say how much truth there is to these assertions. As is often the case, the picture in the media tends to be overdrawn. For instance, in the same *New York Times* article that declares the humbling of the Harvard man, there is an insert which reports that "the norm is still success."[6] And more optimistic forecasts about job prospects for college graduates are beginning to appear.[7]

Nonetheless, that there are many people suffering out there is patently clear. That membership in the educational elite provides no immunity against financial hardship is equally clear. It does, however, stand to reason that the educational elite will continue to be less vulnerable to whatever reversals of fortune afflict others; and they will continue to have the lion's share of choice career opportunities no matter how many businesses downsize or professions get restructured. The fate of the educational elite is obviously tied to that of the nation as a whole, yet relative to others they are always likely to be better off. For example, in June of 1993, 91 percent of Stanford business school graduates had job offers with median starting salaries of $65,000 for M.B.A.s. "It was a tough job market," says the director of the Career Management Center. "They may not be hiring as many as in past years, but they still want the best candidates they can find. We didn't have a fall-off among the major employers who recruit here."[8]

While we have not conducted a formal study of the current undergraduates at Stanford, career counselors who work with them have a good sense of the current attitudes and expectations of these students. These counselors report that students are now keenly aware of the new realities in the marketplace, as are their parents, and they are quite concerned. As a consequence, more are heading for professional and graduate schools right after graduation. Those who are unwilling to take the plunge into further study are seeking temporary jobs or going into public service opportunities (applications to the Peace Corps and VISTA have risen sharply). Hardest hit are those who had planned on going directly into management training programs right after college, since these opportunities have been cut back sharply.

These considerations will no doubt influence the academic and career choices that undergraduates make. Hence, the experiences of the class of 1991 may well be different in some ways from those of the class of 1981, but we do not think that these differences will be of more than modest significance. As to the impact of current economic trends on the career futures of our participants over the next decade, we shall turn to that issue at the end of this chapter.

WAS IT WORTH IT?

Is the enormous investment of these years during and after college justified by what these men and women accomplish in their careers and personal lives? The short answer is a resounding yes. Nonetheless, do they have regrets about their choices? Do they question the wisdom of their decisions? Would they do things differently if given the chance?

ASSESSMENT OF THE UNDERGRADUATE EXPERIENCE

We asked our participants to assess their undergraduate education at Stanford, using the same set of evaluative items we used in their senior survey questionnaire. For the most part, their responses are very positive. They rate the overall quality of Stanford undergraduate education at 4.4 (on a 5-point scale where 1 = poor and 5 = excellent). They also give very high marks to the faculty as scholars and to their courses in their majors.

The overseas study program gets the single highest rating of all (4.8). As one of them said: "Studying at an overseas campus probably had the most direct impact on my life because it influenced my choice of a major, graduate school, and career (international journalism). On a less tangible level, study overseas gave me a greater appreciation of foreign cultures, as well as a different, more critical perspective on the United States."

They are somewhat less satisfied, but still quite positive, about the quality of teaching, graduate school preparation, and the liberal education program (average ratings of "very good"). The only problem areas identified (rated between "average" and "poor") are faculty accessibility and faculty advising, especially general advising (before students declare their majors). Women are more positive about faculty teaching and accessibility than men, but this finding may simply reflect the fact that a greater proportion of women majored in the humanities where classes are smaller, and hence faculty is in closer touch with students. Intellectuals also rate these items significantly higher, for probably the same reasons. After all, they interacted more with the faculty and were more influenced by them than any other group was.

To assess the long-term impact of their liberal education outside of their majors, we asked them to assess their current abilities and knowledge in a range of substantive areas that correspond to those covered by courses required for their general education (distribution) requirements (three courses each in the humanities, natural sciences, and social sciences, and a yearlong course in Western culture).[9] Their strongest self-rated ability is writing clear English (at just above the "very good" level). Almost all other items get mean ratings between "average" and "good." Two items fall below the "average" level of competence: using a foreign language and understanding non-Western cultures.

Women give themselves higher ratings for traditionally "female" areas of academic endeavor: foreign languages, literature and fine arts, understanding gender issues. Men are equally traditional in their strengths—the natural sciences, technology, and understanding international problems. Given the relatively small differences between women and men in their subsequent graduate training and current professions, the persistence of these gender differences is surprising.

Significant typology differences pertain mainly to the Intellectuals, who, as expected, rate themselves higher than other types in literature, arts, and foreign languages and lower in natural science and technical areas. Other types do not reveal any systematic patterns. As for the major occupational groups, lawyers rate themselves highest in more areas (nine of fourteen) than any other professional group, including most areas related to writing, the humanities, and the social sciences. Unlike medicine and business, the study of law does not have narrowly defined prerequisites for admission, thus allowing prelaw students to get a broader education. Moreover, the study and practice of law exposes them to a wider range of areas that they must be informed about. Hence, lawyers see themselves as most broadly informed.

Despite the passage of time, neither their evaluations of Stanford nor their self-assessments of abilities had changed much by the end of the decade. What they liked as graduating seniors they still rate highly, and what they did not like then, they like no more now. Ability assessments did decline somewhat—they may be a bit more realistic about their own capacities now, and they may have higher standards—but the patterns have persisted, particularly with respect to gender and typology differences.

SECOND-GUESSING

No one gets to live life over again, but second-guessing past decisions is an enduring human proclivity. We asked our participants to second-guess their choices: if they had to do it again, what would they do differently?

Almost all (92 percent) would attend Stanford again. Such institutional loyalty is quite characteristic of the educational elite; institutions count on it in raising the immense sums of money from their alumni that they need to survive.[10] Only 5 percent say they would prefer another school, and 3 percent are unsure. Many (70 percent) have a strong or very strong sense of identification with Stanford by feeling part of it and connected to it; only 6 percent feel a "weak" link. Although three of five attended graduate school somewhere other than Stanford, their loyalty to Stanford dominates: Only 10 percent felt strongly identified with any other institution. Gender makes no difference here, but type does: Careerists identify with Stanford most, the Unconnected least.

In the Stanford/Harvard survey, 91 percent of alumni wanted their children to attend the schools they went to.[11] Our participants are no different. Those with a Stanford "legacy," especially one reaching back more than a single generation, often found special meaning in their undergraduate experience. It was a source of great pride for one man to follow in his father's and grandfather's footsteps, but a special burden for another, who felt trapped and resentful for being locked into his family tradition.

Several of our participants were already eager to see their children at Stanford one day, even though some of the children were hardly out of diapers. One woman said, "I wish I could promise my three-week-old son that he could go to Stanford." This is much more than the simple desire to ensure that one's children get a good education. It is an expression of the desire for continuity within the elite, as if to say, "My daughter/son will pick up right where I left off." The intensity of such feelings is demonstrated each spring in the torrent of abuse heaped on the dean of admissions by some of the alumni whose sons and daughters do not make it into Stanford.

When asked explicitly whether Stanford was worth the time and money, over 90 percent of our participants said it was (63 percent "definitely," 28 percent "probably"). Only 1 percent felt that going to Stanford was definitely not worth it. There were no gender or type differences here, except for the Unconnected being less certain than any other type that Stanford was worth it.

Sixty-five percent said they would choose the same major (thus, one-third would not). Ironically, the Unconnected are most satisfied with their choice of major, the Careerists the least. But the tables are turned with respect to career choices, about which the Unconnected have the most regrets: only 55 percent would pick the same career, compared with at least 75 percent of each other type. If following the beat of a different drummer seems to have left them behind in career development, it should be noted that it is mainly those truly Unconnected who could be so characterized.

Physicians are most apt to say they would choose the same career (91 percent), a response partly attributable to their having had the least experience in practicing their profession. Also, having invested so much in their education and training, to think otherwise would perhaps be more painful. Regrets in other professions are uniformly moderate, about one-quarter saying they wish they had chosen a different career.

We also inquired about how they would use their time if given a second chance at college. By and large, they were satisfied with what they had done. If they felt a change was in order, however, almost always they said they would put in more time and effort on various activities, not less. Sizable proportions wish they had spent more time on their majors, on service activities, on social life, on academic work outside the classroom—on almost everything. In addition, more than half our participants express the wish to have taken more courses outside their majors and liberal arts courses. This ringing endorsement of liberal learning (with the benefit of hindsight) is particularly striking for Careerists and Strivers, most of whom (72 percent and 62 percent, respectively) wish they had given more time to liberal arts courses.

The demanding preprofessional training of two professions is most likely to crowd out liberal education: medicine and engineering. Many physicians strongly regret having been forced to slog their way through tough premedical science courses that were not of much intrinsic interest and of unclear value to their medical studies. Others are appreciative of the contributions of their liberal learning. One of them said:

> As a physician, what I have found most memorable and applicable from my undergraduate education are not the organic chemistry or math courses but the overseas studies, history, social science, and humanities classes. I know this isn't a surprise to me now, but I do remember as a freshman griping about the distribution requirements. However, by the time I was a junior, I appreciated those requirements, and ten years later even more so. Maybe that sums up what the impact is all about—an appreciation of the humanities and history which I have found most practical in approaching, understanding, and enjoying life.

Engineers were likely to echo these thoughts, as exemplified in the following comments:

> I chose Stanford mostly because of its engineering program. I think that I got a good engineering education, and that as a result of Stanford's training and reputation, I was able to obtain a good job at an excellent corporation. I believe that the training that I received has

helped me a lot in my career. However, I find that I am in a very specialized area and that very little of my training is directly applicable to my job. In that sense, I wish I had spent more time studying in areas outside my major.

I do feel that I would have benefited more by taking a wider range of courses, and I don't think I would have been hurt by taking fewer engineering courses.

IMPACT OF THE STANFORD EXPERIENCE

What, in the final analysis, is the overall impact of the college experience on the lives of the educational elite? What is the "value added" to a student by a highly selective institution? What is its lasting effect over the ensuing years? We sought our participants' perspective on these issues through an open-ended question: "What impact has your Stanford education had on your life?" Their responses were virtually unanimous in attesting to Stanford's major impact. They used words or phrases like "tremendous," "immense," "the most important experience of my life," and "probably changed the direction of my life." Even when the experience had been negative, there was no question that it had been compelling. For instance:

> Clearly, my decision to attend Stanford was the most significant decision of my life. All other events followed from that decision. First, my career choice: medicine. I probably would have arrived at this choice independent of a Stanford experience. However, the path through medical education (M.D./Ph.D. programs) and a career in research all are likely a consequence of my Stanford education. Second, my partner: now wife. We met at Stanford, became friends, and now share our lives. Third, my friends: my closest friends are those I have from Stanford.

Only a few participants felt uncertain about the importance of the undergraduate experience, and when they did, they usually blamed themselves. "Due to my immaturity at the time, I did not take the necessary steps to avail myself of what Stanford had to offer. In hindsight, therefore, it has had much less of an impact than I wish it could have," said one woman. Another questioned the specific significance of any experience as such: "To be honest, I'm not sure *what* influences my life. I have a feeling my career would be the same regardless of Stanford, but, at the same time, I value greatly my experience at Stanford."

The question of "value added" is a difficult one, since it could be argued that students who go to elite institutions would do well in any case. As one of them put it aptly, "Since I have had only one life, I have nothing to compare myself to. I am my own control." More commonly, they acknowledged the combination of what they brought to Stanford and the contributions of the institutional environment that nurtured their talents, an environment in which they continued to grow and learn, especially from each other:

> My Stanford education helped to keep my standards high for many things: written work, logical thought, moral responsibility, and thoroughness in every task. But for the most part, I had those standards before I came to Stanford. Stanford did not produce them in me but rather provided a rich environment in which they could develop and mature. Everyone I met at Stanford was special before they got there. I have thought many times that Stanford students are special because they arrived there, not because they left there. Stanford does not create exceptional people, it attracts them. In that sense, Stanford is doing something right. To a Stanford student trying to learn, the greatest assets available are fellow students.

> There was something special about nearly every student I knew at Stanford. They had taken ten years of dance, or they were state champion in their sport, or they were a concert violinist. And they were very smart. They were from different backgrounds, different places. They had different interests. Exposure to these people had as much impact on my life as anything I learned in the classroom. The most lasting impression I have of Stanford is that people of a thousand different backgrounds, with a thousand different interests, can excel in a thousand different ways.

> The years I spent at Stanford were the years I experienced the most rapid spiritual, emotional, political, and intellectual growth. I think this would have been true regardless of which college I attended, but I think the Stanford environment, especially the other students and teachers, facilitated and stimulated this growth.

Beyond these general comments, there was a great deal more said about the specific impact of the educational elite experience. We have grouped these comments under five categories: the development of the intellect, careers, personal relations, the sense of self, and institutional critique.

IMPACT ON THE INTELLECT

One of the phrases that recurs frequently is "Stanford taught me how to think critically." Others referred to their enhanced abilities to think "analytically," "creatively," or "independently"; to "become a better problem solver"; to "learn to ask why" and be "introspective." The following statements elaborate on these themes:

My college education encouraged me to think critically and to question the common wisdom in analyzing issues and events. These facilities have served me well in my career and in life. They are, I feel, more important than any specifics I learned in my courses.

I think one of the most important skills I came away with was critical thinking: being able to take the endless stream of information that keeps coming at me in day-to-day life and analyze it in a rational way, throwing out the superfluous and getting to the pertinent points. I think this is essential not only in research, medicine, or business, but in order to maintain a healthy, balanced existence in this busy world!

Most importantly, my Stanford education taught me to truly appreciate learning and to never lose the thirst to discover more. It is my "academic" development at Stanford that I value most and that keeps me forever curious about what more there is to learn.

IMPACT ON CAREER

For some students, usually in engineering, Stanford provided the actual professional training that launched their careers. One engineer said: "Stanford gave me the opportunity to learn my trade. I pursued it because I thought it was 'neat,' not because of later career chances. Now I feel lucky that what I thought was 'neat' lets me not worry about money. I'm lucky because I have a highly salable skill. I'm financially comfortable. I can make time to become emotionally comfortable."

Much more typically, undergraduate education does not impart specialized knowledge or readily marketable skills. Instead, it provides the background or preparation for graduate study and professional education where such expertise is acquired. This is the critical phase for moving from the educational to the professional elite. In referring to this progression, the operative phrase our participants used over and over was "My Stanford education opened doors for me" (with variations: "without me hardly knocking on the door," or, "beyond my fondest dreams").

> Professionally, my diploma from Stanford has meant more than I ever thought it would. My New York University law degree may get me an interview, but my Stanford degree gets me the job. Even here on the East Coast, among the Ivies, my Stanford degree jumps off my résumé, providing entrée to job interviews and employment opportunities. The external value of a Stanford degree in employers' eyes is something which I never really considered or expected, but which is very tangible.

> A Stanford engineering degree is like a medal in a way—you can always wear it, it's always yours, you'll always be respected for it, you'll always be proud of the effort required to earn it.

> My Stanford education has catapulted me into the league of achievers. While I may not have been changed fundamentally by my years at Stanford, people's image of me has been altered. The Stanford name has opened doors and raised expectations. It got me a job in the White House and five breathless years in the front row of the government show. It gave me the confidence to compete for a job in the Foreign Service. And now it allows me to modestly lower my head and confess the name of my alma mater at cocktail parties. No excuses necessary.

Our participants explained why a Stanford degree opens doors typically by referring to expectations of excellence—a reference not so much to the content of their education as to the general assumption of greater competence. As one man put it, "The Stanford name seems to tell people that I am intelligent, I am capable, I can think! There is no need for me to prove it." Another noted, "When people see that name on the résumé, they tend to put a job applicant on a different tier; they assume a higher level of competence." Others referred to "instant credibility," "stamp of legitimate intelligence," "the Good Housekeeping seal of approval," "the aura of being special," "having come from the breeding ground of leadership." These phrases were used with pride as well as a measure of reservation and embarrassment. ("It's not fully deserved. . . . I am not sure I was that much better than the others.") The aura of high quality sometimes spilled over into other interactions as well. One woman said, "Socially, the same thing happens: People assume a higher socioeconomic background (although not always true). Our current landlord chose us over several applicants because we went to Stanford—we were somehow better tenants. Why? It beats me, but it often seems to work."

The association with "Big S" can also be something of a burden because it imposes certain expectations—not only to be successful but to be successful in specific ways and all the time. This reaction on the part of some of our participants is as much a function of how they feel as of how they are made to feel by others.

I often feel pressured to perform exceptionally at any endeavor to uphold the "Stanford" image. I don't want people to think Stanford erred in judgment by admitting me.

For the past nine years, I have taught math at a public school. My high school students are often curious to learn of where I attended college, and every year they are amazed to hear that I went to Stanford. Almost always their next comment is, "What are you doing here?" Their consensus opinion is that such graduates should be doctors, lawyers, engineers, or successful businessmen—certainly not public high school math teachers! (I didn't even major in math!)

IMPACT ON SOCIAL AND PERSONAL RELATIONSHIPS

The Stanford experience has two general effects on social and personal relationships. The first is to broaden social horizons. Participants made repeated references to the positive effect of "exposure to people from different backgrounds," a "sense of becoming part of a larger society," and "appreciating diversity." These occur more through the experience of living together in the residential system than through learning in the classroom:

It taught me to learn from people with vastly different perspectives, backgrounds, and values from my own.

Having grown up in small, relatively isolated communities, the exposure I got at Stanford to the diversity of thought, culture, and ethnicity was significant in shaping my perspective on the world.

There was a tremendous amount of learning about people, politics, society, and human nature in general—education really, though not in the "book" sense—that I acquired through my residential experience at Stanford (living in for three years, and managing, for one year, a co-op). I think students who miss this experience miss a major educational opportunity.

Such exposure is said to lead to "greater tolerance" and "being broad-minded." One man said, "I'm a much more tolerant person than average, and I think this is partly due to the diversity of people I crossed paths with during my years at Stanford." Others refer to "developing political beliefs" and "learning to be socially concerned." "Stanford opened my eyes to the world," said one woman. "It taught me to care about others."

Although, like all institutions, Stanford may have its share of prejudice and intolerance, what these men and women recall of its social climate is mainly positive. As a black woman physician remarked: "I have never again found an environment where, although not perfect, there was more awareness of fairness, equality, and tolerance. It is a terrible thing to leave Stanford and enter the 'real world' of blatant sexism, on-the-job discrimination; to see people resigned to intolerance and desperate actions to protect their jobs, and general apathy towards social issues."

The second social effect of the Stanford experience was on the personal relationships that developed during college. As we noted earlier, about one in ten of our participants met their spouses while at Stanford—which stands out as one of the most important consequences of their college experience. ("In sum, it's fair to say that my Stanford education has had a major impact on my life. If nothing else, I met my husband there!") But more broadly, they focused on the friends they made at Stanford. One woman spoke for many when she wrote:

My first response is a personal one—the strongest impact on my life has been through the people I met at Stanford. Although we're spread across the country, my strongest, most long-lasting friendships are with women from my freshman dorm. We went through a lot together at Stanford, and we continue to face the same challenges and opportunities—marriage, parenthood, and the difficulties of combining children and careers.

IMPACT ON SENSE OF SELF

The many facets of a young adult's life affected by the Stanford experience coalesce in shaping his or her sense of self. This transformation of the self reflects the changes students undergo; hence it counterbalances the earlier questions about "value added," which highlight what students bring to college as against what they get out of it. Our participants recognize that during their college years they passed through a crucial developmental phase. ("Stanford is the place where I 'grew up'"; "It was a bridge between my adolescence and adulthood.") They referred to their evolving sense of "independence" and a process of "self-definition" that continued throughout their twenties.

This developmental phase is inherent in the life cycle. It is much more intensely experienced, however, in residential educational settings. Living in close proximity for four years with other gifted and accomplished young men and women stimulates and encourages these students to explore, achieve, and consolidate their identity, including their feeling of being "special." The experience may also subject them to enormous pressure, requiring adjustment and accommodation. Usually, but not always, that process results in enhancement of their self-esteem.

One major component of this transformation of the self is recalibration. Coming from a wide variety of high schools where they were stars in their respective firmaments, they suddenly find themselves eclipsed by the even brighter stars they encounter among their college classmates. ("After twelve years of being excellent, I found I was only average after all.") This new reality is bound to generate considerable self-doubt, especially at first blush. What they often do not realize is that they themselves can be as intimidating to their classmates as they are to them. One participant stated it well by modifying a worn-out metaphor: "Stanford took me from being a big fish in a small pond in Washington State, to a *very small* fish in the most creative, challenging, exciting learning ocean *anywhere!*" Another said: "I (along with 90 percent of entrants) thought my getting accepted at Stanford was a fluke. (People outside don't think so.) I didn't think that of any *other* students I met at Stanford—they all had various outstanding traits that got them there." Once they have recalibrated themselves on this new and more demanding life scale, most are motivated to surge forward:

My Stanford education transformed me from a small-town, rather narrow-minded youngster into a (hopefully) well-rounded adult capable of coping with and understanding the larger and more complex world outside of my environs.

Some of the achievements and notions of excellence of the other Stanford students rubbed off on me. My goals and ambitions in life are probably higher due to that Stanford influence. Instead of simply admiring or envying success, I have a more "I can do that as well" attitude.

Stanford let me in on the secret that the "elite" is just the people with the courage to go after something. In the end, all the money my father (a cash-poor farmer with a solid net worth precluding financial aid) spent on my education bought me a big name and a boost of self-confidence.

The atmosphere created by the professors, the caliber of the other students, and the possibilities of youth, gave one an unlimited sense of potential and future achievement. Stanford gave its graduates a feeling of efficacy, that you could do almost anything, that you could "change the world."

My Stanford education gives me confidence. This is symbolized by my (admittedly ridiculous) habit of wearing my Stanford class ring to take law school exams, pass bar exams, and so on.

Not everyone shares this experience of self-affirmation and boundless expansion. Ambivalence continues to cloud the memory of the Stanford experience for a number of our participants (perhaps as high as 5 percent). Elite education can be a mixed blessing, and occasionally a downright curse, when it leads to a serious and lasting loss of self-esteem.

Ten years ago being "a Stanford student" was nearly everything in terms of my self-image, how I defined myself, how others saw me. Right now, in terms of my self-esteem, the simple fact of my Stanford education has two lingering, conflicting effects: first, when I feel worthless and underachieving, I can still get a bit of a lift by reminding myself that not everyone can earn a degree and Phi Beta Kappa from Stanford. On the other hand, when I read about all the achievements of my classmates, I feel more worthless and underachieving than ever. I suppose this will continue either until what I did when I was twenty ceases to be meaningful or until I pull off some achievements of my own.

My experience at Stanford may have exacerbated my self-image problems. I had a difficult time with my classes and relating to some of my classmates. For the first time in my life, I thought that I must not be as intelligent as my classmates. I was surrounded by people who were much more talented than I was, in academics, sports, arts, music, sophistication, knowledge of the w. rld, etc. I remember feeling at times like I did not fit in and that somehow I was less of a person because I was, at least in my mind, not as smart or talented as other people.

A few participants suffered serious damage. Jimmy is the son and grandson of Stanford alumni. His father is a highly successful attorney, and both of his parents had high expectations that Jimmy would prepare for a prestigious career and excel at it like his father and grandfather. Despite his obvious intelligence, however, Jimmy had neither the interest nor the drive to pursue any of the standard roads to career success. He felt out of place, trapped, and resentful. He had hoped his college experience would broaden his intellectual horizons, help him build up his self-esteem, and see him through the process of "individuation" to adulthood. Instead, he says, "My Stanford experience represented the most crushing disappointment of my life, reinforced an already low self-image, and in many ways seems to have set the tone of my professional and adult lives."

INSTITUTIONAL CRITIQUE

The personal sense of dissatisfaction for some participants arises from and spills over into a broader critique of institutional values and practices. These criticisms are usually aimed at the way careerist and materialistic values overwhelm the educational aims and purposes of higher education. We had heard some of these complaints during the cohort study, with the more trenchant ones coming from the Unconnected. As one of them put it at that time: "There is a lot more to life than studying. . . . My goal is learning how to think critically. . . . I've been more and more frustrated by the whole approach to education. . . . Though we're reading all these great books . . . I expected to discuss them, grapple with issues. But that hasn't happened. They praise Socrates' methods but use the methods of the Sophists that he denounced. I've heeded the advice not to let school get in the way of education."

These views reverberate a decade later:

I have always been very goal-oriented. Stanford fostered this, but it was not necessarily great for exploring intellectual curiosity in great depth.

Stanford made me a more capitalist-minded person.

My Stanford experience didn't include the encouragement of development of personal morals and ideals. Issues concerning honesty, integrity, and responsibilities as a friend/lover/family member seemed of secondary importance as compared to career-track thinking.

And then we have Ian's damning indictment of the very core of Stanford's educational and social values. After graduation, Ian attended a nontraditional institution for a year, then worked as a managing partner in a restaurant. Eight years after college, he became an elementary school teacher. He earns $21,000 a year and lists "God" as being responsible for his family's financial well-being. His most important objective is "being a role model for others." His goal for his children is to provide them with "complete freedom to follow their destiny." Ten years from now he expects to be "awakening young people and strengthening their will and resolve to be moral, productive members of society." His expected income at the peak of his career: $25,000. His job title: "world citizen." As to what Stanford did for him and to him, this is what he has to say:

Stanford gave me a glimpse of the paths in life that were not for me. This gave me the opportunity to exercise my freedom to deny false paths. It offered a view of the Western-scientific-materialist philosophy that was both breathtaking and essentially morally bankrupt. The impact was that I "dropped out". . . for a number of years to pursue art and the good life in service to others. This time was required to digest my experience at Stanford. I can now say that Stanford—the flagship for Western materialism and the attendant workshop of the technical solution—operates with an inner untruthfulness that acts as poison to the sensitive soul. This untruthfulness pervades every department. One could call it denial of spiritual fact. One could say the emperor has no clothes. One could say that the promotion of conscience-free science is unconscionable.

Now I can look back and see that the impact of Stanford University on my life is that it offered the full picture, the entire scope of the problems facing mankind. That picture, combined with my current worldview—all new and improved—gives me a stronger resolve to bring wisdom to the land of knowledge and give hope to the poor in spirit. Not to mention giving the cynical an opening to cure themselves with wonder and respect.

What are we to make of these critical comments about Stanford? Are they the idiosyncratic views of a few individuals or do they give expression to a wider and deeper problem? What is the faculty's place in all this?

Most of our participants are immensely appreciative of the benefits they derived from their undergraduate experience. Yet that sense of gratitude seems directed mostly at an entity called "Stanford" rather than at sharply etched images of the men and women who taught them, advised them, and managed their academic and institutional lives. Nor do they convey a clear sense of the institutional goals and purposes that presumably helped shape their lives in college.

In concluding our previous book, we referred to our students as the "silent partners" in the educational enterprise who did not have much of a voice in determining the nature and quality of their undergraduate experience. Ten years later, have the faculty become the silent partners?

If so, there are two possible explanations. The first is methodological. The focus of our study was the graduates, not the faculty or the institution as such. When we asked our participants about their evaluation of the faculty, their responses were quite positive except with regard to faculty accessibility and advising functions, as we noted earlier in this chapter. However, we did not specifically inquire as to how many or which faculty members had left a lasting impression on them. There is no doubt that, had we put these questions to them directly, many would have come up with specific answers.

On the other hand, we did not expressly inquire about their peers either. That did not prevent them from telling us a good deal about their friends' continuing importance throughout the decade. This suggests that the impact of the faculty is not so compelling that it gushes forth with the slightest turn of the spigot. If this silence about the faculty is not a methodological artifact—if faculty encounters with students have not left much of a trace—then we do wonder about the nature, strength, and durability of the bonds that college students form with their academic elders.

A similar set of concerns relates to institutional objectives. Our participants enumerate many specific benefits of their college education but do not convey a broader perspective on what their education was all about. The Stanford catalogue has a brief statement on liberal education but does not offer a description of the broader goals of undergraduate education.[12] This problem (if it is a problem) of a lack of clearly stated institutional goals is not specific to Stanford. Ernest Boyer, in his comprehensive survey of the undergraduate experience in America, encountered it at every turn:

> A prestigious eastern college we visited, with about two thousand students and more than a century of tradition behind it, has no statement of objectives. The registrar told us: "We've had a half-a-dozen committees at different points in the past looking at what our goals are, were and should be. Then, sometimes, they get as far as making a statement, which doesn't provide for any action, and of course is lost or forgotten by the time someone else decides in a year or two that we really need a committee to set goals.[13]

The fact that Stanford does not articulate its institutional objectives in specific terms does not mean that it is aimless. Other important functions in the university are also not spelled out in black and white. For example, faculty have no written contracts specifying their roles and responsibilities. Nonetheless, they generally have a clear enough idea about what is expected of them. With respect to undergraduate education, two broad areas where they perform a central role are taken for granted—career preparation and liberal education.

Recapitulating what we have learned from the experience of our participants, it is clear that the faculty, or Stanford as an entity, does an outstanding job of leading students to their careers, and we assume the same would be true for other elite institutions. Whether they do this simply by attracting outstanding students or by the quality of what they teach, or by opening doors through their reputations, they provide the surest prospects for joining the professional elite and pursuing rewarding careers on many counts. Admittedly, the elite institutions are not the only ones to do so, nor do they perform this service for all of their graduates. Yet on balance, their success in this respect is so clear that to say more than we already have would be gilding the lily.

The results are more mixed in the matter of liberal education. Here we encounter more diversity of outcome than with regard to career success, both at Stanford and among select institutions in general. The smaller liberal arts colleges appear to do a better job in liberal education than the large research universities (which have their own advantages); institutions with more structured programs convey a clearer sense of intellectual purpose than those that provide greater choice (which have their own virtues).

What concerns us about our segment of the educational elite is the tremendous disparity in the breadth and depth of their liberal education, as assessed both at the time of graduation and a decade later. Too much seems to ride on individual interests and career proclivities, too little on institutional efforts to provide a better educational balance (such as by teaching more humanities to scientists and engineers and more science to humanists). Moreover, it is not clear whether the purpose of liberal learning is to provide a general education (teaching "something about everything") or to provide intellectual, esthetic, social, and philosophical perspectives (ways of thinking, feeling, and behaving) that will pervade all aspects of an individual's life and are not just 'n add-on to more basic concerns like career and family.

The faculty clearly have a stake in the career preparation and liberal education of undergraduates. But do their responsibilities end there? In the previous chapter we raised the prospect of greater commitment of students to public service and a more sustained focus on their moral development. How willing and able are the faculty to participate in such efforts? Do they have a clear collective view about these matters to transmit to their students?

In 1866, in his inaugural address as the founding president of the Syrian Protestant College (now the American University of Beirut), Daniel Bliss said:

> This college is for all conditions and classes of men without regard to colour, nationality, race or religion. A man white, black, or yellow; Christian, Jew, Mohammedan, or heathen, may enter and enjoy all the advantages of this institution for three, four or eight years; and go out believing in one God, in many gods, or in no God. But it will be impossible for any one to continue with us long without knowing what we believe to be the truth and our reasons for that belief.[14]

Daniel Bliss and his handful of faculty colleagues were Christian missionaries in the Ottoman empire who were driven by a clear vision of what they believed in. In the context of his time, Bliss and his colleagues were actually no different from other American college presidents and faculty who also tried to convey to their students their deeply held convictions.

Times have changed. No one would now expect the one thousand strong Stanford faculty to speak with one voice. But does that mean that they have no responsibility to provide guidance to their students about the proper use or potential abuse of what they learn? To help them integrate learning into their lives? To provide moral energy for social commitment and genuine leadership?

We expect the faculty would readily recognize the value of these objectives but would be exceedingly cautious about their own role in helping students achieve them. There are several reasons for this.

Most important is the dominant conviction that the role of the faculty, above all, is to do research and teach. In these contexts, they have no problem with articulating basic values—such as intellectual integrity, loyalty to the data, and freedom of thought and expression for all concerned—that are necessary for the generation and transmission of knowledge.

Serious difficulties arise when we expect the faculty or the administration to take a collective or institutional stand on specific social and moral issues, or encourage, induce, or compel students to do so. Their unwillingness to take a stand, no matter how crucial the issue, disappoints and dismays some students and faculty who feel passionately about one or another issue. Inaction makes an institution look indifferent and callous, if not in league with the offending entity. When sufficient pressure builds up over a volatile issue, even a minor provocation will result in a student eruption which then takes on a life of its own.

Yet, the majority of the faculty is unwilling to go along with this more activist perspective. At the practical level, there is now such a wide diversity in constituency interests, attitudes, and values that the selection of what to espouse would be largely arbitrary. The experiences of the 1960s are also fresh enough in the minds of the older members of the faculty that they may be forgiven for choosing peace and reason over "social relevance." And although the heady days of the 1960s are over, the 1990s have their own issues that could be just as divisive and disruptive. Therefore, if members of the faculty were to take public positions on social issues collectively (beyond speaking out as individuals, which they already do) or plunge themselves into the political maelstrom, many feel that is likely to hopelessly distract from their primary academic mission as currently defined.

Yet, none of this exonerates the faculty from encouraging and guiding students in the exploration of social and ethical issues (as we discussed in chapter 9). They can best achieve this through doing what they know how to do best: Eliciting the facts, assessing the logic and cogency of arguments, engaging in open and untrammeled debate are the standard ways in which institutions of higher learning ordinarily carry on their business.

In an address on ethnic and cultural diversity, Stanford's president, Gerhard Casper, speaks to this issue:

> While universities do not have a particular ideological mission, universities are dedicated to the search to know. The university is an institution

dedicated to the search to know, the search to know of each member in her or his individual capacity. Students are admitted to Stanford or any other university as individuals, not in groups. No university can thrive unless each member is accepted as an individual and can speak and will be listened to without regard to labels and stereotypes. While the university has no right to tell students who they should become, with what groups to associate or not to associate, university citizenship entails the obligation to accept every individual member of the community as a contributor to the search to know.

. . . If what I just said suggests to you that I see the university as by and large neutral territory where cultures clash, interact, adapt and change while the institution itself is committed to 'ultural relativism, with no ideas and values of its own, you would be quite wrong. A university has a culture, an identity of its own. Its identity is tied to its work. Its work, as I said, consists of the search to know. The search to know is carried out by critical analysis, according to standards of evidence that themselves are subject to examination and reexamination. They cannot be set by a political diktat. Thomas Jefferson spoke of freedom as "the first born daughter of science." . . . [F]reedom (not just academic freedom), nondiscrimination (you will be heard regardless of your sex, race, ethnicity, religion), and equality of opportunity. It is not a mere coincidence that these are also the values, if at times distorted or forgotten, of our country.[15]

TEN YEARS FROM NOW

The first decade after graduation has been a momentous one. Our participants have completed their education, started careers, and settled down. They have bought homes and fashioned comfortable lifestyles. Most have married; many are parents. Thus, they are now established as successful young adults. Where will they be in ten years?

Less than half (41 percent) anticipate staying on their current career tracks; an almost equal proportion (38 percent) see major career change coming. The remainder are uncertain; in all likelihood, most of them will also make at least moderate changes in their career direction. Thus, the considerable degree of nonlinearity we discovered in their career development to this point is apt to continue in an economic world in which linearity is becoming more the exception than the rule.

The major change they anticipate in their working lives lies not in actually changing careers but in striking out on their own. Exactly half expect to own their own businesses or be partners in professional organizations within ten years, almost a tripling of the current rate. Many of those now in technical or line positions expect to move into managerial jobs. Just over one-fifth see themselves working in the public sector, more than double the current rate.

On the other hand, most of them see their current occupations as clearly related to their long-term careers. If they are lawyers, they may end up as politicians or judges, but they will not leave the legal world. If they are in business, they will stay there, and if they are physicians, they are even more certain to stay in medicine. (As one family practitioner said, "I want to deliver babies and then the babies of those babies.") Those who do see new careers on the horizon are for the most part those who have not yet established themselves firmly in any career.

Women are not more likely than men to anticipate major career changes in the next decade, but a considerably higher proportion of women (30 percent versus 13 percent) express uncertainty about the future. This finding is in line with their relatively lower level of career commitment and greater dissatisfaction with their incomes, both of which are rooted mainly in their concerns about how they can reconcile careers with child rearing. And some of the career changes anticipated by women include startling shifts. One woman with a Ph.D. from MIT thinks she may start a business in needlepoint designs (an interest going back to her high-school days).

As for type, we find what we would expect: Careerists are the least likely to expect major career change (36 percent), Intellectuals are the most likely (76 percent). Intellectuals appear to be increasingly aware that the relatively little attention they have paid to career matters is making them fall behind their peers. Careerists, on the other hand, simply plan on continuing the linearity that has marked their lives ever since high school and, at least in material terms, has served them well so far.

If we turn to their futures using the career development models we discussed earlier (chapter 4), many of those on linear fast tracks will continue toward positions of greater prominence. Some of those in business will become CEOs; many of the lawyers will become partners. But as the gradient of their career trajectory gets steeper, others will fall behind. They will find that there are limits to their abilities, drive, and energy. Some other man will get that crucial promotion; some other woman will land the judgeship; some other doctor will develop the new surgical technique that leads to national acclaim. Although they have so far progressed rapidly into the occupational elite, their climb will not always lead ever upward. Those in fields like medicine and teaching are likely to stay on a steady course; their increasing experience and competence will not lead to externally discernible shifts in their career patterns. By contrast, significant numbers of the more restive engineers, lawyers, and businesspeople will go into "spiral" shifts, seeking self-fulfillment in new careers. And a few who have yet to settle down in definite occupations will continue to seek career objectives, which may always remain beyond their reach.

Turning to their personal lives, over half anticipate significant change in the next ten years: the singles expect to get married or find a partner (85 percent); the childless anticipate having children (80 percent). Neither sex nor type makes any difference in this regard. But in a more general sense, gender does matter greatly: women are more likely than men (69 to 42 percent) to anticipate some form of major personal change in the next decade. The difference is once again due to childbearing and child care: 76 percent of women but only 22 percent of men plan to take parental leave from work. The two-thirds of women who do not yet have children are fully aware that motherhood will change their lives profoundly. Parenthood will also have an impact on men's lives, which nevertheless are not likely to change as dramatically as women's lives; men are likely to go on with their careers without, or with less, interruption.

The single most important challenge these couples will face is the continuing struggle to mesh careers and families, particularly because of the gender disparities inherent in this struggle. Some of the "toughness of the times" is likely to persist, owing to structural changes to which our culture has not yet fully adapted. In particular, the shift from the single-breadwinner model of the family to the two-income family has not been fully worked out. The ideology of equality dictates that women, too, should work, should want to work, and can feel valued and empowered only by working outside the home in regular paid employment. It also dictates that men should assume an active role in child rearing and housekeeping. Thus, life gets tougher for both women and men—more equal certainly, and even perhaps more meaningful, but definitely tougher.

Apart from these issues, the wear and tear of living together and raising children will lead to the breakup of some of the shakier marriages. Even currently committed marriages may go stale without proper maintenance. As their children enter puberty and their parents begin to suffer the burdens of old age, these couples will face new stresses and strains. Illness, disability, and death will begin to exact their toll, as distant as they may seem to most of our participants at present.

At least some among the educational elite may not be well prepared for such travails. They have lived charmed lives, always succeeding and always finding the internal resources required to handle the new challenges that come their way. Like the Greek heroes, hubris may be their Achilles' heel. Disappointment and failure, when they come, will constitute a shock that will be experienced as all the greater because most are so unaccustomed to severe adversity.

We suspect that considerable change is likely to occur with respect to the typology in the next ten years as well, but it may not be so much in the way of shifts in new directions as of recapturing the past. The heavy demands of career establishment, young children, household management, and so on, which now so thoroughly consume the lives of our participants, have had a generally leveling effect on the four types. As our participants reach their middle years, they should find it easier to renew long-standing interests, easier (especially for women) to devote time to their careers if they so desire, and more feasible to revivify dormant dreams about how they want to live their lives. We may find Intellectuals who now look unconnected returning to the intellectual mode, Strivers who have had to choose between intellectualism and careerism again engaging in both spheres, and so on. In other words, stability over a twenty-year span may well be greater than that of the first decade after college.

We hope to go back to our participants in the year 2001, when they have been out of college for twenty years, for the next installment of our longitudinal study. The adequacy of our approach to analyzing careerism and intellectualism in these future studies is likely to diminish as our participants move into the middle phase of life, since questionnaire data may well become less useful for distinguishing the four types. So we will need to rely more on the insights that can be gleaned from interviews to explore the new facets of careerism and intellectualism appropriate to successive phases of life.

In the best of all worlds, the next decade should see a flourishing of the intellectual lives of our participants and a greater measure of social involvement. With their careers more consolidated and their children older, they will have more time and energy to devote to these areas. Questions remain, nonetheless, as to what ends their engagements will serve. Will they become patrons of the arts as a way of further enhancing their class status or will they use cultural activities to enrich their inner lives? Will they get into politics to protect their group interests or to secure greater equity and justice for all? Will their greater involvement with religious institutions mainly serve conventional purposes or carry more personal meaning for them?

The educational elite will never have enough time to do all they would like to do. Their futures depend, once again, on how they order their priorities. Good intentions are not enough. As Kirsten Buchanan put it: "I think that at the end of our careers, if we are called upon to answer the same questions asked at graduation, the responses would sound familiar. We would spend more time on our minds, on service activities, on social life, on relationships, on almost everything. By that time, however, it will be too late."

The potholes in the road ahead notwithstanding, for the great majority of our participants the next decade should be one of the happiest and most productive periods of their lives. In Levinson's developmental terms, they will have graduated from the stage of young adulthood by the end of the decade and will be entering the period of the midlife transition. They will hit their stride in their careers and become their own persons. They will fulfill their Dream or adjust their sights to their lesser accomplishments through the device of "de-illusionment" (not to be confused with dis-illusionment), which places matters in a more realistic perspective.[16] And if they heed the advice of Sir Thomas Browne, offered two centuries ago, they will continue to progress in their lives, making the most of what each period has to offer:

> Confound not the distinctions of thy life which nature hath divided; that is, youth, adolescence, manhood, and old age: nor in these divided periods, wherein thou art in a manner four, conceive thyself but one. Let every division be happy in its proper virtues, nor one vice run through all. Let each distinction have its salutary transition, and critically deliver thee from the imperfections of the former; so ordering the whole, that prudence and virtue may have the largest section.[17]

APPENDIX A

Tables

TABLE 1
Distribution of Graduate Degrees Earned *(percentages)*

	Total	*Men*	*Women*
M.B.A.	20%	18%	25%
J.D.	29	30	26
M.S.	16	17	16
M.D.	16	17	14
Ph.D.	8	10	3
M.A.	7	7	7
Teaching certificate	4	1	9
Total degrees	100	100	100
No graduate degree	26%	21%	33%

Abbreviations—M.B.A.: master of business administration; J.D.: doctor of jurisprudence; M.S.: master of science; M.D.: medicine doctor; Ph.D.: doctor of philosophy; M.A.: master of arts. Individuals who received more than one degree are listed under the highest degree received.

TABLE 2
Distribution of Graduate Degrees, by Type *(percentages)*

	Careerists	Intellectuals	Strivers	Unconnected
M.B.A.	23%	23%	19%	17%
J.D.	33	23	31	30
M.S.	10	19	16	17
M.D.	23	7	12	13
Ph.D.	3	12	6	10
M.A.	7	8	10	7
Teaching certificate	0	8	6	6
Total degrees	100	100	100	100
No graduate degree	19	33	20	35

TABLE 3
Current Occupation, by Sex *(percentages)*

	Total	Men	Women
Manager/business	27%	26%	28%
Attorney	17	21	12
Physician	11	14	8
Engineering/technical	9	11	6
Teaching (all levels)	7	6	8
Homemaker	7	0	15
Other professional	5	3	8
Sales/bookkeeping	4	5	2
Graduate student	4	5	3
Scientist	3	4	2
Artist/writer/actor	2	3	1
Manager/public sector	2	2	2
Health professional	2	1	4

TABLE 4
Current Occupation, by Type *(percentages)*

	Careerists	Intellectuals	Strivers	Unconnected
Manager/business	25%	30%	25%	28%
Attorney	25	12	22	11
Physician	19	2	10	6
Engineering/technical	11	10	8	6
Teaching (all levels)	0	10	2	17
Homemaker	8	8	10	2
Other professional	0	8	2	6
Sales/bookkeeping	6	5	5	2
Graduate student	3	2	2	9
Scientist	3	2	2	6
Artist/writer/actor	0	0	2	4
Manager (public sector)	0	2	5	0
Health professional	0	8	2	0

TABLE 5
Median Yearly Income, by Sex *($ × 1,000)*

	Participant	Spouse*	Nonwage**	Total
All	54.0	40.0	10.0	104.0
Men	60.0	30.0	10.0	100.0
Women	47.0	53.0	9.0	109.0

*About 60 percent of participants reported spouse income.
**Household nonwage incomes for participants with partners.

TABLE 6
Median Yearly Income, by Type and Sex *($ × 1,000)*

	Careerists	*Intellectuals*	*Strivers*	*Unconnected*
Men				
Participant	70.0	52.0	56.0	50.5
Spouse*	20.0	30.0	35.0	25.0
Nonwage**	5.0	31.0	10.0	10.0
Total	95.0	113.0	101.0	85.5
Women				
Participant	60.0	45.0	57.5	40.0
Spouse	93.5	57.0	50.0	45.0
Nonwage	11.5	5.5	24.0	8.0
Total	165.0	107.5	131.5	93.0
Both Sexes				
Participant	69.0	45.0	56.0	46.0
Spouse	30.0	40.0	48.0	37.0
Nonwage	7.5	8.0	15.0	10.0
Total	106.5	93.0	119.0	93.0

*About 60 percent of participants reported spouse income.
**Household nonwage incomes for participants with partners.

TABLE 7
Social Mobility

	Participant Social Class					
	Lower-middle-class	*Middle-class*	*Upper-middle-class*	*Upper-class*	*Total*	*N*
Parental Social Class						
Below middle	15%	48%	37%	0%	14%	27
Lower	0	67	33	0	2	3
Working	40	20	40	0	5	10
Lower-middle	0	64	36	0	7	14
Middle	4	50	46	0	22	44
Upper-middle	4	17	75	4	57	114
Upper	0	14	36	50	7	14
Column totals	5	28	61	6	100	199

TABLE 8
Social Mobility, by Sex, Type, and Ethnicity *(percentages)*

	Upwardly Mobile	Steady	Downwardly Mobile	N
Entire Sample	26%	58%	16%	197
Men	25	63	11	112
Women	27	51	21	85
Intellectuals	18	60	22	38
Careerists	30	57	13	37
Strivers	32	55	13	42
Unconnected	30	57	13	46
White	23	61	16	164
Minority*	70	24	6	17
Asian-American	15	77	8	13

*Black, Hispanic, and Native American.

TABLE 9
Participants Ever Married, by Sex and Type *(percentages)*

	All	Careerists	Intellectuals	Strivers	Unconnected
Men	59%	62%	50%	59%	72%
Women	68	77	74	50	75
Both	63	68	62	55	73

TABLE 10
Parenthood
(percentages ever married, with a child)

	All	*Careerists*	*Intellectuals*	*Strivers*	*Unconnected*
Men	58%	74%	43%	61%	57%
Women	56	40	59	88	41
Both	57	60	52	73	52

TABLE 11
Typology Stability and Change over Ten Years

	Follow-up Study Type				
	Careerists	*Intellectuals*	*Strivers*	*Unconnected*	*N*
Cohort Study Type					
Intellectuals	10%	45%	10%	36%	31
Careerists	38	0	54	8	24
Strivers	17	28	47	8	36
Unconnected	37	21	8	34	38
N	32	32	36	29	129

Reconstructing the Typology of Academic Orientation

To evaluate stability and change in the typology that we developed in the cohort study, we began by reproducing the methods of that study as exactly as possible but using data from the follow-up questionnaire. Thus, to determine items that clustered together, we conducted factor analyses of the items related to (a) reasons for attending college, (b) characteristics desired in a career, (c) life goals, and (d) goals for one's children. As before, these analyses produced factors that clustered items related to intellectualism as one set and items related to careerism in another set. Technical variations and adjustments in the factor analysis procedures yielded two quite stable clusters of items.

We then produced summary measures of intellectualism and careerism by combining responses on the relevant items. The resulting intellectualism scale and careerism scale ended up with twenty-two items each, giving them theoretical scores ranging from 22 to 110. (All items were rated on 5-point scales.) The lowest intellectualism score was 43, and the lowest careerism score was 24; the maximum values were 85 in both cases. The median values for the two scales were 68 and 53, respectively.

As before, the zero-order correlation between the two scales was very close to zero (-.02), showing that they are essentially unrelated to one another. It therefore was reasonable to construct the follow-up typology by simply cross-tabulating the two variables, each divided at its median value. Hence, Intellectuals are again those with intellectualism scores above the median value and careerism scores below the median value; the Unconnected are those with below-median scores on both scales; and so on.

Having thus classified our participants according to their responses in the follow-up study, we then could conduct analyses of change and stability in the typology by comparing current (1991) classifications with those from ten years earlier. It is these results that we report in chapter 10. We also conducted analyses using core members of each type, that is, participants whose scores lie in the top or bottom thirds (rather than halves) of the respective scales. These individuals are unambiguously classified because their scores are more extreme, while those with scores near the median values are not well differentiated and may not be typical of the types to which they are assigned.

For a variety of technical and practical reasons, we could not exactly reproduce the methods used in constructing the original typology, so we replaced certain items with other items for each of the two scales, on the basis of theoretical considerations. Other variants involved typologies based on the intellectualism and careerism factor scores yielded by factor analysis rather than on additive combinations of the relevant items.

We found that all variants largely agreed with each other, classifying upwards of 75 percent of students identically. In addition, the degree of stability in the typology indicated by the variants was quite uniform. In almost every variant we analyzed, we found between 40 and 50 percent stability in the typology over the ten years, and no variant deviated sharply from this range. This uniformity of results, despite the considerable variation in methods used, gives us confidence that our conclusions about change and stability are satisfactorily reliable. Particular aspects of change (such as the propensity of Intellectuals to become Unconnected) should be treated cautiously, as exact change figures are not likely to be reliable. Overall patterns, however, can be accepted with confidence.

Notes

CHAPTER 1: CROSSING THE TWENTIES

1. To protect the identity of our study participants, all names have been changed and some of their biographical details have been altered. For the two profiles in this chapter and the eight profiles in the next, we have assigned full names; for the more numerous shorter references and some of the quotations, we have used only first names, for the sake of simplicity. Some of the more common first names that belong to actual participants may also appear in the text, but they refer to different individuals. For instance, there are several men named "John" in our sample, but the "John" in the text is not any of them.

2. The present time referred to is 1991, when most of the questionnaires and interviews were completed.

3. We are mindful of the significance of how our examples were chosen. Our guiding principle was to be descriptive rather than prescriptive. Thus, if we wanted to give an example of a schoolteacher, we picked a woman, since almost all of the teachers among our participants are women. (In that sense, the choice of Alicia Turner is not entirely random.) We do not mean to suggest that teaching should be a female profession. Moreover, while we tried, in choosing our examples, to maintain a reasonable balance of gender, ethnic, and other social characteristics, not all groups are represented in each and every case. Our primary interest has been remaining true to the realities of the lives of our participants.

4. Boyer (1987), 1.

5. For example, Yale President (and Stanford alumnus) Richard C. Levin, in his inaugural address, cited a list of Yale alumni that included fourteen members of the Continental Congress, four signers of the Declara-

tion of Independence, three of the last five presidents of the United States, and ten of one hundred senators in office. Honan (1993).

6. The gender and ethnic distribution of Stanford undergraduates has changed considerably since our first study. In our cohort study sample (which was representative of the class of 1981), 56 percent of the students were men and 44 percent women. White students comprised 78 percent of the total: Asian-Americans (5 percent), African-Americans (6 percent), and Mexican-Americans (or Hispanics) (6 percent) added up to 17 percent for minority students, including two Native Americans. The balance of 5 percent came from foreign countries or other ethnic groups. The 1993–94 freshman class was evenly split between men and women. Whites now account ʿor 50 percent of the ethnic minorities, and other minorities for the other half. This change is largely due to large increases in the number of Asian-American students at Stanford, who now account for 24 percent; the proportions of Mexican-Americans (10 percent), African-Americans (9 percent), Native Americans (2 percent), and foreign students (5 percent) show more modest increases. All 50 states and 43 foreign countries are represented, the largest proportion of students (42 percent) coming from California. (Stanford Undergraduate Admissions Office.)

7. Katchadourian and Boli (1985), app. 2.

8. Ibid., 1. This is an issue that goes to the heart of the debate on the role of higher education. For a recent historical survey, see Carnochan (1993).

9. Given the method we used to ascertain the four types, roughly equal numbers had to end up in each category. After we looked at the interview reports of those in the core groups, we estimated 35 percent to be Strivers, 15 percent Intellectuals, 25 percent Careerists, and 25 percent Unconnected.

10. The questionnaire phase of our investigation was carried out in conjunction with Stanford University's Self-Study Report to the Western Association of Colleges and Schools. We are grateful to Professor William Massey and Professor Myra Strober for their contributions to the design of the questionnaire, and to the staff of the self-study for their help with the collection and coding of the questionnaire data.

11. These five members were John Bunnell, associate dean of admissions, Anne Coxon, former director of the advisory center, Jean Fetter, assistant to the president and former dean of admissions, Sally Mahoney, former registrar, and Steven Peeps, associate vice president, Office of Development. In addition, two interviews were conducted by Elizabeth Hirschhorn, doctoral candidate in the School of Education.

12. Carnegie Foundation for the Advancement of Teaching (1988).

13. *UNESCO Statistical Yearbook* (1984).

14. Boyer (1987), 2.

15. See the discussion on policy implications of the impact of college in Pascarella and Terenzini (1991), 637–38.

16. Stanford usually admits about 20 percent of nearly 14,000 applicants. These figures are roughly comparable to those of Harvard, Princeton, and Yale, which are its main competitors. For the freshman class of 1993–94, 73 percent had high school GPAs of 3.8–4.0; 72 percent had verbal SAT scores, and 89 percent had math SAT scores, of 600–800. Almost 90 percent ranked in the top 1 percent of their high school class. Public schools accounted for 70 percent and private schools for 30 percent. Stanford also enrolls some 120 sophomore and junior transfer students a year; their characteristics vary somewhat from those of the freshman class.

17. The ranking of a given institution varies from one survey to the next and tends to be somewhat arbitrary. Like all else, universities also go in and out of fashion. *U.S. News and World Report* (1993), 110.

18. Skelly (1986), 18–25.

19. Boyer (1987), 26.

20. Moll (1985).

21. See, for example, Fischgrund (1993), or Fiske (1994).

22. The COFHE institutions are Brown, Columbia, Cornell, Dartmouth, Duke, Georgetown, Harvard, Johns Hopkins, MIT, Northwestern, Penn, Princeton, Rice, Stanford, Chicago, Rochester, Yale, Amherst, Carleton, Oberlin, Pomona, Swarthmore, Trinity, Wesleyan, Williams, Barnard, Bryn Mawr, Mount Holyoke, Radcliffe, Smith, Washington, and Wellesley.

23. The "public Ivys" are University of California, Miami University, University of Michigan, University of North Carolina, University of Texas, University of Vermont, University of Virginia, and William and Mary College. The "best of the rest" are University of Colorado, Georgia Institute of Technology, University of Illinois, New College of the University of South Florida, Pennsylvania State University, University of Pittsburgh, State University of New York at Binghamton, University of Washington, and University of Wisconsin. The Association of American Universities, with about fifty institutions, and the Association of American Colleges, with over six hundred, constitute far less exclusive affiliations. Moll (1985).

24. *Barron's Profiles of American Colleges* (1992).

25. A former dean of admissions, Jean Fetter, has provided a thoughtful inside view of the admissions process (but not a guide on how to get admitted to Stanford). See Fetter (in press). Stanford University bulletins, like those of other schools, provide more specific information.

26. Howe and Strauss (1992), Gross and Scott (1990); Zinn (1992).

27. The term "yuppie" (or "yuppy") may have been first used by Alice Kahn in her articles published in the *East Bay Express* in 1983; Howe and Strauss, in their *Atlantic* article, refer to the term's use in 1981 but do not cite a source. None of the uses cited in the *Oxford English Dictionary* precede 1984. Derivative terms include "guppie" (gay urban professional) and "puppie" (pregnant urban professional).

28. Lasch (1978).

29. *Time* Jan. 9, 1984. Patterned after Lisa Birnbach's *The Official Preppy Handbook* (1980), *The Yuppie Handbook* not only pokes fun at but catalogs the distinctive features of the group. Piesman and Hartley (1984). Their lives were also chronicled for a time in the ABC television series "thirtysomething." Kahn (1987a) and Kahn (1987b).

30. Lee (1993), pp. 14–15.

31. Howe and Strauss (1993).

32. *Time* July 16, (1990), 57.

33. Ibid.

34. Everett, Ladd. Quoted in Morin (1994), E 7.

35. Moss and Sussman (1980), 546; Bee (1992), 65.

36. Brim and Kagan (1980).

37. Shakespeare (1988).

38. Ariès (1962).

39. Hall (1904).

40. For an overview of the biological development to adulthood, see Katchadourian (1978). Various aspects of adolescent development into adulthood are discussed in Feldman and Elliott (1990).

41. Pearlin (1980). For an overview of theories of adult development, see Bee (1992); Stevens-Long and Cummins (1992); and Cavanaugh (1981). For a more technical source, see Schaie (1983).

42. Erikson (1963); Erikson (1980).

43. Levinson (1978b).

44. Vaillant (1977).

CHAPTER 2: FOUR PATHWAYS

1. Each pair in our profile group is meant to be illustrative rather than representative of a given type. Thus, the persons we have chosen are not typical in the sense of portraying the "average" person in a group. Rather, they have been chosen because they represent relatively pure versions of their type. Hence, their characteristics tend to be more sharply defined than for other members of their group.

2. Martin MacMillan is "Profile 4.2: Martin—Premed," in Katchadourian and Boli (1985), 86–87.

3. Cynthia Eastwood is "Profile 4.3: Cynthia—Future Financier," in Katchadourian and Boli (1985), 87–88.

4. Kirsten Buchanan is "Profile 5.2: Kirsten—Cosmopolitan Life," in Katchadourian and Boli (1985), 123–24.

5. Christopher Luce is not profiled in Katchadourian and Boli (1985).

6. Katchadourian and Boli (1985), 133.

7. Ibid., 124.

8. Ibid., 128.

9. George Mehta is "Profile 6.2: Pierre—Renaissance Man," in Katchadourian and Boli (1985), 155–56.

10. Geraldine Jones is "Profile 6.1: Geraldine—Actress," in Katchadourian and Boli (1985), 154–55.
11. Ibid., 161.
12. Ibid., 162.
13. Katherine Johnson is not profiled in Katchadourian and Boli (1985).
14. David Levy is "Profile 7.4: David—Waiting to Be Free," in Katchadourian and Boli (1985), 189–90.
15. Ibid., 207.
16. Ibid., 211.
17. Ibid., 220.

CHAPTER 3: EDUCATION FOR SUCCESS

1. Weber (1930).
2. U.S. Department of Labor, *Dictionary of Occupational Titles* (1991).
3. This is the first of nine major occupational categories in the Department of Labor classification. It contains nineteen occupational groups, each subdivided into numerous categories. Ibid.
4. Erikson (1968), 156.
5. Krumboltz (1992).
6. For a comprehensive review of these theories by some of the key authorities in the field, see Brown and Brooks (1990).
7. Super (1985), 197–262.
8. John Krumboltz, personal communication. See also Mitchell and Krumboltz (1990), 145–96.
9. Bachman, O'Malley, and Johnston (1978).
10. Summaries of this area of research are presented in Bee (1992) and Stevens-Long and Commons (1992).
11. D'Andrade (1966), 174–204.
12. Holland (1985).
13. Super (1985).
14. John Krumboltz informs us that "Zeteophobia" is the special label for the protracted fear of settling on career options.
15. The first law to license the practice of medicine in the American colonies was passed in New Jersey in 1772. It imposed severe fines on those who practiced medicine without a license but exempted those who drew teeth, bled patients, or gave medical help for which they were not paid. The first medical degree was awarded by the University of Pennsylvania in 1768; the first law degree was conferred in 1864 at Columbia University. Kane (1964).
16. A number of studies have shown that graduates of highly selective schools are more likely to attend graduate school and to gain entrance to elite graduate programs, even after taking into account student ability, grades, and other factors. See Pascarella and Terenzini (1991), 374–76.

17. Boyer (1987), 275.
18. Ibid., 272.
19. Ibid., 274.
20. Figures released by the American Council on Education show that only 12 percent of Ph.D.s awarded in 1992 were earned by ethnic minorities. Of these, 565 doctorates were received by black women, only one more than the number in 1982. The number of black men getting Ph.D.s is lower (386) and has declined over the same decade. Other minority groups have shown significant increases. The number of doctorates won by Hispanics has risen 41 percent (to 755), among Asian-Americans it has gone up by 83 percent (to 828), and for Native Americans it has nearly doubled (to 148, with nearly half women) over ten years. Mane-gold (1994).

CHAPTER 4: LAUNCHING CAREERS

1. Fuchs (1983), 125.
2. Bee (1992).
3. Hall (1986).
4. Levinson (1978).
5. Ibid., 58.
6. Ries and Stone (1992).
7. Bee (1992).
8. Moen (1985), 113–55.
9. Bee (1992), 305.
10. Krumboltz (1991).
11. Hall (1990).
12. Organizational behavior, a relatively new field often associated with schools of business or management, studies the behavior of individuals within organizations. Though the roots of the discipline go back to the early 1930s, organizational behavior as a formal interdisciplinary field of study emerged in the 1960s. For a general introduction, see DuBrin (1984).
13. Brown (1990), 338–64.
14. Erikson (1963).
15. Vaillant and Milofsky (1980), 1348–59.
16. Super (1990).
17. Super and Thompson (1981).
18. Schein (1977).
19. Driver (1979), 84.
20. Ibid. See also Driver and Rowe (1979), 141–82.
21. To complicate matters further, it was the goddess Athena who disguised herself as a nobleman of Ithaca called Mentor so as to act as the adviser of the young Telemachus. *Oxford English Dictionary* (1971), 1771.
22. Levinson (1978).

23. U.S. Bureau of the Census, *Statistical Abstract 1993* (1993), 405–7.

24. Pascarella and Terenzini (1991), 442–43.

25. Ibid., 448–49.

26. U.S. Bureau of the Census, *Statistical Abstract 1993* (1993), 184–85.

CHAPTER 5: MAKING IT

1. U.S. Bureau of the Census, *Current Population Survey* (1991), 51.

2. The mean figure was $141,400, which is inflated by a few very high figures. We use median values, the point at which half the incomes are higher and half are lower, because they are a more meaningful measure of the overall distributions.

3. Pascarella and Terenzini (1991), ch. 20.

4. U.S. Bureau of the Census (1993), 465.

5. Ibid.

6. Rosenbaum (1984).

7. Ibid.

8. Bray and Howard (1983).

9. Neugarten (1976).

10. Perrow (1986).

11. Glenn and Weaver (1985).

12. Vaillant (1993).

13. Ratings on these dimensions (and the personal dimensions discussed later in chapter 8) were done by the senior author alone. We have confidence in these ratings because he had conducted almost all the interviews and knew the participants well, and we used only three-category scales to make rating easier. Nevertheless, we have no systematic reliability check on these ratings; it would have been too time-consuming and expensive to have an independent rater listen to the interview tapes and read the reports with the care needed to conduct the ratings process properly.

14. We get a more global assessment of career satisfaction by combining the scores of the four C's into an overall career engagement index (CEI), with a minimum score of 4 (low in all four dimensions) and a maximum of 12 (high in all four). Given the overall high levels of satisfaction in the separate dimensions, the mean for this index is quite high, 9.3. Men have slightly higher mean CEI scores than women (9.7 versus 8.9), reflecting their moderately greater commitment and compensation. Differences by type are small but in the expected order—Careerists are highest, Intellectuals and the Unconnected lowest, Strivers midway between. We also find that career engagement is greater for respondents who have followed a linear career trajectory, had mentors, and foresee continuing on their present career path for the next decade.

15. *New York Times.* January 28, 1993, A 8.

16. Bee (1992).
17. Sims (1993).
18. Ibid.
19. Swiss and Walker (1993).
20. Stone (1980).
21. Katchadourian and Boli (1985), app. 4.
22. Jackman and Jackman (1983), 18.
23. Jencks (1979).
24. Featherman and Hauser (1978).
25. To a large extent, individual mobility is a result of what is known as structural mobility—changes in the overall structure of the service, white-collar, and professional occupational system. For example, the 1973 data show that nearly 30 percent of men were in occupations of upper, white-collar status, but only 18.5 percent of the occupations of the fathers of those men were at this level. The entire structure has moved upward, quite apart from mobility among individuals. Maintaining higher class standing is relatively problematic, even when structural mobility is significant. In this respect, the educational elite does much better than the general population: 75 percent of them maintain their upper-middle-class status, compared with only 52 percent in the national study. Jackman and Jackman (1983), 18.

CHAPTER 6: PAIRING UP, SETTLING DOWN

1. U.S. Bureau of the Census (1993), 102, 54.
2. Ibid.
3. Skolnick (1978).
4. Tennov (1980).
5. Sternberg (1988).
6. This question was suggested by George Vaillant in a personal communication.
7. Murstein (1976).
8. Collins (1982).
9. Lee (1974).
10. *Time* (1986), 45.
11. Gerson (1993), 6.
12. There is as yet no convenient term for cohabiting couples (Howton [1994], 4). "My cohabitor" or "significant other" sound stilted; "boy/girlfriend" has an adolescent ring to it; "friend" is too vague, "lover" too explicit; "the man/woman I live with" is cumbersome; "partner" is too businesslike, "life partner," pretentious. In Sweden, where cohabiting is common, a well-entrenched term is *sambo* (short for *samboende*), literally, "one who is living together."
13. U.S. Bureau of the Census (1993), 54.

14. Reiss (1980).
15. Richardson (1993). Unlike at the time of the cohort study, gay and lesbian couples at Stanford are currently entitled to graduate student housing on the same basis as married students.
16. Billy, et al. (1993). Extrapolations from the Kinsey surveys, conducted over forty years ago, placed the prevalence of male homosexuality at 10 percent. A new national study carried out in 1991 for the Alan Guttmacher Institute shows that about 2 percent of the men surveyed (age twenty to thirty-nine) had engaged in homosexual sex in the previous year, and 1 percent considered themselves exclusively homosexual. The figure for those who have engaged in sporadic homosexual contacts sometime during their lifetime would be higher.
17. According to the sociologists Bell and Weinberg (1978), 28 percent of homosexual women and 10 percent of men live together in long-term relationships, essentially like married couples.
18. Richardson (1993), 18.

CHAPTER 7: PATTERNS OF FAMILY LIFE

1. Juster and Stafford (1985).
2. Gerson (1993), 8. For primary sources, see Mischel and Frankel (1991) and Goldscheider and Waite (1991).
3. Pascarella and Terenzini (1991), 324–25.
4. Stevens-Long and Commons (1992), 234.
5. Feldman and Aschenbrenner (1983).
6. Zeits and Prince (1982).
7. Erikson (1963).
8. Similar reactions are reported from the study of women graduates of the professional schools at Harvard. "Regardless of training and professional level, physicians, MBAs, and lawyers said they were caught off guard by the intensity of their desire to be with their children. . . . No measure of professional reward can equal the love and affection of a child, these feminists say." Swiss and Walker (1993), 56.
9. National Center for Health Statistics (1990).
10. Bee (1992), 233.
11. Veevers (1980).
12. Chira (1993).
13. In the Harvard study, one woman who left investment banking for part-time work when her second child was born says, "If you have children, ask yourself what is a 'good' mother. Be sure to sustain the level *you* define as 'good.'" Swiss and Walker (1993), 63.
14. Eckholm (1992).
15. Abrahamson and Franklin (1986).
16. Eckholm (1992).
17. Rossi (1980).

CHAPTER 8: IS THIS WHAT I WANT?

1. Birchler, Weiss, and Vincent (1975).
2. Pascarella and Terenzini (1991), 543–44.
3. Marjorie Hansen Shaevitz, author of *The Superwoman Syndrome,* after her losing struggle to get her husband to share housework, says, "I spend a lot of time smoldering internally over his recalcitrance . . . I took it one step further by judging that if he really loved me, he would see how hard I was working, how tired I was, and would come to my rescue with cheerful resourcefulness. Need I tell you this never happened?" Quoted in Hochschild (1989), 27.
4. When Shaevitz tells her husband that women no longer want to be with a man who wants to be taken care of, he responds, "Marjorie, that's really infuriating to most men. . . . What men find difficult to accept is that they get little credit for what they do, and an incredible list of complaints about what they don't do. . . . Women continue to set ground rules for what they expect, what they want, and how they want it delivered. I can tell you that most highly competent successful men—the kind of men most women look for—simply will not respond to a behavioral checklist." Ibid., 28.
5. See, for example, Tannen (1990).
6. Rollins and Feldman (1970).
7. Abbott and Brody (1985).
8. Anderson, Russell, and Schuman (1983).
9. Housenecht and Macke (1981).
10. Belsky and Kelly (1994); Belsky and Rovine (1990); and Cowan and Cowan (1992).
11. Gerson (1993).
12. Cherlin (1992).
13. U.S. Bureau of the Census, *Statistical Abstract 1993* (1993), 102.
14. Schwartz subsequently published a book on the same topic (1992).
15. Swiss and Walker (1993), 2.
16. Ibid., 10–11, 89–90.
17. Methodological and sampling considerations may also play a role in the differences between the two studies. The Harvard study did not include men, so it is hard at times to identify to what extent some problems are intrinsic to a profession, not to being a woman. The response rate of Harvard women was considerably lower than ours (54 percent as against 70 percent); if those who are more distressed are more likely to participate, the more negative responses would be exaggerated. The authors of the Harvard study also take an activist and prescriptive approach, which tends to magnify the problematic aspects by focusing on them.
18. LaMothe (1989).
19. Hochschild (1989).
20. Swiss and Walker (1993), 89–90.

CHAPTER 9: BEYOND THE SELF

1. Carnochan (1993).
2. Yale College, *Reports on the Course Instruction in Yale College by a Committee of the Corporation and the Academic Faculty,* 1828.
3. Commission on the Humanities (1980).
4. Katchadourian and Boli (1985), 11.
5. Pascarella and Terenzini (1991), 549–50.
6. Stevens-Long and Commons (1992).
7. Schor (1991), 1.
8. Bloom (1987).
9. The Stanford School of Engineering places more emphasis on the liberal education of its students than do other engineering schools. Because of its much higher burden of departmental requirements, however, engineering students have fewer opportunities to take elective courses or attend an overseas campus than most other students.
10. Hofstadter (1963).
11. Commission on the Humanities (1980), 64.
12. Sanford (1967), 33.
13. Barzun (1993).
14. Skelly (1986).
15. Donald Kennedy, "You Can Make a Difference" Conference, Stanford, Calif., February 25, 1984.
16. Wang (1963), 10. We would like to thank Anne Coxon for suggesting this quote and Lee Yearly for identifying the source.
17. Skelly (1986), 21.
18. Pascarella and Terenzini (1991), 223–24.
19. Skelly (1986), 21.
20. Wingspread Group on Higher Education (1993), 4.
21. Ibid., 1.
22. Tyack (1966), 29–41.
23. Bok (1982).
24. Ibid., 125.

CHAPTER 10: LOOKING BACK AND LOOKING FORWARD

Epigraph from Eliot (1971), 13.
1. Lewin (1994), 11.
2. Church (1993), 35.
3. *Time* (1993), 27.
4. Uchitelle (1994), Sec. 3, 7.
5. Newman (1993).
6. Greenwald (1993), 36.
7. Kilborn (1994), 1.
8. *Campus Report* (1993), 3.

9. These requirements have since been changed and are again under review by a commission on undergraduate education appointed by President Gerhard Casper in 1993.

10. While Harvard has the largest endowment and Princeton the highest endowment per student, Stanford currently raises the most money of all institutions of higher learning. Its centennial campaign yielded $1.2 billion over five years, and its income from donations in 1993 topped all educational institutions. This is despite the fact that the giving rate of Stanford alumni is paradoxically low (about 20 percent)—which means that a relatively small group are contributing a great deal.

11. Skelly (1986).

12. *Stanford University Courses and Degrees* (1993–94), 10.

13. Boyer (1987), 59.

14. Bliss (1920), 198.

15. Casper (1994), 6.

16. Levinson (1978).

17. Browne (1878).

Bibliography

Abbott, Douglas A., and Gene H. Brody. 1985. "The Relation of Child, Age, Gender, and Number of Children to the Marital Adjustment of Wives." *Journal of Marriage and the Family* 47:77–84.

Abramson, Jill J., and B. Franklin. 1986. *Where Are They Now?* Garden City, N.Y.: Doubleday.

American Council of Education. 1982. *Higher Education and National Affairs* (newsletter) November 12.

Anderson, Stephen, Candyce Russell, and Walter Schuman. 1983. "Perceived Marital Quality and Family Life-cycle Categories: A Further Analysis." *Journal of Marriage and the Family* 45:127–39.

Ariès, Philippe. 1962. *Centuries of Childhood.* New York: Alfred A. Knopf.

Bachman, J. G., P. M. O'Malley, and J. Johnston. 1978. *Youth in Transition,* vol. 6. Ann Arbor, Mich.: Institute for Social Research.

Barron's Profiles of American Colleges, 19th ed. 1992. Woodbury, N.Y.: Barron's Educational Series, Inc.

Barzun, Jacques. 1993. *The American University,* 2d ed. Chicago: University of Chicago Press.

Bee, Helen L. 1992. *The Journey of Adulthood,* 2d ed. New York: MacMillan.

Bell, Alan P., and Martin S. Weinberg. 1978. *Homosexualities.* New York: Simon and Schuster.

Belsky, Jay, and John Kelly. 1994. *Transition to Parenthood: How a First Child Changes a Marriage, Why Some Couples Grow Closer and Others Apart.* New York: Delacorte.

Belsky, Jay, and M. Rovine. 1990. "Patterns of Marital Changes across the Transition to Parenthood: Pregnancy to Three Years Postpartum." *Journal of Marriage and Family* 51: 6–19.

Billy, John O., Koray Tanfer, William R. Grady, and Daniel H. Klepinger.

1993. "The Sexual Behavior of Men in the United States." *Family Planning Perspectives* 25:52–61.

Birchler, G. R., R. L. Weiss, and J. P. Vincent. 1975. "Multi-dimensional Analyses of Social Reinforcement Exchange between Maritally Distressed and Non-distressed Spouse and Stranger Dyads." *Journal of Personality and Social Psychology* 31:348–60.

Birnbach, Lisa. 1980. *The Official Preppy Handbook.* New York: Workman Publishers.

Bliss, Frederick J. 1920. *The Reminiscences of Daniel Bliss.* New York: Revell.

Bloom, Allan. 1987. *The Closing of the American Mind.* New York: Simon and Schuster.

Bok, Derek. 1982. *Beyond the Ivory Tower.* Cambridge, Mass.: Harvard University Press.

Boyer, Ernest L. 1987. *College: The Undergraduate Experience in America.* New York: Harper and Row.

Bray, Douglas W., and Ann Howard. 1983. "The AT&T Longitudinal Studies of Managers." In *Longitudinal Studies of Adult Psychological Development,* edited by K. Warner Schaie, 266–312. New York: Guilford.

Brim, Orville G., and Jerome Kugan, eds. 1980. *Constancy and Change in Human Development.* Cambridge, Mass.: Harvard University Press.

Brown, Duane. 1990. "Summary Comparison and Critique of Major Theories." In Brown and Brooks, *Career Choice and Development,* 338–64.

Brown, Duane, and Linda Brooks, eds. 1990. *Career Choice and Development,* 2d ed. San Francisco: Jossey-Bass.

Browne, Sir Thomas. 1878. *Christian Morals,* part 3, sect. 8. Boston.

Campus Report (Stanford University), 3. August 11, 1993.

Carnegie Foundation for the Advancement of Teaching. 1988. *A Classification of Institutions of Higher Education.* Princeton, N.J.: Carnegie Foundation for the Advancement of Teaching.

Carnochan, Bliss. 1993. *The Battleground of the Curriculum.* Stanford, Calif.: Stanford University Press.

Caro, Robert. 1974. *The Power Broker: Robert Moses and the Fall of New York.* New York: Knopf.

Casper, Gerhard. 1994. "Concerning Culture and Cultures." *Campus Report* (Stanford University), 6. March 16.

Cavanaugh, John C. 1981. *Adult Development and Aging.* Belmont, Calif.: Wadsworth.

Cherlin, Andrew. 1992. *Marriage, Divorce, Remarriage.* Cambridge, Mass.: Harvard University Press.

Chira, S. 1993. "Census Data Show Rise in Child Care by Fathers." *New York Times,* September 22.

Church, George J. 1993. "Jobs in an Age of Insecurity." *Time,* 31–39. November 22.

Collins, Randall. 1982. "Love and Property." In *Sociological Insight: An Introduction to Non-Obvious Sociology,* chap. 5. New York: Oxford University Press.

Commission on the Humanities. 1980. *The Humanities in American Life.* Berkeley: University of California Press.

Compact Edition of the Oxford English Dictionary. 1971. New York: Oxford University Press.

Cooper, Cary L., ed. 1979. *Behavioral Problems in Organizations.* Englewood Cliffs, N.J.: Prentice-Hall.

Coupland, Douglas. 1991. *Generation X.* New York: St. Martin's Press.

Cowan, Carolyn P., and Philip A. Cowan. 1992. *When Parents Become Partners.* New York: Basic Books.

D'Andrade, Roy G. 1966. "Sex Differences and Cultural Institutions." In *The Development of Sex Differences,* edited by Eleanor E. Maccoby, 173–204. Stanford, Calif.: Stanford University Press.

Driver, Michael J. 1979. "Career Concepts and Career Management in Organizations." In Cooper, ed., *Behavioral Problems,* 79–139.

Driver, Michael J., and Alan J. Rowe. 1979. "Decision-Making Styles: A New Approach to Management Decision-Making." In *Behavioral Problems in Organizations,* edited by Cary L. Cooper, 141–82. Englewood Cliffs, N.J.: Prentice-Hall.

DuBrin, Andrew J., ed. 1984. *Foundations of Organizational Behavior: An Applied Perspective.* Englewood Cliffs, N.J.: Prentice-Hall.

Eckholm, Erik. 1992. "Learning If Infants Are Hurt When Mothers Go to Work." *New York Times,* October 6.

Elder, Glen H., Jr., ed. 1985. *Life Course Dynamics.* Ithaca, N.Y.: Cornell University Press.

Eliot, Thomas S. 1971. "Burnt Norton." In *Four Quartets,* by T. S. Eliot. New York: Harcourt Brace Jovanovich.

Erikson, Erik H. 1968. *Identity: Youth and Crisis.* New York: W. W. Norton.

———. 1963. *Childhood and Society,* 2d ed. New York: W. W. Norton.

———. 1959. *Identity and the Life Cycle.* New York: International Universities Press. Reissued 1980, New York: W. W. Norton.

Exner, T. 1987. "How to Figure Your Chances of Getting Married." *American Demographics* (June): 50–52.

Featherman, David, and Robert Hauser. 1978. *Opportunity and Change.* New York: Academic Press.

Feldman, Shirley S., and Barbara Aschenbrenner. 1983. "Impact of Parenthood on Various Aspects of Masculinity and Femininity." *Developmental Psychology* 19:278–89.

Feldman, Shirley S., and Glen R. Elliott. 1990. *At the Threshold: The Developing Adolescent.* Cambridge, Mass.: Harvard University Press.

Fetter, Jean. (in press). *Questions and Admissions: Reflections on 100,000 Admissions at Stanford.* Stanford, Calif.: Stanford University Press.

Fischgrund, Tom, ed. 1993. *Barron's Top Fifty.* Hauppauge, N.Y.: Barron's Educational Services.

Fiske, Edward B. 1994. *The Fiske Guide to Colleges.* New York: Times Books.

Fuchs, Victor. 1983. *How We Live.* Cambridge, Mass: Harvard University Press.

Gerson, Kathleen. 1993. *No Man's Land: Men's Changing Commitments to Family and Work.* New York: Basic Books.

Glenn, Norval D., and Charles N. Weaver. 1985. "Age Cohort Job Satisfaction in the United States." In *Current Perspectives on Aging and the Life Cycle: A Research Annual,* vol. 1, edited by Zena S. Blau, 89–110. Greenwich, Conn.: JAI Press.

Goldscheider, Frances K., and Linda J. Waite. 1991. *New Families, No Families?* Berkeley: University of California Press.

Gross, David M., and Sophronia Scott. 1990. "Twentysomething." *Time,* 57–62. July 16.

Hall, Douglas T. 1990. "Career Development Theory in Organizations." In Brown and Brooks, *Career Choice and Development,* 422–54.

Hall, G. Stanley. 1904. *Adolescence: Its Psychology and Its Relation to Physiology.* New York: Appleton.

Hall, Richard H. 1986. *Dimensions of Work.* Newbury Park, Calif.: Sage.

Hochschild, Arlie R. 1989. *The Second Shift.* New York: Viking.

Hofstadter, Richard. 1963. *Anti-Intellectualism in American Life.* New York: Vintage Books.

Holland, John. 1985. *Making Vocational Choices,* 2d ed. Englewood Cliffs, N.J.: Prentice-Hall.

Honan, William H. 1993. "Yale Installs Dean as Its 22nd President." *New York Times.* October 3.

Housenecht, Sharon K., and Anne S. Macke. 1981. "Combining Marriage and Career: The Marital Adjustment of Professional Women." *Journal of Marriage and the Family* 43:651–61.

Howe, Neil, and William Strauss. 1992. "The New Generation Gap." *Atlantic Monthly* 270:67–89.

Howe, Neil, and Bill Strauss. 1993. *13th Gen: Abort, Retry, Ignore, Fail?* New York: Vintage Books.

Howton, Elizabeth. 1994. "Not Everyone Loves a Lover." *Palo Alto Weekly.* March 9.

Jackman, Mary R., and Robert W. Jackman. 1983. *Class Awareness in the United States.* Berkeley: University of California Press.

Jencks, Christopher, ed. 1979. *Who Gets Ahead?: The Determinants of Economic Success in America.* New York: Basic Books.

Juster, Thomas F., and Frank Stafford, eds. 1985. *Time, Goods, and Well-Being.* Ann Arbor, Mich.: Institute for Social Research.

Kahn, Alice. 1987a. "Where Have All the Yuppies Gone?" In *My Life as a Gal,* 41–54. New York: Dell.

———. 1987b. "Yuppie!" In *Multiple Sarcasm,* 83–91. Berkeley, Calif.: Ten Speed Press.

Kane, Joseph Nathan. 1964. *Famous First Facts,* 3d ed. New York: H. W. Wilson.

Katchadourian, Herant. 1978. "Medical Perspectives on Adulthood." In *Adulthood,* edited by Erik H. Erikson, 33–60. New York: W. W. Norton.

Katchadourian, Herant, ed. 1979. *Human Sexuality: Comparative and Developmental Perspectives.* Berkeley: University of California Press.

Katchadourian, Herant, and John Boli. 1985. *Careerism and Intellectualism Among College Students.* San Francisco: Jossey-Bass.

Kilborn, Peter T. 1994. "College Seniors Finding More Jobs But Modest Pay." *New York Times.* May 1.

Krumboltz, John D. 1992. "The Dangers of Occupationism." *The Counseling Psychologist* 20:511–18.

———. 1991. *Manual for the Career Beliefs Inventory.* Palo Alto, Calif.: Consulting Psychologists Press.

LaMothe, Louise A. 1989. "Endangered Species." *Stanford Lawyer* 14.

Lasch, Christopher. 1978. *The Culture of Narcissism: American Life in an Age of Diminishing Expectations.* New York: W. W. Norton.

Lee, Elizabeth 1993. *U: The National College Magazine,* 14–15. May.

Lee, John A. 1974. "Styles of Loving." *Psychology Today* 8:43–51.

Levinson, Daniel J. 1978a. *The Seasons of Man's Life.* New York: Alfred A. Knopf.

———. 1978b. "A Conception of Adult Development." *American Psychologist* 41:3–13.

Lewin, Tamar. 1994. "Low Pay and Closed Doors Greet Young in Job Market." *New York Times.* March 10.

Maccoby, Eleanor E., ed. 1966. *The Development of Sex Differences.* Stanford, Calif.: Stanford University Press.

Manegold, Catherine S. 1994. "Fewer Men Earn Doctorates, Particularly Among Blacks." *New York Times.* January 18.

Mischel, Lawrence, and David M. Frankel. 1991. *The State of Working America.* Armonk, N.Y.: M. E. Sharpe.

Mitchell, Lynda K., and John D. Krumboltz. 1990. "Social Learning Approach to Career Decision Making: Krumboltz's Theory." In Brown and Brooks, *Career Choice and Development,* 9.

Moen, Phyllis. 1985. "Continuities and Discontinuities in Women's Labor Force Activity." In *Life Course Dynamics,* edited by Glen H. Elder, Jr., 113–55. Ithaca, N.Y.: Cornell University Press.

Moll, Richard. 1985. *The Public Ivys.* New York: Viking.

Morin, Richard. 1994. "'Generation X?' No Such Animal." *San Francisco Chronicle.* February 4.

Moss, Howard, and Elizabeth Sussman. 1980. "Longitudinal Studies of Adult Development." In *Constancy and Change in Human Development,* edited by Orville G. Brim and Jerome Kagan, 530–95. Cambridge, Mass.: Harvard University Press.

Murstein, Bernard I. 1976. *Who Will Marry Whom?* New York: Springer.

National Center for Health Statistics. 1990. *Vital Statistics of the United States, 1988,* vol. 1, *Natality.* DHHS Pub. No. (PHS) 90–110. Washington, D.C.: Public Health Service.

Neugarten, Bernice L. 1976. "Adaptation and the Life Cycle." *The Counseling Psychologist* 6:16–20.

Newman, Katherine. 1993. *Declining Fortunes: The Withering of the American Dream.* New York: Basic Books.

New York Times. 1993. January 28.

Pascarella, Ernest T., and Patrick T. Terenzini. 1991. *How College Affects Students: Findings and Insights from Twenty Years of Research.* San Francisco: Jossey-Bass.

Pearlin, Leonard I. 1980. "Life Strains and Psychological Distress among Adults." In Smelser and Erikson, *Themes of Work and Love in Adulthood,* 174–92.

Perrow, Charles A. 1986. *Complex Organizations: A Critical Essay.* New York: McGraw-Hill.

Piesman, Marissa, and Marilee Hartley. 1984. *The Yuppie Handbook.* New York: Pocket Books.

Reiss, Ira L. 1980. *Family Systems in America,* 3d ed. New York: Holt, Rinehart, and Winston.

Richardson, Lynda. 1993. "Unmarried New York Couples Proud of Partnerships' New Official Status." *New York Times.* August 1.

Ries, Paula, and Anne J. Stone, eds. 1992. *The American Woman 1992–93: A Status Report.* New York: W. W. Norton.

Rollins, Boyd C., and Harold Feldman. 1970. "Marital Satisfaction over the Family Life Cycle." *Journal of Marriage and the Family* 32:20–27.

Rosenbaum, James E. 1984. *Career Mobility in a Corporate Hierarchy.* New York: Academic Press.

Rossi, Alice S. 1980. "Aging and Parenthood in Middle Years." In *Lifespan Development and Behavior,* vol. 3, edited by P. B. Bates and Orville G. Brim, Jr., New York: Academic Press.

Sanford, Nevitt. 1967. *Where Colleges Fail: A Study of the Student as a Person.* San Francisco: Jossey-Bass.

Schaie, K. Warner, ed. 1983. *Longitudinal Studies of Psychological Development.* New York: Guilford.

Schein, Edgar H. 1977. "Career Anchors and Career Paths: A Panel Study of Management School Graduates." In *Organizational Careers: Some New Perspectives,* edited by John Van Maanen, 49–64. New York: John Wiley and Sons.

Schor, Juliet B. 1991. *The Overworked American.* New York: Basic Books.

Schwartz, Felice. 1992. *Breaking with Tradition.* New York: Warner Books.

Schwartz, Felice N. 1989. "Management Women and the New Facts of Life." *Harvard Business Review,* 65–76. January–February.

Shakespeare, William. 1988. *Complete Works.* New York: Oxford University Press.

Sheehy, Gail. 1974. *Passages.* New York: E. P. Dutton.

Sims, Calvin. 1993. "The Unbreakable Glass Ceiling." *New York Times.* June 7.

Skelly, Florence. 1986. "To the Beat of a Different Drum." *Stanford Magazine,* 18–25. Spring.

Skolnick, Arlene. 1978. *The Intimate Environment: Exploring Marriage and the Family.* Boston: Little, Brown.

Smelser, Neil J., and Erik H. Erikson, eds. 1980. *Themes of Work and Love in Adulthood.* Cambridge, Mass.: Harvard University Press.

Stanford University Courses and Degrees, 1993–94. Stanford, Calif.: Stanford University.

Sternberg, Robert J. 1988. "Triangulating Love." In *The Psychology of Love,* edited by Robert J. Sternberg and Michael L. Barnes, 119–38. New Haven, Conn.: Yale University Press.

Stevens-Long, Judith, and Michael L. Cummins. 1992. *Adult Life: Developmental Processes,* 4th ed. Mountain View, Calif.: Mayfield.

Stone, Allison. 1980. "Gymnast Remains Paralyzed After December Accident." *Stanford Daily.* January 14.

Super, Donald E. 1990. "A Life-Span, Life-Space Approach to Career Development." In Brown and Brooks, *Career Choice and Development,* 197–261.

———. 1985. "Coming of Age in Middletown." *American Psychologist* 40:405–14.

Super, Donald E., and A. S. Thompson. 1981. *The Adult Career Concerns Inventory.* New York: Teachers College, Columbia University.

Swiss, Deborah J., and Judith P. Walker. 1993. *Women and the Work Family Dilemma.* New York: Wiley.

Tannen, Deborah. 1990. *You Just Don't Understand.* New York: Morrow.

Tennov, Dorothy. 1980. *Love and Limerance.* New York: Stein and Day.

Time. 1993. November 22, 27.

Tyack, David. 1966. "Forming the National Character: Paradox in the Educational Thought of the Revolutionary Generation." *Harvard Educational Review* 36:29–41.

Uchitelle, Louis. 1994. "The Humbling of the Harvard Man." *New York Times.* March 6.

UNESCO Statistical Yearbook. 1984. Paris: UNESCO.

U.S. Bureau of the Census. 1993. *Statistical Abstract of the United States 1993,* 113th ed.

———. 1992. *Statistical Abstract of the United States 1992,* 112th ed. Washington, D.C.: Bureau of the Census.

———. 1991. *Current Population Survey.* Washington, D.C.: U.S. Government Printing Office.

U.S. Current Population Reports P-20, No. 418. Washington, D.C.: U.S. Government Printing Office, 1986.

U.S. Department of Labor. 1991. *Dictionary of Occupational Titles,* 4th ed. Washington, D.C.: U.S. Government Printing Office.

U.S. News and World Report. 1993. October 4.

Vaillant, George E. 1993. *Wisdom of the Ego.* Cambridge, Mass.: Harvard University Press.

———. 1977. *Adaptation to Life.* Boston: Little, Brown.

Vaillant, George E., and Eva Milofsky. 1980. "Natural History of Male Psychological Health: IX. Empirical Evidence for Erikson's Model of the Life Cycle." *American Journal of Psychiatry* 137:1348–59.

Van Maanen, John, ed. 1977. *Organizational Careers: Some New Perspectives.* New York: Wiley.

Veevers, Jean E. 1980. *Childless by Choice.* Toronto: Butterworth.

Wang, Yang-ming. 1963. *Instructions for Practical Living and Other Neo-Confucian Writings,* translated by Wing-tsit Chan. New York: Columbia University Press.

Weber, Max. 1930. *The Protestant Ethic and the Spirit of Capitalism,* translated by Talcott Parsons. New York: Scribner's.

Wingspread Group on Higher Education. 1993. *An American Imperative: Higher Expectations for Higher Education.* New York: Johnson Foundation.

World of Learning, 43d ed. 1993. London: Europa Publications.

Yale College. 1828. *Reports on the Course Instruction in Yale College by a Committee of the Corporation and the Academic Faculty.*

Zeits, Carol, and Robert Prince. 1982. "Child Effects on Parents." In *Handbook of Developmental Psychology,* edited by Benjamin B. Wolman, pp. 751–65. Englewood Cliffs, N.J.: Prentice-Hall.

Zinn, Laura. 1992. "Move Over, Boomers." *Business Week,* 74–82. December 14.

Index